negative poetics

negative poetics

edward jayne

university of iowa press ◆ iowa city

University of Iowa Press,
Iowa City 52242
Copyright © 1992 by
the University of Iowa Press
All rights reserved
Printed in the United States of America

Design by Richard Hendel

No part of this book may be reproduced or utilized in any form or by any means, electronic or mechanical, including photocopying and recording, without permission in writing from the publisher.

Printed on acid-free paper

Library of Congress Cataloging-in-Publication Data
Jayne, Edward, 1934–
Negative poetics/by Edward Jayne.—1st ed.
p.   cm.
Includes index.
ISBN 0-87745-362-4
1. Deception in literature. 2. Truthfulness and falsehood in literature. 3. Literature, Modern—History and criticism.
4. Criticism. I. Title.
PN56.D46J39   1992   91-39624
801'.95—dc20   CIP

96 95 94 93 92   C   1 2 3 4 5

TO ELAINE

CONTENTS

Acknowledgments, ix

Introduction, 1

One. A Short History of Deception Theories, 21

Two. Austen, Dickens, Conrad, and Stein, 59

Three. A Homeostatic Model, 86

Four. Shakespeare, Coleridge, and Frost, 111

Five. The Paranoid Dialectic, 133

Six. Young Goodman Brown, 155

Seven. The Affirmative Fallacy, 175

Eight. Roland Barthes, 215

Nine. Three Affirmists and a Brief Negative Manifesto, 242

Notes, 277

Index, 313

ACKNOWLEDGMENTS

Original versions of chapters 4, 5, and 8 appeared, respectively, in *College English*, *Genre*, and the *Minnesota Review*, and the last was reprinted, somewhat reduced, in *Contemporary Literary Criticism*. Among my professors who influenced some of my arguments were Thomas Parkinson and Josephine Miles of the University of California at Berkeley; Lionel Abel, Norman Holland, and Leslie Fiedler of S.U.N.Y. at Buffalo; and Albert Cook at both schools. Years ago professors Abel and Cook were helpful with early portions of chapter 8, and the mixed influence of professors Holland and Fiedler will be evident in chapters 4 through 6. Colleagues, students, and friends with suggestions useful to my ideas have included Woody Stanley, David Isaacson, Shirley Scott, Clifford Davidson, Kirby Farrell, Charles Eidsvik, Berndt Ostendorf, Eva Hesse, Maria Dührig, Kevin Hughes, and Karen Mailler. Also helpful have been both literary and nonliterary exchanges with friends, students, and/or colleagues in Berkeley, Modesto, Arcata, Buffalo, Amherst, Freiburg, Munich, Minneapolis, Florianopolis, Ann Arbor, and Kalamazoo, many of whom would be surprised (and perhaps disturbed) to be associated by name with my project.

I have received generous support from Western Michigan University. Robert Sundick weaned me from the typewriter to the computer to help bring the book to its completion, and Mary Russell Curran vigorously assisted in minimizing my factual errors and editorial inadequacies. My mother taught me by both precept and example that consensus should be dealt with as probable error, if not fraud, and my wife, Elaine, taught me the complementary virtue of persistence, without which this book would not have been published. Her support and assistance have been invaluable. Needless to say, everything said in *Negative Poetics* is ultimately my own responsibility.

negative poetics

INTRODUCTION

Affirmative words are often, in their operation, negative of other objects than those affirmed; and in this case, a negative or exclusive sense must be given to them or they have no operation at all.
Chief Justice John Marshall, *Marbury v. Madison*, 1803

... if it come to prohibiting, there is not aught more likely to be prohibited than truth itself.
Milton, *Areopagitica*

The final revelation is that Lying, the telling of beautiful untrue things, is the proper aim of art.
Oscar Wilde, "The Decay of Lying"

... for the truest poetry is the most feigning, and lovers are given to poetry, and what they swear in poetry, may be said as lovers, they do feign.
Shakespeare, *As You Like It*

The theory of negative poetics I propose is based on the simple principle that misrepresentation is fiction's *sine qua non*, its distinctive and most irreducible feature. With misrepresentation there is fiction, but not without it. Unless the truth is meaningfully warped, distorted, or reorganized, fiction cannot by definition be fiction. Instead, it becomes history, biography, autobiography, sociology, anthropology, philosophy, or, taken to an unliterary extreme, statistics, as confirmed by adequate verification standards.[1] This distinction is of crucial importance, affording the *principium divisionis* that separates the poetic function (*poeisis*) from knowledge (*episteme*), whether the latter derives from scientific verification or from conventional wisdom.[2] Fiction's primary purpose is not to convey any basic insight but to afford pleasure by making an improvement upon the world as we know it. Unless we try to fathom how or why a text revises experience in this fashion, we cannot understand its function, value, or structure as fiction. We might discern what it tells, but not what it *untells* or how such an untelling appeals to readers. Of course, fiction also conveys its share of truths—partial truths and whole truths partially understood—but it succeeds as fiction only when these truths give credence to a gratifying alternative version of experience.

Saint Augustine's argument may be conceded that deception, as opposed to innocent misinformation, must necessarily be intended.[3] However, it would be a mistake to conclude, based on this principle, that the suspension of disbelief essential to literary experience thereby averts deception.[4] By granting that they fabricate stories, authors do not acquit themselves of misrepresenting the truth. Contrary to Sir Philip Sidney's assurance—"Now, for the Poet, he nothing affirmes, and therefore never lyeth"—the literary muse is ineluctably both intentional and distortive.[5] In every dimension of literary experience, both conscious and unconscious—in both author and reader, and in plot, character, and style—fiction gives intention primacy over cognition. Sidney's distinction, drawn from Aristotle, "Not *Gnosis* but *Praxis* must be the fruit," may be transliterated: Not knowledge but gaining results must be the fruit.[6] Though authors might have a purpose different from those of their characters, to say nothing of their readers, there is no aspect or quality of fiction that escapes intention. There is nothing so passive, or so accidental, in literary experience that the role of motivation can be disregarded.

Moreover, as I try to demonstrate, fiction inevitably features misrepresentation by producing results different from life, sometimes with obvious disparities, sometimes by a very narrow margin. The superficial misinformation acknowledged by authors may be accepted as privileged behavior that escapes the lie based on Augustine's distinction as modified by Sidney's. However, the "truths" authors cherish in their fiction are no less vulnerable to the lure of misrepresentation, comprising the lies they tell at least partially conscious of what they are doing as well as the lies they must first tell themselves in order to share with their readers. The conclusion I would suggest is that if fiction is intrinsically both intentional and distortive, this combination is irreducible and affords the *raison d'être* of literary experience. As Francis Fergusson argues in his interpretation of *Oedipus Rex*, fiction is organized as a hierarchy of actualization, a conative integration of plot, characterization, and style to produce the necessary (or desirable) outcome—an outcome, I claim, that may be appreciated because it differs from the quotidian experience of both authors and readers.[7]

Northrop Frye argued in one of his first metacritical essays that "art deals not with the real but with the conceivable."[8] This may be granted, but if the

Introduction

conceivable is different from the real, any treatment of the conceivable as if it were real becomes an act of deception. When we say "let's make believe," no deception occurs, but as soon as we actually begin to make believe, absorbing ourselves in an alternative experience, to that extent, at least, we deceive ourselves.

Wolfgang Iser has likewise argued that fiction is primarily illusion, a negation of reality that makes experience readable. Gross deception, Iser maintains, falls short of what is needed, since fiction can take effect only by providing a credible interaction between illusion and the personal associations experienced by readers.[9] This, too, may be granted, but *credible* and *true* are two entirely different considerations, and accepting the credible as true has always been important for deception to do its work. Unless a lie is credible, it is not effective as a lie. In his essay "The Play of the Text," Iser compares fiction with play as an act of make-believe (a "world enacted") that "acts out difference."[10] "By allowing us to have absence as presence," Iser explains, "play turns out to be a means whereby we may extend ourselves." But when play substitutes absence (i.e., what isn't here) for presence (i.e., what is), it too becomes an act of deception. Again, it may be granted that most individuals who make believe remain aware that they are doing so, but they may enjoy their play only to the extent that they can disregard this realization. Even if their engrossment in play is almost entirely under the sway of their sense of reality, it is their absorption in alternatives *as if true* that catalyzes their pleasure associated with play. In other words, apropos of fiction, even if only the smallest portion of a novel's meaning is deceptive, as in the *roman à clef*, its credentials as fiction depend on the catalytic effect of this minuscule portion. No matter how tiny, this trace of dishonesty offsets and vitalizes the bulk of the text that is merely true.

Some claim that fiction misrepresents only to permit the articulation of basic truths with greater effectiveness. I maintain just the opposite—that fiction engages an assortment of relatively superficial truths to justify its more fundamental act of misrepresentation. Even when lies are told to convey a more basic truth, I maintain that this, too, very likely constitutes misrepresentation, since truths that derive from untruths cannot be entirely true. Somehow, somewhere, yet more basic lies fester unseen. What results, I suggest, is a dialectic standoff between fiction's declared veracity and the relatively unpleasant truths it denies by substituting believable misinformation. Superficial truths are exaggerated to reject more threatening truths, and fiction's final, most inclusive truth consists of the dialectic interplay between the two.

What, then, is the truth whose neglect is encouraged by literary misrepresentation? In its simplest definition, the truth consists, as I. A. Richards maintained, of relatively "undistorted references," ideas of ourselves and the world about us that may be tentatively established as being accurate.[11] If no absolute truths may be established pertaining to a world "out there," as both pragmatists and neopragmatists have insisted, a bivalent distinction between hard and benign truths may be suggested, with hard (i.e., relatively unpleasant) truths consisting of those that are useful because they confront problems, and with benign truths consisting of those that afford satisfaction by diverting our attention from these problems, often by focusing on other problems that may be dealt with more effectively. All thinking mixes these two versions of the truth, but it is the unique value of fiction that it disposes of hard truths by focusing on benign truths. This substitution is what primarily gives fiction its appeal as an act of deception.

If total accuracy is impossible, close approximations are nevertheless achievable and, in fact, may often be taken for granted, for example, in science, repair manuals, and grocery store bargain advertisements. Comprehensiveness and the allowance for exceptions are often desirable, but just as often a simple epithet or phrase captures the truth well enough to be accepted as such. Aphorisms need be no more than a sentence in length to be appreciated for their veracity, for example, bearing upon my topic, Justice Darling's remark, "Much truth is spoken, that more may be concealed," and Samuel Butler's remark, "The best liar is he that makes the smallest amount of lying go the longest way."[12] News stories are often partially true, as is most of the nonfiction sold today. Even narrative history conveys truths, though, as Hayden White insists, its linear selectivity verges on literary distortion.[13] For the average reader, the vast majority of truths are harmless, for example, telephone numbers, family trees, and the factual information that fills an almanac or encyclopedia. However, the truths that provoke literary misrepresentation are more personal, hence more dangerous, since they bear upon our weakness and sense of inadequacy. These are the truths at stake in the context of literary form.

E. D. Hirsch has argued that an author's private experience is irrelevant to the truth of what he or she tells.[14] In fact, this experience is the most impor-

Introduction

tant of all for both authors and readers. Contradicting himself, Hirsch later declares, "The speaker himself is spoken," and here one may agree, but with two caveats: (1) that the reader is likewise "spoken," and (2) that the spoken identities of authors and their readers primarily consist of ego adjustment rooted in avoidances, i.e., in evasions and prevarications. The personal truths we want to disregard—even, if necessary, to the extent of repressing them—these, I claim, are the truths denied by means of fiction. Ascertain what readers find the most uncomfortable, the most threatening, and avoidance of these truths very likely turns out to be the primary reason for readers' immersing themselves in fiction. Time and again they return to the same narrative formula (or formulas), and time and again literary outcomes help them to overlook what bothers them. Thus, fairy tales help small children to reject feelings of helplessness, and westerns and Harlequin romances help adolescents to reject their sense of entrapment in an adult world. Do adults think their reading habits are fundamentally different? Their sensitivities may be more attenuated, but their objectives as readers are essentially the same relative to their needs.

Fiction's manipulation of the truth is obviously illustrated, for example, by the contrast between literary death scenes and the actual experience of dying that occurs daily in the real world. The reconciliation and transcendent lucidity typical of literary death differ from the way most of us die—either by an abrupt terminal attack or, more likely, after a prolonged infirmity characterized by pain, exhaustion, recoveries followed by relapses, an increasing sense of isolation, and, sooner or later, everybody's tacit gratitude that the suffering and uncertainty are finally done with. This is a common ordeal, and it is far more unpleasant than Shakespeare's death scenes—for example, Hamlet's final eloquence, Lear's cradling Cordelia in his arms, and Othello's body stretched across Desdemona's in their belated rite of consummation.[15] Likewise comforting are the death scenes of Tolstoy's Ivan Ilyich and Emily Dickinson's bedridden woman for whom a fly "interposed." Katherine Anne Porter's depiction of Granny Weatherall's death might seem realistic, but her notion that the moment of death provides the key to life is quintessentially literary. Even Emma Bovary's terminal agony fits the pattern. Its clinical accuracy as a depiction of arsenic poisoning might seem uncompromisingly grim, but Emma's final spasm of ironic laughter at a beggar's song heard through the window is obviously literary. Each of these conventional death tableaux is frightening but on balance preferable to the commonplace act of dying that is almost inevitably devoid of both rapport and redeeming wisdom. I would argue that the same upgrading may be observed in the fictional treatment of love, heroism, bold decision-making, and virtually every dimension of human behavior, if drawn from contrasts not quite so stark.

Of course, fiction should muster enough truths to disguise its usefulness as a lie. For example, it refrains from directly contradicting the truth and declaring *not X* ("The hero is *not* greedy," when he obviously is). Instead, it proposes a Y that may be implicitly accepted as an alternative, either by asserting the contrary affirmation—for example, "She can at times be generous"—or by resorting to indirection—for example, "She is bold and ambitious," and/or "He treats money only as a game." In either case, Y may be accepted as a different version of events whose acceptance diverts one's attention from the truth of X ($Y = \text{not } X$). Any kind of a standoff may be featured between X and Y, as long as denial is either declared or implied. Often this strategy is refined by concentrating on limited truths to deny more inclusive truths, for example, affirming X to deny the blanket validity of $X + Y + Z$. Obversely, inclusive truths may be declared to deemphasize component truths, for example, affirming $X + Y + Z$ to deny the paramount role of X. In the first instance, for example, a suitor's rectitude might be praised to exclude from consideration the wealth and social status that would make him particularly attractive (e.g., in *Tom Jones*); in the second, his wealth and social status might be conceded but in a catalog of virtues that masks their disproportionate importance (e.g., in *Pride and Prejudice*). In both instances denial occurs by the author's imposing an alternative version of events, and of course without any acknowledgment that a substitution has been made. Usually this dialectic blends the truth and its denial in what seems an indistinguishable mixture, but it may be detected whenever readers find satisfaction in stories at odds with what they can see for themselves in their daily lives. In effect, the truth-untruth choice has been tilted and reorganized as an affirmative-negative polarity. The whole of the text has become a negative referent to dispose of unacceptable truths by means of creative expressiveness.

Stanley Fish's sweeping pragmatic question "What does a text do?" may be answered by the Aristotelian dictum that it conveys truth through its imitation of behavior (*praxis*), but I want to maintain, more fundamentally, that *mimesis* itself affords *praxis* if and when a plot's imitation of behavior organizes truths in such a manner as to convey falsehoods.[16] Whenever linear advancement predominates, as it usually does, a text produces results which only seem true to life. What is not true is presented as if it comes true, so a lie is told by advancing from valid uncertainties to a false sense of resolution. This, I propose, is what gives deception its dominant role in literature. Both truth and the lie may be told in the context of fiction, but as *muthos* (or plot), it is only the lie that happens, giving fiction its primary appeal.[17] Aristotle's definition of plot as the imitation (*mimesis*) of action (*praxis*) may accordingly be revised, as Plato would have insisted, with *praxis* incorporated into *mimesis* as plotted by what happens to produce misrepresentation.[18] Suggestive of Aristotle's theory of plot, a sequence emerges in which beginnings at least tacitly acknowledge the truth, ends deny it, and the middle functions to subordinate local snags and resistances to the momentum toward closure through acceptable misrepresentation. There are two plateaus, a *before* and an *after*, and the second contradicts the first. The middle consists of the transition between the two while the lie is in the process of being told.

Unlike metaphor, which almost instantaneously declares or undeclares its truths, a plot's metonymic organization subsumes representation to a protracted substitution based on the principle of denial. *After* signifies *before*, but only by reversing it by means of a suitable (i.e., happy) ending. If what is denied remains in view, as Wolfgang Iser argues, it is as a memory of a preliminary circumstance that serves to intensify one's satisfaction with the results.[19] What can be forgotten is the threatening aspect of this circumstance, which has been erased (or designified) through absorption into a benign and more inclusive context imposed by narrative form. Beginnings and local insights are revised by their outcome, so threat becomes little more than the memory of a challenge surmounted. Moreover, the confessional honesty that appears here and there in fiction's local texture is absorbed and finally denied by narrative closure.

Stanley Fish's question compels three additional questions: (1) where does fiction take us? (2) what does it leave behind? and (3) how does this loss produce satisfaction? As the broadest answer, most texts provide a unique opportunity to deal with problems by means of conventional literary truths. Momentum toward closure (the pseudosolution of these problems) is pitted against subversiveness (their acknowledgment). Usually, but not always, honesty confesses uniqueness (Tolstoy's unhappiness "in its own way," as declared in the first sentence of *Anna Karenina*), and fiction's conventional resolution imposes the appropriate distortions to cope with this honesty in a socially acceptable manner. Sometimes an author consciously works to deceive readers, but more often authors deceive readers by first deceiving themselves well enough to let readers respond in kind by drawing on authorial illusions to buttress their own. Self-deception becomes a collaborative act shared by authors and readers. Here the notion of textual indeterminacy (or *aporia*)— explained, for example, by Iser's "gaps," Derrida's "ruptures," and Barbara Herrnstein Smith's notion of "radical contingency"—essentially concedes the freedom of readers to adapt the author's self-deception to suit their own needs.[20] At one level readers might be trying to adjust the "truth" of fiction to fit their own perspective, but at another and more basic level their effort entails the appropriation of evasiveness, as afforded by narrative form, to suppress their own truths. The reader's freedom of choice may be emphasized, but it is the choice among untruths, not truths, that primarily determines the range of possibilities. Here the "linguistic competence" Fish emphasizes has its counterpart in what might be described as narrative competence, the skill of readers to adapt literary illusion to their own personal needs.[21] If they can draw satisfaction from the illusion intended by the author, it is not of great importance whether they understand or concur with every aspect of the story. What is important to recognize is that misrepresentation constitutes both the source and the final outcome of literary experience. As a conscious and/or unconscious intentional act, literature affirms in order to deny for both authors and readers, and its formal organization provides the structural embodiment of this negative accomplishment. To borrow a term from Alfred North Whitehead's metaphysics, deception "ingresses" literary form, and all readers, the author included, may derive from it any lie they need within the spectrum (or "horizon") of opportunities it provides relative to their experiences. As might be suggested by this more inclusive notion of indeterminacy, the classic as defined by Frank Kermode is merely a text that offers useful evasions for the broadest audience of readers over at least a century or two.[22]

In recent years, Stanley Fish and others influenced by the neopragmatism of Richard Rorty have emphasized a skeptical relativism that challenges the possibility of literal truth. All truth is presumably relative in fiction, so neither literal truth nor, *a posteriori*, the lie as an avoidance of this truth is of concern in hermeneutics. For if truth is impossible, so, too, is the lie as its misrepresentation. In "Interpreting the *Variorum*," published in 1977, Fish proposed that "interpretive acts" by "interpretive communities" provide the only valid basis for explicative objectivity.[23] Each community features its own truths

Introduction

about literature, and no explication is necessarily better than the rest. In *Doing What Comes Naturally*, published in 1989, Fish advocates an "antifoundationalism" based on the recognition that what seems the most impartial opinion still necessarily expresses partial bias.[24] Since all preferences are principled, and, obversely, since all principles are preferences, the relativity of knowledge presumably becomes inescapable. In his article "Rhetoric," Fish takes his argument one step further by insisting that all truths—scientific, literary, and otherwise—are inevitably rhetorical.[25] He cites Thomas Kuhn to dispense with the myth of scientific objectivity and tries to demonstrate that J. L. Austin's "constative" truths are "performative" and hence dependent on persuasiveness rather than factual accuracy.

However, contrary to Fish's arguments, relativism among truths, literary or otherwise, is not so immutable that any truth is as valid or invalid as another. Some truths correspond to reality with a better fit than others, so any rejection of these for alternatives whose comparative inaccuracy affords greater satisfaction may be treated as an act of deception. In nonliterary discourse, any theory or belief rooted in inaccuracy is vulnerable to being superseded by another with better and more inclusive—if not perfect—sufficiency in its depiction of reality. But whatever aspects of the rejected theory still bear a useful fit may be retained and brought into synthesis with later alternatives. The advance in empirical knowledge from one age to the next, as proposed by Kuhn in *The Structure of Scientific Revolutions*, has not led to the wholesale rejection of each age's scientific hypotheses for those of the next.[26] Newton's theory of relativity has not been altogether superseded by Kant's and Darwin's respective theories of evolution, Einstein's theory of relativity, or Hawking's theory of black holes. Certain hypotheses—for example, that of phlogiston and both the geocentric and heliocentric theories of the universe—have been displaced by others, but many other hypotheses have persisted, since the "truths" they convey more or less integrate with later empirical data. The overall trend has been on balance cumulative rather than substitutive, as explained by two of the outstanding classics in the history of science, Alfred North Whitehead's *Science and the Modern World* and Albert Einstein and Leopold Infeld's *The Evolution of Physics*. Like Heisenberg's uncertainty principle, Kuhn's relatively modest thesis has become a nonscientist's crutch for dispensing with science, and one doubts, as John Searle recently indicated, that Kuhn himself would approve of such an effort.[27]

Fish likewise revises J. L. Austin's theory of speech acts to demonstrate the neopragmatic thesis that constative (i.e., literal) truth is always fundamentally performative (i.e., persuasive).[28] Truth, Fish claims, may be judged true only on a rhetorical basis, i.e., in a particular context for a particular audience. Here Fish's skepticism, like Hume's, cannot be refuted in the final analysis, but Fish ignores the prevalence of truths whose performative sufficiency affords relative constative certitude. Moreover, he fails to recognize that the distinction between the two is no more absolute than any of the other true/false distinctions he rejects. In fact, all truths are *both* performative and constative, though on balance favoring one at the expense of the other. Literary truths, for example, are necessarily more performative and scientific truths more constative, but in neither instance is the alternative altogether eliminated. Two corollaries may accordingly be proposed: (1) that any exaggeration of performative value as if it were constative provides the matrix of literary experience, and, vice versa, (2) that any effort to weed out a statement's performative deficiencies probably (but not necessarily) increases its constative value. Any performative truth may be revised to be accepted as being relatively constative, often by merely adding a qualification—"perhaps," "at times," "according to," or, most inclusively, "granted the following exceptions." If, for example, the sentence *Hamlet commits suicide* seems dubious, the revised versions *Perhaps Hamlet commits suicide* and *What Hamlet does is tantamount to committing suicide* are less vulnerable to challenge. Though all truths are performative, some are more constative than others, and perfect accuracy remains a valid goal in nonliterary areas of behavior, whether or not it can ever be achieved. Though at times an endangered species (for example, in politics, media hype, and television advertisements), literal truth does exist, relatively speaking, and so too, therefore, does untruth as its literary avoidance. The use of skepticism to deny this possibility affords probably the biggest lie, the most basic of evasive strategies.[29]

Until the last couple of decades, the unexamined worship of literary truth has been commonplace in literary criticism, and, in what seems an overreaction, Fish and others have replaced it with a notion of indeterminacy as the principal ingredient of literary discourse. What I propose as a synthesis, if such may be possible, is a recognition of the dialectic by which fiction arranges competitive versions of the truth in complementary phases: (1) the rejection of unpleasant truths through (2) the substitution of preferred truths, i.e., whatever diversionary truths are needed to convey the lie. Granted their context, they are true enough, but their truth is misleading relative to the truths

Introduction

their acceptance excludes from consideration. Victory truths, for example, substitute for failure truths, love truths for frustration truths, adequacy truths for inadequacy truths, rapport truths for alienation truths, and, of Menandrine necessity, orthodox heterosexual truths for their androgynous alternatives. Other substitutions feature degree rather than kind, for example, when one finds satisfaction in literary role models that seem more sensitive, more comprehending, more fortunate, more heroic, and/or more attractive to the opposite sex. Subtler variations include the reader's renewed sense of personal worth from acknowledging presumably universal truths (for example, ironically, the seldom useful truth that honesty is the best policy) or from recognizing that no such answers are forthcoming, or that the right questions cannot even be asked (for example, in *Waiting for Godot*). Paradoxically, even the truth that deception is unavoidable (for example, Marlow's final insight in *Heart of Darkness*) may be useful as a lie, as I try to demonstrate in chapter 3.

Sometimes we benefit from identifying with characters whose truth derives from their being more violent and degenerate than ourselves. Transgression truths likewise make us feel good, so we seek them out in stories that deny the inhibitions we cannot otherwise acknowledge. On the other hand, the sense of control while reading fiction can be no less deceptive. Our feelings of adequacy are improved by identifying (or, as Simon Lesser explains, by analogizing) with characters whenever we please and by our ability to share in the author's successful verbalization of the story.[30] One way or another, we find satisfaction in texts that give us what seems a more favorable understanding of ourselves and the world we live in. As Northrop Frye maintains, reading literature establishes an identity that lets us get away from the world we don't like.[31] Otherwise, we would not bother to read fiction.

In the most inclusive sense, we enjoy a text because it substitutes the world of fiction for the world outside fiction—and, once within fiction, because it substitutes an achieved world for the world left behind. Not only is the world of fiction different, but it is susceptible to further change; other improvements can be made, one state of affairs replaced by another. Of course, preferred truths may be declared as an instantaneous act of denial, but they are more effectively imposed by means of narrative reversal that culminates in acceptable closure, with the truths they deny limited to a texture of local images and metaphors quickly forgotten in the flow of reading.[32] Narrative advancement thus consolidates the eventual victory of misrepresentation, its progressive momentum only temporarily impeded by antilinear alternatives.

Like the textual gaps proposed by Wolfgang Iser, these resistant features are more likely to emphasize subjective expressiveness, as opposed to the progressive features whose dominant context of meaning culminates in a pleasantly evasive resolution.

The progressive-resistant dialectic I am suggesting may engage any number of distinctions—for example, at the most simplistic level, between good and evil, between temptation and its rejection, or between timidity and the courage to seek vindication. With greater complexity, it may pit a relatively expressive depiction of villains, as in the case of Milton's Satan, against a relatively conventional depiction of heroes, as in the case of Milton's Adam. Bridging categories, it may pit ambivalent motivation against dramatic convention (as in the case of *Hamlet*), or, as explained in chapter 4, it may pit threatening local connotations against a combination of theme and narrative closure that almost vehemently disavows these connotations. One state of mind is implicit in the images, metaphors, and puns that dominate the attention from one sentence to the next, but an entirely different state of mind prevails once closure is imposed. In effect, the story's resolution denies both its beginning and the way it has been told. Serious fiction might be less obviously escapist than popular fiction, but it likewise provides us with a vacation from ourselves. Its greater sophistication is thus a matter of degree rather than kind. There might be more subtlety and greater psychological complications, and countervailing suggestiveness might be better articulated, necessitating a more circumscribed sense of ending. Nevertheless, any story that produces results better than reality brings into play narrative dynamics rooted in self-deception.

Here the "sense of an ending" I am defining essentially reverses Frank Kermode's definition in his useful book of the same title. According to Kermode, escapist fiction lacks serious fiction's apocalyptic experience of finality. Kermode argues that the two versions of literary experience are qualitatively different and that every novel fits one category or the other, not both. In his view, serious fiction compels our attention by representing improvements (the "world of potency") as being achieved (a "world of act") and by showing narrative movement "through time to an end, an end we must sense even if we cannot know it."[33] I respectfully propose an alternative to Kermode's theory based on three premises: (1) *every* text proposes its own "world of potency" that is realized as act (or *praxis*) in the context of narrative form, (2) *every* text is accordingly organized to provide a sense of an ending that

Introduction

can be somewhat accurately anticipated by readers, and (3) the serious fiction that Kermode admires actually puts up more of a struggle than popular fiction against this narrative inevitability. In serious fiction there is usually a more effective resistance to closure by truths that defy linear simplification, for example, in style and characterization. Closure's victory is consequently less decisive, but this does not diminish its importance.

Through the course of *Negative Poetics*, I explore literary deception based on cognitive, homeostatic, and paranoid models of narrative denial, all of which help to explain closure as an agent of misrepresentation. The cognitive model I am proposing features the use of conventional truths to deny unacceptable experience, the paranoid model features denial as the primary displacement in a projective strategy to act out one's problems in the relatively safe context of fiction, and the homeostatic model treats narrative form as a kind of negative feedback system to produce tension reduction felt as pleasure. Each of these models is explained in one chapter, then illustrated in the next, the cognitive model in chapters 1 and 2, the homeostatic model in chapters 3 and 4, and the paranoid model in chapters 5 and 6. In chapter 7 I propose what might be described as the affirmative fallacy, which manifests itself whenever the denial mechanism is directly linked to a diversionary act of affirmation—for example, at the most harmless level, when one praises the weather to avoid mentioning one's discomfort with the need to converse. In the rest of chapter 7, as well as in chapters 8 and 9, I shift my focus to literary criticism based on the broader application of the affirmative fallacy. Chapter 7 treats the false assumptions of several modern schools of criticism, chapter 8 treats the evasiveness of a particular critic, and chapter 9 treats the evasiveness of three works of literary criticism with declared affirmative viewpoints.

In my first chapter, I resurrect deceptionism (or, to avoid ambiguity, deceptology) as a neglected critical tradition that has included Plato, Rousseau, Hegel, Reynolds, Poe, Nietzsche, Tolstoy, Freud, Mencken, I. A. Richards, Marcuse, Barthes, Steiner, and perhaps two dozen others. I include a wide diversity of perspectives here, many at variance with others. My own approach concentrates on the deceptive impact of narrative form, but I also take into account the full range of opportunities for deception as featured by these others. As I indicated earlier, I reject Sir Philip Sidney's notion that a text tells no lies because it makes no attempt to tell the truth and instead agree with Gerald Graff's argument in *Literature against Itself* that the distinction

Introduction

between true and false propositions is built in to the language of fiction and that it cannot be arbitrarily excluded from literary experience.[34] Contrary to Graff's position, however, I propose that this necessity limits fiction to the category of telling lies. Like any other discourse that draws false conclusions from true premises, fiction cannot avoid being fallacious, since it uses truths for deceptive purposes. In the most restrictive sense, only the uncompromising dedication to truth justifies warranted assertability, for example, as earlier mentioned, in the case of scientific methodology. In fiction, like religion, there is little room for strict verification standards, for the unbiased accumulation of data, or for the full exploration of exceptions. Instead, fiction's truths and untruths inextricably blend with each other, reducing literary truth to verisimilitude as the appearance of truth rather than the truth itself.

I also propose that fiction primarily deceives about the most important issues in life and that authors, like politicians, are probably the most credible when they believe their fabrications. The misrepresentations important to readers may differ from those important to authors, but narrative conventions afford enough flexibility to let readers adopt an author's self-deception for their own purposes. From an author's lies, readers can generate their own, and the more basic the lie, very probably the more universal its appeal. The same act of misrepresentation may serve to deny any number of unacceptable truths, and in any combination for any particular reader. In effect, the opportunity for self-deception is communicated just as words and images are communicated, and a structural residue of deception is built in to each and every text as the tangible record of this shared purpose. It is this structural residue that gives formal validity to a text, providing the vehicle for illusion as communicated from authors to their readers. Obversely, a work of literature becomes irrelevant to readers' feelings if the formal organization of the works discourages self-deception, whereupon readers can be expected to set those aside for other, more interesting books.

With my second model, as I explain in chapters 3 and 4, I revise and update Aristotle's theory of catharsis by treating literary deception as an agent of homeostasis. I maintain that tension (as expressed by fear, anxiety, or simple dissatisfaction) might be temporarily elevated by fiction, but only to be reduced to a steady-state minimum felt as pleasure. As with other types of homeostasis, fiction constitutes a relatively modest commitment of energy, the attention devoted to reading a text, which helps to diminish more pervasive tension levels. Paradoxically, the story's plotted resolution may be affir-

Introduction

mative, but its positive value as illusion derives from the principle of negative feedback, a relatively small diversion of nervous energy (in this case, the cognitive activity of reading a book) for causing homeostatic tension reduction experienced as pleasure. As opposed to the ordinary lie, which usually raises tension levels, literary deception lowers these levels by concentrating the reader's attention on imaginary characters whose behavior produces results that reverse what has *not* been achieved in real life. Something happens contrary to our experience (i.e., denial occurs), and this makes us feel good (i.e., tension levels have been reduced by means of negative feedback).

As Coleridge pointed out, there is also ongoing pleasure ("the attractions of the journey itself") in the process of reading a text independent of its sense of an ending.[35] Local contexts provide homeostatic satisfaction, for example, when ambiguity is suddenly clarified, when rhyme and rhythm effectively contour ideas, or when periodic sentences are brought to a suitable conclusion. However, the sequence of minor homeostatic effects culminates in a final splurge, the broad gratification we feel upon finishing the story—because a suitable resolution has been imposed and also (why not admit it?) simply because completion has occurred. The process is over and done with, followed by a genuine sense of accomplishment.

I devote chapters 5 and 6 to my third model, based on comparisons with the clinical diagnosis of paranoia. I compare literary form with Freud's analysis of the paranoid syndrome as a sequence of denial and projective displacements by which we can blame others for our own problems.[36] I extend Freud's theory to literary analysis by showing how fiction abstracts and reverses these two displacements in a narrative context devoid of recognizable personal animosity. The plot itself becomes an agent of denial, since it imposes a linear arrangement that sooner or later supplants need with vicarious fulfillment. As I indicated earlier, almost any reversal of events may be refashioned by readers to fit their individual circumstances. The denial implicit in Hamlet's revenge, for example, may be enjoyed for any number of reasons, as may the denial implicit in Antony and Cleopatra's martyrdom to love, David Copperfield's rise to success, and most of the other literary success stories familiar to readers.

Because readers only partially immerse themselves in fiction, paranoid defense mechanisms may be utilized as a relatively healthy pattern of evasiveness. Nevertheless, fiction often features such obviously symptomatic paranoid coping mechanisms as the simplistic distinction between good and

Introduction

evil, the conflict between heroes and villains, the exaggerated centrality of heroes in a pseudocommunity of friends and enemies, the undue importance of special truths and secret disclosures, the use of simplistic homophobic stereotypes to deny sexual ambivalence, and the perpetual quest for vindication in the opinion of readers. These classic paranoid traits are benign in fiction, since its make-believe context is limited to the act of reading. As a result, fiction's preparanoid organization of experience becomes a healthy expedient—temporary in its cathartic benefits, permanent (but not necessarily chronic) in its availability as literary reinforcement to our sense of personal worth.

In chapter 7, I propose the affirmative fallacy as an act of denial in its most irreducible manifestation. This occurs when undesirable experience automatically produces compensatory affirmation in something—anything—that may be construed as its opposite. Such a reversal happens, for example, when uncertainty triggers belief; confusion, discipline; resentment, false gratitude; and the diminished sense of personal worth, an overweening loyalty to whatever group or category one can take pride in (church, nation, local sports teams, etc.). I try to show how an intermediate loss of focus occurs, letting this reversal come about without having been recognized as such by those who benefit from it. At one moment, discomfort prevails; at the very next, pride, joy, or indignation crowds it from our minds. Energy is withdrawn from one mental disposition and almost as quickly invested in another—in effect, its opposite. There is a tenor-vehicle interaction, as I. A. Richards has suggested for metaphor, except that its forward metonymic organization depends on a vehicle whose acceptable truth *designifies*, or drives from consciousness, its tenor rooted in unacceptable truth.[37] Metonymic designification occurs in the sense that the image implicit in this vehicle as a final state of affairs substitutes for its tenor's acknowledgment of countervailing difficulties instead of conceding them through its more accessible representation.

Also designified, necessarily, is the recognition that such a displacement has taken place. When our minds shift from unpleasantness to diversionary affirmation, we must exclude from consciousness both the unpleasantness and our effort to divert our attention elsewhere. To reject or ignore an idea, we must also ignore our choice to do so. As E. H. Gombrich maintains, we cannot watch ourselves having an illusion.[38] We can fantasize or be conscious that we are fantasizing, but not both simultaneously. As soon as we recognize this is what we are doing, we no longer, strictly speaking, do it. Similarly, to

Introduction

tell ourselves lies, we must also lie about what we are telling ourselves. If we admit we are lying, the lie dissolves, so the lie we tell must be augmented by the lie that we are not lying. Two acts of denial thus simultaneously occur: (1) the affirmative truth which denies a more basic truth, and (2) a commitment to this truth which denies that denial has occurred. By means of this doubling, we defend our lies with greater energy than the truths we can otherwise take for granted. Our lies assume the value of a belief, or belief system, worthy of strenuous defense—strenuous enough at times that it becomes an imposition, almost an act of aggression.

All in all, in the most general terms, I am proposing a hyperreductionist model of literary experience (1) as self-deception, (2) as a tension-reduction strategy based on self-deception, (3) as a paranoid double displacement that "plots" a self-deceptive outcome, and, most fundamentally, (4) as the intellectual commitment to positive achievement that denies (or designifies) unacceptable experience by engaging in both literary and critical evasiveness. Each of these four reductionist perspectives—respectively explained in chapters 1, 3, 5, and 7—brings into play the same basic principle, the use of affirmation to deny. Each chapter features one particular aspect of denial, focusing respectively on (1) disavowing truths too painful to be acknowledged, (2) giving homeostatic value to the avoidance of these truths, (3) utilizing preparanoid fantasy as the agent for diminishing anxieties, and (4) automatically substituting an affirmative vision as an acceptable alternative. Organized as a taxonomy, the homeostatic component (of the Freudian id) explains the biological aim of literary illusion, the deceptionist component (of the ego) explains the cognitive realization of this aim, and the paranoid component (of the superego) explains the ethical bias involved in trying to make this self-serving fabrication seem true to life. With the affirmative fallacy, finally, I reduce to its essence the use of literary illusion to deny (or designify) unacceptable experience. Each of these particular models stands alone, but any combination may be emphasized to help clarify how fiction's distortions let us adjust to our own modestly distorted circumstances—our frustrations, empty successes, and lost opportunities.

Readers should be forewarned that my four explicative chapters—chapters 2, 4, 6, and 8—primarily illustrate the negative dialectic implicit in these models by concentrating on what seems in my opinion fiction's most problematic evasive strategy, the homophobic rejection of androgyny by means of literary convention. Fiction that disposes of anxieties bearing on death, failure, alienation, or heterosexual frustration would be no less relevant to my thesis, but for the most part I find that the homophobic rejection of androgyny best and most dramatically illustrates the negative dialectic I am proposing. Moreover, homophobia (or, with less pathological violence implied, "homoaversiveness") seems rampant in fiction, especially in stories of romantic love that feature exaggerated heterosexual stereotypes, but also in tragedies, stories of male bonding through shared violence against enemies (the Starsky and Hutch syndrome), and stories of unfulfilled quests typified by the *Epic of Gilgamesh* and "The Rime of the Ancient Mariner." Often the choice between the two is exacerbated to such an extent and with such total ignorance of what is happening on the part of both author and readers that the negative dialectic I am trying to define may be explored with relative confidence. For this reason, my explicative chapters concentrate on this particular issue.

It also seems appropriate, however, to acknowledge my agreement with two apparently contradictory tenets of the gay perspective: that homophobia is rampant in society and that literature is replete with overlooked androgynous implications. Where I disagree stems from my willingness to explore the dialectic between androgyny and its homoaversive denial that occurs in the context of literary form, granting androgyny's relative freedom in local contexts but also conceding homoaversion's final victory through an outcome whose gender distinctions are satisfactory to the average heterosexual imagination. As a metonymic transfer from androgynous suggestiveness to homoaversive reassurance, this dialectic affords many texts their presumably undefinable fascination. Sheer androgyny necessarily deprives itself of most of its potential audience, while the crude homophobia that features violence and exaggerated role differentiation primarily appeals to the lowest common denominator. As organized by literary form, however, androgyny may be granted a certain measure of freedom once readers can relax, confident that homoaversive denial ultimately predominates. In effect, androgyny may be tolerated, even explored, as long as there are adequate homoaversive defenses to confirm its harmlessness, as, for example, when Rosalind's multiple transvestitism in *As You Like It* culminates in her marriage to Orlando, or, even more obviously, when the eager pursuit of Marilyn Monroe justifies transvestitism in the film *Some Like It Hot*. By means of this compromise, most individuals experience both catharsis (as illustrated by laughter in response to

Introduction

both examples indicated here) and a renewed commitment to heterosexual love, sexual reproduction, and the nuclear family.

In chapter 2 I balance relatively simple homoaversive explications of *Pride and Prejudice* and *David Copperfield* against more subversive (and potentially androgynous) explications of *Heart of Darkness* and Gertrude Stein's "a rose is a rose is a rose is a rose." In chapter 4 I emphasize a plot-metaphor dialectic in more complicated homoaversive explications of *Hamlet*, "Mending Wall," and "The Rime of the Ancient Mariner." I show that in *Hamlet* androgynous tendencies lead to tragic self-destruction, while in "Mending Wall" and "The Rime of the Ancient Mariner" they oblige continuing vigilance, respectively against transgressing heterosexual barriers and against too eagerly capitulating to the marriage ritual. I explicate "Mending Wall" as perhaps the *locus classicus* of homoaversive vigilance and both *Hamlet* and "The Rime of the Ancient Mariner" as "antiepithalamiums" that reject heterosexual marriage without more than hinting at homosexual alternatives. In chapter 6 I explore the short story "Young Goodman Brown" as a story of paranoid ambivalence whose rejection of the marriage ritual helps to clarify the sexual ambivalence implicit in the frontier myths of American literature featured by Leslie Fiedler and others. Finally, in chapter 8 I trace Roland Barthes's lifetime career as a literary critic as an example of androgynous commitment elevated to the status of literary criticism. Barthes proposed a rapid succession of theories to challenge the importance of mimesis because of its connection with *doxa* (heterosexual orthodoxy), presumably the worst of literary sins. Only in one of his final books, *Camera Lucida*, did Barthes pay his respects to truth based on the mimetic value of family snapshots in reinforcing his intense rapport with his dead mother.[39] At last a radical theory of mimesis (i.e., the snapshot's certitude in recording a specific moment in the past) imposed closure on Barthes's career, both inverting the narrative dialectic I propose and lending urgency to his suicidal eagerness to rejoin his mother in death.

In chapter 9 I shift to politics by exploring as a sequence the compensatory affirmative perspective of three critics—Lionel Trilling, Wayne Booth, and John Gardner—all of whom played a role, each more decisively than the last, in both documenting and justifying our culture's withdrawal from its anarchistic obsession with authenticity during the sixties. I discuss Trilling's *Sincerity and Authenticity*, published in 1972, as a historic reassessment of the dialectic between truth and evasiveness that let him justify his rejection of the

New Left's extravagant commitment to "letting it all hang out."[40] Booth's *Modern Dogma and the Rhetoric of Assent*, published in 1974, I discuss as a manifesto for "systematic assent" that effectively precludes skeptical inquiry (Bertrand Russell having been the godfather of the protest movement, in Booth's opinion); I also try to demonstrate how Booth's proposal that affirmative value might be built into the universe as a hierarchy of explanatory systems suggests a more inclusive *negative* hierarchy, one that advances from quarks and photons to carbon molecules, tissue permeability, cell reproduction, homeostasis, the complex physiology of the human brain, and, at the apex of biological evolution, literary form as perhaps denial's most refined manifestation.[41] Finally, I end the chapter by challenging the compulsively superficial litany of affirmative prescriptions for good writing advocated by John Gardner in his book *On Moral Fiction*, published in 1978.[42] By categorizing and systematically reversing these prescriptions, I am able to conclude *Negative Poetics* with an iconoclastic manifesto that emphasizes the value of self-deception for all writers with something to say—if not exactly what they mean.

one

A SHORT HISTORY OF DECEPTION THEORIES

It is told that Solon, the ancient Athenian statesman, attended one of Thespis's tragedies to see for himself why this new type of spectacle had gained such wide popular appeal. Shocked by its factual liberties, he asked Thespis after the performance if he were not ashamed to tell so many lies before such large crowds of people. In his defense Thespis argued that no harm had been done, whereupon Solon angrily struck his staff against the ground, declaring, "If we honour and commend such play as this, we shall find it some day in our business."[1] This first known instance of theater criticism has been widely cited for its naiveté, but it accurately foretold the almost inextricable blend of truth and fiction taken for granted today in all walks of life. Who, after all, can deny Oscar Wilde's iconoclastic view that life imitates art and that our understanding of nature is necessarily the product of our education by art?[2] If Solon could visit the modern world, he might be offended by Wilde's perverse delight in this outcome but hardly by the validity of his judgment. It almost seems as if Thespis's aesthetic liberties both anticipated and set in motion the creation of modern literature. Whether we like it or not, literary distortion has become indispensable to human experience, valid because it codifies nonliterary modes and trends that it itself has so effectively encouraged. Poetic license has escaped Pandora's box, and many of our best and most useful insights, as well as our most dangerous, may be traced to its literary wellspring.

Much in the spirit of Solon's warning, Plato argued in the tenth chapter of *The Republic*, almost two centuries later, that poetry should be banned from the ideal republic because its depiction of experience is necessarily twice removed from the truth of ideal forms. The poet's description of a chair, for example, only partially replicates the artisan's handiwork, and this in turn only partially replicates the ideal concept of a chair. First the concept gains concrete realization when the artisan constructs a version of the chair, after which the product may be depicted by poets and artists within the context of literary expression. This sequence took place, for example, when Thoreau boasted, "I had three chairs in my house: one for solitude, two for friendship, three for society," and when F. Scott Fitzgerald beckoned, "Draw your chair up close to the edge of the precipice and I'll tell you a story." Both authors proposed versions of a chair twice removed from its essence and purest conceptualization in order to express their respective views of privacy and the magic of storytelling. The chairs they described fell short of the ideal conception, and their description compounded this departure from the truth in a manner acceptable to literary convention. In similar fashion, all poetry doubles signification in giving free rein to bias and emotional manipulation at the expense of factual accuracy. Therefore, Plato argued, poetry should be excluded from the perfect society that encourages an uncompromising dedication to both honesty and emotional health.

Plato's notion of aesthetic deception would probably have had a far more oppressive influence if Aristotle had not reversed his arguments by focusing his metaphysics of ideal forms upon tragic action as the purest literary ideal. According to Aristotle, tragedy is more true to life than either history or philosophy—the former because it is too particular, the latter because it is too general. Through its refined use of *mimesis*, Aristotle suggested, tragedy tells the truth by imitating a single action, the fall and self-discovery of a flawed protagonist that produce an appropriate dose of catharsis in a sympathetic audience. In effect, this limited use of *mimesis* duplicates a specific instance of behavior (or *praxis*) so that emotional release can be duplicated too. By identifying with a tragic protagonist, playgoers experience an appropriate mixture of pity (objective) for the protagonist and fear (subjective) for themselves.³ The principle of *mimesis* accordingly expands from the simple congruence between an event and its aesthetic representation to a dynamic interaction between staged and subjective self-discovery.

However, Aristotle's model of literary experience sacrificed thoroughgoing mimesis (the *trompe l'oeil*, slice of life, etc.) to the extreme selectivity needed to evoke catharsis. As Emerson proposed in "Circles," Aristotle himself "Platonized," in this instance by featuring the destruction of characters because of their deviation from established norms and conventions. Moreover, not just any behavior could be imitated but only the approved stories of kings and mythic personages whose destinies exemplified a reversal from high estate tarnished by ignorance to low estate redeemed by defeat and self-recognition. Aristotle claimed, in fact, that it is this radical selectivity that makes fiction superior to history. Probability takes precedence over actuality, he argued, since events are described as they *ought* to be, not as they are, cluttered by accident and random circumstances. This normative obligation bore obvious Platonic implications contrary to Aristotle's mimetic prescriptions explained elsewhere in *Poetics*. Aristotle also emphasized the plot's relatively abstract reversal dynamics at the expense of both idea and characterization, and he limited the scope of tragedy to its achievement of dénouement through ritualized self-destruction. He thus minimized the full complexity of human experience by stressing the importance of formal purity. Tragic form as a unity of action provided the aesthetic realization of Platonic ideals, since plot (*muthos*) led from genuine deficiency (*hamartia*) to purification through self-discovery (*anagnorisis*). Unfortunately, Aristotle did not explore the contradictions implicit in this model. He judged tragedy for both its mimetic accuracy and the transcendent purity of its form as if these two virtues are necessarily harmonious with each other. He also fell prey to the pleasant assumption that tragic recognition epitomizes human understanding, which it does not. Something else happens in life, and its radical simplification by tragedy necessarily diminishes tragic form's accuracy as pure representation.

A second theoretical effort to salvage poetry from Plato's indictment came with the advent of Neoplatonism in the third century. Like Aristotle, Neoplatonists turned Plato on his head, in their case by ascribing truth to ideal beauty as defined by Plato himself in *The Symposium*. Here Plato had explained love as the urge to perpetuate or reproduce ideal beauty, and Plotinus took the obvious additional step of featuring Plato's concept of ideal beauty as irradiated symmetry expressive of the ideal good. During the Renaissance, Neoplatonists took the final necessary step of treating poetry as the best medium for the depiction of ideal beauty. Italian aesthetician Girolamo Fracastoro claimed that the poet plays a special role as one "who is moved by the true beauty of things—by their simple and essential beauties, not merely apparent ones."[4] Poetic inspiration supposedly discloses the truth by capturing the essential beauty of the universe as ruled by God. Poets could therefore be confident they were telling the truth as long as they restricted their discourse to the appreciation of beauty. Plato's concept of poetry as a twofold departure from absolute truth was accordingly reversed to establish aesthetic expression as the primary means of regaining this truth. If the artisan's handiwork necessarily falls short of the idealized chair, the poet's inspiration purifies the chair of its imperfections, restoring its idealization through the vision and language of poetry. As a result, the poet's worship of beauty becomes our primary access to higher truth, not its final and most unavailing abandonment. This Neoplatonic reversal took on enormous importance through the seventeenth century, and vestiges have persisted into the nineteenth and twentieth centuries. At first poetry could be defended for expressing the poet's dedication to Platonic love (in the poetry of Petrarch and Sidney); later it could be defended for expressing the poet's comparable dedication as a prophet of nature (in Wordsworth), of society (in Whitman), and even of civilization's decline (in T. S. Eliot).

Christian doctrine perpetuated Plato's original views of literary deception despite their modifications by Aristotelian and Neoplatonic theory. In *The Confessions* St. Augustine complained of "poetic fictions" as the "choice spectacle of his vanity" during his youth. In comparable fashion, secular literary experience was rejected by Christian polemicists such as Salvianus, Stephen Gosson, William Prynne, and Jeremy Collier, all of whom excoriated both the theater and literature in general as temptations to sinfulness.[5] If scripture alone embodies Christian truth, they argued, literary experience necessarily diminishes this truth, especially when classical gods and heroes are venerated by secular poets who try to elevate their creativity to the same plane as that of scriptural revelation. In effect, these polemicists adopted Plato's rejection of literature to the equally stringent tenets of orthodox Christianity. Once the worship of God could be substituted for Plato's theory of ideal forms,

A Short History of Deception Theories

Plato's rejection of literary deception could be resurrected for the purposes of guaranteeing spiritual purity.

Only with the advent of the Renaissance did it become possible to make a virtue of artistic license as the best means of teaching morality. Perhaps the first such defense of aesthetic distortion was offered by Francesco Robortelli, a translator and relatively minor critic of the mid-sixteenth century who more directly took his inspiration from Aristotelian doctrine that poetry "deals with things as they ought to be, rather than as they are."[6] The primary objective of poetry, Robortelli suggested, should be not mimetic accuracy but the encouragement of virtue, which it accomplishes by proposing improvements upon the real world. In "An Apologie for Poetrie," written in 1583 and published in 1595, Sir Philip Sidney likewise praised poetry for "making things either better then Nature bringeth forth, or, quite a newe, formes such as never were in Nature." According to Sidney, poetry's unique achievement was its "divine consideration of what may be, and should be," apparently with the aim of elevating *praxis* (action) over *gnossus* (knowledge) through the encouragement of "vertuous action" in readers.[7] In 1658 the French critic Guez de Balzac likewise praised literary deception as a pedagogical device for conveying valuable lessons through duplicity: "O la bonne trahison que celle-là!"[8] This ethical defense of literary deception has persisted over the centuries. Essentially the same argument, for example, has been made in the twentieth century by Thornton Wilder: "It [the theater] lives by conventions: a convention is an agreed upon falsehood, a permitted lie." In Wilder's opinion, the whole purpose of literary misrepresentation is the lesson it teaches:

> The myth, the parable, the fable are the fountainhead of all fiction and in them is seen most clearly the didactic, moralizing employment of a story. Modern taste shrinks from emphasizing the central idea that hides behind the fiction, but it exists there nevertheless, supplying the unity to fantasizing, and offering a justification to what otherwise we would repudiate as mere arbitrary contrivance, pretentious lying, or individualistic emotional association spinning.[9]

In other words, literary deception imposes standards of behavior superior to those observed in the real world—exactly opposite Plato's view. As my twelfth-grade English teacher fervently argued, we must first imitate virtues in order to acquire them. Fiction accordingly suggests improvements, and readers benefit from observing, then absorbing them. The obvious hypocrite merely fails to complete this transition from pretense to actualization.

By the eighteenth century, the Baron von Bielfeld, a Prussian encyclopedist, was able to shift from ethics to the psychological value of literary deception with his striking declaration, "L'art de'exprimer les pensées par la fiction." By means of aesthetic distortion, ideas could be the most effectively expressed. Bielfeld's pronouncement was later quoted by Edgar Allan Poe to challenge the obtrusive didacticism of Longfellow's poetry.[10] The essence of literature is hardly truth, Poe argued, but rather the artistic effort of the poet to manipulate the reader's feelings. As an artisan, the poet must reorganize experience to produce the necessary aesthetic effect, thus giving precedence to creativity over the raw experience used for this purpose. By implication, the writer must distort the truth in order to mold the reader's psychological response in the context of literary form. Whereas Robortelli, Sidney, Balzac, and Wilder were willing to manipulate the truth in order to encourage morality, Bielfeld and Poe preferred doing this to produce aesthetic experience for its own sake. Literary form imposed a different version of morality—but with a comparable sacrifice of mimetic accuracy.

The German metaphysician Friedrich Schlegel also acknowledged the central role of literary deception, in his case by emphasizing its value as autobiographical evasiveness. Schlegel proposed that fiction necessarily conceals truths important to the author and that critics must therefore "spy on what he [the author] wanted to hide from our sight or at least did not want to show himself at first: on the author's secret intentions, which he pursues in silence and of which we can never assume too many in a genius."[11] The task of critics was to recognize these intentions despite the various distractions used by poets to defend themselves. This romantic vision of artistic mystery anticipated the psychoanalytic theory of literary displacement in the twentieth century, if without suggesting the extent to which the latent content of a text can be submitted to systematic examination.

In one form or another, Platonism seems to have been revived in the eighteenth century both to praise and to reject aesthetic expression for its departure from mimetic accuracy. In his 1758 antitheatrical essay *Letter to d'Alembert Concerning Spectacles*, Rousseau challenged the construction of a public theater in Geneva by mingling complaints against acting as false representation with a variety of arguments to demonstrate the immorality of public entertainment. On the other hand, the English painter Sir Joshua Reynolds offered perhaps the simplest and most pragmatic version of Neoplatonism as the elimination of superficial imperfections through artistic craft:

> Upon the whole, it seems to me, that the object and intention of all the arts is to supply the natural imperfection of things, and often to gratify the mind by realizing and embodying what never existed but in the imagination.[12]

No mystery was involved in this simplified defense of Platonic ideals, merely the effort of a portrait painter (or poet) to exclude unsightly blemishes from the representation of ideal beauty. By glossing over such detail—the redundant streaks of the tulip decried by Johnson—the artist was better able to capture this perfection in his portraits.

More thoroughgoing in his metaphysics, G. W. F. Hegel emphasized the distinction between illusion and reality by arguing that uncompromising artistic honesty becomes a lie if judged in light of our substantive interests in life. He claimed aesthetic truth is limited to our highest cognitive faculties, so it necessarily conflicts with the world of appearance associated with our practical needs:

> Art liberates the true content of phenomena from the pure appearance and deception of this bad, transitory world, and gives them a higher actuality, born of the spirit. Thus far from being mere pure appearance, a higher reality and truer existence is to be ascribed to the phenomena of art in comparison with those of ordinary reality.[13]

Nevertheless, Hegel found that artistic beauty also depends upon appearance, necessitating the use of deception to give expression to transcendent reality:

> If, finally, art is regarded as a means, then there always remains in the form of the means a disadvantageous aspect, namely that even if art subordinates itself to more serious aims in fact, and produces more serious effects, the means that it uses for this purpose is deception.[14]

Like earlier Platonists, Hegel stressed the truth of ideal form by describing serious art as equivalent to religion and philosophy in its representation of "the highest ideas in sensuous form." But he also acknowledged the appeal of concrete immediacy and established a dialectic tension between the two that revitalized Plato's distinction between art and reality. As opposed to Plato, Hegel approved of art's drawing upon the world of appearances to express the countervailing "reality" of eternal truth, but in what seems a compromise between Plato and Neoplatonists, he proposed that art's elevation of ideal form over tangible immediacy means that each challenges the integrity of the other. Like the Neoplatonists, he felt the pursuit of transcendence through immediacy is worthy, but like Plato he recognized the insurmountable differences involved. The truth of ordinary life falls short of art, while art inescapably deviates from ordinary life by letting higher truths be felt as sensible experience.

As early as the seventeenth century, scientific methodology began to take precedence over classical philosophy in explaining the physical universe, but most empiricists were willing to permit literature and science to coexist as separate disciplines, each valid on its own terms. The nineteenth-century utilitarian philosopher Jeremy Bentham was the first empiricist willing to attack fiction as a frivolous exploration of the make-believe that was unworthy of serious consideration:

> Between poetry and truth there is a natural opposition. . . . The poet always stands in need of something false. When he pretends to lay his foundations in truth, the ornaments of his superstructure are fictions; his business consists in stimulating our passions, and exciting our prejudices. Truth, exactitude of every kind, is fatal to poetry. The poet must see everything through coloured media, and strive to make everyone else to do the same. It is true, there have been noble spirits, to whom poetry and philosophy have been equally indebted; but these exceptions do not counteract the mischiefs which have resulted from this magic art.[15]

Bentham advocated scientific methodology as the single most valid means of judging the human condition, and he rejected literary experience as a distraction qualitatively no different from children's games: "If poetry and music deserve to be preferred before a game of push-pin, it must be because they are calculated to gratify those individuals who are most difficult to be pleased." Bentham's purist demands resembled Plato's except that he substituted scientific fact for ideal forms.

Two generations later Friedrich Nietzsche likewise took science as his point of departure, but from an entirely different vantage. Influenced by the current debate over evolution, Nietzsche proposed a post-Darwinian concept of blind purposefulness that restored literary deception to its central role in culture. Literary deception is beneficial, Nietzsche argued, because it helps the public to cope with matters otherwise beyond its grasp. As he insisted in one particularly disarming pronouncement, "We possess *art* lest we *perish of the truth*" (italics in the translation).[16] In *Beyond Good and Evil* Nietzsche went so far as to emphasize the necessity of deception as a principle more essential to the perpetuation of life than ethics itself—thus providing the title of his book:

> [W]e are fundamentally inclined to maintain that the falsest opinions (to which the synthetic judgments *a priori* belong), are the most indispensable to us; that without a recognition of logical fictions, without a comparison of reality with the purely *imagined* world by means of numbers, man cannot live—that the renunciation of false opinions would be a renunciation of life, a negation of life. *To recognize untruths as a condition of life*: that is certainly to impugn the traditional ideas of value in a dangerous manner, and a philosophy which ventures to do so has thereby alone placed itself beyond good and evil.[17]

The revolutionary importance of Nietzsche's ethical inversion should not be underestimated. Neoplatonists and Hegel had salvaged art from Plato's hostile aesthetics by promoting ideal form as a literary truth, but Nietzsche reversed priorities by expanding Plato's theory of aesthetic deception to embrace all human experience, including ethics, artistic creativity, and the metaphysics of ideal forms. If Plato's concept of a higher truth could be adopted to supersede his theory of aesthetic deception, the latter could just as easily take precedence by reducing every dimension of human attainment to the artistic lie:

> "Life *ought* to inspire confidence": the task thus imposed is tremendous. To solve it, man must be a liar by nature, he must be above all an *artist*. And he *is* one: metaphysics, religion, morality, science—all of them only products of his will to art, to life, to flight from "truth," to *negation* of truth. This ability itself, thanks to which he violates reality by means of lies, this artistic ability of man *par excellence*—he has it in common with everything that is. He himself is after all a piece of reality, truth, nature: how should he not also be a piece of genius in lying![18]

Like Oscar Wilde, Nietzsche extolled the mimetic arts for their paradoxical honesty in articulating the dishonesty that inescapably dominates human affairs. All conscious behavior is deceptive, he declared, and by far the most deceptive, even more than philosophy, is art, so art becomes quintessential in its distortion of everything we know. Like Plato, Nietzsche treated falsehood as the matrix of art, but unlike Plato, he therefore praised art for its transcendent value as an expression of human fallibility. If the whole world, every shred of human intercourse, is dishonest, then art, which is fully naked in its dishonesty, affords a more accessible correspondence to this reality than does any other mode of discourse. Similar tributes to aesthetic dishonesty enjoyed iconoclastic vogue among Nietzsche's contemporaries, as illustrated by Wilde's radical aestheticism, Mallarmé's enthusiasm for "*ces glorieux mensonges*," and Henry James's bland assurance that fiction is "after all only a 'make believe.'"[19] But it was primarily Nietzsche who restored misrepresentation to its theoretical pinnacle. From the ashes of intermediate philosophical systems emerged the phoenix once again, Solon and Plato's recognition that literary fiction epitomizes the lure of misrepresentation in human intercourse.

In the brief essay "Hymn to Truth," H. L. Mencken, the American journalist and author of *The Philosophy of Friedrich Nietzsche*, explained Nietzsche's principles of literary misrepresentation with unusual iconoclastic vivacity, if without mentioning Nietzsche by name:

> The two elements, of untruth, and of beauty, are both important, and perhaps equally. It is not sufficient that the thing said in poetry be untrue: it must also be said with a certain grace—it must soothe the ear while it debauches the mind.[20]

Most poets and authors defend literary truth, Mencken conceded, but only to encourage the acceptance of their lies:

> Poets, of course, protest against this doctrine. They argue that they actually deal in the truth, and that their brand of truth is of a peculiarly profound and esoteric quality—in other words, that their compositions add to the sum of human wisdom. It is sufficient answer to them to say that the chiropractors make precisely the same claim, and with exactly the same plausibility. Both actually deal in fictions. Those fictions are not truths; they are not even truths in decay. They are simply better-than-truths. They make life more comfortable and happy. They turn and dull the sharp edge of reality.[21]

Mencken identified the love of poetry as one of the most primitive of human traits, "the love of the agreeably not-so," but he also claimed that the same

A Short History of Deception Theories

quest for pleasurable fictions occurs at all levels—in the college professor's appreciation of Browning's poetry as well as the Kiwanian's pleasure with Edgar Guest's poetry. How can this universal appeal of literary disingenuousness be accounted for? Mencken quickly answered by reminding us of human nature:

> No normal human being wants to hear the truth. It is the passion of a small and aberrant minority of men, most of them pathological. They are hated for telling it while they live, and when they die they are swiftly forgotten. What remains to the world, in the field of wisdom, is a series of long-tested and solidly agreeable lies. It is out of such lies that most of the so-called knowledge of humanity flows. What begins as poetry ends as fact, and is embalmed in the history books.[22]

Published in 1927, this brief article provides a model for the expression of Nietzsche's viewpoint in American idiom.

In *Abbey's Road*, published roughly fifty years later, the American author and naturalist Edward Abbey similarly explains his role as a writer absorbed with deceiving both himself and his audience:

> The writer puts the best of himself, not the whole, into the work; the author as seen in the pages of his own book is largely a fictional creation. Often the author's best creation. The Edward Abbey of my own books, for example, bears only the dimmest resemblance to the shy, timid, reclusive, rather dapper little gentleman who, always correctly attired for his labors in coat and tie and starched detachable cuffs, sits down each night for precisely four hours to type out the further adventures of that arrogant blustering macho fraud who counterfeits his name. You can bet on it: No writer is ever willing—even if able—to portray himself as seen by others or as he really is. Writers are shameless liars. In fact, we pride ourselves on the subtlety and grandeur of our lies. Salome had only seven veils; the author has a thousand.[23]

With comparable flair, Ursula K. Le Guin argues more or less the same case in her introduction to her science fiction novel *The Left Hand of Darkness*, but with due respects paid to the social need for literary deception:

> Fiction writers, at least in their braver moments, do desire the truth: to know it, speak it, serve it. But they go about it in a peculiar and devious

way, which consists in inventing persons, places, and events which never did and never will exist or occur, and telling about these fictions in detail and at length and with a great deal of emotion, and then when they are done writing down this pack of lies, they say, There! That's the truth!

They may use all kinds of facts to support their tissue of lies. They may describe the Marshalsea Prison, which was a real place, or the battle of Borodino, which really was fought, or the process of cloning, which really takes place in laboratories, or the deterioration of a personality, which is described in real textbooks of psychology; and so on. This weight of verifiable place-event-phenomenon-behavior makes the reader forget that he is reading a pure invention, a history that never took place anywhere but in that unlocalisable region, the author's mind. In fact, while we read a novel, we are insane—bonkers. We believe in the existence of people who aren't there, we hear their voices, we watch the battle of Borodino with them, we may even become Napoleon. Sanity returns (in most cases) when the book is closed.

Is it any wonder that no truly respectable society has ever trusted its artists?

But our society, being troubled and bewildered, seeking guidance, sometimes puts an entirely mistaken trust in its artists, using them as prophets and futurologists.[24]

Le Guin's argument here seems even more despairing than Nietzsche's explanation of literary deception as a coping mechanism to maintain collective sanity. Without rejecting Nietzsche's assessment, her final words emphasize literary deception's status as a symptom of chronic social malaise, whether or not there is any possibility of relieving the disorder.

In *What Is Art*, published in 1898, Leo Tolstoy drew upon essentially the same assumptions about literature, but from a substantially different viewpoint.[25] Instead of using the evidence of literary deception to challenge the adequacy of the average mind, he used it to justify the wholesale rejection of literary experience as the best means of salvaging the average mind. In effect, he merged the perspective of Plato and early Christian polemicists with contemporary standards of artistic deception implicit in the pronouncements of Nietzsche, Wilde, and Mallarmé, but with the view of resurrecting religion as a substitute for literary temptation. He advanced the fundamentalist notion that fiction should serve the ends of revealed Christianity through both its sincerity and its accessibility to the average reader. Valid art, he claimed, was limited to that which promotes Christian values in the simplest stories of human sympathy. Few works of fiction met his stringent specifications—the rest he rejected, including his own major novels.

In the twentieth century, literary deception has become a source of speculation in a wide variety of fields, and only the most significant innovations can be explored here. No clustering, no line of descent, no effort to systematize and interconnect various approaches has occurred to justify the title deceptology or deceptionism, and, as Mencken warned, most contributions have rather quickly fallen into obscurity. Hans Vaihinger's neo-Kantian theory of "as if," for example, deserves comparison with Gustov LeBon's theory of the group mind, with Vilfredo Pareto's sociological distinction between residues and derivations, and with Jean-Paul Sartre's existential concept of "bad faith."[26] Only the latter, however, has been successfully diluted for popular consumption. The others continue to be studiously neglected as oddities of epistemological speculation. It seems taken for granted that they were arguing separate cases, as if there were no meaningful convergence in their shared vision of civilization's universal dependence on lies and misinformation.

The same problem has affected twentieth-century literary criticism. Any suggestion that dishonesty might be an intrinsic feature of literature has been vigorously attacked for its wrongheadedness, then ignored. I. A. Richards tested possibilities when he proposed his theory of literary pseudostatement in *Science and Poetry*, then quickly redeemed himself with his complementary theory of sincerity in *Practical Criticism*.[27] In the first of these books, published in 1926, Richards argued that pseudostatement reduces the truth of fiction to a willing suspension of disbelief; in the second, published in 1929, he proposed that literary value ultimately depends upon the author's sincerity. Richards left unexplored the basic contradiction between these two perspectives, but if he had tried to integrate them, he would probably have been obliged to admit that the final standard of poetic merit he was proposing depended on the poets' ability to believe in their own fabrications. Other examples of nervous fascination with literary deception include Christopher Ricks's refinement of the lie as a literary figure and Lionel Trilling's cryptic final words in *Beyond Culture* lamenting modern fiction's recreation of Bacon's idols "in its own contrivance." Trilling's ambivalence was even more pronounced in *Sincerity and Authenticity*, in which he sought to expose the pathological extremes of authenticity that he despised in the protest movement of the sixties.[28]

Undoubtedly, the twentieth century's most influential contribution to the concept of literary deception has been Sigmund Freud's theory of repression and unconscious displacement. In *The Interpretation of Dreams*, Freud proposed that dream formation provides the most fertile (or "overdetermined") vehicle of unconscious displacement, but he also suggested that all consciousness resembles dream formation because of its frequent dependence upon unconscious displacements to satisfy particular needs:

> Thought is after all nothing but a substitute for a hallucinatory wish; and it is self-evident that dreams must be wish-fulfillment, since nothing but a wish can set our mental apparatus at work.[29]

Just as our residue of recent experience is reorganized by dream work, our daytime consciousness sifts and reorganizes perception in the service of desirable ends—either as a concrete effort to achieve these ends or as the fantasy that such an effort has been successful. In other words, we conceptualize substitutes to improve upon our material circumstance, usually by formulating a specific plan of action but almost as often by entertaining harmless illusions that satisfy our hopes without really fulfilling them. William James proposed a similar motivational (or conative) model of cognition in *Principles of Psychology*, published a decade before *The Interpretation of Dreams*:

> Every actually existing consciousness seems to itself at any rate to be a *fighter for ends*, of which many, but for its presence, would not be ends at all. Its powers of cognition are mainly subservient to these ends, discerning which facts further them and which do not. . . . The brain is an instrument of possibilities, not of certainties.[30]

Here thinking was shown to occur as a preliminary exploration of alternatives, with differences tentatively explored in the separate realm commonly described as consciousness in order to choose the appropriate concrete behavior for making changes. But as both the curse and joy of the human mind, those changes that cannot be made for one reason or another may nevertheless be entertained in this realm as fantasy and hypothetical conjecture, and with beneficial results anyway. Merely an instrument of *praxis* at its most primitive level, consciousness becomes in and of itself a substitute for *praxis* through the dynamics of wish fulfillment. James Ward, William McDougall, and others have also stressed this motivational basis for consciousness, but Freudian metapsychology seems to offer the most convenient model for treating consciousness as the tentative exploration of behavioral alternatives. To the extent that an idea deviates from the actual circumstance it draws upon, Freudian theory shows how each alternative gives the lie to the other. "This might be this," the individual recognizes, "but if it were that [i.e., a perceived substitute], I could be happier, so let it be that, either by making genuine changes *or* by fantasizing them." As Freud emphasized throughout his career, the cognitive and conative ingredients of the mind (respectively, the reality and pleasure principles) can be so perfectly blended in this manner that our desire seems realistic, our circumstances capable of "literary" outcome.

In effect, Freud's volitional psychology elevated instincts (or drives, which he described as *Triebe*) to the status of Plato's eternal forms—if from below (or within) instead of above. Like Nietzsche, Freud treated survival as the final most important issue, but he emphasized the relatively circumscribed benefits that come of minimizing anxieties through the effective gratification of drives. He consequently expanded traditional epistemology to embrace a more inclusive division between our conscious-perceptual apparatus at one pole, the ego, and, at its opposite, the volitional demands composing the id. According to Freud, these two vectors of experience interact in all behavior, so the misguided pursuit of either at the expense of the other is inevitably harmful to emotional adjustment. Freud preferred the ego, but without diminishing the tentative harmony between the two in fantasy associated with literary experience.

As to be expected, Freud argued in his brief essay "The Relation of the Poet to Day-Dreaming" that fiction appeals to readers precisely because of fantasy content's departure from real-life expectations:

> Now the writer does the same as the child at play; he creates a world of phantasy which he takes very seriously; that is, he invests it with a great deal of affect, while separating it sharply from reality.[31]

Formal adequacy is primarily important to fiction, Freud maintained, because it grants wish fulfillment as an outcome both aesthetic and seemingly true to life:

> The writer softens the egotistical character of the day-dream by changes and disguises, and he bribes us by the offer of a purely formal, that is, aesthetic, pleasure in the presentation of his phantasies.[32]

In other words, both form and descriptive accuracy are subservient to affective needs. They let fiction effect the same benefits as the dream or daydream by giving credibility to illusions that yield emotional satisfaction:

> I am of the opinion that . . . the true enjoyment of literature proceeds from the release of tensions in our minds. Perhaps much that brings about this result consists in the writer's putting us into a position in which we can enjoy our own day-dreams without reproach or shame.[33]

An author's willingness to believe in daydreams reinforces our own, helping us cope with our baggage of normal anxieties. Freud attributed the universal appeal of fiction to this stimulation of pleasure through fantasy as a substitute gratification of needs.

Unfortunately, ego psychologists and literary response theoreticians such as Norman Holland and David Bleich have tried to minimize the importance of this conscious-unconscious dialectic emphasized by Freud. Even Norman O. Brown has criticized the Freudian model for "having the basic dynamic of a flight from reality" and for reducing art to "an opiate of the people, an escape into an unreal world of fantasy indistinguishable from a full-blown neurosis."[34] In part this concern seems justified, but it should also be acknowledged that fiction loses its appeal if the dynamics of repression (and thus the unrecognized lie) are totally eliminated from literary expression. By emphasizing the relatively simple response dynamics when readers match a text's truths with their own, response theoreticians neglect the opportunity to explore how the author's distortions built in to a text help readers to fabricate distortions more relevant to their individual circumstances—often by so completely stretching distortion that even the text itself goes virtually unrecognized as a vehicle of substitute experience. It may nevertheless be proposed as a basic principle that readers' personal responses to a text seem best explained by their collaborative willingness to share in its fantasy content. Their primary task—which they are capable of performing with great ingenuity—is to appropriate its distortions of the truth to help justify their own.

Contemporary Marxist doctrine offers fewer possibilities than does psychoanalysis as an explanation of literary deception. Ignoring Matthew Arnold's definition of literature as "spilt religion," too many Marxists fall victim to the glaring contradiction of on the one hand dismissing religion as an opiate of the people but on the other praising literature, presumably its derivative, for its unique and transcendent honesty. For example, in *What Is Literature?* Jean-Paul Sartre emphasized the obligation of all authors except lyric poets to confront their readers with the truth, specifically consisting of a progressive vision of historical necessity in the victory of socialism. Christopher Caudwell and Georg Thomson likewise emphasized tragedy's secularization of primitive ritual without concerning themselves with Solon's objections to its veracity. But how, exactly, can religion embody a lie or be the "opiate of the masses" while its secular adaptation remains totally purified of this deficiency? Only Marxists of the Frankfurt School entertained the possibility of literary misrepresentation, and among them Herbert Marcuse has professed a deceptionist interpretation of fiction that is most accessible to the American reader. Marcuse first dealt with literary deception in *Eros and Civilization*, his early treatment of Freudian doctrine, and later in *One-Dimensional Man* and *Counter-Revolution and Revolt*, in which he drew upon psychoanalytic distinctions to support Marxist conclusions. According to Marcuse, fiction draws upon an extra dimension of consciousness to expose and challenge the capitalist irrationality that dominates our society:

> Like technology, art creates another universe of thought and practice against and within the existing one. But in contrast to the technical universe, the artistic universe is organized by the images of a life without fear—in mask and silence because art is without power to bring about this life, and even without power to represent it adequately. Still, the powerless, illusory truth of art (which has never been more powerless and more illusory than today, when it has become an omnipresent ingredient of the administered society) testifies to the validity of its images. The more blatantly irrational the society becomes, the greater the rationality of the artistic universe.[35]

Like Hegel, Marcuse praised literature as an entry into a second and improved realm, but he joined in the Marxist effort to put Hegelian doctrine on its head by envisaging this realm as an idealized socialist future rather than a prelapsarian garden or the timeless domain of Platonic forms. To promote such a future, valid art actually doubles alienation, thus exposing its stranglehold upon bourgeois society today:

> [A]rt retains that alienation from the established reality which is at the origin of art. It is a second alienation, by virtue of which the artist dis-

sociates himself methodically from the alienated society and creates the unreal, "illusory" universe in which art alone has, and communicates, its truth.[36]

Fiction can be praised because it undermines existing values and institutions by advocating obviously superior alternatives. Its referential content concedes the status quo, but its style suggests a world more worthy of our aspirations:

> By becoming components of aesthetic form, words, sounds, shapes, and colors are insulated against their familiar, ordinary use and function; thus they are freed for a new dimension of existence. This is the achievement of the style, which is the poem, the novel, the painting, the composition. The style, embodiment of the aesthetic form, in subjecting reality to another order, subjects it to the "laws of beauty."[37]

The meaning of words draws upon one dimension, the world as we know it, but the stylistic use of words imposes as a second dimension a world of fantasy that suggests an improved alternative. As a vehicle for this extra dimension, fiction conveys truths at odds with received opinion because they conflict with the world as we know it. Perhaps fiction deceives because of its celebration of unrealized ideals, but just as deceptive is the nonliterary and one-dimensional belief that our ideals cannot be fulfilled in a better future. These ideals can indeed be attained, Marcuse claimed, through a permanent commitment to revolution as encouraged by fiction.

A less militant deceptionist model is suggested in Fredric Jameson's study of the Frankfurt School, *Marxism and Form*, in which there is passing reference to dialectical reversal, alternative structural realizations, and the "secret dynamics" of the subject-object relationship.[38] Jameson praises literary form as the working out of content in the realm of the superstructure, and his discussion of the intrinsic-extrinsic integration of a text and the compensatory interaction between overdeveloped and underdeveloped elements bears useful implications. Contrary to deceptionist priorities, he maintains that the truth is the source of "determinate negation," but he also warns of a resistance (or *mauvaise foi*) to socioeconomic truths that might become strong enough to usurp these truths in the context of literary form. Unfortunately, he rejects the importance of plot. He mentions its foregrounding but claims it is "mere hypostasis" that stands out in relief from the work as a whole.[39] This failure to recognize plot's dialectic value as an agent of deception affords perhaps the most important difference between his approach and the model of negative poetics I will later be proposing. However, Jameson does praise Humboldt's concept of inner form (obtained from Plotinus and Goethe) as a "negative and anxiety-ridden type of work [based on] a positive fantasy."[40] According to Jameson, "Art which can no longer in good conscience put up with this deception . . . has already dissolved the only element in which it can realize itself."[41] To exist as art, he suggests, fiction depends on the dialectic by which fantasy misrepresents the truth.

Substantially at odds with both Marcuse's and Jameson's revolutionary perspectives is Roland Barthes's conservative, even reactionary, vision of literary deception. Barthes found the rejection of deceptive motivation to be a key flaw in the Marxist insistence upon political engagement. He enthusiastically praised Brecht's aesthetics of alienation (or *Verfremdungseffekt*), but he also criticized socialist realism for its insufficient commitment to literary deception:

> All literature knows that like Orpheus, it cannot, on pain of death, turn around to look at what is behind it: it is condemned to mediation—that is, in a sense, to lying. . . . [I]t is because socialist realism, in its very project, rejects any mediation that (at least in our Western countries) it asphyxiates itself and dies: it dies of being immediate, it dies of rejecting that something which hides reality in order to make it more real, and which is literature.[42]

Using Hegelian nomenclature, Barthes attacked the immediacy of socialist realism that prevents writers from freely modifying (or mediating) their truths with aesthetic liberties. Because of its flat depictive style, he claimed, socialist realism loses its deceptiveness, hence its value as art. By way of contrast, Barthes gave special status to Kafka because his fiction exposes the lie as an ethical issue at the root of self-expression:

> That is Kafka's paradox: art depends on truth, but truth, being indivisible, cannot know itself: to tell the truth is to lie. Thus the writer *is* the truth, and yet when he speaks he lies: a work's authority is never situated at the level of its esthetic, but only at the level of the moral experience which makes it an assumed lie.[43]

If the truth consists of indivisible experience, any selection of this experience deceives by diminishing this totality. Good fiction therefore lies because of its selectivity, and writers can be admired because they accept the moral burden of making the necessarily distortive selection of experience they consider important. They must try to take into account the full truth, but they must also recognize that their effort is doomed to failure. Authors capable of this transcendent ambivalence, including Kafka, Brecht, and Robbe-Grillet, retain their integrity by acknowledging in their fiction its unavoidably dishonesty.

Probably Barthes's most intriguing contribution to deceptology is his explanation of language as a linear and propositional mode of symbolic representation that necessarily compounds literary deception. Fiction deceives as imaginative representation, as explained by Freud, but, even more manifestly, it deceives as a combination of words:

> [I]n relation to objects themselves, literature is fundamentally, constitutively unrealistic; literature is unreality itself; or more exactly, far from being an analogical copy of reality, literature is on the contrary the very consciousness of the unreality of language: the "truest" literature is the one which knows itself as the most unreal, to the degree that it knows itself as essentially language.[44]

With this semiotic twist, Barthes attributed to the language of fiction a radical selectivity that necessarily reinforces the compositional distortions of literary form. Thinking biases factual accuracy, language biases thinking, and fiction takes this departure from the truth to its extreme by its "intentional misuse of language which can only convey the truth through recognition of its failure to do so." In effect, Plato's two stages of departure from reality are revised and expanded to three, with verbal distortions sandwiched between those of conceptualization and literary expression.

The inevitability of verbal deception emphasized by Barthes was likewise recognized by Emerson in "Nominalist and Realist": "No sentence will hold the whole truth, and the only way in which we can be just, is by giving ourselves the lie."[45] Similarly, the contemporary novelist John Barth lets Jacob Horner, his protagonist in *The End of the Road*, disparage the truth value of language: "To turn experience into speech—that is, to classify, to categorize, to conceptualize, to grammatize, to syntactify it—is always a betrayal of experience, a falsification of it; but only so betrayed can it be dealt with at all."[46] For George Steiner in *After Babel*, this limitation affords an ethic—in fact, a theory of civilization—that gives renewed importance to literary deception as an agent of survival and social harmony. Steiner describes the

A Short History of Deception Theories

brain's supposition of alternatives as proposed by both Freud and William James as a feature of verbal communication that lets us deal with our problems on a hypothetical basis:

> *Language is the main instrument of man's refusal to accept the world as it is.* Without that refusal, without the increasing generation by the mind of "counter-worlds"—a generation which cannot be divorced from the grammar of counter-factual and optative forms—we would turn forever on the treadmill of the present. Reality would be (to use Wittgenstein's phrase in an illicit sense), "all that is the case" and nothing more. Ours is the ability, the need, to gainsay or "unsay" the world, to image and speak it otherwise. . . . It is not, perhaps, "a theory of information" that will serve us best in trying to clarify the nature of language, but a "theory of misinformation."[47] (Italics in the original)

Steiner goes on to describe misinformation as perfectly normal behavior in the choice of words and syntactic constructions:

> We communicate motivated images, local frameworks of feeling. All descriptions are partial. We speak less than the truth, we fragment in order to reconstruct desired alternatives, we select and elide. It is not "the things which are" that we say, but those which might be, which we would bring about, which the eye and remembrance compose. . . . Information does not come naked except in the schemata of computer languages or the lexicon. It comes attenuated, flexed, coloured, alloyed by intent and milieux in which the utterance occurs.[48]

According to Steiner, our very survival skills depend upon our ability to use language as an instrument of deception:

> It is unlikely that man, as we know him, would have survived without the fictive, counter-factual, antideterminist means of language, without the semantic capacity, generated and stored in the "superfluous" zones of the cortex, to conceive of, to articulate possibilities beyond the treadmill of organic decay and death.[49]

And again:

> The relevant framework is not one of morality but of survival. At every level, from brute camouflage to poetic vision, the linguistic capacity to

conceal, misinform, leave ambiguous, hypothesize, invent is indispensable to the equilibrium of human consciousness and to the development of man in society. Only a small portion of human discourse is nakedly veracious or informative in any monovalent, unqualified sense.[50]

The value of poetry, then, comes from its unique intensity in expressing this dishonest potential of human intelligence:

A poem concentrates, it deploys with least regard to routine or conventional transparency, those energies of covertness and of invention which are the crux of human speech. A poem is maximal speech.[51]

By "maximal" Steiner refers to the extremes to which verbal deception can and should be brought in the context of fiction. Here Steiner entirely agrees with Nietzsche's and Barthes's inversions that make the pursuit of illusion the single most important mode of human behavior. He concedes the warnings of Solon and Plato but shows that literary deception epitomizes civilization. Without deception, human institutions—literature included—could never have evolved beyond the most rudimentary levels of tribal cooperation.

In his *Atlantic Monthly* article "Lies, Lies, Lies," Anthony Brand effectively summarizes Steiner's argument pertaining to verbal deception in and of itself, independent of the cultural implications featured by Steiner:

George Steiner observes that "our outward speech has 'behind it' a concurrent flow of articulate consciousness"; there is our outward talk, and there is the flow of words in our minds, our talking to ourselves, our "thinking." Between them, Steiner goes on, there is never anything more than partial congruence. But behind *that*, behind the thinking, the articulate consciousness, there is the flow of feeling, while behind that there is still more feeling, deep, abiding patterns of feeling; and the more layers we peel away the more difficult it becomes to see how to put into words all that is going on inside, how to be anything but dishonest no matter what we say. *Anything* we say is a selection from the flow of consciousness; it is a construct, something we build up from certain elements and not others; it is a consistency chosen from among numerous apparent inconsistencies, from the general mess of imprecision of feeling; in short it is, or at least it follows the same principle of selectivity as, a work of art no matter what we say.[52]

A Short History of Deception Theories

Brand concludes, "When we must speak to others we speak ironically, holding truth and falsehood in balance, knowing that nothing we say is strictly true, that the best we can hope for is a vague approximation, and that no matter what we say, seeming true or seeming false, the ones inevitably most deceived by it will be ourselves."[53]

The variety of deceptionist theories listed here is formidable, and many seem to contradict others. Oscar Wilde rejoiced in the genius of literary deception, whereas Tolstoy, his contemporary, found it a source of despair. Like Tolstoy, Plato attacked literature because of its immorality in misleading the public, whereas Thornton Wilder, like Sidney, praised it for exactly the opposite reason, that it teaches people morality by misleading them. Bentham deplored the uselessness of literary deception, while Nietzsche emphasized its universal necessity. Hegel stressed the value of deception in expressing higher truths, Mencken redefined "higher" as a better-than-truth, and Freud located the source of this better-than-truth in fantasy and wish fulfillment. Bielfeld, Steiner, and others have shown deception to be functional at an even more basic level, embedded in both language and consciousness. More specifically, Schlegel saw literary deception as the sharing of unacknowledged secrets; Barthes, as verbal paradox; Poe, as the key to literary craft; I. A. Richards, as a useful substitute for belief; and Marcuse, as an agent of political subversiveness. How, then, does one classify the critics listed here?

I propose the four relatively distinct categories shown in figure 1.1 to combine the binary distinctions between theories emphasizing fiction's honesty and dishonesty and between theories emphasizing fiction's resemblance or lack thereof to objective discourse. These four categories may then be listed as shown in table 1. Categories 1 and 2 characterize objectivist theories that treat fiction as the vehicle and highest exemplification of the truth, while categories 3 and 4 characterize all deceptionist theories that treat fiction as a departure from the truth. Together, the second and third categories differentiate fiction from objective discourse based on their conflicting truth value, but with opposite priorities. Critics in the second category—such as Plotinus, Hegel, and Marcuse—find literature to be more honest than objective discourse, while those in the third category—such as Plato and Freud—invert this distinction by finding greater honesty in such nonliterary expression as dialectic inquiry and diagnostic thoroughness. Of course, both Plato and Freud paid their respects to literary inspiration (Plato in the *Ion*), but the

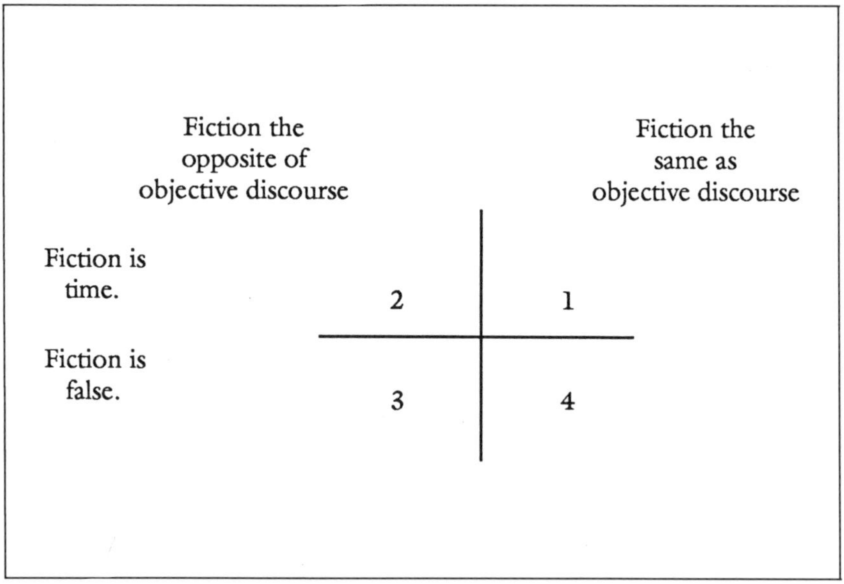

A Short History of Deception Theories

```
                    Fiction the                    Fiction the
                    opposite of                    same as
                    objective discourse            objective discourse

        Fiction is
        time.
                              2           |           1
                            ──────────────┼──────────────
        Fiction is
        false.
                              3           |           4
```

FIGURE I. *Matrix of critical categories*

truths they themselves articulated lay elsewhere. In contrast to the second and third categories, the first and fourth enjoy the benefits of consistency; analysts in the first insist that fiction epitomizes the honesty typical of objective discourse, and those in the fourth—for example Nietzsche, Barthes, and Steiner—insist that fiction instead epitomizes its rampant dishonesty.

What is the relative popularity of each of these four categories? Arguments of the first category, based on the assumption that both fiction and objective discourse tell the truth, have been dominant in published literary criticism, while arguments of the second, based on the notion of fiction's higher truth, take up most of the exceptions. Many critics who despair of hypocrisy and venality in our normal daily affairs revere fiction for its comparative honesty in subordinating fantasy to universal truth. Nevertheless, a few critics may be found whose views fall into the third and fourth categories. Category 3, embracing the view that fiction is less honest than objective discourse, primarily includes theories of fiction as fantasy gratification, while category 4, committed to the view that both fiction and nonfiction are inescapably deceptive, is restricted to the handful of hard-core deceptionists including Nietzsche, Wilde, Barthes, and Steiner. Among this tiny minority, fiction is appreciated

A Short History of Deception Theories

TABLE I. *List of Critical Categories*

		Objective Discourse	Fiction
1.	Aristotle and most orthodox approaches to criticism	... is capable of telling the truth.	... epitomizes the truth.
2.	Plotinus, Hegel, and Marcuse	... usually falls short of the truth.	... epitomizes the truth.
3.	Solon, Plato, Augustine, and Freud	... is capable of telling the truth.	... epitomizes the lie (or fantasy).
4.	Wilde, Nietzsche, Barthes, and Steiner	... usually falls short of the truth.	... epitomizes the lie.

for its unique achievement in epitomizing the myths and illusions that are crucial to our pleasure, self-respect, and perhaps our very survival.

Some critics escape all four of these categories by arguing that fiction tells lies in order to convey more fundamental truths. Authors supposedly resort to aesthetic misrepresentation to expose readers to the valid insights at the heart of their stories. The final product of this effort, they suggest, is a consummate honesty otherwise inaccessible to readers. This truth-untruth paradox, in conflict with the holistic deceptionist insights already quoted by Edward Abbey and Ursula Le Guin, was emphasized by D. H. Lawrence in his "Studies in Classic American Literature":

> The curious thing about art speech is that it prevaricates so terribly, I mean it tells such lies. I suppose because we always all the time tell ourselves lies. And out of a pattern of lies art weaves the truth.[54]

Norman Mailer expressed a similar view in his "Appeal to Lillian Hellman and Mary McCarthy," in which he tried to defuse the controversy arising from Mary McCarthy's remark that "every word she [Lillian Hellman] writes is a lie, including 'and' and 'the.'" Insists Mailer.

> To say that Lillian Hellman is dishonest is blarney. No writer worthy of serious consideration is ever honest except for those rare moments—for which we keep writing—when we become, bless us, not dishonest for

an instant. Of course Lillian Hellman is dishonest. So is Mary McCarthy, Norman Mailer, Saul Bellow, John Updike, John Cheever, Cynthia Ozick—name 500 of us, Willa Cather, Edith Wharton, Henry James—we are all dishonest, we exaggerate, distort, we use our tricks, we invent.[55]

Similarly, Grace Paley has explained in an interview, "The story is a big lie. And in the middle of this big lie, you're telling the truth. If you lie [in the middle, too], things go wrong. You become sentimental, opaque, bombastic, you withhold information" (brackets added).[56] Like Lawrence and Mailer, Paley argues that authors extract basic truths from relatively superficial lies. Of course, committed deceptionists such as Nietzsche and Mencken would point out that the use of superficial lies to tell basic truths usually conveys even more basic lies—those by which authors fool even themselves. Authors resort to the surface appeal of literary verisimilitude in order to confirm other, more impelling fictions they continue to accept (literary deception's "deep structure"), and they can best do this if they remain at least partially unaware of their strategy. Fiction seems sentimental, opaque, bombastic, and uninformative exactly when authors become consciously or unconsciously ashamed of the self-deception at the heart of their stories. When the central lie begins to crumble, embarrassed insincerity follows.

Lawrence, Mailer, and Paley also overlook the important distinction that any truth becomes misrepresentative if and when authors unduly exaggerate it, as authors are prone to do. Sir Francis Bacon used his Idol of the Den to describe any idea one's mind "seizes and dwells upon with peculiar satisfaction," and he argued that this idea is to be held in suspicion for precisely this reason.[57] Similarly, in his essay "Intellect," Emerson explained, "If a man fasten his attention on a single aspect of truth, and apply himself to that alone for a long time, the truth becomes distorted and not itself, but falsehood."[58] Almost by definition, the intended truths of fiction fit this description, since authors usually fasten upon them with enough "peculiar satisfaction" to impose a sense of reality for material that is in large part fictional. As urged by both Bacon and Emerson, such truths must necessarily be held in suspicion. Moreover, if aesthetic liberties are needed to tell the real truth, the use of these liberties probably conceals distortion that authors themselves might not be able to recognize. The honesty at the core of a text sought by Lawrence, Mailer, and Paley might be more valid than the conventions used to express

A Short History of Deception Theories

it, but it very likely diverts the attention of both the author and readers from truths that acknowledge whatever inadequacy gives fiction its compensatory value. The more threatening these underlying truths become, the more energetic everybody's insistence on the text's honesty, and the more energetic this insistence, very probably the bigger the lie.

An alternative strategy for rejecting the inevitability of literary deception has been based on exactly the opposite argument that since fiction makes no effort to tell the truth it cannot be accused of lying. This approach avoids defending the truth value of literature, but in doing so it also undermines the notion of literary deception. Sir Philip Sidney was perhaps the most succinct in articulating this noncommittal aesthetic when he declared, "Now, for the Poet, he nothing affirmes, and therefore never lyeth."[59] Coleridge loosely concurred by proposing the author's and the reader's dependence on a willing suspension of disbelief.[60] As I indicated earlier, I. A. Richards revitalized the concept when he proposed in *Science and Poetry* that fiction appeals to readers as pseudostatement, which can neither be proven nor disproven and whose value primarily depends on its conscious effect rather than its truth content:

> A pseudo-statement is a form of words which is justified entirely by its effect in releasing or organizing our impulses and attitudes. . . . [A] statement, on the other hand, is justified by its truth, i.e., its correspondence, in a highly technical sense with the fact to which it points.[61]

Richards borrowed the distinction between statement and pseudostatement from logical empiricism and expanded its meaning to explain fiction's temporary reinforcement of traditional beliefs among readers demoralized by the empirical skepticism of the twentieth century. Readers must depend on fiction for a renewed commitment to tradition, religion, and social custom, Richards suggested, since these have otherwise lost their credibility in the face of hard scientific evidence. If divine retribution, for example, no longer seems inevitable in the conduct of our affairs, fiction's capacity as pseudostatement lets us trust in its power at least within the artificial world of a novel or poem. Having ceased to be true to life, poetic justice remains true to fiction and consequently immune to scientific verification. Fiction tells us what we want to think, and it does so without the excessive intrusion of verifiable truths. As a result, it escapes the lie, technically speaking. Nothing is scientifically or historically affirmed, so the poet's honesty is not at stake.

Richards's concept of literary pseudostatement was at first angrily challenged by critics and aestheticians, and he responded by backing off from the more radical implications of his argument. But then New Criticism gradually absorbed and granted respectability to his assumptions. William Empson and Cleanth Brooks proposed theories of irony and ambiguity that subordinated the conventional truth value of literary texts to the author's right—indeed, obligation—to load words with significance in excess of their denotative meaning. Yvor Winters likewise proposed the fallacy of imitative form as the misguided exaggeration of factual accuracy for its own sake. Later René Wellek offered a formalist explanation of this principle when he declared in *Theory of Literature*: "Art imposes some kind of framework which takes the statement of the work out of the world of reality."[62] Likewise, Northrop Frye limited fiction's raw truth content to a category of experience and subordinated this to the category of innocence in his hierarchy of literary archetypes. Only satire and "low-mimetic" naturalism were sufficiently burdened by experience (i.e., the truth) to violate the dominant role of innocence, so these could be relegated to what seems an inferior status among literary genres.[63] Proponents of New Criticism continued to reject the pejorative implications of the term *pseudostatement*, but the idea of fiction's special validity independent of its objective truth gained popularity once a more suitable wording could be found.

Nowadays the concept of pseudostatement, cleansed of logical positivism and rehabilitated as indeterminacy, is commonplace among postmodernists, deconstructionists, and loosely identifiable poststructuralists. Jonathan Culler, for example, emphasizes the myths and formal devices that give shape to fiction without necessarily communicating ideas; John Ellis stresses that literature consists of fiction *not* to be acted on; Barbara Herrnstein Smith emphasizes fiction's "absence of truth claims" as its *defining* convention; Raymond Federman claims fiction's production of meaning abolishes both reality and the notion that reality is truth; and Paul de Man proposes a "paradoxical" language for fiction (as opposed to "steno-language") that deconstructs itself by calling attention to its own fictiveness.[64] In each instance poetry has been absolved of verification. Its informational content is seen to be superfluous, and its propositional content is deemed empty except pertaining to the context of fiction itself. What results, in the words of Gerald Graff, is a "radical unaccountability" of literary meaning in its reference to real experience. Fiction does not tell the truth, these critics concede, but then again it does not

A Short History of Deception Theories

lie either, because it does not claim to tell the truth. Consequently, both deceptive and objective theories of fictive meaning can be rejected for being irrelevant to fiction.

In *Literature against Itself*, Graff challenges this notion of literary unaccountability by claiming that the propositional and informational functions of language are just as applicable to fiction as to any other mode of communication. He insists that fiction's sentences inevitably express subject-predicate equations conveying information whose validity must sooner or later be tested against the real world. He acknowledges that fiction can be largely hypothetical but argues that its value as fiction nevertheless depends upon its "convincing understanding of the world." Its reorganization of experience may be creative, but it must also be true to the world as we know it. As perhaps we could expect, the committed deceptionist finds no problem in agreeing with Graff's emphasis on the truth value of fiction, but with the caveat that fiction's most basic propositional content must accordingly be treated as false, not true. Fiction does indeed tell a great variety of truths, but these truths are almost always used to justify its more fundamental distortions. Fiction provides a convincing understanding of the world, as Graff maintains, but it is untruth, not truth, that dominates fiction's most inclusive organization of experience, thus reducing verisimilitude to the use of both truths and untruths to confirm a text's more basic fabrication. For example, when a happy ending is totally unrealistic, the accumulation of accurate detail and genuine human insight used to confirm its vision of experience is no less fictitious than the ending itself *if* the work is to be considered an aesthetic whole. No matter how accurate particular words, images, and sentences might seem, these remain part of the whole, and if the whole consists of a lie, so, too, do these portions of it to the extent that they give it believability.

This basic and unshakable role of literary deception seems confirmed by formal logic's so-called material implication, which provides that no matter how true the premise is, a logical implication becomes invalid if its conclusion is false. If true information supports true conclusions, then the material implication is valid in logical discourse. An implication is equally valid if false information supports false conclusions, for example, by declaring absurdities that bear absolutely no claim of verisimilitude. Even if false information supports true conclusions, the implication remains valid according to the laws of deduction. But if true information is used to couch, justify, and give immediacy to false conclusions—for example, by telling "realistic" stories of pure love and total selflessness—then the implication is invalid. The literary application of this simple logical distinction seems plain. No matter how accurately a work of fiction depicts the life and times of its characters, its supportive informational content imposes a false deduction if its primary appeal is based on the falsehoods implicit in the conventions of form, theme, and narrative closure. When truths are put on display—for example, to legitimize a happy (or "appropriate") ending—every detail, no matter how accurate, becomes just as fictive as the fantasy content it reinforces. In all such cases, literary truths become untruths if and when they are used to make other untruths come true. Factual authenticity has been absorbed by its fictional context to confirm its appeal as an attractive alternative to our normal expectations in life.

Graff praises fiction for exposing readers to straightforward, uncompromising honesty. Literary truth, he insists, encourages similar behavior in its readers:

> One of the most useful functions that literature and the humanities could serve right now would be to shore up the sense of reality, to preserve the distinction between the real and the fictive, and to help us resist those influences, both material and intellectual, that would turn lying into a universal principle.[65]

Here, paradoxically, Graff calls upon fiction to help us eliminate literary misrepresentation from our thinking. He thereby ignores both the etymology of the word *fiction* (*fictio* as a making, or fabrication) and the current pervasiveness of deception in language, social intercourse, and indeed consciousness itself, to say nothing of our public myths and simplistic theories of collective achievement. How much of our shared sense of history amounts to anything more than historic romance? How many of our personal insights derive from fictional conventions? To what extent do we simplify, exaggerate, and foreshorten? And to what extent does our sense of individual and group destiny depend upon a confidence in benign outcome as a happy and appropriate resolution that derives from fiction's conventional sense of an ending? As Solon might have predicted and Oscar Wilde indeed boasted, the basic choice confronting us in almost every sphere of human endeavor is not between truth and myth but between competing myths, some of which are more useful than others.

If fiction helps us to adjust to life, it is not by teaching us to abide by stringent tenets of veracity.[66] Instead, fiction plays the more useful role of helping us to adopt the best and most convenient distortions of the truth—the most credible euphemisms and simplifications for glossing over what really matters, what really happens in life. The primary benefit of literary distortions (as opposed to the nonliterary varieties) has been to help buttress our sense of personal worth without producing harmful consequences. Too often the raw truth—as experienced, for example, by Plato's cave dweller when he reaches the outside world—exceeds our tolerance except in small and manageable doses. Literary deception can be admired because it diminishes this threat, thereby contributing to our survival as individuals, as a society. A new and more fundamental truth therefore emerges with the recognition that most truths are best utilized if, in the words of George Steiner, they are "attenuated, flexed, coloured, alloyed by intent and milieux." The value of better-than-truths was Nietzsche's discovery as a philosopher and Pareto's as a sociologist—it seems just as valid in the field of literary criticism.

My own view of literary deception approximates those of Nietzsche, Freud, Barthes, and Steiner. Ideal form does not especially interest me, nor does ideal beauty, nor any realm of ideas that transcends human fallibility. However, I agree with the notion that our emotional balance probably depends upon a healthy dose of self-deception and that we must reconcile ourselves to its inevitability in both our personal lives and the literature we enjoy. I acknowledge that verisimilitude's use of untruths to express the truth is harmless and of relatively superficial importance, but I find this priority to be reversed in fiction's more inclusive context of meaning, since fiction's so-called basic truths almost always mask even more fundamental distortions. This is demonstrated, I think, by the importance of literary conventions, especially those associated with narrative closure.

I also take it for granted that literary misrepresentation can be fully credible only when authors themselves believe in their distortions. They are best able to deceive readers by first deceiving themselves, then persuading readers of their sincerity. The cold-blooded fabrication of a story recommended by Edgar Allan Poe probably fails for this reason, since authors should be no less dishonest with themselves than with their readers in order to give credibility to the truths they consider important. This perhaps more demanding tenet of literary deception usually obliges authors to be at least partially ignorant of their feelings and motives. They might try to tell the truth, but they should also be willing to take whatever liberties seem necessary to dramatize and invigorate those truths that seem important to them. This is the exemption, the hidden clause, that permits self-deception to predominate in the craft of fiction. Of course, an ardent defense of fiction's truth value can be expected from authors and critics who share a vested stake in treating fiction as the fount of human wisdom. They can bestow life upon their lies only by considering them true. However, like Mencken, we need to treat their defense of literary truth as a sales pitch essential for producing and marketing the product. The more convincing their protestations, the more unassailable their roles as purveyors of the truth. To tell the lies they want to believe in while fully acknowledging what they are doing is more than should be expected of them.

If there is any truth in literary experience important to authors, I find it to be more or less pragmatic, as explained by William James in his two books *Pragmatism* and *The Meaning of Truth*.[67] James insisted that the truth is "only the expedient in the way of our thinking" and that it necessarily emphasizes the attainment of beneficial consequences. Literary fiction likewise affords an expedient manner of thinking that is beneficial to readers. James argued that the truth is not absolute but happens to an idea and is made true by events. The same may be said of fiction, which seems true to life because of its believable recombination of events. James also explained that truths "emerge from facts," then "dip forward into facts again and add to them." Once again, the same principle applies to fiction, whose verisimilitude depends on an ongoing interplay between apparent factual accuracy and the liberties needed to produce a desired effect. James praised truths that lead to "consistency, stability and flowing human intercourse" and that "lead away from eccentricity and isolation, from foiled and barren thinking." Again, the same may be said of fiction, which absorbs and tolerates eccentricity but only to give final precedence to conventional truths. James also took personal need into account by explaining that the truth consists of what each individual "'troweth' at that moment with the maximum of satisfaction." Here, too, the parallel seems obvious, since the art (or behavior) of fiction lets authors and readers redefine experience to their own satisfaction. And finally, James explained that "our obligation to seek truth is part of our general obligation to do what pays." James subverted the notion of an objective truth by arguing that "the payments truths bring are the sole why of our duty to follow them." This principle even more obviously applies in the case of fiction, whose payoff

A Short History of Deception Theories

depends almost entirely upon misrepresentation. Most of the assumptions important to James's pragmatic definition of truth are equally valid, *mutatis mutandis*, in judging the merits of fiction. Honesty abounds, but its truth value depends on the author's confidence (or belief) in those ideas that cannot, and should not, be exposed to uncompromising skeptical investigation.

However, as I indicated in my introduction, the pragmatic truth of fiction in its formal context cannot be altogether isolated from the countervailing truths it helps to eliminate from consideration. Relative to all the other truths with which it cohabits in both fiction and whatever personal associations the reader brings to bear in enjoying it, the truth of fiction is indeed true. But relative to the real world, and relative to the alternatives intentionally excluded from this literary context, this truth is very likely false, the product of denial, negation, and reaction formation—all of the Freudian negative displacements that give literary wish fulfillment its appeal to the reader. In this sense, the pragmatic usefulness of literary truth primarily derives from its not being true, at least not in the most inclusive sense. It comforts as truth precisely because it denies other, less comfortable truths whose elimination provides the *raison d'être* of literary experience. At one level literary truth is on a pragmatic "float," but on another level this float may be judged untrue relative to the psychological benefits it provides. If denial is at work, as more often than not seems the case with literary experience, the affirmative value of whatever truths afford denial must be judged relative to the experience denied.

My second basic assumption, then, divides the act of deception into two complementary aspects, the rejection of one account of reality by the promotion of another that serves as its opposite. Every lie, every distortion and misrepresentation, may be divided in this fashion into two propositions, one true and the other false. When everyday liars falsely declare, "I mailed my rent this morning; the check is in the mail," they resort to this kind of substitution, and the truth they obscure may be deduced as a contrary proposition, "In fact, I have not paid my rent yet." An unpleasantness is thus denied by affirming whatever effectively substitutes for it. Chief Justice John Marshall explained the exclusionary impact of this displacement in his celebrated *Marbury v. Madison* opinion: "Affirmative words are often, in their operation, negative of other objects than those affirmed; and in this case, a negative or exclusive sense must be given to them or they have no operation at all."[68] In other words, to affirm anything is necessarily to deny whatever in fact provides its opposite. Often the choice as to what might be affirmed as an act of denial seems random, but its usefulness depends on the implicit contrast between what it declares and what it thereby denies. This dialectic occurs even when subtler modes of indirection are employed to diffuse the implied contrast between the two. "The money is on its way," delinquent tenants might insist, neglecting to mention that they plan to send it later. Or they might resort to mock equivocation: "What do you mean have I paid my rent? Haven't I always been a good tenant?" Here the truth is denied by an enthymemic construction whose minor premise deserves to be rejected (that the liar has *not* been a good tenant, at least to the extent that the rent has not been paid). In all instances, whatever evasiveness is brought to bear by delinquent tenants, proposition X denies proposition Y in order to obscure the fact that they have not yet made their payment. Literary evasiveness, I think, possesses comparable value as denial, for example, as explained by Freud, when the image or epiphany of a silent and beautiful young woman denies one's fear of death.[69] Other, more obvious examples include stories of bravery that deny timidity, stories of romance that deny frustration, etc. Inevitably, deception is rooted in substitution (useful truths supplant real truths), and just as inevitably substitution expresses denial. Denial is thus very likely the most basic ingredient of literary expression if, in fact, this expression appeals to readers for its value as wish fulfillment. Unless denial plays a central role, I would conclude, a text ceases to be literary.

It is my contention here that all literary distortions, no matter to what extent they are diluted by partial truths, can be reduced in this fashion to denial, the simplest of the Freudian displacement mechanisms. One version of experience is rejected by fastening onto another that provides a more comfortable explanation of events. No obviously schematic opposition is needed between these alternatives. Any X may be affirmed as long as its acceptance permits the conscious or unconscious denial of Y. Blatant lies may be concocted, as in westerns, horror tales, and the like, but for sophisticated readers partial truths may be even more effective in crowding from consideration the relevance of less pleasant truths (e.g., the sensitive young woman who presumably finds her unique purpose in life, or who discovers that her second choice is probably better for her). Moreover, the more truths used to convey the lie, the better. In all such cases, there is felt necessity to give credence to X, affording felt subversiveness to Y once this necessity has been accepted. Authors enjoy wide latitude in their choice of literary truths, and readers enjoy comparable latitude in substituting these truths for the real truths they wish to avoid—often truths substantially different from those avoided by the authors they read.

This principle of substitutive freedom applies at every level of consciousness. Just as any lie may be divided into two alternatives, one supplanting the other, any psychological displacement that originates in denial may be identified as an exercise in self-deception based on the substitution of one idea or frame of mind for another. Freud, for example, explained paranoia as a projective strategy that lets the individual deny problems by blaming them on others (not my fault, but theirs), and Robert Waelder expanded Freud's theory by claiming that all neurotic behavior originates in denial.[70] One step further, I claim that literary fiction likewise depends upon denial—not because it is neurotic but because it plays a comparable but healthy psychological role, providing a manageable dose of catharsis and self-justification in a relatively harmless medium. Denied (or repressed) ideas are not entirely isolated in a recessive zone reified as the unconscious. Instead, fiction provides a unique arena for their interplay with the ideas that finally prevail. As in dream formation, the literary text becomes a medium for putting affirmed truths and rejected truths into a closer, more engaged relationship with each other. Dominant form (or plot) gives credence to desirable truths, but a countervailing texture of implications via metaphor, irony, and ambiguity expresses subversive truths. Censorship occurs in the sense that dominant form ultimately prevails, but not without first giving vent to this figurative subversiveness. The conflict between these competing truths may be enjoyed without being understood, but it also discloses itself to readers who, like Schlegel, are willing to seek out authors' secret intentions—so secret, in fact, that authors themselves very likely overlook the fullest implications of what they are saying.

My third basic assumption emphasizes the deceptive function of literary form as an advancement from one plateau of experience to its opposite—in other words from X to *not X*, from an undesirable circumstance to its denial through narrative closure. I fully agree with Barthes and Steiner that both thought and language offer ample opportunity for literary self-deception, but I also emphasize plot (or narrative form) as its primary vehicle. Aristotle's notion that a plot's primary feature is its linear advancement from beginning to end may be expanded, I think, to accommodate the principle that this transition produces gratification (or catharsis) by denying an original state of affairs. In effect, the sequence is a metonymic transition from *maybe X* to *Y* as *not X*, shifting from tension to relief, from need to gratification, from perceived difficulties to their effective elimination. Stanley Fish argues that criticism itself marks out beginnings, middles, and ends, but here he exaggerates the responsibility of the critic.[71] As Sartre maintains, it is the telling about life that necessarily imposes beginnings that imply their own ends.[72] Moreover, Gotthold Lessing's insistence upon fiction's linearity may be refined based on the principle that its affirmative outcome fulfills and consolidates the denial displacement, completing the unity of action by making its transition from beginning through middle to end. By means of narrative reversal, a plot advances from the potential confession of dissatisfying truths to the substitution of better-than-truths that declare a satisfactory alternative.[73] The text's resolution actually denies (or designifies) the original state of affairs expressed or implied at its beginning. This principle also applies to the simplest anecdote, but it is literary form that invests the denial displacement with its full global sufficiency relative to human need.

Once linear narrative achievement is recognized as the primary vehicle of literary deception, it becomes possible to resume Fracastoro's effort to integrate the aesthetics of Plato and Aristotle, but on an entirely new basis. Both the author's imagination and necessarily distorted use of words, as explained by Barthes and Steiner, may be recognized to compose Plato's first stage of removal from the truth of human affairs (due to the limitations of human consciousness), while plot's built-in reversal dynamics (the product of the author's skills as an artisan) may be recognized to compose the second stage by telling a lie *in media res*, not simply as an accomplished fact. At the initial level of misrepresentation, the author's experience signified by particular words necessarily distorts the truth, but plot, at the second level, becomes even more vitally distortive in bringing about the achievement here and now of an appropriate ending that denies a mood or state of affairs implicit in its origins. Misrepresentation is doubled by fiction so that whatever unacceptable truths survive conscious and verbal selectivity can be altogether vanquished by means of the plot. As a cumulative sequence of events, plot terminates the circumstances that give rise to its appeal. In this sense, the plot advances from a *signified* original state of affairs to its *designification* produced by narrative closure. Of course, the summary retelling of already formulated misinformation is just as common in fiction as in other modes of discourse. However, readers take greater pleasure when actively participating in the

A Short History of Deception Theories

quest for those alternative truths they want to believe in. *The lie must happen.* It must also be earned if the reader is to be lured to share in making it happen. There must be a sense of attainment, of producing benign results, and this is the most basic purpose of plot (or *muthos*) for both the author and the readers.

I also want to stress that the truth and its misrepresentation must actively coexist in struggle against each other within a serious work of fiction. For Homer, Shakespeare, Dostoevsky, and other major authors, the plot acts out the denial displacement as a conflict of moral and intellectual precariousness from beginning to end. Its affirmative resolution can be tentatively earned only at the expense of genuine self-perception. Its value as denial is necessarily achieved, not told, and this means that the experience denied must be included in the recipe as a danger worthy of elimination. Only then does aesthetic form gain credible linear realization, disavowing one vision of life that is accurate but unpleasant through the energetic affirmation of another that is pleasantly inaccurate. Hard truths nevertheless fester on the brink of disclosure and oblige continuing effort to confirm their rejection. The entire text thus becomes a moral battlefield, with hard truths pitted against surface truths that encourage ethical simplicity and exaggerated self-respect. A reaching out for credible misrepresentation dominates plot development, and the eventual victory of such an effort can be only partial. Anything more decisive seems unlikely, even undesirable. To understand texts organized by this dialectic, critics must seek out their unpleasant truths that make the affirmation of their superficial truths attractive to both authors and readers. Only then, paradoxically, does the final truth emerge that a lie has been told and why it might be gratifying. When formally structured, this truth becomes fiction's defining feature, its most irreducible ingredient.

My fourth basic assumption comes from my willingness to speculate on the sources of anxiety denied within the context of fiction. It is one thing to declare that we are all liars but quite another to explore with any thoroughness what we might be lying about. Like the gifted dissembler, fiction reserves its misrepresentation for only the most important issues. As an act of denial, it is not the product of empty avoidance but expresses aversions that pose a genuine threat to our sense of personal worth. What fiction helps us to deny in ourselves must be sufficiently dangerous to justify the extra investment of psychic energy required by misrepresenting the truth. As a shared act of self-deception, it exacts a price that we are reluctant to pay unless this investment is exceeded by its benefits. This means that the matters we deceive ourselves about are almost inevitably embarrassing, even humiliating, and that our felt surge of gratification once they are denied expresses our resistance to thinking about them. For this reason, it is often even distasteful to confess that lying has been hypothetically possible. In defense of our benighted innocence, we must convince ourselves that we are dealing exclusively with honest approximations of the truth—hence our compensatory insistence upon the honesty of fiction. The more vital the lie, the more vigorously we defend it—especially when the literature we venerate for its insight is called into question. As Nietzsche recognized, fiction's universal appeal derives from epitomizing, and thus conceding, those lies we depend on lest we perish of the truth. This is fiction's final obligation, which authors, critics, and readers find so difficult to acknowledge.

two

AUSTEN, DICKENS, CONRAD, AND STEIN

In her 1971 manifesto, "When We Dead Awaken," Adrienne Rich concedes the necessity of literary distortion by arguing that good poetry demands an energetic pursuit of meaningful differences. Passive fantasy alone falls short of adequacy, she claims, since effective writing depends on the active quest for alternatives:

> Most, if not all, human lives are full of fantasy—passive daydreaming which need not be acted on. But to write poetry or fiction, or even to think well, is not to fantasize, or to put fantasies on paper. For a poem to coalesce, for a character or an action to take shape, there has to be an imaginative transformation of reality which is no way passive. And a certain freedom of the mind is needed—freedom to press on, to enter the currents of your thought like a glider pilot, knowing that your motion can be sustained, that the buoyancy of your attention will not be suddenly snatched away. Moreover, if the imagination is to transcend and transform experience it has to question, to challenge, to conceive of alternatives, perhaps to the very life you are living at that moment. You

have to be free to play around with the notion that day might be night, love might be hate; nothing can be too sacred for the imagination to turn into its opposite or to call experimentally by another name. For writing is renaming.¹

There is little to disagree with in this passage except the use of the word *perhaps* in indicating the importance of seeking substitutes—better and more interesting versions of experience than the life one is living at the moment. Unavoidably, personal circumstances dictate the renaming of one's experience. The use of opposites is needed in revising the world one knows, and to persist in exploring opposites means at least provisionally rejecting part, or all, of this particular world. A certain amount of personal dissatisfaction is probably integral to the effort to call day "night" and love "hate," and, *mutatis mutandis*, an intense rejection of the status quo seems beneficial to the effort to reinterpret and thereby rename the most sacred experiences (parenthood, marriage, confidential experiences with others, etc.) in the context of literary form.

Of course, this quest for alternatives is not adequate in and of itself as a formula for good writing. It must also be given credibility by style and literary form. Differences provide the raw material of art, but they must be sorted out, depersonalized, and subordinated to an aesthetic whole acceptable to authors and their readers. Denise Levertov explained the formal benefit of this more elaborate strategy in her brief 1979 manifesto, "On the Function of the Line," in which she praises the use of deletions to bring the poet's inner feelings into the context of literary form:

> Excess of subjectivity (and hence incommunicability) in the making of structural decisions in open forms is a problem only when the writer has an inadequate form sense. When the written score precisely notates perceptions, a whole—an inscape or gestalt—begins to emerge; and the gifted writer is not so submerged in the parts that the sum goes unseen. The sum is objective—relatively, at least; it has presence, character, and—as it develops—needs. The parts of the poem are instinctively adjusted in some degree to serve the needs of the whole. And as this adjustment takes place, excess subjectivity is avoided. Details of a private, as distinct from personal, nature may be deleted, for example, in the interests of a fuller, clearer, more communicable whole.²

Austen, Dickens, Conrad, and Stein

Literary form's intrinsic evasiveness depends upon the combination of Rich's and Levertov's prescriptions for good poetry. Rich's pursuit of alternatives obliges selectivity, while Levertov's emphasis on formal integrity that defines this selectivity as a use of exclusions is best achieved by narrative form. Undue subjectivity is thus avoided, and, more inclusively, structure itself becomes the vehicle for imposing alternatives. By means of linear organization, specific events and identities may be deleted in order to dispense with those concessions and complications the poet prefers to ignore. The experience may be actively renamed, as Adrienne Rich recommends, or it may simply be left out, as Denise Levertov recommends. Some experience may be deleted to keep it from the reader, some other experience because the poet wants to avoid confronting it too. Inevitably, certain private feelings are more expendable than others, and their deletion may be justified entirely in the interest of formal adequacy. Other feelings might be too embarrassing to acknowledge, and their deletion (tantamount to denial) might oblige the full resources of literary form.

Both deletions and the active pursuit of alternatives are rooted in denial, and both may be found throughout the history of literature from the epic to the sonnet, from seventeenth-century prose characters to the *Bildungsroman*, from spy escapades to Harlequin romances. If the truth is almost totally sacrificed, the result is empty fantasy. On the other hand, if deletions and reversals are minimized, the result is a tedious documentation of the habits and distractions that clutter our daily behavior. The truth and literary form therefore depend on each other. Alone, each lacks appeal, but once combined and brought into suitable equipoise, they vitalize literary expression. A basic dialectic thus emerges that features both honesty and the substitution of a more satisfactory point of view as justified by narrative outcome. The universal expectation of readers that useful truths will ultimately prevail at the expense of unpleasant and apparently meaningless truths (no less unpleasant) gives fiction its vitality, its inspiration, even its formal structure as an act of denial plotted from beginning to end.

A work of fiction loses its audience whenever its particular combination of selectivity and renaming ceases to be useful to readers. Few of us find pleasure today, for example, in works of romantic self-pity, unmitigated Victorian innocence, or *fin de siècle* unconventionality. Likewise, the simplistic political enthusiasm of Depression-era strike novels, the propagandistic stereotypes of

World War II, and the canned existentialism of the fifties have all faded by now into deserved obscurity. Works of fiction uncompromisingly committed to these once fashionable truths (and "truths" they were) are no longer relevant to human needs, so they have predictably sunk into oblivion. In order to write permanent fiction for a permanent audience, writers need to make better and more lasting omissions reinforced by better and more lasting renamings. Those classics in which this balance is achieved effectively resonate in the minds of their readers for decades, sometimes centuries.

Specific distortions of the truth abound in fiction, but perhaps the most obvious example is the use of exaggerated motivation to deny the bland monotony of our daily routine. Our reduced sense of accomplishment may be revitalized by our sharing in the undiminished energy of literary figures who pursue important goals with an almost guaranteed predictability of achieving them. In real life, everyday habit blunts our expectations; in fiction, deletions and renamings support the illusion of unusual attainment. Also deceptive is fiction's exaggerated ethical righteousness, which denies the pragmatic flexibility typical of normal relationships. Contrary to our daily experience, fiction sets virtue against evil based on a simplistic distinction between "good guys" and "bad guys," or, with slightly more sophistication, between good intentions and the tarnished goals of less admirable figures—faithless lovers, grasping relatives, meddlesome neighbors, etc. Again, this kind of Manichaean exaggeration denies the boring, if intricate, balance of strengths and weaknesses found in the real people we know. Only in fiction does one meet individuals who are uncompromisingly malicious or unavailingly generous. Only in fiction are people rigidly stereotypical in every choice they make. Even when characters seem endowed with unusual complexity—for example, Saul Bellow's Herzog in his novel *Herzog*—their stories hinge upon relatively simple-minded literary discoveries, in Herzog's case his belated recognition that he should avoid throwing himself at the first woman who comes along. We are expected to believe that he at last abandons his romantic impetuousness and learns to be more realistic in his pursuit of female companionship. This happens in Herzog's late forties, when such a basic reform seems unlikely, therefore necessitating at least a modest suspension of disbelief when the novel concludes with his commitment to maintaining his bachelor status.[3] Even when fiction challenges conventional morality by sympathetically exploring grand ethical transgressions—for example, in the works of Homer,

Goethe, and Dostoevsky—it distorts reality by representing these transgressions as the epitome of human achievement. Odysseus, Faust, and Raskolnikov possess extraordinary values quite beyond the purview of the average citizen. Their stories evoke the sense of a cosmic breakthrough that can only flatter and befuddle the ordinary mind.

Most of all, it is the verbal competence of writers that deceptively reorganizes the truth. With almost inexhaustible sufficiency, fiction's flow of vocabulary generates problems, then surmounts them simply by talking them out. Experience accessible to words becomes organized, then resolved by words, since language altogether dominates behavior in the context of story. There is no stuttering, no redundancy, no failed expression that drifts into hiatus and half-hearted reformulation. Only in poems and novels can language fully declare subjective feelings or dissolve behavior into intangible effects presumably transcending the words that describe them. Only in poems and novels can the thoughts and utterances of characters be supplemented by an authorial omniscience that probes the feelings they express. Only in poems and novels can there be uncompromising authorial license to impose whatever deletions and renamings seem useful in reconstructing interior consciousness. In these and dozens of other ways—the excitement that denies boredom, the confidence that denies embarrassment, the romantic vitality that denies impotence and frigidity, and the presumed capacity for ambivalence that denies simplistic authoritarianism—literary experience serves up one kind of truth, both attractive and compelling, in order to reject other truths that come closer to what we know about ourselves, our family, and our friends and acquaintances.

The dialectic between truth and fiction's active pursuit of alternatives may be examined in the works of such admired novelists as Jane Austen, Charles Dickens, and Joseph Conrad, all of whom used literary insight to delete and rename the worlds they lived in. Three of their major novels—respectively *Pride and Prejudice*, *David Copperfield*, and *Heart of Darkness*—were written more or less at fifty-year intervals, providing a measure of historical continuity to the analysis of their misrepresentations. The same strategy may also be found in the briefest of lyrics, for example, "a rose is a rose is a rose is a rose" by Gertrude Stein, a *tour de force* in ambiguity that can be treated as an exception to prove the rule. For each of these four texts, including Stein's poem, I want to discuss the use of deletions and reversals to emphasize literary truths at the expense of more threatening truths. I also want to speculate on why these substitutions were made, how they occurred, and the extent to which rejected truths continue to play a subversive role.

In *Pride and Prejudice,* there is remarkable insightfulness by both the heroine, Elizabeth Bennet, and the implied narrator, whose perspective seems a close approximation to that of Jane Austen herself. As a result, the reader quickly grants credibility to the novel's depiction of provincial family life and the ironic treatment of most of the characters. Not more than a couple dozen pages into the text, we share Elizabeth's embarrassment with the ignorance and fallibility of her mother and younger sisters, her impatience with the gossipy pretensions of her neighbors, her tolerant disagreement with the eccentricities of her father, and her fascinated indignation with the brittle rectitude of Darcy, whom she finally marries. Also realistic is the complex interaction among these characters that finally leads Elizabeth, a young woman of the middle class, to surmount her pride in winning an advantageous match. What is the most valid truth of this perceptive novel? Probably the sustained interplay of feeling, behavior, and language which Austen works out with such precision that we find ourselves caught up in the courtship strategies of late-eighteenth-century rural gentility. Likewise important are the standards of politeness observed by this class in its daily behavior. The novel can be treated, in fact, as a textbook in rural etiquette that documents the personal lives of a rural middle-class family from day to day through the cycle of a single year.

A different and more inclusive vision of the truth prevails in *David Copperfield,* written fifty years later, in which society is viewed on a grander scale and with a social conscience more appropriate to the mid-nineteenth century. London has become even more dominant as the hub of England, and so Dickens's novel appropriately traces the centripetal activities of individuals drawn into this center. The story of young David's being buffeted from one household to the next illustrates the restless migration in and around London during this period of social dislocation. We watch David's character evolve as he surmounts his handicap as an orphan, works his way into the world, and at last establishes himself as a novelist, perhaps the author of his own story. Vivid is the depiction of all the crises and challenges that provide the milestones for his slow but inexorable growth through early life. The shadow-side of mid-century British culture is also explored in depth as a realm David must transcend as he makes his ascent to become the master of his own destiny. Portraying a broad range of characters from thieves and opportunists to honest simpletons unable to cope with social demands, Dickens provides in this novel a better sense of Britain's social malaise at mid-century than may be found in most, if not all, textbooks of economics and social history. If *Das Kapital* by Karl Marx furnishes the statistics and historic evidence of urban despair, *David Copperfield* fleshes it out by bringing to life the visible misery of believable characters. Marx's data afford truth for the scholar willing to endure his exhaustive treatment of the topic, but far more vivid is Dickens's truth for those willing to subject themselves to his eager use of poetic license.

With Joseph Conrad's vision of human degradation in *Heart of Darkness*, published fifty years after *David Copperfield*, we encounter a new and more complex vision of honesty based on the skeptic's stoic acceptance of primordial forces at the root of civilization. We are first confronted with the violence of European colonization in Africa, then with its historic necessity as the source of affluence among presumably civilized nations. Imperialism works, we learn, though it might have borne ugly consequences for the exploited African people during the final decades of the nineteenth century. But the truth becomes an issue in the novel, for example when Marlow, the narrator-protagonist, declares his aversion to hypocrisy:

> You know I hate, detest, and can't bear a lie, not because I am straighter than the rest of us, but simply because it appalls me. There is a taint of death, a flavour of mortality in lies—which is exactly what I hate and detest in the world—what I want to forget. It makes me miserable and sick, like biting something rotten would do. Temperament, I suppose.[4]

His allegiance to the truth as an abstract principle is supposedly in harmony with his faith in liberal values. However, he soon discovers more important truths, first in the actual behavior of Kurtz, a legendary ivory hunter in the Belgian Congo, then in the need to lie to Kurtz's bereaved fiancée, who continues to admire Kurtz for what she believes is his altruistic sacrifice to benefit the natives. Marlow decides it would be too great a shock to reveal to her Kurtz's final dying words, since Kurtz had only been able to utter "The horror!" presumably referring to his genocidal practices as an ivory hunter. His final truth thus consists of the recognition, like that of Plato's cave dweller, that the truth is too harsh for most people to endure.

The novel's central irony arises from Marlow's blurting out the lie to Kurtz's fiancée that Kurtz's final utterance was to name her, inadvertently identifying her as the real horror at last recognized by Kurtz. "The horror," he said, and, indeed, he was referring to her—to her ignorance of his crimes and her liberal reasons for justifying them without recognizing their necessity for protecting her standard of living. Reinforcing this irony, the word horror can be easily slurred into whore, an insult that suggests her dependence on imperialistic profits in exchange for her misplaced faith in his idealism—*her* service for the pay he offers. By stumbling on this unspeakable equation, Marlow delivers the novel to its culminating vision of truth, the price of Victorian respectability in the exploitational violence that must be committed abroad. Conrad accordingly exposes the disparity between late-nineteenth-century colonial atrocities, almost entirely committed by men, and the blind progressivism of European liberals who encouraged them, epitomized by those women whose genteel life-style finally depended on these atrocities.

Conrad's ironic message seems to be that imperialism was "worthy of its hire" (to borrow the words of Marlow's aunt), since it brought enough wealth to Europe to justify overlooking the raw brutality at the root of all human behavior. Vice versa, Victorian purity was no less worthy of its hire as the inspiration for Victorian imperialism. If murder and exploitation were inevitable, it was better committing these crimes to sustain the genteel innocence of Europeans rather than letting them happen randomly and with comparable brutality, as they would have if Europeans had not intervened, but without any benefit to civilization. If idealists recoiled from this insight because of their misguided humanitarianism (strictly a by-product of their affluence), these gentle souls needed to be kept in ignorance of the system that supported them. Violence in the service of blind idealism was consequently the key to progress. This was Kurtz's discovery, which he finally shared with Marlow. Their rationalization, of course, persists even today among some self-styled conservatives, but most critics have tried to defend *Heart of Darkness* as a humanistic testament that effectively transcends this cynicism. We cannot overlook, however, its most basic message, the reactionary conviction (consistent with Lenin's theory of imperialism) that if colonialism was a nasty business, it nevertheless remained indispensable as the principal source of Europe's surplus wealth, thus guaranteeing bourgeois stability over the several decades preceding World War I.

Austen, Dickens, Conrad, and Stein

In one way or another, each of these three novels declares a particular vision of the truth based upon the experience and judgment of its author. And of course this is the case for all fiction. No matter how rigid, chaotic, big, small, or devoid of intelligible organization a scrap of creativity might seem, it affirms a truth (if not exactly *the* truth) about human experience. Essentially the same dynamics are at work in the tiniest lyric as in the epic novel. With just as much conviction, for example, Gertrude Stein's epic fragment "a rose is a rose is a rose is a rose" offers a tautological affirmation of Keats's truth—"That is all ye know on earth, and all ye need to know." The noun rose is incessantly repeated, for, according to Stein, "You can love a name and if you love a name then saying that name any number of times only makes you love it more, more violently more persistently more tormentedly"; she thus drums the flower's verbal representation into our consciousness well enough to be able to boast, "I think that in that line the rose is red for the first time in English poetry for a hundred years."[5] In effect, Stein reduces to its simplest formulation Emerson's argument in "Self-Reliance" that roses make "no reference to former roses or to better ones," that "they are for what they are," and that "there is no time for them. There is simply the rose; it is perfect in every moment of its existence."[6] Stein also short-circuits Friedrich Engels's use of an empty double negative (or *Negationsnegierung*), which he bases on the example of the rose:

> Or I negate the sentence, "The rose is a rose," when I say: "The rose is not a rose"; and what do I get if I then negate the negation and say, "After all, the rose is a rose?"[7]

On the contrary, Stein claims, the rose cannot be diminished in this fashion. It is not "not not" a rose; it is simply a rose is a rose. Just as relevant, therefore, is the line's significance as a rejoinder to Juliet's famous romantic outcry, "What's in a name? That which we call a rose by any other word would smell as sweet." In other words, "I love this man no matter what he is called, even Romeo Montague." To which Gertrude Stein replies that Romeo's name— or any name, for that matter—is nevertheless a legitimate object of adoration that fully appropriates to itself the appeal of what it represents. If Rose is intended as a female name, as was the case for several of Stein's fictional heroines over the span of her career, then the incantation of her name reinforces her memory. In either case, the poem proposes its vision of truth comparable to that of fiction, if on a briefer and more compulsively insistent note.

As I have already indicated, literary truth also tells untruths based upon the negative equation $X = \textit{not } Y$. Authors such as D. H. Lawrence, Norman Mailer, and Grace Paley have argued that writers necessarily accept an overbalance of dishonesty as the price they must pay for unexpected illumination.[8] However, this ephemeral expression of the truth often excuses a sustained disingenuousness almost out of control, since only a modest dose of accuracy is needed to permit the deletion and renaming of experience crucial to literary experience. For example, Gertrude Stein's insistent equation "a rose is a rose is a rose is a rose" deceives by its tautological repetition, which emphasizes the sound of *rose* at the expense of its connotations. Unavoidably, one version of the rose, primarily auditory, crowds from consideration all the rest. Driven from consciousness are associations pertaining to gardening (blight, aphids, Japanese beetles, etc.), as well as the full range of implications this variety of flower has acquired throughout the history of Western civilization—its ancient symbolism as the flower of Aphrodite, its use as the basic ingredient for thirty-two medical remedies listed by Pliny, and so on. A rose is *only* a rose, and none of these others, Stein implies. Also crowded from thought are its dirt-rootedness, its hybrid cultivation, its frequent use in poetry, and its relevance to the Wars of the Roses, which decimated English chivalry. Rejected as literary convention are Blake's vision of a rose destroyed by the invisible worm that flies by night and Friar Lawrence's prediction of roses in lips and cheeks fading to wanny ashes.

More specifically, if the poem's rose bears any reference to Rose Johnson, the object of lesbian desire in *Three Lives* by Gertrude Stein, Johnson's complex appeal as an individual human being is denied by the diminutive repetition of her name—"my little flower is my little flower is my little flower, etc." Or, more disparagingly yet, "an attractive companion is *just* an attractive companion, is *just* an attractive companion." And quite so, according to the law of identity: "X is X and exclusively X, even if it refers to a lover or a beautiful flower." Fortunately, life is more complex than the law of identity, lending credibility to the inclusive negative proposition, "a rose is *more* than a rose, is *more* than a rose." An individual is more than a flower, sex is more than sex, and the wealth of additional implications attached to the symbolism of the rose is almost impossible to ignore.

Austen, Dickens, Conrad, and Stein

In Austen's *Pride and Prejudice*, a judicious use of surface truths obscures the unlikely fiction that Elizabeth Bennet's quick wits win her the region's most advantageous match despite her narrow background, her lack of dowry, and the prudishness that prevents even a kiss throughout the entire course of the novel. Not that Darcy ever tries to force the occasion. True to her high standards of morality, Elizabeth marries Darcy untouched, the virgin proprietress-to-be of one of the largest estates in England. Far more typical of human affairs, however, is the indifference of wealthy bachelors to plain and financially modest middle-class women with an excessively critical temperament, no matter how intelligent and vivacious they might seem at parties and dances. The sexual adventurousness of Lydia, Elizabeth's foolish younger sister, might have gained temporary accessibility to the wealthier classes, but seldom, if ever, did marriage with one of the nation's most eligible bachelors come to the likes of Elizabeth Bennet.

The very title *Pride and Prejudice* both reverses and domesticates the conventional notion of pride, worst of the seven deadly sins. Pride is obviously attributed to Darcy and prejudice against Darcy to Elizabeth, of course, because she resents his pride. Yet contemporary opinion at the time Austen wrote her novel would have reversed this judgment. Any young woman who aspired to marry beyond her social position would have been accused of pride, and she could expect to evoke prejudice against herself from those of the class she tried to join. This attitude was prevalent among the country gentry known to both Elizabeth and Jane Austen. Of course, Elizabeth is depicted as making no conscious effort to arouse Darcy's matrimonial inclinations, but it is hard to overlook the romantic possibilities that result from her repeated attendance at social gatherings, her prolonged visit to Bingley's house, her several provocative conversations with Darcy, and her accidental visit to his estate. The best way for a young woman to avoid entanglements with an arrogant young man she thinks she despises is to stay away from him, but this Elizabeth seems unable to do. Miss Bingley is vilified because of her jealousy of Elizabeth, but her suspicions seem entirely justified, despite Elizabeth's frequent protestations to the contrary. For who is fooling whom? It is Elizabeth who wins Darcy, not Miss Bingley, and the latter cannot be faulted for her more accurate anticipation of romantic developments— intended by Jane Austen, if not by Elizabeth herself.

Also to be noted is the novel's selective loading of villainy onto characters who express or embody the prohibition against marrying beyond one's class.

Miss Bingley and Lady de Bourgh are afforded heavy-handed characterization precisely because of their snobbishness, while the "dark" males, Reverend Collins and Wickham, are viciously personified to discredit the two worst alternatives this taboo might suggest among eighteenth-century English gentry. In Collins Austen invokes the unpleasant prospect of conventional union with a pompous fool from similar middle-class circumstances; in Wickham she invokes the threat of disgrace and the loss of social position through seduction (i.e., falling in love). Both these possibilities are vilified by the characterization of those whose respective destinies they represent, clearing the path for Elizabeth's remarkable success, undisturbed by second thoughts about her accidental good fortune. Total victory—she wins the social position she deserves, and without sacrificing her middle-class righteousness, a feat of enormous vicarious appeal to readers at the turn of the nineteenth century.

A slightly different kind of lie may be found in *David Copperfield*, where Dickens's unforgettable portrayal of human behavior overshadows the contrary insight that real people usually exceed in complexity the simplistic caricatures of Dickens's novels. Real-life flesh-and-blood parents, for example, are usually complex enough to oblige by combining the generous love bestowed by Peggotty and her family with the fallibility of Micawber, the eccentric rectitude of Betsy Trotwood, and the hatefully punitive authority of the Murdstones. Readers need to merge and integrate these guardian identities to gain a composite portrait approaching the full complexity of the parental role. Or take David himself, by the end of the novel a successful and well-adjusted self-made man. Surprisingly, he survives his childhood ordeal as a balanced individual who is surrounded by a variety of freaks and obsessive-compulsive eccentrics. Common sense would suggest an entirely different outcome, that David's worldly success might be accompanied by comparable emotional instability as the by-product of his compensatory ambition. In all likelihood, he himself would be maladjusted, and others around him would be trying to cope with the idiosyncrasies he developed from his desperate struggle to escape his origins. It would be David, not Uriah Heep, who cultivates the art of obsequious flattery for maneuvering himself into job advancements. Likewise, it would be David, not Steerforth, who transgresses social propriety, for example, by discarding Dora, his frail and childish first wife, in order to gain a more advantageous marriage with Agnes. Instead, both Uriah Heep and Steerforth are steeped in evil, while David, pure of heart, rises in society by a magic principle of levitation that is never fully explained. Through authorial complicity, Dora is permitted to die (in effect, murdered by her unsympathetic novelist), but David remains faithful until the end, after which he is free to turn his attention to Agnes, who provides a far more desirable match.

Contrary to real life, David eats his cake and has it too. He wins everything he might ever have wanted against almost insurmountable odds, and there is no scar tissue, no debt to be paid, no psychic damage of any consequence resulting from his overcompensatory victory over his situation. This portrait is misleading, especially as implied autobiography, since Dickens himself was reputed to be intensely ambitious and to have aggressively sought out the advancements David could take for granted. Like David, Dickens rose to success from an impoverished family background, but the strenuous effort to improve his circumstances seems to have produced an irritability significantly different from David's sweetness of temper. Moreover, Dickens, like David, was dissatisfied with his first wife, Catherine Hogarth, but she was a real woman who could not be consigned to an early death by authorial license. Instead, eight years after the publication of *David Copperfield,* Dickens obtained a formal separation from her to devote his attentions to Ellen Ternan, an attractive eighteen-year-old actress who joined him in his public readings. In other words, he finally eliminated his wife, just as he had eliminated David's, but, like Steerforth, he could only achieve this end by transgressing social propriety—in his case by resorting to abandonment. The exaggerated distinction between virtue and evil in David's story consequently distorts reality as a self-exculpatory success story in which blame is both heightened and diverted to an appropriate scapegoat. David Copperfield wins the day in fiction, but Steerforth's rejected alternative finally prevails in real life. The ethical struggle takes on the proportions of a morality play, and internal ambivalence is reorganized so that the hero is clearly differentiated from a problem character who is equally expressive of one or more of Dickens's personality traits. By the Freudian principle of splitting, Steerforth absorbs and focuses the waywardness found socially unacceptable, while David, the lucky widower, benefits from this waywardness without paying any price for it.

My last example, Joseph Conrad's *Heart of Darkness,* offers the typical protestations of late-nineteenth-century jingoists that, whether vicious or not, colonialism had become an unavoidable economic necessity. Enormous profits at least temporarily accrued to Europe from its colonial practices in Africa, and these profits supported its economic stability, only incidentally aggravating the precarious balance of power between England and Germany. Moreover, as Marlow insists, the progress of civilization since the beginning of time has depended upon such wholesale exploitation, even during the Roman occupation of Great Britain centuries earlier. Consequently, it might have seemed better to come to terms with this historic necessity, accepting the hypocrisy it entails, than to commit oneself to the foolishness of trying to bring about radical change. However, this defense of imperialism implicit in Conrad's novels has been overtaken by historic developments in the years that have elapsed since the 1902 publication of *Heart of Darkness*. Many changes have occurred in third-world nations such as the Belgian Congo, now Zaire, site of the novel, and overt European domination has been reduced if not altogether eliminated. In part this reduction has resulted from humanitarianism, in part from the flexibility of governments and multinational corporations, the latter now able to maximize profits without incurring unnecessary administrative costs. It turns out both that African natural resources may be utilized without resorting to colonial administration and that these resources are far less important to civilization than once thought. Of course, African nations are still beset with serious problems, but their leadership is presently indigenous, and the genocidal exploitation typical of the closing two decades of the nineteenth century has been terminated.[9] Modest progress began with the reaction of European public opinion against the excesses of King Leopold's administration after the publication of Conrad's novel. This was not because of Conrad's influence but because of the efforts of such figures as H. R. Fox-Bourne, John Holt, Herbert Samuel, E. D. Morel, and Roger Casement. Once friendly with Conrad, Casement unsuccessfully tried to enlist him to their cause. Less willing than Conrad to accept the grotesque discrepancy between Europe's delusions of the "white man's burden" and its brutal mercenary tactics in Africa, Casement and his associates attacked public misconceptions with enough effectiveness to force King Leopold and the British government to liberalize their colonial administrations. The European economy survived, as did its standard of living, without totally subjecting the African people to indentured servitude. Liberalization occurred, and this has been better for Western civilization, contrary to the final message of *Heart of Darkness*.

Why is there a basic contradiction in these four works between asserted truths and those that are concealed? Why does each tell a story both true and

Austen, Dickens, Conrad, and Stein

false? One may resort to psychohistory for an explanation, but authorial biography is not necessary to shed light on the use of misinformation to organize fiction. Authors' personal circumstances remain secondary to their strategies, leaving room enough for whatever deletions and renamings readers want to make in meeting their own needs. Authors pursue alternatives, but so do readers, and often with just as much license. Authors deny, but so do readers, and usually by bringing to literary forms their own denial strategies akin to those intended by authors but seldom the same. Self-deception becomes a subjective choice, letting readers allay their anxieties by means of denial, the simplest and most independent coping mechanism available. No matter what authors themselves try to reject, those readers able to benefit from their authorial license possess the flexibility to fit it to their own circumstances. If Jane Austen, for example, tells a story of successful courtship to create a happy alternative to her own courtship disappointments, married women may find satisfaction because of nostalgia, romantic illusion, or fantasies of unviolated sexual power. Men, too, may experience rapport in the vicarious pleasure of being "trapped" by a sensitive and talented young woman. The same vicarious satisfaction may be experienced with *David Copperfield* and even with *Heart of Darkness*. If Joseph Conrad tells a tale of abandoning liberal values for the real truth about human fallibility, the reader may empathize for the purpose of escapism, mystery questing, existential dissatisfaction, or liberal indignation potentially in conflict with Conrad's intentions in writing his novel. Each, or any combination, of these motives may be involved, and our flexibility as readers in merging and focusing our sympathies increases the possibility of satisfaction. We disguise our own sense of need by projecting our attention upon imagined accomplishment, which indirectly disposes of problems we cannot otherwise confront. $X = \text{not } Y$ (the author's aversion) but also *not A*, *not B*, *not C*, etc. This gives universality to such authors as Austen, Dickens, and Conrad, and it helps to explain the unique appeal of Stein's laconic dedication to tautology.

As I have already indicated, fiction does more than declare one set of truths in order to deny another. It also shapes and organizes the linear transition between the two, an advancement from insufficiency and confessed anxiety to the affirmation presented as its opposite. Hence the progress of any story from challenge to victory, from uncertainty to apparent clarification, from a tacit acknowledgment of awkward and unpleasant compromise to the gratifying fulfillment of aspirations involving love, marriage, financial gain, self-discovery, aesthetic transcendence, the defeat of enemies, and so on. High truth may also be affirmed in this manner, for example, when Conrad's novel culminates with a vision of tragic irony that turns out to be irrelevant to future trends in Africa. The experience of closure or finality that we gain at a story's conclusion is evidence that narrative transition has been effective, that denial has been satisfactorily attained. If we come away from reading fiction with a sense of fulfillment (i.e., of feeling good), we know that the act of misrepresentation has been communicated, that literary truths have glossed over more unpleasant truths best left unexamined. And we judge a plot to be compelling the more resoundingly it carries out this Aristotelian sequence from beginning to end, from problems to their pseudosolution. Plot's linear forcefulness gratifies because it drives from thought distasteful alternatives, telling a success story even if its success might paradoxically involve ambivalence, absurdist despair, or martyrdom to a transcendent cause typical of tragedy. There is movement from partial acknowledgment of the reality principle (the intrusion of unacceptable experience) to its rejection by literary accomplishment supportive of the pleasure principle (the desirable outcome anticipated by readers). At the beginning obstructive elements are likely to dominate, but by the story's conclusion these have been convincingly eliminated.

In Jane Austen's novel, the plot begins cluttered with irritating domestic circumstances and a variety of social lapses that impede the innocent pursuit of eligible bachelors. Three hundred pages later the resolution is pure fantasy: The glass slipper fits Cinderella, our plain but resourceful young heroine wins the bachelor catch of the nation. Entirely in the spirit of free enterprise, if reduced to courtship maneuvers, Elizabeth's match with Darcy confirms the laissez-faire values of the world she lives in, stable and impervious to disruption except for Elizabeth's upward mobility, which results from her natural superiority. A similar optimistic transition occurs in *David Copperfield*, in which David's nightmarish entrapment by family, education, marriage, and job situation is successfully overcome by a happy turn of circumstances owing to death, coincidental reunion, and the opportune disclosure of villainy. In like fashion, Conrad's novel begins with Marlow's astonishment at Europe's willful ignorance of its murderous policies in the Congo but then concludes with his acceptance of the inscrutable wisdom that this problem is inevitable, in fact the paradox at the root of all civilization. In each of these novels, a problematic beginning is brought to its appropriate resolution, and the transition from one to the other is produced or mediated by the plot. Change has been produced that affirms one truth at the expense of another.

Even Gertrude Stein's fragment offers this kind of linear transition since it begins with the simple equation, "a rose is a rose," thereby suggesting the importance of the rose in and of itself compared to its various extraneous associations. However, this equation is twice repeated, flattened to a minimalist tautology that deprives the rose of its referential impact. The sequence involves a buried incremental repetition:

a rose is a rose $\longrightarrow$ a rose is a rose is a rose, etc.

By doubling and then tripling the law of identity, Gertrude Stein suggests both the necessity of reexamining the truth she first seems to acknowledge and her confidence that to do so obliges an entirely different conclusion:

this is this (maybe symbolic) is exclusively this (*not* symbolic)

Paradoxically, she uses potentially endless repetition to produce the closure that desymbolizes the rose. Her line's initial declaration ("a rose *is* a rose") suggests that a rose might be more than a rose, but its repetition imposes a perpetual tautology to insist that a rose is *only* a rose. In trying to explain her inspiration for the poem, Stein claimed that she repeated the word rose to achieve a "continuous present" comparable to the art of Cézanne and Picasso in their liberation from Aristotelian constraints, but of course this effect could be only illusory. Repeating words necessarily produces succession, thus transition, and this transition is resolved when brought to its end. First explained by Gotthold Lessing, this temporal limitation applies to any end-stopped sequence of words, necessarily creating a before and after as well as linear advancement from one to the other. Accordingly, the transition from identity to repeated identity constitutes the advancement from "this now" to "this forever." Closure is produced at a new level of meaning ("this forever"), so the trace of a plot emerges, letting Stein deny those feelings that really concern her. As with other, more obvious works of fiction, her brief poem thereby diminishes the truth, as Plato insisted poetry inevitably does, but by means of linear organization as emphasized by Aristotle. This negative principle is just as true of the briefest poem as of the novels of Austen, Dickens, and Conrad. It typifies all fiction, both high and low, that possesses any sustained audience appeal.

Last but not least, an undercurrent of denied feelings persists throughout serious works of fiction. As a subversive influence, it acknowledges alternatives authors would not be able to explain. The less these alternatives are recognized, the more effectively they undermine the story's overt interpretation. Helter-skelter, deletions undelete themselves, renamings unname themselves, and the linear momentum of narrative form almost comes unhinged. Plot's momentum toward satisfactory closure is persistently challenged by tone, metaphor, nuance of characterization, and unnecessary narrative detours. Works of fiction in which this resistance almost but not quite predominates include some of the most revered classics of our Western literary tradition, from the *Epic of Gilgamesh* to the novels of Dostoevsky, D. H. Lawrence, and William Faulkner. Their adequate interpretation is possible only if this ongoing struggle is fully taken into account.

Countervailing subversiveness may be detected, for example, in Jane Austen's obsessive and perhaps unconscious dependence upon commercial vocabulary—such words as *fortune, property, possessions, terms, means*, etc.—when she is presumably concerning herself with the romantic impasse between Elizabeth and Darcy.[10] Elizabeth may think that she is strictly responding to Darcy's moral and intellectual worth as a gentleman, but pecuniary intrusions in both dialogue and narrative style confess a more calculating objective that might justify the apprehensions of a wealthy suitor. Also subversive is the heightened vilification of Mr. Wickham and Reverend Collins that prejudices the reader against both the capitulation to physical love and the necessity of marrying into a moderate income. Wickham's seduction of Lydia is entirely incongruous, since an unscrupulous social climber would not bother with a young woman as resourceless as Lydia. Only later, after they have run away together, does he learn that he might profit from his adventure with her. The sin implied is therefore not fortune hunting but its opposite, the abandonment of fortune in favor of physical love. Collins, in turn, is led to write a foolishly pompous letter advising Elizabeth not to marry Darcy, though a prudent individual in his position would hedge his bet, restrained by family ties as well as by loyalty to his patroness. Moreover, it seems obvious that Collins would benefit more by persuading Lady Catherine de Bourgh to accept Elizabeth's marriage with Darcy, since it would establish an indirect family connection reinforced by Elizabeth's close friendship with his wife, Charlotte. His worst possible course of action would be to antagonize Elizabeth by opposing her marriage with Darcy and then to fail in his efforts—exactly the choice Austen imposes upon him. That Collins is depicted as being rash enough to make this mistake (and without agonizing over it) unnecessarily stunts his characterization, then penalizes him for being depicted in this fashion. As I earlier indicated, the vilification of both Wickham and Collins apparently discloses the two transgressions the most offensive to Austen—sexual passion and a modest income. Elizabeth escapes both of these by means of her marriage to Darcy. As a matrimonial catch, Darcy provides the *deus ex machina* that releases Elizabeth from social, economic, and biological coercion, and, happy coincidence, the high virtues that attract his advances can now be cultivated in her enviable role as mistress of a wealthy household.

Half-confessed subversiveness likewise provides a counterpoint to David Copperfield's story of emotional growth by restricting the personality traits found totally unacceptable to bona fide villains. Steerforth's romantic destructiveness, for example, expresses a potentially harmful freedom from ethical constraints, while Uriah Heep's grasping duplicity expresses a dependence on manipulative shortcuts useful to those who want to rise in the business world. The almost exuberant vilification of these two figures imposes a Scylla and Charybdis through which David Copperfield must pilot his career toward ultimate success. Each epitomizes a complementary flaw to be avoided in David's struggle to improve his circumstances in life—reckless extravagance and prudence verging on greed. Paradoxically, however, Dickens's use of vilification (at times far heavier than Austen's) suggests a lack of emotional integration—in narrative point of view, if not in David's personality. The emphatic projection of blame upon others is somewhat at odds with the story of David's emotional growth. A better distribution of strengths and weaknesses would be shared by the characters if the novel's overall point of view were proportionate to David's presumed attainment of maturity. Superior balance in the interpretation of personality may be observed, for example, in *The Way of All Flesh* by Samuel Butler and in *Sons and Lovers* by D. H. Lawrence, each of which is comparable as a *Bildungsroman* recounting the youth of its author. With similar objectivity, positive virtues could be more graciously acknowledged in David's enemies, and, vice versa, David himself could be shown to possess a few of the negative qualities so generously bestowed upon these others. There would be no clearly defined heroes or villains *per se* in a mature world inhabited by a mature David Copperfield. The unctuous irony of Uriah Heep's final declaration that others besides himself might likewise benefit from serving prison terms could be recognized to contain more than a grain of truth, and the virtues of love and undying loyalty attributed to David and his friends and benefactors could be acknowledged as at least an incipient tendency in the personalities of Uriah Heep and the Murdstones. Manichaean vividness would give way to the equitable judgment of a healthy and generous author, his style and characterization serving to confirm the outcome of his story.

More complex is the subversiveness that undermines Conrad's defense of European colonial excesses in *Heart of Darkness*. His theme of universal corruption is challenged by his use of women to symbolize the blind liberalism of Europeans. In general, women bear the brunt of Conrad's cynicism, as illustrated by his depiction of Kurtz's fiancée and of Marlow's aunt, who praises imperialists for "weaning these ignorant millions of their horrid ways." Appropriately, Kurtz's allegorical painting is of Justice as a blindfolded woman swaddled in darkness, and the two old women knitting black wool in the outer office where Marlow is first hired are apparently envisaged as Fates (or *moirai*) who weave the destiny of all men entering the portals of Africa. By limiting women to the role of ignorant liberals who support imperialism, Conrad implies that to be liberal is to be female, or effeminate, the ignorant beneficiary of extreme delusions. In turn, masculinity is shown to be stupidly methodical in its pursuit of imperialistic gains, for example, as illustrated by the behavior of the station chief and subordinate administrators Marlow first encounters in Africa. Only the few men who possess superior minds, for example, Kurtz and Marlow himself, are shown able to understand and implement the savage contradictions that have presumably supported civilization since the beginning of time. Reluctantly, these geniuses sacrifice themselves—even their integrity, if necessary—in order to protect the interests of the idealists and to give them a standard of living they deserve. These superior men presumably do the dirty work that provides women the leisure to find good reasons to justify their effort, producing a symbiosis essential to civilization based on the unbridgeable discrepancy between the sexes. True honesty is possible, but only among these superior men who are frustrated by their obligation to serve womanhood but who share a profound empathy in their silent recognition of this obligation.

However, problems of sexual identity somewhat diffuse the sexist logic implied by Conrad. The shared secret that Marlow establishes with Kurtz takes precedence over heterosexual rapport, and with enough insistence to suggest latent homosexual affinity, a role confusion that calls to mind exactly the feminine qualities to be denied, including the eager dedication to liberal causes.[11] As a result, Conrad cannot entirely escape the sentimental generosity he attributes to women, as demonstrated by his novel's disproportionate outrage against colonial practices at the expense of its intended final message, the defense of these practices as the cost of civilization. There is enough emphasis on Conrad's initial repugnance against colonial brutality that most readers overlook his entirely different concluding judgment, the cynical acceptance of colonialism as the price that must be paid to guarantee Europe's high standard of living. By linking political vision with sexual roles, Conrad transfers his ambivalence from one domain to the other, undermining his final acceptance of imperialistic necessity and thereby suggesting a modest loss of control in his narrative. If mild homophilia subverts Conrad's vision of complementary roles, it is no accident, given his logic, that his sense of revulsion about Congo atrocities is powerful enough to obscure his novel's final vision of unmitigated skepticism.

Among the meaningful encounters scattered throughout *Heart of Darkness*, two in particular confirm this sexual disorientation: Kurtz and Marlow's marriage of minds in a Congo steamer's cabin just before Kurtz dies, and, balanced against this, Marlow's uncomfortable visit to the apartment of Kurtz's fiancée at the novel's conclusion. Both meetings are shrouded in darkness, just as Marlow himself is shrouded in darkness aboard the *Nellie* when he tells his tale. As the novel ends, there is a convergence among these three episodes in the representation of darkness, but there are also important differences in their respective uses of darkness for symbolic purposes. The darkness of the riverboat cabin at Kurtz and Marlow's last meeting symbolizes their shared moral obligation to serve civilization by uncivilized means, thereby sealing their conspiracy to delude women. This inner truth produces the novel's key insight, "the horror," Kurtz's ambiguous remark, which is later understood by Marlow to capture the paradox at the root of civilization. In the second meeting, with Kurtz's fiancée, darkness symbolizes the collective ignorance that imposes this horror. Marlow's visit thus becomes the final and most harrowing ordeal in his quest for ultimate truth. Having barely survived the jungle, he finds himself in a lair of archetypal temptation (a modern Den of Error) that at last exposes his reluctant debt to feminine ignorance. And he bows to this heterosexual necessity because of the most compelling of truths, that the truth cannot be told. Like Kurtz, he finally recognizes the necessity of perpetuating gender differentiation to guarantee high civilization, but he does so without sacrificing either his disgust with Congo atrocities or his fascination with the transgression he shares with Kurtz. *Heart of Darkness* is thematically complex enough to have enabled Conrad to explore these contradictions important to himself, but in doing so he necessarily cast doubt upon his novel's intended message of stoic acquiescence to imperialistic brutality.

Interestingly, *Heart of Darkness* documents its own composition, and even here its distortions suggest the denial displacement at work. The rapport between Marlow and Kurtz exhibits a curious parallel to the relationship between Conrad and Ford Madox Ford when they collaborated in writing the novel in the winter of 1898–99. They sequestered themselves in the library at Pent Farm to work up an acceptable final draft while their wives and children kept to other parts of the household, obviously with a sense that they had a stake in the project but without otherwise participating in it.[12] The close working relationship between Conrad and Ford in a project they hoped and expected might help to support their families seems to have resembled the sense of shared genius between Kurtz and Marlow, while the exile of Conrad's and Ford's families to other parts of Pent Farm resembled the role of women in the novel as ignorant beneficiaries eager to applaud dirty work they could not even begin to understand. A decade later, Conrad used comparable symbolism in his short story "The Secret Sharer" to dramatize the uncomfortable temporary breakdown in his working relationship with Ford. Once again Conrad's plot tells of two men who experience intense rapport, one of them a fugitive murderer, the other a neophyte captain who must prove himself with his crew, symbolizing society at large. As in *Heart of Darkness*, Conrad plays the mariner and gives Ford the role of reluctant killer. By making a dangerous nautical maneuver, the captain proves his worth as a seaman (i.e., novelist) and simultaneously lets his double escape into the world again, presumably to make his own nautical maneuvers (i.e., to write his own novels).

Even so brief a poem as "a rose is a rose is a rose is a rose" bears subversive implications that cast doubt upon its deceptively simplistic pretensions, and with far more threatening implications for homophobic readers than are present in Conrad's novel. In a casual reading the poem seems entirely innocent, but its obsessive repetition of "a rose is a rose" suggests a variety of puns with lesbian connotations that become evident in later versions published by Stein.

Austen, Dickens, Conrad, and Stein

For example, in "Sacred Emily," published in 1913, the line begins with *rose* capitalized as a name and with the first indefinite article omitted: "Rose is a rose is a rose is a rose." Here a woman, Rose, is obviously identified with the flower whose identity is its most definable feature. In "Objects on a Table," published in 1922, Stein then added a second female persona when she revised the line as a provocative question: "Do we suppose that all she knows is a rose is a rose is a rose is a rose." Here the reader is expected to ask why such a tautology is important enough to dominate a woman's imagination. In at least three instances—Gertrude Stein's stationery, the design upon her dishes, and the cover of her autobiography, *The Autobiography of Alice B. Toklas*—she organized the line as a linked circle to suggest not only the shape of the rose but also the permanence of spatial form and the closed circle of feminine identity:

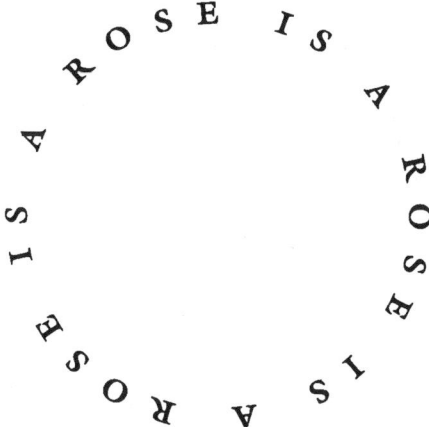

More threatening connotations dominate the line's almost unrecognizable variation in *Tender Buttons*, published in 1914:

> a charm a single charm is doubtful. If the red is a rose and there is a gate surrounding it, if inside is let in and there places change then certainly something is upright. It is earnest.

The passage is deliberately cryptic but features symbolism that bears almost oneiric sexual implications. Unswerving commitment to heterosexual love would necessarily be limited to a "single charm," but alternatives can be sought "if inside is let in" through what is presumably a gate (i.e., an opening that might be closed to those who want to enter) as represented by the rose's vulviform configuration of petals. But once this gate is entered, "places change" (i.e., roles are reversed), since "upright" denotes both an erection and earnestness (i.e., superior love). "Earnest" might also be a pun for "her nest," further reinforcing the suggestion of penetration by a woman rather than a man.

In her children's novel *The World Is Round*, published in 1938, Stein once again uses the motto "a rose is a rose" in a linked circle. She also tells the story of a young heroine, Rose, who seeks her destiny in a dreamlike landscape with obvious symbolism. On the first day of Rose's journey, she enters a cave behind a waterfall (obviously feminine) to find glowing on its walls the words "Devil Devil Devil." The triple graffiti reinforces the heterosexual threat implied by the identity of Satan, whose name at least is inscribed under the waterfall. However, the devil is denied the next day when Rose carves "Rose is a Rose is a Rose is a Rose" on a tree trunk. The explanation for her choice soon follows when Rose discovers an entirely new and comically disgusting variation carved on a tree nearby, "Rose and under Rose was Willie and under Willie was Billie." Willie is her harmless male companion and Billie is a lion. Their pileup reduces to clownishness the bestiality of heterosexual love (man, woman, and animal), but it is described with the preterite *was*, not *is*. Significantly, Rose is located at the top of the heap and Billie at the bottom, with Willie defenselessly trapped in the middle. As to be expected, Rose decides that she prefers whatever is signified by her name's repetition to the heterosexual pileup she would share with Willie and Billie.

If incessantly repeated as if an incantation, the simplest version of the poem—"a rose is a rose is a rose"—also discloses the pun "arose is," suggesting the aftermath of arousal, the memory of desire just consummated. Uttered four (or more) in a row with descending cadence, its tense-oxymoronic sequence belabors the triumph of postponed gratification:

    arose IS
        arose IS
            arose IS
                arose

The final verb indicates completion as a coda that exclusively depends on the verb in its past tense. This sequence can also be reversed to make Rose a woman who has been aroused:

a ROSE is arose is arose is arose

In this variant the use of *arose* to signify *aroused* mixes tenses in its combination with *is*, perhaps suggesting black dialect to recall Rose Johnson's lesbian appeal in *Three Lives*.

The rose-arose pun likewise introduces a grammatical distinction that seems to have been important to Gertrude Stein's creative intentions when writing the poem. In "Lectures in America," she proposed that nouns are the proper medium of poetry. As she explained, the singular appeal of her poem consequently resulted from its obsessive repetition of one particular noun: "I made poetry and what did I do I caressed completely caressed and addressed a noun."[13] However, the redivision of a noun and its article into two verbs, *arose* and *is*, challenges this nominal and supposedly poetic expression. From the harmless rose emerges an alternative possibility of arousal that reduces aestheticism to sexual provocation. The jarring of tenses between arose and is likewise undermines the line's monosyllabic repetition that supposedly purifies a flower of its additional connotations. The standoff between these two interpretations of the line's meaning accordingly sets in conflict these two dimensions, active (*arose*) and substantive (a *rose*), each only partially effective in offsetting the other. At its simplest interpretation, the line is strictly affirmative in its triple insistence upon the flower's identity to the exclusion of everything else. At other levels, very probably overlooked by the reader, its meaning forces a standoff between androgynous desire and the radical aestheticism that both expresses and disguises it. For the homoaversive middle-class reader, Stein insists a rose is a rose and only a rose, but for Stein and her acolytes a rose can also be *arouse*, the ecstasy of forbidden pleasure.

The issue of sexual compatibility is important to Austen and Dickens, but they deal with it on a conventional heterosexual basis, each by rewarding true virtue with marriage. Austen uses romantic love as the needed machinery to guarantee happiness and financial security for Elizabeth, while Dickens reverses this process by affording David enough success in life to be able to switch partners, finally joining the woman he truly loves. Whether Elizabeth knows it or not, aristocratic status is her goal, while David's is the pursuit of ideal companionship. Their objectives are linked with "normal" heterosexual ends despite their differences—social climbing versus the lonely restlessness of a self-made man. Both accept the literary conventions that mix marriage and social advancement, but with opposite priorities.

The problem of sexual adjustment is more effectively obscured in the works of Conrad and Stein. However, it remains just as essential to their appeal, if not more so. If conventional goals cannot be won after overcoming a variety of obstacles, at least unconventional alternatives can be implied, and this in itself is an accomplishment of no little importance. In one instance this subversiveness might involve the symbolism of a flower unsullied by alien energies, in the other an antiepithalamium of a man and woman unable to communicate, rapidly sinking into darkness isolated from each other. Conrad pays his due to heterosexual demands, but Stein more daringly befuddles bourgeois judgment—her intentions perhaps fully as defiant as might be suggested by her portrayal in Picasso's celebrated painting. Both Conrad and Stein employ symbolic displacements, one featuring an inward journey into the heart of Africa and the other the aesthetic imminence of a common flower. In each instance, socially unacceptable implications are smuggled into the story without being recognized. For both, the homophobic taboo necessitates heavy disguise, further strengthening the dialectic between declared intentions and an implicit rejection of conventional standards.

All four writers seem to have been troubled by role limitations too unpleasant to be directly acknowledged. By means of fiction, Jane Austen expressed her aversion to middle-class spinsterhood, Charles Dickens his aversion to both failure and entrapment in an inferior marriage, Joseph Conrad his anxious conservatism rooted in severe identity crisis, and Gertrude Stein her rejection of orthodox heterosexual standards. All of these authors declare socially acceptable truths in their works, but these truths take on additional significance as the denial of countervailing truths that were just as relevant to their lives. This is integral to the success of their fiction, giving it the energy needed to let readers adapt its avoidances for their own particular needs. Conflicting motives are organized into fierce dialectic tension that can only be resolved by imposing pseudosolutions with obvious conventional appeal. In the novels of Austen and Dickens closure comes with the age-tested Menandrine comic formula of marriage; in Conrad's novel it comes with Marlow's final acceptance of the fallibility of the human condition; and in Stein's poem it comes with sheer aestheticism asserted at the expense of anything it might imply. In each instance a surface vision of the truth is presented in the best possible light, but its selective reversal brings antithetical implications that continue to challenge its sufficiency. Literary form provides the medium for this confrontation, which is resolved by a conventional sense of an ending.

three

A HOMEOSTATIC MODEL

"God offers to every mind," Emerson warned, "its choice between truth and repose. Take which you believe—you can never have both."[1] Among the exceptions Emerson overlooked was the gratification of both scientific and nonscientific discovery (Archimedes's "eureka"), but he seems to have been correct that any exaggeration of either truth or repose is probably at the expense of the other. A useful corollary may be proposed that the two often function as reciprocals, since a bigger commitment to one tends to produce commensurate losses in the other, except, perhaps, when our major lies have been so completely ingrained that new and relatively minor lies produce disproportionate gratification, as, for example, with the experience of fiction. For it is pleasure, the experience of having obtained repose, that reigns supreme in fiction. As Kenneth Burke maintains, "The reading of a book on the attaining of success is in itself the symbolic attaining of that success."[2] There is satisfaction not from acquiring knowledge about literary incidents and personages, but from the effect of this knowledge in letting us overlook what we already know about ourselves. Our literary experience might be additive in the wealth of human experience it depicts, but far more important is what it subtracts by imposing believable alternatives. In effect, we walk out on ourselves. This is why we read fiction—because our departure makes us feel better, as if relieved of a burden that we cannot quite understand.

The explanation of pleasure as the product of loss rather than gain is hardly new. It was first identified by Hippocrates as catharsis, a medical term for the elimination of surplus humors. Plato found catharsis in music as an agitation that calms the soul, and Aristotle extended its application to tragedy as vicarious relief produced by pity and fear—pity for the tragic protagonists matched by the playgoers' fear for themselves.[3] Though Aristotle's functional definition of catharsis was sketchy (the thorough analysis that he promised in *Politics* was either lost or never written), it established the basis for later efforts to define the unique sense of fulfillment provided by tragedy. Others have since spoken of tension reduction as a universal principle, for example, Ali ibn Hazm of the eleventh century, who is quoted as having argued, "No one is moved to act, or resolves to speak a single word, who does not hope by means of this action or word to release anxiety from his spirit."[4] In the nineteenth century, Gustav Fechner explained the principle on a more scientific basis:

> In so far as conscious impulses always have some relation to pleasure or unpleasure, pleasure and unpleasure too can be regarded as having a psycho-physical relation to conditions of stability and instability. . . . According to this hypothesis, every psycho-physical motion rising above the threshold of consciousness is attended by pleasure in proportion as, beyond a certain limit, it approximates to complete stability, and is attended by unpleasure in proportion as, beyond a certain limit, it deviates from complete stability.[5]

In other words, any increase in tension beyond a steady-state equilibrium produces pain or discomfort, which leads to the effort to restore equilibrium. If successful, this effort is rewarded by the experience of pleasure.

Sigmund Freud based his neurological investigations early in his career on Fechner's concept of tension reduction, and he drew upon this concept along with the research of Hermann Helmholtz and Ernst Brücke in proposing his economic (or "hydraulic") explanation of personality. Fascinated by the so-called neuronic inertia of stimulated nerve cells during their recovery phase, Freud tried to apply this concept on a holistic basis to the entire personality, explaining all behavior, both conscious and unconscious, as the effort to evoke pleasure associated with such a recovery phase. According to Freud, deficiency is experienced as desire, and the satisfaction of desire signals the elimination of deficiency. The reality principle takes into account an environment accessible to cathexis (i.e., the satisfaction of desire through attachment to an object or its representation), while the pleasure principle embraces the dynamics of cathexis, dynamics that produce a recovery phase experienced as pleasure. In other words, reality is used or reorganized by the individual in order to produce pleasure, and, not accidentally, pleasure expresses the elimination of physical and/or emotional deprivation. What we perceive is used to grant us what we want.

This model of human consciousness was central to Freud's metapsychology. He proposed it in *The Interpretation of Dreams*, published in 1900, and in "Instincts and Their Vicissitudes," published in 1915, and he summarized his arguments in his *General Introduction to Psychoanalysis*, published in 1917:

> It seems as though our total mental activity is directed towards achieving pleasure and avoiding unpleasure—that it is automatically regulated by the *pleasure principle*. . . . Pleasure is *in some way* connected with the diminution, reduction or extinction of the amounts of stimulus prevailing in the mental apparatus, and . . . similarly unpleasure is connected with their increase. An examination of the most intense pleasure which is accessible to human beings, the pleasure of accomplishing the sexual act, leaves little doubt on this point.[6]

In "Beyond the Pleasure Principle," published in 1920, Freud went so far as to treat tension reduction as an organic consequence of the inorganic principle of inertia:

> The pleasure principle, then, is a tendency operating in the service of a function whose business it is to free the mental apparatus entirely from excitation or to keep the amount of excitation in it constant or to keep it as low as possible. . . . It is clear that the function thus described would be concerned with the most universal endeavor of all living substances— namely to return to the quiescence of the inorganic world.[7]

Throughout his career Freud persistently adhered to this economic explanation of the pleasure principle, and his more generally accepted dynamic model seems to derive from it in most particulars. Virtually every term in Freud's psychoanalytic lexicon may be explained in economic terms. *Neurosis*, for example, derives from an accumulation of unrecognized tensions; *displacement* produces tension reduction by shifting *cathexis* from one mode of discharge to another; the *superego* aggravates tension by introjecting parental standards; and the *unconscious* stores drives and memories whose conscious recognition would increase tension to unacceptable levels. The pleasure principle cannot be deprived of its centrality in Freudian metapsychology, as ego psychologists have tried, without depriving the Freudian approach of its most basic assumptions.

The body's effectiveness in maintaining a steady-state equilibrium has also been fruitfully investigated in the field of biology, first and most notably in the mid-nineteenth century, when Claude Bernard proposed his theory of the body as a *milieu intérieur*.[8] According to Bernard, our skin, the largest of our organs, is dry on the outside and wet on the inside in order to guarantee the maintenance of a precise steady-state balance in temperature, salinity, and so on. Good health depends on the successful perpetuation of this steady-state balance, while sickness expresses a breakdown, or disequilibrium, that obliges restitutive behavior. In 1932 this concept of sustained equilibrium was definitively applied to human physiology by Walter Cannon, who gave it the name *homeostasis* and traced its complex reflex circuitry for maintaining equilibrium.[9] According to Cannon, deficiencies automatically produce negative-feedback signals that initiate the necessary changes to restore an appropriate balance. Cannon's theory of homeostasis was soon extended to behavioral psychology and applied to the personality as a whole. As early as 1934, Ives Hendricks recognized its close similarity to Freud's explanation of the pleasure principle, and by 1945 Otto Fenichel could describe homeostasis as the basis for all instinctual behavior explained by Freudian theory; by the early fifties, the concept of homeostasis was expanded by G. L. Freeman and Ross Stagner to apply as a comprehensive explanation of the entire personality comparable to Freud's pleasure principle.[10]

In *The Vital Balance*, published in 1963, Karl Menninger, Martin Mayman, and Paul Pruyser systematically treated neurosis as a product of unacceptable tension levels, and they proposed a new approach to psychotherapy that emphasized the effective reduction of these levels based on the principle of homeostasis.[11] As explained by the authors, homeostasis plays a dominant role in all human behavior and drives, including sex, hunger, making friends, acquiring wealth, or pondering philosophy. With the autonomic nervous system, homeostasis operates as a rigid, invariable signal system for producing the necessary changes to sustain an optimal biochemical balance. For example, as explained by Walter Cannon, excessive salinity initiates a variety of automatic restitutive functions in the kidneys and elsewhere in order to bring sodium and potassium levels back into balance without any conscious effort on the part of the individual. However, as also explained by Cannon, conscious behavior may be included in the feedback loop when behavior is needed either to avoid pain or to satisfy perceived appetites. When consciousness is involved, a wish or sense of need triggers the pursuit of objectives that result in tension reduction. In the case of hunger, for example, a glycogen deficiency in the stomach muscles signals the brain that food is needed, whereupon we become conscious of the desire to feed ourselves. As with the kidneys, the need for modification is signaled by negative feedback, and the energy expended to send this signal is small compared to its beneficial effect. The only difference is that conscious behavior is included in the loop. Mental activity joins in the effort to produce the restoration of a steady-state minimum, and its reward for a job well done is the experience of pleasure.

Many biologists and systems theoreticians have argued that the concept of homeostasis cannot be extended to include conscious behavior. However, Freudian metapsychology successfully meets the three basic requirements of homeostasis listed by R. C. Davis, a systems theoretician who was dubious about its psychological applications:

1. We should know what the system is, at least to the extent of identifying its input and output.
2. We should be able to demonstrate that the energy is, or at least can be, carried in a reverse direction as a signal.
3. We should know that this energy has a negative sign with respect to the original process when it reenters the main path of the system.[12]

First, a feedback circuitry of one or more loops should be identified whose input and output are organized to produce tension reduction; second, restitutive dynamics should be identified that are specifically targeted to produce this result; and third, the limited output of energy (called negative feedback) needed to carry out this function should be identified. In the broadest sense, contrary to Davis's thesis, conscious behavior does in fact meet these three requirements. As explained by Freudian nomenclature, input represents instincts (or, more exactly, *Triebe*—organized drives), output represents their payoff experienced as pleasure, and negative feedback describes the specific

A Homeostatic Model

behavior that yields this payoff via *cathexis*. If pleasure is the conscious by-product of negative feedback, the success of feedback mechanisms will be indicated, though not always explained, when our efforts are rewarded by the sense of pleasure. The more intense our gratification, the more effectively these mechanisms have functioned, regardless of whether their exact *modus operandi* can be pinpointed. Consciousness has performed the needed tasks, and when pleasure is felt, something, somewhere, has brought about tension reduction.

Several reservations nevertheless seem in order when discussing homeostasis as a function of consciousness. First, it must be conceded that conscious (and literary) patterns of negative feedback lack the near-perfect predictability of their somatic counterpart, for example, the complex regulatory behavior of the kidneys. When thinking is involved, flexibility takes precedence over reliability, and sometimes to an extraordinary degree. As explained by Robert Waelder's "principle of multiple function," this is often because complex means are used to produce a relatively simple end.[13] The brain's synaptic complexity favors variety over rigid consistency, but its purpose is the same as its somatic counterpart—to expend a relatively modest amount of energy for a more homeostatic restitution. Needs produce tension, consciousness finds the means to gratify these needs, and its success results in tension reduction experienced as pleasure. The unpredictable pattern of mental activity compared to the simple reflex arc probably results from the disproportionate involvement of higher brain centers when thinking occurs. Because of vast neural dispersion within the brain, a complex network of byways becomes available to complete the feedback loop, activating a stimulus-response sequence whose precise definition cannot be ascertained. Yet this dispersion can act just as effectively to transform tension buildup into tension reduction felt as pleasure.[14] For example, laughter, temper tantrums, and righteous indignation can equally relieve anxieties, if without any clear explanation why. Nevertheless, it may be assumed in each instance that consciousness participates in the feedback loop to produce satisfaction through tension reduction.

Another difference between somatic and conscious behavior is that we sometimes pursue activities to increase stimulation instead of diminishing it, thereby setting in motion positive rather than negative feedback dynamics. We want to be challenged and to test our capabilities for the sheer satisfaction of doing so. Additional tension seems our goal instead of tension reduction, so homeostasis necessarily plays a more complicated role. Greater strain is pursued in one sphere of experience because it produces relief in another, for example, when we play a hard game of tennis to diminish stress from the day's frustrations. The body may be exhausted by physical exertion, but, more important, this exertion relieves anxieties and leads to physical relaxation. Likewise, our analytic skills may be taxed by a game of chess, but by accepting the challenge we can temporarily ignore simpler but more threatening problems. In both instances, limited stimulation has produced negative feedback leading to overall tension reduction. Such activities are pleasurable not because they stimulate but because they stimulate to calm. Chess, tennis, and good novels tax our energies in one sphere so we may relax in another. This is why positive feedback can be gratifying despite its apparent stress and excitement. Even if there is no obvious expectation of a later payoff, homeostasis remains the objective.

Finally, mental activity cannot bring about a perfect return to the previous equilibrium, as with simpler modes of homeostasis. Complete restitution of the *status quo ante* takes place for somatic feedback mechanisms, but for consciousness a new and more inclusive harmony is produced based on new modifications in psychological adjustment. As maintained by Ludwig von Bertalanffy, dean of systems theoreticians, consciousness must therefore be explained as an open rather than a closed system, since feedback produces growth and increased complexity rather than a constant balance sometimes confused with the nirvana principle (or death wish).[15] Taking into account this difference, Ross Stagner has proposed a concept of dynamic homeostasis to explain "an active effort of the entire organism" toward an overall reduction in tension levels.[16] Conscious growth is beneficial to the extent that it refines and improves our adaptability, but it retains the same goal of maintaining a steady-state equilibrium that guarantees our physical and emotional survival. Disequilibrium is beneficial only to the extent that it leads to a more inclusive equilibrium, i.e., a better and more sufficient harmony of organization. Any structure or organism dooms itself if its growth is disproportionate. The pyramid letter club, for example, collapses once it exhausts its new membership, and cancer ultimately destroys itself by destroying its host body ("no host, no party," quipped a friend shortly before dying of Hodgkin's disease). Growth is important, but so is adjustment, the effective recovery from dislocations produced by growth. In fact, growth is beneficial only to the extent that it may be accommodated by these adjustments. For this reason, moderate growth both serves and is served by the dynamics of homeo-

A Homeostatic Model

stasis. The open-feedback qualities of romance, discovery, and cultural fulfillment advance the human condition, but only if they lead to happiness and stability, once again as dictated by steady-state maintenance.[17]

Of course, the pleasure principle is irrelevant to the dynamics of homeostasis that occur independent of consciousness, for example, with the functions of the liver, kidneys, pancreas, and so on. However, when consciousness is included in the loop, any experience of pleasure indicates by its felt payoff that homeostasis has occurred here too. When a particular act seems enjoyable, we know that it has served its purpose well enough for consciousness to be rewarded with the experience of pleasure. Our quest for pleasure leads to the fulfillment of needs we might otherwise ignore, since pleasure acts as a signal system, the language our body uses to instruct consciousness where to concentrate its effort. Pleasure is the body's incentive for setting consciousness to its appropriate tasks, and without explaining why these are important. The mind is thereby encouraged to pursue ends it need not understand, and pleasure takes on an importance of its own as payment for having attained them. By means of pleasure, the body compensates mental activity for the role it plays in maintaining a balance of functions ultimately crucial to our survival as individuals and as a species.

But does homeostasis bear any relationship to literary experience? Can a concept borrowed from biology really help to elucidate fiction, or, more specifically, to clarify fiction's role as an agent of deception? Very definitely, I think, since the principle of homeostasis underlies any experience of pleasure, even the most attenuated moment of intellectual satisfaction. Let the reader finish a novel with nothing more than the sense of relief that it is over and done with, and the pleasure principle is operative at least to this extent. As opposed to the cognitive and affective aspects of literary response, the conative response features a quest for satisfaction that, when resolved, produces pleasure. Even more basic than Gerald Else's Aristotelian sequence from *hamartia* to *anagnorisis* is the sequence from need (conation) to satisfaction (catharsis) as articulated by literary form.[18] What complicates homeostasis in literary response is its catalytic function in the written text as a milieu external to the negative feedback dynamics that produce satisfaction.[19] Unlike somatic feedback circuits, the physical existence of the text is located outside the body, yet it, too, guides and sustains the reader's feelings in a linear circuit that leads to biological restitution. By concentrating their attention on the text in its forward momentum, word for word, episode for episode, readers lock their entire conscious-perceptual apparatus into automatic pilot and let their experience of the text do the work for them. They draw upon their own fund of experience to comprehend it, but the text itself organizes the necessary modifications for producing satisfaction. They experience pleasure while this process completes itself and for a brief period thereafter, but this feeling slackens and disappears as soon as relaxation has completed itself, and only when tension has increased and been reduced again by comparable means can pleasure recur as a conscious by-product of need satisfaction. "Shall I read Fowles or Burgess?" the reader asks, trying to ascertain which of these authors is the most suitable antidote for the mood (or sense of need) felt at that particular time. The choice is made, the book read, and the reader comes away from it with a feeling of gain. As a catalyst, the story takes effect without being used up. Its text is consumed, but it also remains to be used many times again—as long as it continues to produce tension reduction.

The dynamics of homeostasis also provide a functional explanation of narrative form as a story of events brought to a resolution that most readers find satisfactory. This can be seen, for example, with Aristotle's theory of catharsis as the audience's sense of relief once a tragic protagonist learns to accept fate.[20] A transition in feelings occurs based on the advancement from tension to relaxation resulting from both discovery (*anagnorisis*) and reversal (*peripeteia*). From a psychoanalytic perspective, Peter Brooks has persuasively argued that all plot, not merely that of tragedy, provides such a transition, since it necessarily originates in tension that seeks quiescence:

> For plot starts (must give the illusion of starting) from that moment at which story, or "life," is stimulated from quiescence into a state of narratability, into a tension, a kind of irritation, which demands narration. Any reflection on novelistic beginnings shows the beginning as an awakening, an arousal, the birth of an appetency, ambition, desire or intention. . . . [Thereafter] the development of a narrative shows that the tension is maintained as an ever more complicated postponement or *détour* leading back to the goal of quiescence.[21]

Every work of fiction organized by plot somehow features this linear movement from tension to relief, from dissatisfaction to its elimination felt as pleasure. Such an outcome terminates stories of romance, martyrdom, triumph, moral insight, existential despair, and righteous vindication. There is one invariable function—the experience of change that produces gratification. When a book fails to produce both change and gratification, we abandon it (unless assigned to read it for a literature course). "It was boring," "I just couldn't get into it," and "It was going nowhere" are a few of our stock excuses for setting it aside as being irrelevant to our needs. A pleasant experience had been our purpose, and not enough was offered to justify sticking with the book.

Most conscious activities fragmentize, recombine, and put to trial a variety of routes to gratification. The brain is free to operate in countless ways, and, as earlier indicated, any number of alternatives can be explored for producing roughly the same results. In contrast, fiction drastically curtails conscious freedom in order to stretch the resources of the imagination to their limit. Paradoxically, verbal expressiveness is enhanced by the author's creativity, but only within a fixed linear pattern—the immutable one-dimensional sequence of words, sentences, and episodes that constitute the story as told. The reader's relatively amorphous feelings and impulses are organized by a text's irreversible advancement from Aristotle's beginning, characterized by high tension, to Aristotle's end, producing relief and the restoration of a steady-state minimum. Like the simplest feedback loop, the text as a fixed sequence of words mediates the necessary passage between the two. Variety can (and must) be tolerated in one's response to a text, but only to the extent that it can accommodate itself to this linear advancement, since mounting tension (the dominant aspect of Aristotle's middle) must eventually culminate in an experience of release that reduces tension levels to the anticipated steady-state minimum. In its role as an agent of negative feedback, the plot organizes consciousness to bring about this result.

Of course there is considerable local satisfaction experienced by readers as they linger over a work of literature page by page, as Coleridge insisted in *Biographia Literaria*:

> A poem is that species of composition, which is opposed to works of science, by proposing for its *immediate* object pleasure, not truth; and from all other species (having *this* object in common with it) it is discriminated by proposing to itself such delight from the *whole*, as is compatible with a distinct gratification from each component *part*.[22]

More specifically, as he explained a few lines later:

> The reader should be carried forward, not merely or chiefly by the mechanical impulse of curiosity, or by a restless desire to arrive at the final solution; but by the pleasurable activity of mind excited by the attractions of the journey itself. Like the motion of a serpent, which the Egyptians made the emblem of intellectual power; or like the path of sound through the air; at every step he pauses and half recedes, and from the retrogressive movement collects the force which again carries him onward.

Indeed, the "local" satisfaction described by Coleridge is not to be discounted, especially in the experience of poetry, since each local context bears its impact, both heightening and satisfying tension within the compass of the reader's short-term memory. However, local effects are quickly forgotten except for the relatively few that are retained in the long-term memory, most of which help to clarify the story being told, thereby reinforcing the anticipation of closure at the expense of these effects.[23] As explained by Stephen Booth (and paraphrased by Stanley Fish), there is a "temporal experience in the course of which meanings become momentarily available, before disappearing under the pressure of other meanings, which are in their turn superseded, contradicted, qualified, or simply forgotten."[24] Moreover, once a linear sequence establishes itself, the mounting anticipation of closure dominant in the long-term memory increasingly crowds from consciousness the significance of local contexts (metaphor, imagery, etc.) that compete for time and space in the short-term memory. As the plot advances, tension is increasingly brought to focus on anticipated developments—the relatively simple understanding, for example, upon the completion of act 3, scene 2, of *Hamlet* that Hamlet must be careful now that he has alerted Claudius to his knowledge of his fratricide and, upon the completion of act 3, scene 4, that his task is more difficult now that he has killed Polonius. This linear emphasis continues to accumulate until it produces its final payoff in suitable closure. Local effects are thus absorbed in the momentum toward a resolution whose culminating satisfaction crowns and gives final definition to the memory of the entire text.

Critics such as I. A. Richards, Norman Holland, and David Bleich have emphasized the wide range of response among readers to any particular text.

A Homeostatic Model

Each reader presumably brings to fiction a unique mixture of personal associations, and no two individuals can be expected to share exactly the same response. However, the more a reader's attention is fixed on plot's linear organization of words and episodes toward acceptable closure, the more predictable (i.e., universal) the response becomes. The more intense the anticipation of the story's eventual outcome, the closer its linear effect upon the reader's consciousness resembles a simple reflex arc more or less shared by all readers. There might be enormous variety in the personal associations that readers bring to bear upon this linear sequence, and their intellectualized retrospective assessments of the text can be expected to reflect this variety, but while narrative form asserts itself *in media res* during the telling of what happens, a shared anticipation of acceptable closure takes precedence over this variety. At least in their experience of mounting tension and homeostatic relief, readers do not significantly differ from each other. Before and after their exposure to a text, their ideas and feelings might be different; however, during their reading of it—while the story takes place—these converge, and sometimes to an extraordinary degree. Why? Because fiction's conative dimension (the pursuit of wish fulfillment) takes precedence over both its cognitive dimension (the reader's personal knowledge relevant to the story being told) and its affective dimension (the reader's feelings in response to this story). Since the conative demands of readers—to be told something different from what they already know—necessarily dissolve upon the completion of the story, readers must cope with the husk of their satisfaction, i.e., their affective and cognitive responses, whereupon variety necessarily reasserts itself at the expense of uniformity. But it is a profound mistake to document this variety as if it were intrinsic to literary experience, since the shared quest for satisfaction dominates while a story is in progress, not the memories and associations readers (or playgoers) bring to this sharing.

Readers need not be ashamed of the way they have focused their interest on the story. For only by projecting themselves into its narrative momentum can they benefit from its negative feedback, guided word for word, episode for episode, from one end of its loop to the other. Every phrase, every described event, becomes important only if it helps to refine and modulate the advancement toward a suitable resolution. For this reason, readers can take up a text wherever they please, confident that they are joining a narrative loop destined to complete itself. They can also risk trying out a text, aware that they are free to break the circuit at any time. This is the ultimate freedom offered by fiction—its escape clause for those who find they are unable to suspend disbelief.

The narrative momentum of a text almost inevitably produces an allopathic centering of the reader's dissatisfactions on either a single problem or a relatively limited group of problems. As David Hume proposed in his classic essay "Of Tragedy," subordinate movement is converted into predominant movement, whose relative simplification produces a better sense of control over an undefinable spectrum of personal difficulties.[25] Like the scapegoats of ancient ritual, fiction gives focus to problems so they can be eliminated more effectively. Random, nonspecific irritations with job, money, family, friendships, and quality of life converge in a definable literary crisis whose resolution, equally literary, produces an improved sense of personal worth. For example, in the case of *Hamlet* the playgoers' broad spectrum of problems and aggravations converges in the single issue of botched revenge, whose final catastrophe wipes the slate clean for the playgoers as well as for Hamlet.

There is also homeopathic relief in the sense that the problems solved by fiction almost inevitably exaggerate real-life circumstances. Most readers' emotional needs are normal, and the corrective produced by fiction, like that of aspirin, is likewise relatively superficial. However, ordinary difficulties must be intensified to be eliminated, usually by converting affect (a feeling or disposition) into active emotion that is triggered by specific events of a dramatic nature. For example, horror stories convert the reader's timidity into outright fear that can be denied by acts of courage, success stories convert the reader's mild dissatisfaction into intense frustration that can be denied by great achievement, and so on. In effect, fiction hyperbolizes—it imposes stories of acute crisis to exemplify the chronic problems familiar to readers. By exacerbating these problems to a sufficient degree, it justifies the pursuit of a solution that is sufficiently dramatic to diminish anxieties and thus help readers to stay on an even keel in real life. Hamlet's intense struggle to decide how, when, and for what reason he wants to revenge his father's murder gives almost cosmic proportions to the range of uncertainties most of us endure in our lives. Nevertheless, through literary exaggeration the story of Hamlet engages our feelings, permitting a sense of relief that would otherwise not occur. If ordinary events are recounted at a level of intensity comparable to our daily expectations, the story would bore us, and its resolution would produce little if any tension reduction. The minimalist fiction in vogue today

A Homeostatic Model

might seem an exception to this rule, but it, too, hyperbolizes, and perhaps more than its advocates realize. Nevertheless, to the extent that they succeed in avoiding exaggeration, their uncompromising dedication to aesthetic purity deprives them of mass audience appeal. Both the allopathic concentration of experience and its homeopathic exaggeration are needed to guarantee homeostasis.

But it is probably the reader's anticipation that is the most important ingredient of literary experience. There must be an expectation of closure for local contexts to be taken seriously by most readers. Forepleasure might be experienced in the early stages of a text (comparable to sexual petting, or the smell of food cooking), but it can be enjoyed primarily because a suitable resolution is guaranteed later on. Readers, for example, may become absorbed in the myriad encounters of Tom Jones, Elizabeth Bennet, and David Copperfield because of their confidence that everything that transpires will later be ironed out. The pattern is even more dominant in popular fiction, in which heightened expectations obviously impose both allopathic focusing and homeopathic exaggeration. It may be observed, for example, in the film *An Affair to Remember*, directed by Leo McCrary in 1957, in which Cary Grant plays a successful artist who cannot forgive his ex-fiancée, played by Deborah Kerr, for having jilted him the day they were to marry at the top of the Empire State Building and then for never having contacted him to apologize. What he never learns is that she had been struck and crippled by an automobile when she rushed across 34th Street to reach the marriage ceremony on time and that she refused to contact him to avoid his marrying her through pity. The story reaches its climax years later when he finally makes an unexpected visit to her modest apartment where she lives alone. At last confronted, she sits motionless on her living room couch with tears in her eyes as he berates her for having abandoned him at the altar. When he turns to leave, she bids him good-bye, also without rising. Suddenly a different possibility dawns on him. While talking, he glides to her bedroom door and pushes it open far enough to see a wheelchair and, on the wall, his earlier portrait of her, completed during their romance, which was recently purchased by a mysterious woman in a wheelchair. Suddenly he realizes that something terrible must have happened, and when he turns back from the bedroom door to see her sitting on the couch with her legs carefully tucked under a blanket (no wonder she had not risen to greet him!), he sees she sees he finally knows, and of course he melts in both forgiveness and contrition.

A Homeostatic Model

At this point the entire audience is on the brink of tears—even those the most offended by the mawkish sentimentalism by which their emotions are being manipulated. Everything about the episode is fraudulent—the feelings, the situation, the script, and the acting. But there can be no mistaking that a determinate organization of expectations has been plotted with mounting expectation based on both allopathic focusing (awaiting Cary Grant's discovery of what had happened) and homeopathic exaggeration (a sentimental organization of events contrived to maximize the impact of his discovery). Contrary to the most basic assumptions of response theory (as I will explain in chapter 7), this organization of expectations both sharpens the effect for the individual moviegoer and brings this response into relatively close harmony with the response of everybody else in the theater. The same emotion occurs with roughly comparable homeostatic value for all who keep up with the story without leaving the theater or somehow diverting their minds to other topics. Many will actually experience a much stronger emotion than they might feel upon the death of a personal friend or close member of the family. Some gladly accept the emotion; others reject it, but their rejection does not mean they haven't experienced a comparable effect. Moreover, few are going to be entirely honest in explaining their response, since whatever appeals to them in the episode is too lugubrious to be directly acknowledged. Instead, they may be expected to resort to a variety of diversionary rationalizations to explain themselves to those with whom they are discussing the film. Nevertheless, a preposterous fabrication has been foisted on the audience, and there is almost unanimous complicity—almost everybody at least temporarily cooperates in the illusion in order to benefit from its effect.

Many critics reject the cathartic explanation of fiction based on the dynamics of allopathy, homeopathy, and intensified expectations. Morse Peckham, for example, has emphasized disorientation rather than satisfaction as fiction's most important feature. According to Peckham, literary disorientation improves the reader's adaptive skills.[26] Tension predominates instead of narrative closure, and as a result education (*utile*) takes precedence over escapism (*dulce*). The value of fiction presumably derives from exposing readers to new experience so they are better able to cope with life. Obviously, this creative priority appeals to literary specialists and a small coterie of sophisticated readers who seek out confusion, allusion, and presumably meaningful juxtapositions instead of linear coherence and narrative closure. However, as in the case of minimalism, this pursuit is irrelevant to the needs of most readers,

A Homeostatic Model

who are bored by excessive aesthetic dislocations. What most of us seek is temporary escapist gratification, and this gratification comes from reading as an *immediate* adaptive response based on imminent gain here and now rather than the *postponed* adaptive response of educating ourselves to deal with future uncertainties. How many readers tell themselves they want to enhance their adjustment strategies for coping with life, so maybe it's time to read another novel? Very few. Most fiction draws readers because it subordinates positive feedback to the homeostatic benefits of poetic justice, happy endings, and the usual stereotypes taken for granted in the experience of fiction. Closure and simplification predominate, and their homeostatic benefit comes from a rage for order (i.e., the achievement of gratifying results), not from any rage for chaos.

All psychological displacements bear homeostatic value in fiction—otherwise, they would not be brought into play. But denial is probably the most primitive, hence the most basic, of these displacements because of its flat rejection of unacceptable experience (I am *not* cowardly, I am *not* lonely, etc.). In the context of literary form, denial functions as the affirmation of contrary experience (*not* cowardice → bravery, *not* loneliness → love, etc.). Anything affirmed by the final outcome of a text is probably an act of denial (e.g., Elizabeth Bennet gets married and thus does not remain a spinster), and a wide diversity of readers can be satisfied by the relatively abstract function of the denial displacement embedded in narrative form. As a result, fiction appeals to a mixed audience and for a variety of reasons. One reader seeks out adventure stories because they deny ennui, another because they deny daily routine, another because they deny parental authority, and yet another because they deny all three, or any combination of them. Each reader harbors a unique panoply of problems to be denied, and each turns to fiction in order to deny uncomfortable traits or feelings. When a novel helps readers to do this, its structure has played a useful role, but when it falls short of helping them, they are likely to turn to other books more amenable to their style of evasiveness. If science fiction and horror stories fail to improve their sense of personal worth, they can turn to historical adventures and Gothic romances. If Dreiser cannot refract and disguise their problems and inadequacies, let readers try James, or Joyce, or Joyce Carol Oates. All provide the opportunity for denial, but in different ways and to a different degree with different readers.

A broad spectrum of unacceptable experience may be denied by fiction, and often several felt inadequacies may be denied simultaneously. For example, fiction's heightened purposefulness denies habit and indifference, its narrative focus denies random meaninglessness, its closure in a happy ending denies the perpetual need for compromise, and its exaggerated morality denies the pragmatic shortcuts of day-to-day behavior. We also enjoy fiction's sensitivity because it denies obtuseness, its profundity because it denies banality, its glamour because it denies drabness, and its romantic love because it denies loneliness and impotence. The literary convention that persistence finally pays off denies the truth that dogged persistence is often a waste of time; the literary convention that crime never pays denies society's inability to cope with crime; and the literary convention that wealth and status can be gladly sacrificed to true love denies the reality that true love is often poverty's first victim. In each instance, affirmed values gain particular importance because they help to us reject our more realistic expectations in life.

Those readers whose personalities are relatively unencumbered by the denial displacement are likely to be disinterested in literary experience. Since they do not read to deny, they are more prone to consider plot development to be artificial, warm emotion to be histrionic pointlessness, and vibrant characterization little more than predictable stereotyping. For such readers, dramatic confrontation is likely to seem overdramatized, insight pseudoinsightful, and lucky accident the absurdity of the *deus ex machina* swinging out of control from the rafters. As in the case of both Emerson and Bertrand Russell, for example, fiction's truths are likely to be examined, poked once or twice, then set aside for something more meaningful to contemplate. This disinterest is perhaps offensive to professional students of literature, but it seems roughly comparable to an adult's disinterest in children's fiction. It is also exemplified by our changing tastes as we grow older. Only such major figures as Sophocles, Shakespeare, and Tolstoy seem versatile enough to accommodate our needs throughout our entire lifetimes, and even these are vulnerable to abandonment in our advancing years.[27] We can all observe our indifference to authors whose denial skills have lost their relevance to our mature needs, for example, Dumas, Hugo, or Kahlil Gibran. For some of us, Poe, Shelley, and perhaps D. H. Lawrence represent similar milestones in our emotional development—profound when we first read them, and forever to be cherished for this reason, but somewhat embarrassing in later encounters. Most of the authors we read possess an appeal at one stage in our lives that becomes almost inexplicable at another. Dostoevsky might seem extraordinarily insightful to the reader at twenty-five but lugubrious at forty, Jane Austen deliciously ironic at thirty but rather too prim at fifty-five. Or vice versa. And who is to say which opinion is the most valid? For any poem or novel to engage our imagination, it must vitally deceive us, and this means it must help us to deny feelings relevant to our present needs, right now, at this point in our lives. The cumulative result is literary tradition, the overall history of books that have consistently performed this task at one time or another in the experience of readers.

Paradoxically, affirmation usually serves as the vehicle of denial, disguising its aim with what seems a straightforward positive choice. Why affirmation? Because it not only denies but rejects the very possibility that denial might be intended. "Think positive," programmed optimists declare, ignoring the abundance of aversions and dislikes implicit in every positive declaration they make. "We work hard around here," they declare, making it plain that sloth is unacceptable. "Everything turns out O.K." makes it plain that whatever falls short of turning out O.K. is not to be discussed. "They are lovely people" makes it plain that their defects—their marvelous assortment of inadequacies—are not to be discussed. Optimists always talk positively, but it soon becomes apparent that their dominant effort is to impose avoidances, and the more positive the outlook, the bigger the avoidances. Sir Francis Bacon explains in *Novum Organum*:

> [I]t is the peculiar and perpetual error of the human intellect to be more moved and excited by affirmatives than by negatives, whereas it ought properly to hold itself indifferently disposed towards both alike. Indeed, in the establishment of any true axiom, the negative instance is the more forcible of the two.[28]

And since fiction eschews the rigorous establishment of true axioms, it is free to resort to affirmatives via the double negative—the so-called *Negationsnegierung* proposed by Engels: a rose is *not not* a rose. The hero is likewise *not not* a hero, the lover *not not* a lover, and so on. Replace *not not* with *truly* or *finally*, and dialectic becomes amenable to literary solution based, as I explain later, on the affirmative fallacy.[29] Avoidances can be particularized and vitalized by focusing on alternatives bigger and more dramatic than life.

As W. K. Wimsatt maintains in his study of Samuel Johnson's prose style, the dialectic between denial and affirmation seems unavoidable in verbal discourse:

> By every affirmation . . . something incompatible is implicitly denied; and what is denied, or what would be relevant to deny explicitly, varies with what it is relevant to affirm. . . . The negative defines the positive. The more peculiar and complex the affirmation the more it may need the emphasis of negation, the more negation itself, elaborated in its own aspects, may become a relevant and parallel meaning, until which is superior and which is subordinate is hardly to be told.[30]

Johnson's use of Ciceronian antithesis is Wimsatt's topic here, but the principle applies in a more inclusive sense to almost any expression of feelings. It may be proposed, in fact, that the pleasure gained through affirmation is almost always symptomatic of the machinery of denial, whether the topic be religion, patriotism, family, employment, or personal relationships. Beneath the declared affirmative lurks the operative negative, giving homeostatic value to one's positive outlook. The more strenuously this connection is disavowed, the more likely its relevance. And when an author's sincerity is at stake, such as in published fiction, the denied alternative is the most imminent, and the dialectic it necessitates the most intense.

The invisibility of the denial displacement is important, since its homeostatic benefits can be guaranteed only if we remain oblivious to the specific reasons for its appeal. Our heightened involvement in a story must be matched by oversight as to exactly why we want to share in its satisfactory outcome. By concentrating our attention upon fiction, we can avoid recognizing our reasons for doing so. Vice versa, we cannot effectively deny our feelings if we recognize what we are doing. One cannot say, "Right now I am thinking *this* in order to deny *that*." Suddenly *that* leaps into the equation again. By admitting denial, we necessarily cancel out its value except as an intellectualization that brings denial to a new level of abstraction. The moment we recognize, for example, that we enjoy Tom Jones's fistfights because we avoid such encounters at all costs in our own lives, our satisfaction substantially diminishes. Only by diverting our attention to a separate issue—for example, by confessing, "I know my cowardice gives me pleasure in identifying with Tom Jones"—are we able to salvage enjoyment with a new and more inclusive act of denial, presumably the candid admission to be admired as the candid admission "I am not so blind that I cannot recognize my limitations." If confronted with our evasiveness in conceding this (since there is probably far more than cowardice to be confessed), we are likely to beg off altogether by shifting to an entirely different topic. In comparable fashion, denial finds its appropriate level in the enjoyment of fiction based on the particular needs and versatility of readers, some more complicated than others, some more dependent on literary gratification than others. But in all instances, denial is best carried off if we *think* we have kept our two worlds separate from each other—the fiction we enjoy and our personal circumstances whose denial guarantees its enjoyment.

The plot is necessarily fiction's principal agent of denial, since it tells a success story that leads from aggravation to false confidence, from positive-feedback threat to negative-feedback satisfaction. The plot thrusts action forward toward a satisfactory conclusion, a closed-system victory over open-system impediments—the compromises and qualifications that cannot otherwise be avoided. Open-system surprises and challenges might be introduced, but only to be brought under control by literary convention. Both in the story itself and in the minds of readers, there is a shift from confusion to clarity, from problems to their solution, from minor aggravation to temporary relief. Reversal leads from uncertainty to closure at a new plateau of experience that produces an improved sense of personal worth. Through plot, the denial displacement is achieved as well as told, affording a transformation that is stretched out and brought to dramatic realization both through and beyond language. "I am *not* cowardly" becomes "I *discover I am* brave," or, better yet, "I *learn to be* brave." This transformation dramatizes the rejection of our problems by leading from one state of affairs to its opposite, producing homeostasis based on a sense of accomplishment significantly at odds with real experience. If I recognize that I am a coward, tension increases; however, if I can deny my cowardice with credibility, a modest dose of homeostasis occurs. And if I can identify with literary heroes who gain the courage to meet some kind of challenge, homeostasis can be intensified with little threat to my sense of personal worth. This happens, for example, if I can identify with Hamlet when he resolves to take his fate into his own hands, or if I can identify with Tom Jones in one of his foolish, if justified, fistfights.

Obvious examples of a plot's linear organization of denial include the roving cowboy who guns down a band of rustlers and the Rider Haggard adventurer who helps lost tribes to gain their freedom from traditional adversaries. Other examples include lovers who overcome family opposition, troubled individuals who transcend themselves through heroic self-destruction, and even TV sitcom families who sweep away their relatively trivial misunderstandings during the course of an hour, advertisements included. In more sophisticated plots, characters become liberated by learning to accept their weaknesses, by discovering that liberation is not their goal, by committing themselves more sincerely to the quest, or by acknowledging that such purposefulness has been futile and meaningless. But even here closure occurs, and, with closure, satisfaction can be felt as the expression of the pleasure principle.

One of the principal advantages of plot is its gradual and carefully articulated realization of the denial displacement. It is stretched out in linear fashion so that the negation of X through the affirmation of Y is cumulative instead of instantaneous. There is metonymic advancement in the sense that new events resignify old events, until the final stage in this sequence imposes an entirely new situation that denies (or designifies) the original state of affairs. Because of this elongated reversal process, denial yields the appearance of growth and improvement: "Henry Fleming was a coward *until* he was taught under fire to be brave"; "Squire B. played the seducer *until* Pamela convinced him to be an honest man," etc. With ordinary denial individual readers quickly reject unpleasant alternatives, worried that others might doubt the truth of their assertions. On the other hand, with literary denial experience can be more effectively modulated to produce reversal as a cumulative achievement. A better interplay can occur among somatic, conscious, and literary modalities, each brought to culmination in its own sphere: (1) the negative feedback needed to produce homeostasis, (2) the denial needed to produce a felt sense of relief, and (3) the narrative closure needed to produce the satisfaction of having read a good novel. Stated in the simplest possible terms, narrative closure consolidates denial as a psychological displacement governed by the pleasure principle. The entire process is unified in a hierarchy of actualizations, and each of the three levels represents one phase, or dimension, in the orchestrated satisfaction of the text.[31]

Positive-feedback mechanisms that impede the plot as an agent of denial are usually more difficult to recognize, partly because they feature open-system ingredients characterized by complexity and elusiveness. Here a certain measure of Peckham's rage for chaos may emerge, but suitably restricted to its subordinate role as resistance to an affirmative outcome. In popular fiction, positive feedback usually consists of the obvious hurdles to be overcome by heroes, but in more ambitious works it also includes the surprises

A Homeostatic Model

and countervailing insights that temporarily draw attention to themselves at the expense of plot development.[32] Puns, images, and metaphors, for example, often divert the reader's attention by expressing an attitude in conflict with the success story associated with closure. If there are any confessional implications that bear this impact, these may be described as leakage, as defined by Paul Ekman in his recent book *Telling Lies*.[33] Ekman proposes that, without realizing it, liars reveal themselves by means of kinesic signals beyond their control—by voice, facial distortions, slips of the tongue, and various emblematic gestures. In fiction this leakage instead occurs through its texture of overlooked connotations, a texture that essentially contradicts the theme and basic thrust of the story. With each new disclosure there is a surge of countervailing awareness that is quickly forgotten because of the narrative form's momentum toward an acceptable resolution. If enough leakage accumulates, however, an overtone theme emerges as the open-system acknowledgment of repressed truths that resist the use of closure to deny them. Tension increases between this partially recognized cluster of truths and the sequential organization that disposes of them. Positive feedback is not totally absorbed and reorganized by negative feedback, nor are open-system freedom and volatility entirely harnessed by closed-system dynamics. Of course, the plot eventually succeeds at the expense of leakage, but without entirely drowning it out. A compromise formation results, by which the stimulative appeal of local contexts reinforces the more inclusive satisfaction produced by narrative closure as the denial of these contexts. Fiction actually gains by this complexity, since what is denied reinforces the act of denying it. The expression of problems intermingles with their solution, producing a wonderful resonance typical of most works of literary genius. If the dialectic works appropriately, simplification is better realized at the expense of complexity, deception at the expense of truth—in sum, negative-feedback mechanisms at the expense of positive-feedback risk and expansiveness.

Psychoanalytic critics have emphasized a variety of displacement strategies as the source of literary gratification, but without tracing their origins—each and every one of them—to the denial displacement. However, as the primary agent of homeostasis, denial should be recognized to provide the initial impulse that is both particularized and resolved by these strategies, all of which complete its action by means of diversionary effort elsewhere. In each instance, it is the denial displacement that initiates finding a new aim. The particular channels for diverting experience are important, but these remain subordinate to denial itself, which both initiates and energizes the effort to eliminate this experience. First there is an impulse to disavow an idea or impulse, and then a specific displacement takes place to satisfy this impulse by shifting our attention elsewhere. Sometimes denial occurs alone (e.g., the cowardly lion's proof that he is not cowardly), but it is usually preliminary to the imposition of a diversionary positive aim that is brought to completion by one of these other displacements. And of course, fiction guarantees the preeminence of the denial displacement by its stretched-out advancement from one state of affairs to its opposite. By dominating the forward inertia of narrative form, denial both subordinates these other displacements and provides ample opportunity for them to flourish, each after its own fashion.

The role of the Oedipus complex in literary experience—for example, as emphasized by Simon Lesser, Bernard Meyer, and Frederick Crews—originates with denial. A wide variety of neurotic symptoms characterize the Oedipus complex, but their source remains the simplest and most basic displacement—the denial of parental dependency, necessitating the quest for an identity of one's own. First comes denial, then the complex adjustment that satisfactorily determines one's mature relationship with others. By means of self-discovery, a new role substitutes for an earlier one, producing a narrative reversal in the transition from one state of affairs to its opposite. In the case of *Hamlet*, for example, as explained by Ernest Jones, the ambivalent behavior of the mother and the stifling dominance of patriarchy as represented by three father figures—Hamlet senior, Claudius, and Polonius—express a denial of filial subservience intense enough to necessitate a tale of justified revenge.[34] By accepting the obligation to revenge himself, Hamlet finally realizes his status as his father's rightful heir. Similarly, the oral fixation featured by Norman Holland in *The Dynamics of Literary Response* produces denial by emphasizing fantasies characterized by abundance and nourishment as the reward for passive trust. Plenitude is both promised and rewarded, but its efficient cause is denial—the elimination of strain and disappointment through regression to infantile dependency. Likewise, the anal fixation denies mature responsibility by fastening on order, cleanliness, accumulation, enumeration, respect for authority, and the creation of stable boundaries.[35] The initial step is to deny the give-and-take of mature relationships, followed by the gratifying pursuit of regressive virtues associated with the anal stage of development.

A comparable pattern of denial takes place for the compulsion syndrome, which Angus Fletcher emphasizes in *Allegory: The Theory of a Symbolic Mode*.[36] The repetition compulsion helps to protect our sense of personal worth by preventing variety and disruption from aggravating our anxieties to an unacceptable extent. By ritualizing behavior through the use of literary convention, we can reject emotional difficulties in a safely predictable fashion. We cast their threat from our thoughts by resorting to habit and organization. First comes denial—"Those are not my problems"—followed by "undoing" in our dedication to tried and proven formulas—"Only to these alternative outcomes am I willing to devote my attention over and over again." Almost inevitably, readers seek out habitual pattern in the formulaic plots typical of adventure stories, love stories, detective stories, and the like, all of which feature a gratifying predictability.

More inclusively, Hans and Shulamith Kreitler propose in their book *Psychology of the Arts* that literary experience pleases because of its homeostatic value in more efficiently organizing our impulses.[37] Aesthetic harmony is emphasized to deny problems associated with the less organized world we live in. Once again, denial serves as a preliminary displacement mechanism, followed by our seeking action to find an agreeable substitute, in this instance the perfection of aesthetic form. Formalist critics accordingly take pleasure in the dramatic symmetry of *Hamlet* (i.e., three revenging sons, the alternation of family scenes with ritual scenes, and the fact that Ophelia and Laertes both serve as foils to Hamlet, one in actually committing suicide, the other in effectively seeking to revenge his father's murder).

Each literary genre offers its own possibilities for such a compromise formation, but only within the most challenging of its works. In simpler works, pleasure almost entirely derives from the success story implicit in the narrative outcome, with countervailing (i.e., positive-feedback) instances almost entirely limited to the behavior of villains and other such blocking characters. In simple detective stories, for instance, denial is based on a variety of optimistic assurances: that evil is caused by somebody else, that it can be eliminated by the villian's exposure, that doing so is entirely within the capacity of the detective, and that the universe is at least temporarily benign because of detectives who can root out such evil. Only in more complex detective stories, such as *Oedipus Rex* and *Crime and Punishment*, is the criminal act disclosed to express defects even the detective cannot totally disavow.[38] Likewise, simple adventure stories offer optimistic assurances that deny a spectrum of concerns, including boredom, impotence, purposelessness, and the lack of independence. The greater our frustration, the more we enjoy accounts of successful struggles against apparently insurmountable odds. Only in more sophisticated tales of adventure, such as *The Odyssey* and *Moby-Dick*, are weaknesses disclosed at the core of a hero's identity. Each genre offers its own pattern of affirmation, stated or implied, whose accomplishment guarantees its audience appeal, but only in the best and most profound works are problems and their denial brought into the necessary equipoise for preventing the easy achievement of homeostasis.

four

SHAKESPEARE, COLERIDGE, AND FROST

A metaphor can be disorienting, even offensive, when its image expresses a variety of presumably accidental connotations beyond its overt intended meaning.[1] The unsullied youthfulness implied by the image of a rose, for example, may also bear antithetical sexual connotations, especially when associated with the latent implications of other metaphors nearby. To the extent that these additional connotations get out of control and draw attention to themselves as a vehicle of unintended feelings, they are likely to become threatening, thereby producing positive feedback as well as an open-system consciousness that aggravates tension rather than resolving it.

Fortunately, a metaphor's verbal economy helps to obscure these connotations well enough for them to be felt without drawing too much attention to themselves. They verge on recognition but are quickly crowded from consciousness by the accumulation of new metaphors and word combinations, as well as by the demands of narrative momentum toward a suitable resolution. Our capacity to mull over the additional baggage of connotations for any length of time is diminished by questions bearing upon the meaning and plotted outcome of the text in its advancement toward closure. What results is a relative neglect of conscious intentions that enhances metaphor's freedom of expression. Its fugitive suggestiveness can be both felt and overlooked, giving it unusual flexibility in its articulation of repressed feelings. This freedom bears striking results when a metaphor's confessional implications come in conflict with the theme, story, and characterization that dominate the linear momentum toward closure. Because of what is declared (which features negative feedback), what is confessed can be tolerated; and because of the resistance to what is declared by what is confessed (which features positive feedback), the passage seems of unique and profound significance to readers. Of course, whatever locks into dialectic interplay with metaphor's primary process resourcefulness ultimately prevails by imposing, in the words of Mencken, "better-than-truths," but homeostasis at least partly results from metaphor's fugitive expression of less acceptable truths that must at least be well enough acknowledged to be denied. Gratification is doubled when these truths are both acknowledged by metaphor and denied by theme, plot, and all the other dynamics of literary closure.

By means of metaphoric overdetermination, the poet's most intimate feelings can erupt into language, then quickly disappear from view as the reader's attention continues to be drawn forward by new metaphors and mounting thematic and narrative demands. Poets thus enjoy temporary freedom from conventional restraint and can take advantage of the opportunity to express forbidden implications that they themselves might be the last to recognize; they might even be shocked—offended at the suggestion—if these are pointed out to them. Yet poets say what they say, and the accidental implications too often bear an integral relationship—at times, in fact, a vitally contradictory relationship—to the central meaning of their poetry. The same impact is also possible with symbols, puns, ambiguity, and heightened imagery, since they all possess comparable value in conveying unconscious implications. Only when latent associations begin to cluster too insistently do they begin to draw attention to themselves as composing an important dimension of the total poem—perhaps the most important of all.

Sometimes the latent implications come directly in conflict with the text's dominant meaning, as expressed by plot, theme, and the conventional expectations of closed-system gratification. However, these implications can be tolerated as long as they are absorbed and denied by their more respectable narrative framework.[2] According to Freud's theory of dream symbolism, the text's secondary elaboration disguises and renders harmless its metaphors' primary process subversiveness. As Nietzsche might have explained, the Apollonian clarity of narrative form absorbs and ultimately denies the Dionysian intensity of metaphoric extravagance. Philip Wheelwright likewise finds such a dialectic between story and aesthetic innuendo.

> One of the most powerfully expressive kinds of poetic tension is that which exists between the story or scenario of a poem and the suggestions thrown off by its imagery—a tension between statement and aesthetic innuendo. Such tensions are dramatic by their very nature, and give a certain dramatic character, an inherent dialectic, to the poem in which they occur.[3]

A psychoanalytic explanation of this conflict can also be proposed by combining Ernst Kris's theory of metaphor and Norman Holland's theory of form and idea (or theme) as defense. In his article "Aesthetic Ambiguity," Kris demonstrates that metaphor "serves as a stimulus to functional regression" because the primary process itself is metaphoric and imagistic; in *The Dynamics of Literary Response*, Holland explains at length how form, plot, theme, and language serve as defenses that allow primary process fantasy content to be transformed into a pattern of expression acceptable to the ego and superego.[4] Both theories are useful, and a synthesis seems appropriate that features the formal and thematic dynamics proposed by Holland as defenses against the metaphoric infusion of primary process displacements proposed by Kris. Metaphoric confession occurs, but at the cost of redoubled censorship, and if censorship wins, it is only by giving metaphoric confession a major role to play—enough to justify imposing this censorship. The value of what is declared is demonstrated by what it denies, but, then again, what is denied is paradoxically confirmed by the act of denying it. Whenever this dialectic becomes dominant, the key to its interpretation is hardly sincerity (which I. A. Richards proposed as the primary ingredient of good poetry) but in fact an audacious insincerity—audacious enough to touch upon unacknowledged feelings in order to dismiss them, feelings too personal to be explained, yet too important to be disregarded. What results is a modern version of the *psychomachia*, an internal dialogue between conventional truths and a metaphoric expressiveness only partially understood. Each dimension gives the lie to the other, and their continuing struggle both defines and is defined by literary form.

This dialectic may be observed in Donne's "A Valediction: Forbidding

Mourning," in which metaphors of death throes, tantrum storms, a gold filament beaten so thin that it all but disappears, and a compass that can only complete its circle on separate legs repeatedly suggest that Donne might find some gratification in abandoning his pregnant wife for a year or two, contrary to the thematic expressions of extreme distress at their parting. At one level (featuring negative feedback), Donne declares his reluctance to depart, but at another (featuring positive feedback) he implies his eagerness, and it is the tension between these levels that gives vitality to his poem. A more threatening dialectic unfolds in Keats's "Ode on a Grecian Urn," in which the urn's depiction of eternal youth denies the imminence of death. Static figures presumably epitomize life, and an irrefutable equation between truth and beauty presumably guarantees aesthetic permanence, perhaps a perpetuation of life itself. "That is all ye know on earth, and all ye need to know," Keats claims, refusing to acknowledge his mortal illness at the time he writes the poem. By concentrating on the urn's immortality as opposed to its appeal as a fixed tableau devoid of life, he denies his own imminent death. Once again negative feedback absorbs and denies the positive-feedback alternative confessed by the poem's metaphoric content, this time implicit in its imagery.

The dialectic may also be observed in Arnold's "Dover Beach," in which pervasive metaphors of heterosexual seduction successfully undermine the poet's declaration of Platonic fidelity to his companion, "Ah, love, let us be true to one another!"[5] Though not evident until the final stanza, the dominant human relationship in the poem is between the poet and a woman at his side (his fiancée), so the obvious sexual implications of the imagery must first and foremost be recognized to bear upon their relationship. In the first stanza, the Dover cliffs play a masculine role and the water a feminine role, with the ebb and flow of the waves an obvious mimetic suggestion of sexual consummation. In the same vein, the third stanza implies undressing ("a bright girdle . . . I only hear its . . . withdrawing roar," etc.), and the last stanza confesses the fear of their "clash by night" that would next occur, which would lead to "neither joy, nor love, nor light, nor certitude, nor peace, nor help for pain." It is not exactly clear what is meant by *true* after this abundance of imagery that, once revised in its sequence, traces the normal seduction routine. Is the couple's love true enough for them to undress and go to bed together, or for them to stay dressed and remain true Platonic friends? Apparently, the poet asks for Platonic rapport both to justify and avert his halfhearted seduction attempt. Why else his fear of their "land of dreams" (i.e., bed) or of ignorant *armies* that "clash by night," a pun suggesting awkward *arms* (undoubtedly the poet's) in the act of making love. Faithfulness between man and woman seems to be proposed as the only enduring value in a threatened civilization, but this high thematic appeal is undermined by the choice between Victorian chastity and the sensuous abandonment suggested by the poem's metaphoric overdetermination. The final truths declared by Arnold (obviously of negative-feedback value) accordingly deny positive-feedback anxieties that derive from Arnold's timidity as a seducer, as implied by his choice of metaphor.

In Shakespeare's Sonnet 73, a slightly more attenuated dialectic interaction occurs. The empty branches on which birds once sang are described as "bare, ruin'd choirs," using the word *bare* to indicate the absence of birds and leaves, and suggesting that the poet refers to himself in his old age, devoid of poetic inspiration. However, *bare* also implies human nakedness, suggesting the poet's relationship to the individual to whom he addresses his sonnet. This additional possibility is reinforced by the connotations of disgrace implied by the adjacent word *ruined*, suggesting a cause and effect relationship—that the poet is ruined because he has been bare, i.e., that his relationship first stripped him naked, then deprived him of his respectability. Since it is a choir that is bare and ruined, the combination, based on the analogy between birds singing and the poet's verse, also suggests (1) empty of song, (2) nakedness sung, and even the two in combination, (3) nakedness sung *because* empty of song. An even more inclusive possibility consequently emerges—nakedness sung because disgraced and empty of song. However, the two words slip by so rapidly while one reads the passage that their multiple connotations remain unnoticed. As a result, repressed feelings can impinge on the flow of language as overlooked suggestiveness, presumably unrelated to the intended meaning of the poem as declared in its final couplet:

> This thou perceiv'st, which makes thy love more strong,
> To love that well which thou must leave ere long.

Here the sonnet's *carpe diem* theme, the poet's declaration of his confidence that his lover will remain committed to their necessarily transient love, seems to contradict the earlier puns and metaphors that suggest it might in fact be the love relationship that has ruined the poet. But even the wording of this final couplet includes a pun that reinforces the earlier suggestiveness, since the word *leave* in "which thou must leave ere long" may be interpreted as drawing upon the earlier use of *leaves* (of the tree), this time adopting it as a verb to suggest both rejuvenation (to the tree, or poet, to which thou must restore leaves ere long) and deciduousness (which thou must strip of leaves ere long—i.e., which thou must drive into old age ere long, as earlier implied). In either case, the orthodox theme that the poet grows old and is therefore confident of his lover's faithfulness suddenly takes on the additional implication that it is his lover's departure that is making him old.

This antithetical possibility becomes obvious if the heavy consonant parallel between the two words *love* and *leave* is stressed in one's oral reading of the final line, giving additional dimensionality to the commonplace "love them and leave them" predicate combination. Of course, the expression of the poet's doubts pertaining to his relationship with his lover is not exactly intended in the poem and it may easily be overlooked, but one cannot entirely ignore the standoff that emerges between the two essentially antithetical propositions: "I grow old, so do take pity on me" (featuring negative feedback) and "Because you seem entirely willing to abandon me, you aggravate my age" (featuring positive feedback). On the one hand, the sonnet is a stoic complaint; on the other, it is a desperate appeal, perhaps an accusation. Pun and metaphor have told their truth, but this is effectively absorbed and denied by a final thematic better-than-truth, thereby subsuming positive-feedback doubts to negative-feedback gratification.

The dialectic interaction between theme and metaphor intensifies, and sometimes to an extraordinary degree, when one's sexual role is at stake. This happens, for example, when latent homosexuality is both confessed and denied by its sublimation in poetry. Threatening metaphoric leakage must be counterbalanced by invoking the most effective thematic concerns, for example, such cosmic issues as fate, evil, tragic despair, and sin and redemption. In response, metaphors are likely to become further convoluted to give vent to the anxieties denied in this fashion. Both theme and metaphor consequently escalate to levels of intensity the poet and the readers may admire without entirely understanding. Often, for example, the supposedly ineffable genius found in many works of great literature—of Homer, Dante, Milton, Goethe, etc.—may be traced to unrecognized homophobic—or, with greater constraint, homoaversive—ambivalence. Androgyny and even homosexuality might be suggested in puns, metaphors, and local imagery, but only to be either disguised or vehemently denied by narrative form. Metaphoric bisexuality clamors for recognition, but only to be denied by traumatic content invested with the rights of narrative closure.

Coleridge's "The Rime of the Ancient Mariner" illustrates a moderately disguised version of homoaversive satisfaction in which both heterosexual and homosexual alternatives are rejected. Heterosexual marriage is declined, but so, too, is homosexual gratification, obliging cloistered innocence as the only acceptable alternative. At its most obvious thematic level, the poem is dominated by its subversiveness as an antiepithalamium that diverts male wedding guests (hence bridegrooms too) from wedding ceremonies. If the bridegroom himself instead of the wedding guest were detained by the mariner, the rejection of heterosexual marriage would be obvious, so the avoidance of marriage is displaced to the avoidance of other people's marriages, just as the Grimms' fairy tales transform fathers into woodsmen or giants and mothers into stepmothers or witches. Once this elemental disguise has been imposed, the poet can express his ambivalence toward marriage by the story he tells of the Ancient Mariner's voyage and its rampant but presumably inexplicable symbolism. At its face value, there seems to be no moral to the Ancient Mariner's story beyond his guilt for the seemingly motiveless killing of an albatross and his redemption once he can bless sea creatures. However, the bizarre symbolism of his voyage provides an indirect explanation of both his crime and his later effort to detain wedding guests—also an explanation of Coleridge's intentions in writing the poem. At the nadir of the Ancient Mariner's ordeal after killing the albatross, he meets Life-in-Death, the only individualized female in the poem besides the bride of the frame story. Just as Hansel and Gretel are driven into the woods at the behest of their evil stepmother only to be confronted by her even more threatening incarnation as a witch, the mariner has left a world dominated by such conventional observances as the marriage ceremony only to encounter at high sea the oneiric incarnation of marriage as the sun's imprisonment by a hideous female figure described as Life-in-Death. In effect, Life-in-Death emerges as the bride's nightmarish otherworld depiction, a temptress of classical origins (suggestive of Ishtar, Eve, Circe, the Wife of Bath, Error, etc.) who epitomizes not temptation itself but the female entrapment that presumably follows, from which the mariner is trying to save the wedding guest. The masts of her death ship are seen as prison bars behind which the sun is confined, apparently symbolizing the obligation to marriage and suggesting that the killing of the albatross—i.e., not leaving well enough alone—symbolizes getting married as opposed to remaining a bachelor. First comes marriage (the senseless killing of an albatross), then entrapment (the sun's imprisonment by Life-in-Death).

A better and more attractive alternative is suggested by the crew, whose death and resurrection ritualize the mariner's redemption. The androgynous, antiepithalamic implications of their sacrifice become obvious in the extended comparison between their corpses and slimy sea serpents:

> The many men, so beautiful!
> And they all dead did lie:
> And a thousand thousand slimy things
> Lived on; and so did I.
>
> I looked upon the rotting sea
> And drew my eyes away;
> I looked upon the rotting deck
> And there the dead men lay.

Only when the mariner can finally bless these water snakes is he baptized by a stream of rain and lightning from a phallic moon-cloud formation symbolizing true patriarchal redemption. He is then served by the dead crew who have immediately been resurrected and transformed into seraph-like figures, purified "slimy things" able to fly to heaven—as opposed to the patriarchal sun that remains locked behind bars. The crew's new power of levitation also helps to explain the mariner's moral crisis, for, as seraphs, they fly like the albatross (whose killing symbolizes his guilt) while resembling the sea serpents (whose acceptance brings his redemption). Happily, they can fly together, and their destination is a better world where Life-in-Death no longer poses any threat.

The poem's neglected frame story absorbs and denies these implications by its theme of the ancient mariner's eternal effort to expose selected young men to the truths implicit in his story. Enlightened by his ordeal, the mariner advises the wedding guest that it would be far sweeter "to walk together to the kirk with a goodly company" than to enter the kirk to get married (i.e., trapped by Life-in-Death). Such a journey together parallels the homoerotic voyage, the flight of the seraphim, and the mariner's quest for young men who might be diverted by his glittering eye. However, instead of flight, innocent perambulation is recommended—the shared experience of sensitive men who can walk together through the countryside, just as Coleridge and Wordsworth did when "The Ancient Mariner" was written. Not unexpectedly, the mariner indicates this "goodly" company consists mostly of men, since the only women included are specified to be virgins, young women who have not yet imposed life-in-death on their husbands. Once again the mariner repeats his moral, "He prayeth best, who loveth best all things both great and small," a distinct reference to the sea serpents as well as, possibly, to his cosmic baptism. Then he forcibly restrains the young wedding guest from crossing the threshold to the wedding party. Apparently the wedding guest is convinced to forsake marriage altogether. However, instead of turning to the homosexuality implied by the fused imagery of the crew and sea creatures, he opts for celibacy, as implied by his waking up alone the next morning, and probably all mornings thereafter, a sadder but supposedly wiser man.

In *Hamlet* (according to Ernest Jones, Shakespeare's most autobiographical play), tragic dénouement brings under control latent homosexual metaphors that are almost entirely out of control. These metaphors provide an almost infinite interplay of androgynous significations, only to be answered and denied by a tragic resolution that imposes homophobic retribution through the destruction of Hamlet as well as most everybody else. Because of the conventional dynamics of revenge tragedy, a positive-feedback metaphoric intensity expressive of gender confusion culminates in negative-feedback closure that confirms the tendency in a suicidal orgy of destruction that prevents its fulfillment. Homophobic demands finally prevail, but only because of Hamlet's self-destruction as a tragic hero unable to transcend the crisis implied by his use of images and metaphors. Like "The Ancient Mariner," *Hamlet* is an antiepithalamium, but the images and metaphors of role confusion must also be resolved by tragic action, and tragic closure both confirms and denies what has already been implied by metaphor. Like Coleridge's wedding guest, Hamlet allows himself to be steered away from marriage, but his choice bears mortal consequences, ultimately resulting in the destruction of his prospective wife, Ophelia, her entire family, the king and queen (the only married couple in the play), and himself. All vestiges of the nuclear family are terminated, but so, too, is Hamlet, the almost completely passive agent of their destruction. Unable to confront maturity, he fails both in satisfying his true father's demands and in escaping these demands well enough to survive the play.

Dominant throughout *Hamlet*, as W. H. Clemen maintains in *The Development of Shakespeare's Imagery*, are image clusters that seem to take on a life of their own.[6] But Clemen overlooks what we might call the sex nausea implicit in this imagery, which bears a very important role in helping to explain the relationships that transpire between the sexes over the duration of the play. One of the most frequently repeated images, for example, is of an infectious cavity, an ulcer filmed with skin "whiles rank corruption, mining all within, infects unseen." That this cavity is frequently associated with females suggests its cumulative significance as what might be described as a vaginal abscess, a central image of sexual disorientation from which many other metaphors of the play radiate in a multitude of displacements. References to an infected cavity proliferate and converge again in unexpected new combinations, often with the vehicle of one metaphor becoming the tenor of the next. This metaleptic complexity becomes as inclusive as the play itself, imposing open-system implications almost entirely out of control. For example, the cavity image extends from vaginal hell ("Rebellious hell, if thou canst mutiny in a matron's bones") to blackness ("that his soul may be as damned and black as hell, whereto it goes"), and thence to night, melancholy, and Hamlet's indecisiveness. It also extends from the symbolic pregnancy of Ophelia by Hamlet ("For if the sun breeds maggots in a dead dog") to the sun, light, death, and worms, and from there to flowers blighted by worms and holes in the ground penetrated by other burrowing creatures, such as the mole, rat, mouse, and fox. One of these, the mole, becomes a tragic flaw ("some vicious mole of nature") as well as the king's ghost when Hamlet exclaims, "Well said, old mole," suggesting his responsibility for Hamlet's indecision, at one level, at least, composing his tragic flaw.

Obsessive imagery of the ear also amplifies the image of the abscessed vagina, for example in the king's remark, "And wants not buzzers to infect his ear" or the queen's plea, "The words like daggers enter my ear." Other versions of this cavity include the nasty sty, the grave, the oven of the baker's daughter, the basket that tumbles a monkey to its destruction, and, of course, nothing, the suicidal possibility of extinction (a "not to be") that Hamlet finds between the legs of Ophelia. Hamlet amplifies upon this meaning when he expresses his disgust with Claudius—despite his crime, a good husband—by his cryptic remark, "The King is a thing," followed by his explanation, "Of nothing." The sword, dagger, cannonball, and even words, light, "offense's guilded hand," and the massy wheel of fortune drawn into a gulf of destruction are phallic instruments to penetrate this void. Moreover, the king declares the plot itself, both as story and conspiracy, to be an effort to penetrate it when he declares, "But, to the quick of the ulcer." Homosexual penetration is suggested when Hamlet says to Horatio, "Give me that man that is not passion's slave, and I will wear him in my heart's core—aye, in my heart of heart, as I do thee." Hamlet also taunts Claudius, "Nothing, but to show you how a king may go a progress through the guts of a beggar," having already described himself much earlier, "Beggar that I am." As opposed to Ophelia's recurring depiction as a helpless flower threatened by the worm, Hamlet is depicted as a dark mystery that others must try to penetrate. Even the situation of the play seems to feature the cavity metaphor. For example, the original crime was the pouring of poison into the king's ear. Similarly, the first scene begins with confused men standing on a vertical parapet in the midst of darkness, and the central conflict is brought to its climax in the "very witching time of night," when the king must cry out for light, having watched his crime reenacted. Later, Hamlet and Laertes are locked in struggle over Ophelia at the bottom of her empty grave, an abscessed cavity in the earth itself.

Metaphor has almost exhausted itself by act 5, when Claudius, rather than Hamlet, initiates the final catastrophe. By now Hamlet's identity crisis has been amply demonstrated by his inability to revenge his mother's seduction and his true father's death. He cannot shake off his melancholy and take the part of his father, as does Laertes, for example, in his eagerness to punish Hamlet for killing Polonius. For many critics, this reluctance seems to be Hamlet's essential flaw, but they overlook how it is clarified by the metaphors of sexual disorientation that assert Hamlet's fundamental problem and call for its rejection by means of tragic dénouement, as occurs in the final revenge tableau in which all the characters meet their destruction amid symbolism of the sword and chalice. Temptation and aversion culminate in the way characters meet their ends, and with whom. Not by accident Ophelia drowns alone in her garland of flowers, contrary to the fate of Juliet, Antigone, and other tragic heroes who somehow join their true lovers in death. Gertrude unwittingly takes poison, also a feminine death, but one that lets her share with Claudius the chalice supposedly intended for Hamlet. In contrast, Hamlet and Laertes use swords to envenom each other, and Hamlet dies in the arms of Horatio, to whom he has dedicated his heart of heart. Rosencrantz and Guildenstern are beheaded, likewise dying as a pair, so among the men, only Claudius is destroyed in full heterosexual fashion, by both the sword and the chalice, falling united with Gertrude in conjugal shame. A prototypical Oedipal breakdown emerges: the bad father compromises and then destroys his wife by trying to destroy her son, but at the same time her son revenges both his fallen mother and good father by killing the killer—his bad father, the patriarchal figure with whom he refuses to identify.[7] Not incidentally, all three parents are exterminated, and marriage itself—the ultimate proof of Hamlet's identification—has been disgraced.

In *Hamlet* as much as in any tragedy, unconscious needs are fulfilled in the very act of denying them through a tragic dénouement based on the conventional Renaissance equation between sex and death. Once marriage has been discredited and the bride-to-be isolated and driven to watery suicide, Hamlet is able to perish by Laertes, for Fortinbras, and in the arms of Horatio in what seems a triumph of latent homosexual catharsis. Unacknowledged, homosexuality is both consummated and rejected in this orgy of destruction. In effect, latent homosexuality revenges itself upon the nuclear family, but homophobic demands have also been met by Hamlet's suicidal acceptance of his fate. His victory compels his destruction, and flights of angels (like the Ancient Mariner's seraphim) sing him to his rest.

What makes Hamlet's ordeal particularly disturbing—verging on utter nihilism—is his rejection of both life itself and the possibility of his existence after death. He becomes not only an un-male, but an un-person, indeed an un-presence entirely obliterated from the physical universe. In the fullest sense of the word, he, more than Claudius, becomes a "thing of nothing." In his "To be, or not to be" soliloquy, which is deservedly famous but has a relationship to the rest of the play that otherwise seems undefinable, Hamlet uses metaphors describing death as an active quest ("take arms against a sea of troubles," etc.) as opposed to a passive, even masochistic, acceptance of life ("bear the whips and scorns of time," etc.). The reason he resigns himself to the burden of life, he claims, is that he cannot tell whether by dying he would totally perish or experience an afterlife (the dreams that would come "in that sleep of death")—an afterlife that presumably includes hell, since Hamlet expresses elsewhere his eagerness to consign Claudius's soul to this domain. In other words, the soliloquy declares that Hamlet would be entirely willing to die except that he fears punishment in an afterlife, "the undiscover'd country from whose bourn no traveler returns." At what seems the most basic level of interpretation, it is this suicidal ambivalence rather than Hamlet's delay that seems the thematic center of the play—the tragic flaw, or *hamartia*, that Hamlet cannot confront. The importance of this soliloquy is emphasized by its almost random location in the middle of the play. In quarto 1, it occurs in act 2, scene 2, and in both the film productions of Olivier and Zeffirelli it is switched to take place after Hamlet's encounter with Ophelia, in the first instance on a parapet, in the second in a crypt. In fact, it may be transferred almost anywhere in the action preceding act 3, scene 2, that the director might wish, its only requirement that it somehow be included, since it declares the before (or *hamartia*) of Hamlet's ordeal that must be answered and somehow denied by an after, the final revenge scene in which multiple killings preempt the necessity of suicide.

At the thematic level, Hamlet's tragic recognition—the answer, or *anagnorisis*, by which he rejects his earlier fears—must be extrapolated from his effort to discourage Horatio's suicide by telling him, "Absent thee from felicity awhile." Here the word *felicity* absolutely clashes with everything Hamlet concludes about death in his most famous soliloquy. With the word *felicity*, Hamlet rejects his earlier fears by suggesting that Horatio's suicide would bring pleasure instead of eternal punishment. But how would Hamlet characterize what he means by "felicity?" The answer comes in Hamlet's final line, "The rest is silence." Indeed, the rest of the play culminates in silence, since Hamlet will no longer be talking, and the rest of Hamlet's life will likewise be silence, and for the same reason. But even more important, the rest of Hamlet's existence—his afterlife—this, too, will consist of silence, the absence of language. For Hamlet, this is a major transformation, since his status and identity throughout the play almost entirely consist of words—in his words, "words, words, words"—and in a role to which Shakespeare devoted more language than for any of his other characters throughout his entire career. *Praxis* as behavior is obtained by others in the play, not by Hamlet, who does little more than aid them in bringing about their own destruction. Instead, Hamlet primarily dedicates himself to his words, his passionate rhetoric—this is his very *raison d'être*—so by implying his expectation that silence is his destiny after he dies, he is in effect denying his earlier fears of what might happen in an afterlife. No language: no existence, so his death becomes sheer felicity—exactly as he had hoped when he spoke of "a consummation devoutly to be wished." Hamlet covets extinction as his preference to the futile existence he has been living—his gender, his status, his mortal obligations. Horatio declares, "And flights of angels sing thee to thy rest," but these accompany him in his escape, and there is no guarantee of eternal life. "There are more things in heaven and earth, Horatio, than are dreamt of in your philosophy," but more, it turns out, is less—in fact, a something of nothing. The bitterness implicit in Hamlet's metaphors, his soliloquies, and angry repartee is finally resolved to the satisfaction of Hamlet and, in all candor, to the satisfaction of the audience as well, for he has altogether talked himself out. Hamlet's failure as a man, as a prince, as his father's problematic son dissolves into oblivion, his preferred choice. Negative feedback actually attains the nirvana Freud associated with the death instinct, testing the very limits of homeostasis. Some enjoy the play because Hamlet avenges himself, others because his revenge reverses *praxis*, making Hamlet's language, in its sheer virtuosity, the agent of dénouement, and still others because this virtuosity exhausts possibilities and is followed by silence.

Robert Frost was far more wary of unpleasant temptations than either Coleridge or Shakespeare. With wonderful skill he touched upon unconscious feelings without acknowledging them and then renounced his effort without admitting why he chose to do so. Usually he wavered between two alternatives, tantalizing himself and his readers with forbidden implications asserted by metaphor and imagery, but only to reject these for "good" reasons based on acquired rural profundity. Lawrance Thompson has said of Frost, "How to express and how to defend oneself became two inseparable themes for him."[8] Myth and tragedy are not brought into play, as in "The Rime of the Ancient Mariner" and *Hamlet*, but Frost's confessional approach permits a combination of defense and expressiveness that similarly advances from metaphoric parapraxis to its denial through thematic sagacity. First there is nostalgia for an inexplicably attractive earlier experience, and then it is rejected by a profound message of abstinence based on a closer examination of this experience. This shift from nostalgia to denial, somewhat akin to tragic recognition, is what gives Frost's poetry the effect of wisdom. He explores forbidden inclinations within the context of poetry and then denies them there as well. As opposed to Nietzsche's vision of tragedy, Frost briefly tests his Dionysian inclinations but finds good reasons for retreating to safety in the Apollonian world of appearances. Positive feedback primarily intrudes as a suggestion of possibilities to be denied by truths that guarantee intellectual repose. This pattern of discovery and denial can be attributed to a persona assumed for the occasion of the poem, but it is difficult to distinguish Frost's persona from the real poet who hides behind it.

Shakespeare, Coleridge, and Frost

Perhaps the most schematic example of this ambivalence can be found in "The Road Not Taken," in which Frost makes the ironic discovery that one pursuit must be forsaken to undertake the experience of another. He uses affectation ("I shall be telling this with a sigh") to suggest motives he cannot entirely accept, undoubtedly at the expense of Edward Thomas, a friend who often took him hiking in England. Thomas chose their trails, profusely apologizing for those they had to bypass, and Frost transforms this mannerism into ambivalent insight with universal significance pertaining to the different routes to be found through life.[9] In "Stopping by Woods on a Snowy Evening," Frost goes through the same steps by making the pragmatic decision to continue his course in life rather than letting himself freeze to death in the woods. In "After Apple-Picking," he similarly reconciles himself to imperfect harvests in which abortive projects must be sacrificed like bruised apples sent to the cider heap. And in "Birches," he nostalgically recalls his youthful solitude in nature before he was burdened by the inflexibility of his mature years. Masturbation is suggested by the game he describes of climbing birches, then bringing them down to earth, "the right place for love." Only later do girls provide the "truth" that "broke in" his fantasy world.[10]

Perhaps the most threatening latent implications may be found in "Mending Wall," which Frost featured as the initial poem of his first successful volume of poetry, *North of Boston*. As in "The Rime of the Ancient Mariner" and *Hamlet*, sexual ambivalence takes precedence, but with a happy ending guaranteed by the homoaversive symbolism of building and maintaining walls. The overt lesson (or message) is that generosity of spirit cannot be taken to an extreme through the loss of boundary between two men—hence the shared obligation of maintaining the wall or boundary that separates them, each working from his own side to keep it intact. Homosexuality cannot be acknowledged, much less fulfilled, so the wall must be retained to confirm the necessity of homoaversive denial. This dialectic interaction between metaphoric attraction and thematic revulsion is implicit throughout "Mending Wall." The two neighbors rebuilding the wall are constrained to "walk the line" parallel to each other, but they must also swing back and forth to fit stones together with shapes disconcertingly phallic ("And some are loaves and some so nearly balls"). Scattered stones must be heaped in a single pile, symbolizing close cooperation as well as the obstruction separating the two. It occurs to the poet that he might want to eliminate the wall, sacrificing its value as a cooperative endeavor in order to dispose of the social inhibitions it also represents. But he recognizes his neighbor would refuse, so he resigns himself to their isolation and the limited neighborly task of restoring the wall once a year.

Norman Holland has proposed that Frost's temporary inclination to break down the wall suggests the oral fixation to penetrate a veil of isolation and incorporate experience otherwise excluded from possibility.[11] But with what can the narrator achieve oral fusion if there is no wall? Nature is the same on both sides except for the apple and pine trees. The only major difference is the presence of the neighbor himself, so the question of fusion necessarily introduces the relationship between the two men. The wall that separates them also draws them together, if only once a year to maintain their independence by rebuilding it. The poet reflects for a moment that he might prefer eliminating the constraints between them, and then he just as quickly recognizes the imprudence of such a choice. Male bonding is repeatedly implied by an abundance of puns, images, metaphors, and grammatical ambiguities that are answered and resolved by emphasizing the value of barriers. Some of the poem's latent homosexual suggestiveness is possibly accidental, more the product of the explicator's imagination than the poet's. However, the connotations in other contexts seem plain, even blatant, and whenever these compound each other, it is difficult to establish where to draw the line.

The poem's metaphoric overdetermination begins with the first four lines, which may be interpreted as a scrambled invocation to the possibility of homosexual consummation:

> Something there is that doesn't love a wall,
> That sends the frozen-ground-swell under it,
> And spills the upper boulders in the sun;
> And makes gaps even two can pass abreast.

There has been much speculation about the significance of the word *something*. Existential and theological explanations have been offered, as well as the oral interpretation of Holland and the archetypal explanation proposed by Northrop Frye. None of these can be ruled out, but the latent implications of *thing* seem obviously phallic (like Coleridge's "all things both great and small" and Shakespeare's "thing of nothing"). In Frost's poem, *something* is capable of penetration, paradoxically as a denial of love, since "doesn't love" indicates both opposition to the wall and love's failure to break through this barrier. In the second line, the word *swell* implies masculine arousal; and since the frozen ground swell is commonly described in New England as a frost heave, the poet himself is implied to be aroused. The swell spreads *under* the wall, but with the "spilling" of the boulders, the phallic imagery is dislocated so the boulders no longer represent a surface penetrated but the act of penetration itself. That rocks are spilled "in the sun" also bears homosexual connotations based on the *sun-son* pun that is also employed in both *Hamlet* and "The Rime of the Ancient Mariner." In the fourth line, the "gaps" something "makes" also seem personified, as reinforced by the remark "two can pass abreast."

The double entendre of shared isolation is sustained throughout the rest of the poem with almost the proportions of allegory. Later the poet expresses his disgust with hunters who pursue "another thing," or perhaps whose "thing" prefers another object-choice, specifically the rabbit:

> The work of hunters is another thing:
> I have come after them and made repair
> Where they have left not one stone on a stone,
> But they would have the rabbit out of hiding,
> To please the yelping dogs.

Here the metaphor apparently shifts to heterosexual relations. A primordial insistence on dominance and the hunt is implied by helpless rabbits, guns more potent than rocks, and the bestial appetite of "yelping dogs" when they devour rabbits once flushed from their holes. Significantly, the hunters can "have" the rabbits only by leaving "not one stone on a stone," thereby undoing the work of the neighbors. Because of their destructiveness, hunters deny the ambivalence that haunts the narrator, but with the paradoxical result that they enable him to "come after them"—i.e., gain his own satisfaction after they do theirs. The awkward combination "made repair" may also be decomposed into two parts, "made" as a verb of seduction and "re-pair" as a reunion—possibly the reunion between the two neighbors, who have once again come to rebuild the wall. The destruction of rabbits had occurred in late fall, the season of death, but in the spring the poet once again calls his neighbor to their annual ritual of harvesting rocks. Once again they can resort to magic ("to use a spell to make them balance") in piling stone upon stone.

In lines 9–10 the poet suddenly shifts from "yelping dogs" to what seems more important to him, "the gaps, I mean," perhaps because it is the gaps that bring the neighbors together. In line 20 he says, "We wear our fingers rough with handling them," and then goes on to explain casually, "Oh, just another kind of out-door game, one on a side." Here the poet himself seems almost aware of what he was suggesting. In lines 24–26 he asserts that his personified apple trees ("and I am apple orchard") would not "eat the cones under his pines," though, vice versa, a threat merely suggested, the equally symbolic but less civilized pine trees ("he is all pine") might be inclined to devour his apples. Pinecones and apples again evoke the vertical displacement of loaves and balls. In line 27 Frost declares, "Spring is the mischief in me," implying that the season is internalized and to be discharged in a prohibited act of mischief. Such an act might involve jumping, as indicated by the pun *spring*, presumably over the wall to join his startled neighbor. To convey such an inclination to his neighbor is ambiguously described as "putting a notion in his head."

In lines 30–31 the poet argues that the two can safely eliminate the barrier between them because no cows are present (perhaps a reference to women as mothers), leaving the two neighbors unobserved by spectators. In line 34 he resorts to another pun, saying that before he built a wall he would want to know "to whom I was like to give offence." The last word is clearly divisible into the phrase *a fence*—suggesting, as Holland indicates, that he wouldn't want to fence his neighbor out. In line 36 he speculates that whatever it is that could lead his neighbor to overcome his inhibitions might be identified as elves. But then he makes it a point to qualify himself, "But it's not elves exactly." Instead, the word fairies comes to mind, a pejorative reference to homosexuals. Coincidentally, elves and fairies also suggest Coleridge's "seraphim" and Hamlet's "flights of angels." Frost also associates elves with fairies in at least two other poems, "Mowing" and "Spoils of the Dead." In the latter he identifies himself with a corpse in the woods, whose ring and chain lying beside him are "glittering *things*" (italics added) removed to "play with" by creatures interchangeably described as both elves and fairies.[12]

The poet also admonishes the personified stones, "Stay where you are until our backs are turned," and finally says of his silent neighbor, who seems attractive but terrible with a stone in each hand, that "he will not go behind his father's saying," though he "moves in darkness" where such inclinations might be fulfilled. Here the paternal wisdom offensive to the poet suggests homophobic demands connected with the Oedipus complex. The neighbor speaks with partriarchal authority because, unlike Hamlet, he fully identifies with his father (both in his good and bad personae), and consequently with his lineage of fathers receding into a prehistory characterized by darkness. He has successfully internalized his father's wisdom, which the poet finds it difficult to do, affording his mysterious appeal to the poet, who is separated by a wall from the right choice but knows that to cross the wall is the wrong choice. Still, it is the poet's whim to do so, and he must be discouraged by guilt feelings without the benefit of being able to call them his own.

The issue of unresolved Oedipal identification explains the poem's homosexual ambivalence as well as its basically paranoid displacements of denial and projection (it's the neighbor's decision, not his) for suppressing this anxiety. In *Hamlet*, Oedipal crisis is dealt with by splitting the good father and the bad father, the latter coincidentally a good husband; and in "The Ancient Mariner," it is symbolized by the cosmic struggle between the sun's paternal authority and absolution through the power of the moon, a conflict resolved by the mariner's preference for universal love at the expense of marriage. Frost likewise grapples with filial ambivalence, but he comes up with entirely different results, since the tried and true filial relationship is projected to his neighbor on the other side, while its difficulties are represented by his frustrated wish to reach out to him, a fused inclination that combines homosexual attraction with the homophobic restraint that prevents consummation.

The thematic resolution of "Mending Wall" denies its metaphoric implications by means of the conventional paradox that the poet's shared experience with his neighbor actually divides them. Frost concludes by quoting his neighbor's truism to the effect that "good fences make good neighbors," letting it speak for itself as well as implying its perhaps more significant obverse principle—that *good* neighbors make good fences. Yet the line's repetition and the emphasis of its terminal position leave us with no alternative conclusion. The first line has also been repeated, so there is a narrative transition from its stressed exploratory willingness ("something there is," etc.) to the inhibition of the last line, which is more decisive in its commitment to maintaining effective barriers. The possibilities of each are explored by the poet, but in the end restraint overrides exploratory freedom. The two men figuratively "meet," as Frost declares in line 13, but in the shared task of rebuilding a wall to keep them apart. They "make good" by constructing effective barriers ("good" fences) to preserve their virtue. Moral *de-fenses* thereby guarantee moral relationships, allowing the not quite liberated poet to accept with thankfulness his neighbor's inhibitions. His poetic sensibility led him astray for a moment, but it brings him back again to the primitive universal truth evident to his neighbor all along, and with the additional profundity available to a poet. In fact, it is poetry that helps him to recover his equanimity by sublimating his ambivalence within the safe context of theme and metaphor. His strategy of expressive form has encouraged him to test edges and then to back off again, with good reasons for doing so and without having directly confronted the question. Even his renunciation is unacknowledged.

But an additional dimension of complexity must be taken into account, since Frost does not seem to have suffered from acute latent homosexual anxieties. Few of his other poems imply sexual ambivalence, at least to this degree. Beyond his strong attachment to his mother, there seem to be no reports, either published or unpublished, that would suggest latent feminine identification strong enough to have obliged this degree of compensatory homophobic denial.[13] Consequently, we may speculate that the sexual ambivalence of "Mending Wall" was probably triggered by particular circumstances associated with Napoleon Guay (pronounced *gay*), Frost's French-Canadian neighbor at Derry, New Hampshire, with whom Frost once rebuilt a wall separating their property. It was undoubtedly Guay who was depicted as Frost's taciturn neighbor on the other side of the wall. However, Guay's personality was, if anything, excessively friendly rather than reclusive, as would be suggested by his depiction in the poem. Lawrance Thompson's biography of Frost suggests, in fact, that the relationship between Frost and Guay in real life exactly reversed their relationship in the poem. Throughout their experience as neighbors, Guay was persistent in his "continuing and friendly assistance" despite Frost's aloofness. Guay often dropped by to visit and just as often invited Frost and his family to visit, but Frost never reciprocated with similar visits and invitations of his own. Once Guay crept up behind Frost to catch his ax in midair while he was chopping wood—a remarkable gesture of physical superiority—then held the ax back while lecturing Frost about its use. It seems Guay posed a continuing threat to Frost's privacy and compensatory sense of masculine sufficiency.

In "Mending Wall," Frost apparently responded to this threat by switching roles, giving each the persona of the other. In a complicated exchange of identities, he attributed his own reserve to his neighbor and accepted for himself the onus of excessive friendliness.[14] The behavior of Guay brought carefully guarded and perhaps dormant homosexual anxieties to the threshold of recognition, to which Frost reacted with defensive irony by writing as if he himself contemplated the elimination of barriers. His expansiveness could thus be rejected by exactly the individual who caused him this anxiety. Frost then gave literary validity to the transposition by conventionalizing their roles. He became effusively imaginative in his borrowed identity, as might be expected of a poet, while attributing his own reservations to his neighbor as a romanticized New England intractability. His inhibition became his neighbor's patriarchal authority, asserted in a single truism that fixed the boundaries beyond which they could not transgress. However, in his poetic license he transcended these boundaries anyway—the ironic necessity of his task—by merging their identities. Only Frost-Guay could reject Guay-Frost, supposedly to put an end to the matter in a poetry of renunciation, but with affirmation at least in identity confusion. Frost is quoted by C. L. Barber and cited by Holland as once having confided, "As if I weren't on *both* sides of the wall!" Divided by a wall, one identity could respond to the appeal made by the other with a supposedly self-sufficient truism rejecting unconscious feelings too dangerous to acknowledge.

The American public has revered Frost, this century's most important hearthside poet, but without taking into account the undercurrent of needs and inhibitions in his poetry. "Mending Wall" in particular has been widely appreciated for its innocence as a transcendental inquiry into the meaning of barriers. Once deciphered, however, the mystery on the other side poses a challenge to innocence so threatening that even its rejection cannot be acknowledged. An ambivalent restraint emerges which is fully as complicated as that in the verse of Donne and Marvell, or of Wallace Stevens and Hart Crane. Frost's poem explores a doubly inverted theme of homosexual courtship denied and draws upon the American archetype of pastoral fraternity that Leslie Fiedler has found between Natty Bumppo and Chingachgook, Ishmael and Queequeg, Huckleberry Finn and Jim. Here, though, virginal friendship is challenged by imagery, figuration, organ speech, puns both intentional and unintentional, and every other conceivable use of language to complicate the landscape of Frost's imagination. The transitory inclination to tear down a wall gives place to the decision to retain the wall as a barrier, but without necessarily clarifying what it defends against. *Animus* is isolated from *anima*, the poet from his neighbor, and ultimately the two of them from us, the readers, because we cannot quite penetrate the secret of their unfulfilled tableau. The account of two *men doing* a wall (hence, "men-*ding* wall") introduces ambiguities that it takes forty-five lines to explore and deny—thus the fascination of Frost's poem, which seems to have been composed and revised at the brink of consciousness.

five

THE PARANOID DIALECTIC

Simon Lesser's notion that readers analogize by drawing comparisons between fiction and their own lives is best understood not as their introjection of literary experience, as Holland has proposed, but as their projection of themselves into literary experience to share in its accomplishment.[1] As Lesser indicates, readers put themselves into a work of fiction rather than incorporating it into their personalities as a temporary "subsystem." They do not absorb stories—they become absorbed by them. Their purpose in doing this, I claim, is to enjoy fiction's transition from dissatisfaction to satisfaction—a purpose compelling enough that they gladly devote their attention to any story that features such a transition without offending their taste and values.

We can observe this pursuit of fictive change, for example, when we turn on a television program in the middle of an episode. Our eagerness to be swept into its forward momentum becomes evident as we seek out those clues and fragments that expose the essential conflict and the prospects of resolution. With whom can we identify? Who are the bad guys? What are the problems to be solved? What virtues assure eventual success? These are the questions that draw us into the unfolding story. The same search behavior occurs when we start reading a novel or poem in the middle. At every level of sophistication, we seek a suitable outcome, and its appeal depends on promised improvements that are flattering to our sense of personal worth. The benign traits we think we possess we can project upon heroes, while those we cannot acknowledge offer almost as much satisfaction once projected upon villains to be defeated, or, at perhaps a greater level of abstraction, upon discordant relationships to be harmoniously resolved. As a general rule, we take pleasure in literary experience as long as the virtues we can identify with prevail at the expense of our projected weaknesses. By analogizing in this fashion, we improve our attitude toward ourselves, and without necessarily recognizing that we have been trying to do so.

Of all the more global psychological disorders that have been explored to help clarify this projective dimension of literary experience, paranoia is probably the most relevant. A superficial resemblance between fiction and paranoia has often been noted, and, in fact, both depend on the same basic psychological displacements that Freud emphasized in his original definition of paranoia.[2] Like fiction, Freud's model of paranoid consciousness features self-deception, which combines the projection and denial displacements but in a reversed sequence—one that both begins and culminates in denial. With paranoia, hostility is projected against others perceived as enemies; with fiction, individuals project themselves into a story to share in the pursuit of acceptable alternatives—and without necessarily encountering enemies. As Freud explained, the paranoid man harbors delusions of persecution in order to cope with latent homosexual tendencies too threatening to acknowledge. He disavows these tendencies first by denying his attraction ("I am not drawn to this man; in fact I hate him") and then by projecting his homophobic revulsion ("It's not that I hate him—rather, he hates me"). Subsequently he dedicates himself to the gathering of evidence to confirm his suspicion, thereby reinforcing his suppression of his feelings. Freudian doctrine traces the paranoid tendency in women to either homosexual or heterosexual ambivalence, in the latter instance with this particular sequence: "I do not want to submit to this man; in fact I hate him," followed by, "but I'm not unjustified in hating him, since his sexual designs are repulsive and basically hostile." Needless to say, both the heterosexual and homosexual versions of paranoia are often justified—partly because paranoid individuals seek out hostile relationships in the first place, but also because their relentless vigilance even further aggravates these relationships through the dynamics of prophecy fulfillment by which others play the role one expects them to play. Although recent research shows that many instances of paranoia do not stem from sexual repression, the syndrome may be broadly defined as the use of a double displacement combining denial and projection to reject the possibility of masochistic acquiescence to others in a dominant or potentially dominant position. Its tandem sequence combines denial ("I do not want to be submissive to them; in fact I resist their authority") and projection ("It's not that I'm unjustified, since they are plotting to conquer and destroy me"). This second displacement necessarily obliges proof that a conspiracy has transpired, so potentially delusional experience becomes useful in buttressing the necessary supportive evidence. And once again prophecy fulfillment becomes useful, since anybody may be steered into playing out a role as a despicable antagonist. Fortunately, this degenerative pattern of hatred is to a large extent eliminated from fiction, where problems can be resolved rather than obsessively cultivated with an emphasis upon personal victimization.

Comparable to Freud's transactional model of paranoia is the homeostatic sequence proposed by David Swanson, Philip Bohnert, and Jackson Smith in their psychiatric reference book *The Paranoid*.[3] They explain paranoia as a dangerous but useful coping mechanism for reducing unmanageable anxiety levels by means of a six-stage progression from anxiety to the homeostatic relief provided by paranoid delusion. In its simplest outline, this advancement begins with a rejection of any personal responsibility, followed by bewilderment and scanning for an external cause (the acute phase), and finally tension reduction through projecting responsibility onto others (the chronic phase). The parallel features of Freud's model and that of Swanson, Bohnert, and Smith are diagrammed in table 2. Stages 1 to 4 loosely represent the acute phase of paranoia and stages 5 and 6 its chronic phase. At first glance this overall sequence might seem different from Freud's model, but its six stages may be more inclusively grouped as a double displacement of denial (stages 2 to 4) and projection (stages 5 and 6). Swanson et al.'s model is more elaborate than Freud's, and there is no necessary connection to sexual resentment. Otherwise, essentially the same process is described.

As defined by both models, paranoia's denial-projective displacement strategy bears a close similarity to the dynamics of literary response if and when readers bring their deepest anxieties under control by projecting them into a fictive context that serves to deny them. Something akin to a paranoid strategy emerges in the reading experience whenever conflict-dominated fantasies are evoked to relieve anxiety. As in the case of paranoia, the quest for tension reduction justifies a substitution of projective fantasies for a more

TABLE 2. *Parallel Features of Models of Paranoia*

	Cognitive	Economic	Transactional
1.	Perception of pronounced change or threatening feeling	Disequilibrium	Something is wrong.
2.	Unexplainable on the basis of previous experience, or intolerable to the self	Denial	It's not me.
3.	Psychological disequilibrium experienced as bewilderment		
4.	Scanning for explanation (tendency to use projection)	Scanning	Then what is it? (3 and 4)
5.	Identifying an external cause (paranoid conclusion)	Projection	It's them!
6.	Psychological equilibrium	Paranoid stability	So I'm O.K. if only they would treat me right.

direct approach to problem solving that might lead to further complications. In both instances, individuals depend on illusion to obtain gratification without confronting their real feelings.

The relative harmlessness of fiction at least partly results, I suspect, from fiction's reversed sequence in combining the denial and projective displacements. In the case of paranoia, denial initiates evasiveness as an internal rejection of masochistic tendencies, after which the projective displacement dominates in the effort to translate guilt and inhibition into a righteous sense of persecution. In the case of fiction, the effective use of the denial displacement

The Paranoid Dialectic

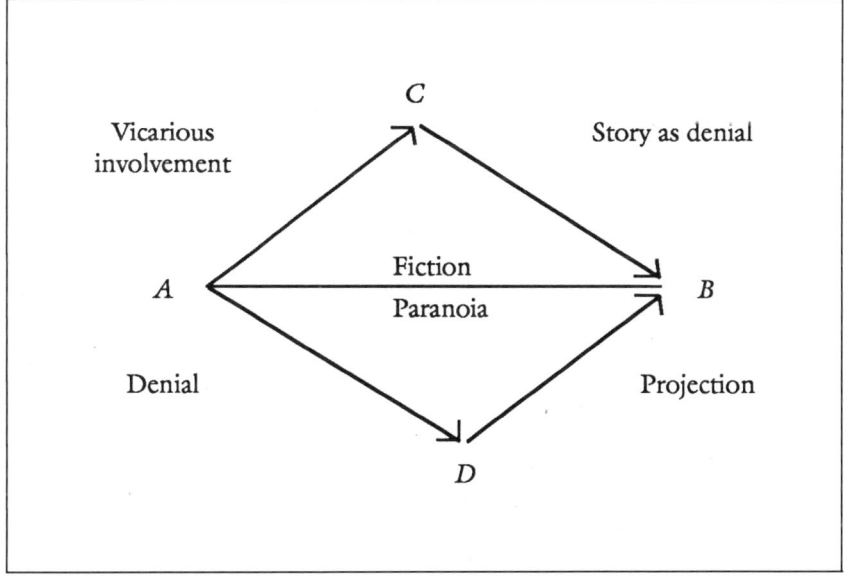

FIGURE 2. *Displacement diagram*

is both postponed and harnessed through plot's linear advancement from one state of affairs to its opposite. As a result, the reader's role can be relatively passive, since fiction itself incorporates denial into its momentum toward closure. Readers need only to project themselves into a story in order to benefit from its achievement as an act of denial independent of their real-life circumstances. The substitution that occurs in these final two stages of displacement is diagrammed in figure 2. If the horizontal advancement AB represents a direct homeostatic reduction of anxiety typical of normal problem solving, ADB represents its reduction through paranoid delusion and ACB its reduction through literary experience. Both depend on the mixture of denial and projection, but fiction's inverted arrangement seems more flexible, since a greater variety of projected feelings can be brought under control by narrative form as the second stage of displacement. Usually, in fact, the normal vicarious involvement of readers lets them choose what is to be denied, a freedom exceeding the relatively narrow spectrum of anxieties tied in with paranoid defensiveness.

It is important to recognize here that for fiction as well as for paranoia the projective displacement necessarily originates in denial, as maintained by

The Paranoid Dialectic

Robert Waelder, but the paranoid denial-projective sequence is enlarged by fiction both to begin and end with denial.[4] The initial rejection of anxiety is obtained by focusing upon the relatively harmless aim of identifying with fictional characters, whereupon narrative form intervenes as the culminating agent of denial. Sandwiched between the reader's personal choice to obtain denial and the text's function as an agent of narrative denial, the projective displacement mediates the experience of fiction as the vehicle of denial—in effect, its agent, the *praxis* that makes it happen (*mimesis* as *praxis*, as opposed to the *praxis* it imitates). In other words, readers first deny their circumstances by projecting themselves into fiction, and then fiction completes the denial displacement by its affirmative resolution. With paranoia, the rigid and simplistic quest for victory over enemies justifies one's delusions of crisis and relentless struggle; with fiction, a more inclusive narrative momentum literally plots denial once readers can involve themselves in its linear advancement from search behavior to accomplishment. More or less fixed in its locus as the initial displacement of paranoia, the denial displacement becomes the final and crowning achievement of fiction by organizing the unity of action defined by Aristotle. As a result, the experience of fiction remains flexible and relatively healthy compared to paranoia itself.

I should also emphasize that the paranoid dynamics of fiction offer little appeal to victims in the advanced stages of paranoid decompensation. These individuals are frequently too wrapped up in their own difficulties to be able to identify with literary characters. On the other hand, literary illusion seems altogether accessible to readers who are relatively free of paranoid tendencies, able to relax and share in narrative experience without granting it total credibility. They may experience considerable anxiety in their personal lives, but they recognize the destructiveness of projective strategies that have not been packaged by narrative form. Instead of cultivating hostile relationships, they turn to fiction, whose temporary demands let them escape delusional extravagance that might be harmful to their relationships with others. While paranoid individuals incessantly brood over their victimization, normal readers harbor relatively benign anxieties and dissatisfactions that can be eliminated by a conventional sense of an ending. As opposed to the obsessive recapitulation of grievances typical of paranoid delusion, fiction focuses and discharges tensions on a voluntary basis and with much greater variation from text to text. Fiction appeals to readers because it affords provisional gratification that is unlikely to overwhelm them in their own rationalizations. Its sedative effect may be compared with that of aspirin rather than that of an opiate or major surgery.

However, as I earlier indicated, many resemblances between fiction and the paranoid syndrome cannot entirely be ignored. Just as delusions of persecution work as a coping mechanism to minimize anxieties, the suspension of disbelief puts most readers in a better-managed world of fantasy that successfully distracts them from their chronic everyday problems. Just as the victim of paranoia resorts to an elaborate reconstruction of experience to gain control over an emotional crisis, readers turn to fiction so as to share in its better and more exciting reconstruction of experience. For both fiction and paranoia, an unrealistic conflict is intensified and elaborated in order to deal with genuine anxieties that may otherwise be difficult to suppress. In each instance fantasy becomes a coping mechanism to reduce anxieties without disclosing their source in personal inadequacy.

As perhaps to be expected, a variety of widely accepted literary conventions suggest the paranoid syndrome. The tendency may be recognized whenever a story, novel, play, or poem depends on a heightened sense of conflict and intense motivation to bring this conflict to its resolution. Also paranoid is fiction's subordination of personality to a relatively simplistic question of intentions. As Aristotle recommended, character is reduced to the agency of action, thereby sacrificing individuation to the use of recognizable stereotypes and archetypes. As Northrop Frye has suggested, these stereotypes and archetypes relieve us from the strain of trying to be fair-minded. Also paranoid is fiction's mixed insensitivity and "hyperalertness" to the hidden implications of human conduct. Fiction features remarkable discoveries and sudden insights at the expense of a balanced perceptiveness typical of normal social adjustment. Likewise paranoid are fiction's simplistic ethical distinctions between good and evil, between friends and enemies, and between moral deficiency and just restitution. Whenever ethics is invoked to project guilt rather than acknowledging it, a surplusage of paranoia may be assumed additional to the paranoid organization of experience harnessed by literary form.

Other literary conventions illustrate fiction's indebtedness to paranoia:

Like paranoia, fiction resolves personal conflict by fixing the blame on villains and adverse circumstances. Extropunitive motivation focuses and diverts the reader's attention from nonspecific anxieties to concrete problems that can be effectively resolved.

The Paranoid Dialectic

Like paranoia, fiction exaggerates cause and effect relationships among people. As a result, heroes are more virtuous than usual and villains more villainous.

Like paranoia, fiction is obsessed with justifiable causes, with victims and their saviors. It flourishes in its role as an "injustice collector" pitted against crime, sin, vulgarity, etc.

Like paranoia, fiction thrives on crisis. Each work of fiction resolves its crises, but literary tradition as a whole returns time and again to the same problems and the same formulaic coping mechanisms for dealing with them.

Like paranoia, fiction tends to dispense with compromise. Trade-offs might seem possible in the early stages of a story, but they are usually eliminated through narrative closure. Instead of concessions, a clear-cut victory is both sought and gained.

Like paranoia, fiction tends to dispose of confusion. If and when there is ambivalence or complexity, it is preliminary to the attainment of new and greater clarification.

Like paranoia, fiction puts intricacy in the service of desirable conclusions. Nothing is purely accidental. Everything is deciphered relative to the necessary final reckoning.

Like paranoia, fiction is capable of homicide—both by characters and by authors able to do as they please with their characters. Death is much more frequent in fiction than in our daily lives, inflicted by both heroes and villains. When dying is supposedly natural, the author alone becomes the agent of homicide.

Like paranoia, fiction often puts individuals at the mercy of cosmic forces beyond their control—religious, political, extraterrestrial, etc.

Like paranoia, fiction thrives on bizarre theories of apocalypse and divine intervention. Its often pathological religious tendencies have been amply documented by sympathetic exegetical interpretations of Dante, Milton, Blake, and a host of other authors.

Like paranoia, fiction gives centrality to a character who is nearly always at stage center where important things can be expected to happen. This central role is equally important for poets who draw upon their personal experience to generalize about the human condition.

Like paranoia, fiction pits a pseudocommunity of enemies against the hero. It also creates a pseudocommunity of friends whose interests are protected by the hero.[5]

Like paranoia, fiction exaggerates stereotypical role differences between the sexes. The masculine paranoid imagination divides women into devouring temptresses and/or women on pedestals who accept their subservient virginity. The feminine version reduces masculine behavior to a comparable spectrum of stereotypes from rapist aggressors to tame and harmless brother or father figures.

Like paranoia, fiction resorts to convincing but simplistic "real" truths and clues to these real truths (epiphanies, revelations, etc.) that mask the more fundamental deception involved.

Like paranoia, fiction expresses an ambivalent authoritarianism. There is fierce commitment to personal freedom, yet narrative form imposes its own rigid and conventional standards of behavior.

Like paranoia, fiction engages in elaborate self-justification. This is obvious in its meticulous documentation of behavior to rationalize its dispensation of rewards and punishment. It takes great pains to clarify why characters deserve what they get.

Like paranoia, fiction parades its honesty by means of overabundant documentation. There is an obsessive use of concrete detail to justify its biased vision of human behavior.

Like paranoia, fiction depends upon the *folie à deux* (or, more accurately, the *folie collective*), a delusional system fabricated by the author to be shared with sympathetic readers.

Like paranoia, fiction imposes an inflexible context of meaning, the text as meticulously organized by its author—exactly identical, word for word, every time we return to it.

Finally, like paranoia, fiction offers an "unshakable delusional system," a complete story that is credible and coherent and that effectively obliges the suspension of disbelief among its sympathetic readers.

The Paranoid Dialectic

The resemblances between fiction and paranoia are manifold, especially in the movies and the pulp fiction that appeal to mass audiences. As seems obvious today, the more paranoid the organization of a story, the more likely its appeal to readers. Those who find satisfaction in it are not necessarily paranoid themselves, but they do benefit from a denial-projective organization of fantasy content that bears obvious resemblances to paranoid delusion.

The central role of denial that I am proposing here as the central displacement of both paranoia and literary form reverses the negative function of art as explained by Keats's notion of negative capability and by the dialectic theories of aesthetics that define negativity as a radical expressiveness that transcends orthodox social constraints.[6] Quite the opposite, I am suggesting that fiction subordinates this presumably negative expressiveness to the more basic function of denial or negation as an avoidance strategy typical of conventional authoritarianism (*Doxa*, as discussed in chapter 8). As Freud explains, "Negation [or denial] is, at a higher level, a substitute for repression," for it "is a way of taking account of what is repressed; indeed, it is actually a removal of the repression, though not, of course, an acceptance of what is repressed."[7] In fiction, denial predominates by acting out the elimination of unacceptable experience. Since expressiveness plays a relatively fugitive role in eluding (or denying) this objective, a dialectic interplay may be expected between these complementary alternatives of experience, as explained by Engels's concept of *Negationsnegierung*. Fiction's presumably negative creativity—i.e., its spontaneity and freedom of expression—can be tolerated because these are ultimately denied by means of narrative closure. Certain passages might suggest Keats's negative capability, as exemplified by bizarre images and strikingly unconventional standards, but narrative momentum brings these under control by means of an acceptable sense of ending. Particular figures and metaphors might deny orthodox social expectations, but these in turn are denied by conventional form. Whatever negative expressiveness entails is itself negated by the stronger and more inclusive process of denial, since local contexts are absorbed and reversed by narrative closure.

The model I am proposing also complicates Norman Holland's explanation of form as a defense against unconscious fantasy content. Holland maintains that literary experience appeals to readers because of its compromise formation between fantasy and fantasy management, the latter as structured by form.[8] Fantasies, rather than needs and anxieties, are treated as the problem, even though needs and anxieties are usually the cause of fantasies. In

The Paranoid Dialectic

effect, we entertain fantasies to cope with our needs and anxieties. In contrast, the paranoid model of literary form that I am proposing integrates form and fantasy by explaining form as the organization of fantasy content in order to reduce anxieties. Specifically, it is anxiety, not fantasy, that provokes denial, and fantasy itself is actually structured, or plotted, by form as a more sophisticated use of denial to bring anxiety under control. One side of the equation comprises the anxiety that needs to be diminished, and the other comprises fantasy as organized by form to bring this about. As in the case of paranoia, form organizes fantasy as a version of events whose outcome affords self-justification, thereby reducing anxiety levels.

Similar to the model I am proposing is Kenneth Burke's explanation of form as "an arousement and fulfillment of desires . . . the creation of an appetite in the mind of the auditor, and the adequate satisfying of that appetite"; as Burke explained, this satisfaction "involves a temporary set of frustrations, but in the end these frustrations prove to be simply a more involved kind of satisfaction and furthermore serve to make the satisfaction of fulfillment more intense."[9] I agree with Burke's explanation, but with the caveat that his "involved kind of satisfaction" results from self-deception based on the paranoid double displacement that combines denial and projection. Burke also describes linear advancement as literary form, though it seems more useful to limit this role to plot, reserving to literary form the overarching dialectic interaction between plot's forward inertia and countervailing metaphoric expressiveness. Metaphors disclose frustrations, plot diminishes them, and form articulates and gives definition to the dialectic interaction between the two. Literary form's final importance depends on integrating the input-output dynamics at work between these two basic vectors of literary experience.

As indicated earlier, plot denies by mediating the transition from free-floating anxieties to a relatively simplistic resolution. The reader's multiple uncertainties can be focused on a one-dimensional advancement from problem to solution, from nonspecific conative alertness to a gratifying if misleading sense of an ending. Such a transition is almost painfully obvious in potboiler novels and movies that generate apprehension to be dispelled through victory against stereotypical villains. But the same transition also occurs in high art—for example, in romantic odes in which uncertainty is resolved by means of insight and spiritual rejuvenation and in sonnets in which the octave's romantic despair is effectively answered by the sestet's counterstatement of stoic acceptance. Here, too, the plot consists of a linear advancement from the acknowledgment of problems to a renewed sense of adequacy. Explained in Aristotelian terms, the plot creates a unity of action by making its transition from beginning to end, as clarified by Gerald Else's notion of advancement from *hamartia* (or flaw) to *anagnorisis* (or discovery) and as clarified by Hegel's notion of advancement from abstraction (partial truth) to absolute knowledge (the whole truth).[10] However, contrary to Else's model, the pattern applies to all fiction, not merely to tragedy, and, contrary to both Else's and Hegel's models, it features deception instead of the truth. If anything, it progresses from potential accessibility to the whole truth to those partial truths that help to drive the most offensive aspects of the whole truth further from consciousness.

Sometimes plot's negative advancement is difficult to recognize, but it plays a decisive role in determining the shape and control of virtually all fiction. An apparent exception that illustrates plot's importance as denial is Gertrude Stein's "a rose is a rose is a rose is a rose," discussed in chapter 1. Another is Ezra Pound's equally famous poem, "In a Station of the Metro":

> The apparition of these faces in the crowd;
> Petals on a wet, black bough.

How can there be any plot to these fourteen words? Close examination, however, reveals two noun phrases, the second of which acknowledges the misanthropy implicit in the first. Pound himself claimed that he tried to express in his poem his sense of wonder when he had seen some beautiful faces one day at a subway entrance.[11] However, his appreciation of these faces seems obviously counterbalanced by the potentially ominous image of a "wet, black bough." In a complicated reversal, the funneled darkness of the subway is turned inside out by the glistening bark of a wet branch. The subway's dark interior from which the crowd is flowing has been inverted to become the image of a bough that brings life to the flowers growing on it. Like flower petals, the human faces seem blank, delicate, and harmless, but they are obviously nourished and interconnected by biological and potentially disgusting forces bigger than themselves. The frail, misguided individualism implied by the petals is possible only because of shared nourishment from the bough, which is also attractive, but for different reasons, as implied by its aesthetic contrast. The poet's wonderment at commuters spilling from a subway entrance thus puts the crowd in its place—ephemeral, yet organic—no less victimized by its bovine proclivities than the crowd, or social horde, described, for example, in Gustav LeBon's *The Crowd*, which was popular at the time Pound wrote his poem. How, then, does such a vision distort the truth? One need only take into account the humanist perspective of Pound's contemporaries, such as Shaw, H. G. Wells, and Sidney and Beatrice Webb. Just as a rose is *more* than a rose, faces in a crowd are *more* than petals on a wet black bough. In both instances, the personification of flowers aestheticizes to simplify the human condition.

In those rare examples of poetry in which less narrative transition is detectable, such as concrete poetry, there is at least negative movement from the context of language to the silence following it. As a model of concrete poetry, I offer this:

$$\text{noise noise noise} \longrightarrow \text{the rest is silence}$$

This has virtually the same aftereffect as the image of a haiku, which resists being forgotten in the moments that follow. The transition that occurs is important, albeit subtle and hardly detectable. In his popular text *How Does a Poem Mean?* John Ciardi argues that every poem has a major fulcrum that divides its statement from its counterstatement.[12] The transition from one side of this fulcrum to the other constitutes a plot, since there is advancement from one plateau to another. A linear and one-dimensional progress takes place from expectation to closure, from *A* to *not A*, culminating in a resolution that denies and thereby designifies preliminary uncertainties.

Plot's movement toward gratification may be strenuously resisted by a variety of truths that defy simplistic resolution. Whenever confusion arises, or ambivalence, or the concession to exceptions, the progressive momentum of plot expressive of the denial displacement is impeded, and the resulting complexity appeals to serious readers. As Robert Penn Warren maintained: "[A] poem, to be good, must earn itself. It is a motion toward a point of rest, but if it is not a resisted motion, it is a motion of no consequence."[13] Northrop Frye concurs: "What corresponds to content is the sense of otherness, the resistance of the material, the feeling that there is something to be overcome, or at least struggled with."[14] J. Hillis Miller mentions fiction's "nagging loose ends" that keep the narrative from reaching "final clarity."[15] And Roland Barthes explains this interaction as a linguistic strategy:

> [W]hereas the sentences quicken the story's "unfolding" and cannot help but move the story along, the hermeneutic code performs an opposite

action: it must set up *delays* (obstacles, stoppages, deviations) in the flow of the discourse; its structure is essentially reactive, since it opposes the ineluctable advance of language with an organized set of stoppages.[16]

All serious fiction, in fact, seems to be dominated by the negative tension between motion and countermotion, i.e., between demands for acceptable closure and a nagging awareness of its impediments. The author must justify closure by overcoming these impediments. Rivals, enemies, hostile prospective fathers-in-law, etc., must be defeated, but, even more important, the constantly varying blend of latent implications that challenges plot's forward momentum must be brought to the surface in order to be denied, as I demonstrated in chapter 4. The more powerful the obstructive features, the more likely the forward momentum must be exaggerated to dispose of them. This struggle finally ends, as with the example of *Hamlet*, in silence, the psychic space that follows successful closure, but only because of plot's conditional victory as guaranteed by the conventional dynamics of fiction.

Metaphor epitomizes the resistance to plot's linear organization of experience, since it can project a full spectrum of personal feelings relatively unfettered by conscious restraint, as demonstrated by the texts of Shakespeare, Coleridge, and Frost discussed in chapter 4. As positive feedback, a metaphor's projective capacity disrupts expectations by suggesting open-system relationships at odds with narrative closure. Like dream symbolism, its image (or vehicle) conveys latent implications that express an ambivalence and complex motivation to be harnessed and eventually denied by the momentum toward a suitable resolution. According to Umberto Eco, any sign substitutes and therefore potentially lies.[17] As signification, a metaphor necessarily distorts the truth, but it also helps to convey the truth since it doubles signification, its image (or vehicle) intervening between the *signified* and *signifiers* of words. As opposed to the "sign situation" of a simple word—an idea represented by its sign—a metaphor expands to include three members: (1) an idea expressed by (2) an image represented by (3) a sign. The eidetic spectrum of possibilities implicit in the image, plus the necessary additional step in the dynamics of representation, gives metaphor an expressive freedom that increases the possibility of exposing, or leaking, the truth in its fullest and most dangerous implications. On the one hand, metaphor's conscious tenor helps to convey experience obviously supportive of the plotted chain of events dominated by wish fulfillment, but on the other its latent sugges-

The Paranoid Dialectic

tiveness at least temporarily undermines this linear advancement. Thus the dialectic between metaphor and plot. If metaphor confesses anxiety, plot denies it; if metaphor implies unacceptable feelings, plot, like paranoia, represses these by diverting the reader's attention to a conflict that can be brought to its satisfactory resolution. The more unacceptable the feelings to be denied, the more aggressive the use of plot for this purpose.

When the dialectic between plot and metaphor becomes particularly intense, plot actually takes on the role of metonymy that *designifies* metaphor, since its deferment of signification until closure lets it deny the existence of its antecedent (after = *not* before). Partial signification has already occurred through metaphor, but through *praxis* as deferred metaphor (results signifying their preliminary circumstances), plot both revises signification and slows it down to the time the plot takes to complete itself. In effect, the plot's narrative resolution *resignifies* metaphor, and, by resignifying it, very likely *designifies* it, denying or somehow diminishing its fullest implications. It absorbs the cumulative meaning of earlier figurative representations by substituting its latest representation, the end by which characters receive what they deserve.

This function of plot in compounding metaphor to purify it of its objectionable signification is suggestive of the French psychoanalyst Jacques Lacan's treatment of metonymy as "a signifier of desire" whose deferred representation endlessly reappears in other guises.[18] As Lacan suggests, a basic "signifying game" occurs between the plot as a "horizontal signifying chain" and metaphors as its "vertical dependencies in the signified," but one must disagree with Lacan's characterization of metonymy—in fiction, at least—as "eternally stretching forth towards the *desire for something else*" (p. 167). Instead, Lacan's principle of metonymy as words signifying words may be extended to apply to a new and more inclusive level—of narrative portions that signify narrative portions, or, more specifically, of terminal word combinations that signify earlier word combinations, i.e., of Aristotle's end signifying (or designifying) its beginning. In this instance, which is literary, closure becomes essential to the dynamics by which metonymy at least temporarily prevails over metaphor, contrary to Lacan's null-Aristotelian assumption that competition between the two goes on indefinitely in fiction—"until the match is called, there where I [Lacan] am not, because I cannot situate myself there" (p. 166). With even the most restrictive definition of metonymy—of words signified by other words—a *before* and an *after* become necessary, and, if literary form occurs, closure is obtained by any *after* that fully signifies or designifies its *before*. For most readers, metonymy, like both signification and metaphor, depends upon a capping experience, a plateau effect—perhaps momentary, perhaps longer—that occurs when a signifier asserts itself as an adequate substitute for what it signifies. "Ah yes," readers fleetingly tell themselves in the case of metaphor, "the rose indeed represents the first blush of youth"; but in the case of metonymy, as represented, for example, by the final impression of Gertrude Stein's brief poem already interpreted, "Ah yes," readers conclude, with pause tantamount to belief, "a rose is, in the final analysis, nothing more than a rose." The second instance imposes closure, a metonymic denial of metaphor—here in Gertrude Stein's poem the denial of a single metaphor, but in most instances, for example, both in *Hamlet* and in Pound's "In a Station of the Metro," the denial of a cumulative impact of metaphors. In effect, literary form is an organization of experience by which metonymy (a linear seeking of closure) both caps and designifies metaphor's simultaneity. As Emerson explained, "That which proceeds in succession might be remembered, but that which is coexistent knows not its own tendency."[19] More specifically, that which proceeds in succession *helps to prevent* that whose signified and signifier are coexistent from being too closely examined. Hence the value of narrative form as a displacement strategy based on the use of closure to supplant complex and relatively threatening experience with a gratifying alternative. Through sequence less can be told in the the sense that more has been untold via metonymic designification.

As a countervailing liberation of experience, metaphor plays a more important role than usually recognized, since it embraces any signification whose eidetic value in doubling the sign situation encourages confessional primary process displacements that need to be excluded from the reader's purview. Other literary devices may accordingly be described as being metaphoric whenever they expose an undercurrent of countervailing motives at odds with narrative closure. What might seem simple imagery often bears metaphoric implications, for example, when the obsessive depiction of violence (guns, reckless driving, broken windows, etc.) expresses aggressiveness disproportionate to the final happy ending imposed by narrative closure. Ambiguity can also be metaphoric if alternative meanings undermine the appeal of narrative closure, as can poetic texture if tension arises between the forward momentum of ordinary usage and stylistic deviations that express disruptive associations. Irony likewise falls into the same category if connota-

The Paranoid Dialectic

tions and declared meaning divide along lines relative to the process of denial carried out by the plot. This division can occur between what is told and implied, between what is told and seen, or between what is told and remembered from personal experience. Characterization, too, can be metaphoric, if torn between progressive stereotyping (in the sense that it justifies the plot's momentum toward acceptable closure) and occasional interludes that concede the exceptions and modifications typical of human complexity. Literary caricatures deserve their fate—real people don't, exactly. The same is true of the story, as opposed to the plot, if it meanders into episodes that hinder its momentum toward resolution. Sometimes these narrative byways seem to be temporary distractions from the issues and feelings resolved by the plot. Often, however, they contribute to a countervailing pattern of signification that obstructs the plot's impetus toward closure. Paradoxically, the more effectively they resist closure, the greater the felt need for closure. At best, literary form focuses and dramatizes this dialectic opposition by imposing a resolution that at least suggests the possibility of genuine synthesis.

If literary form's struggle between progressive and obstructive components (respectively, plot and metaphor) is explained according to Roman Jakobson's dichotomy between the metonymic and metaphoric dimensions of language, the plot once again becomes metonymic, since it is organized forward in time and depends upon the cumulative advancement of words and episodes from beginning to end.[20] On the other hand, the metaphoric dimension represents the dynamics of signification, including metaphor and all obstructive features whose referential associations compound signification, thereby slowing down metonymic advancement. In general, metaphor tends to expand the range of experience signified, as opposed to metonymic linkages that impose a second order of reference more likely to diminish or constrict the range of experience signified. Each word or word combination expresses both tendencies, on the one hand drawing the reader's attention to the signified experience, on the other helping to organize this experience in a sequence that emphasizes certain aspects—those that feature a desire for something else—at the expense of others—those that feature the world as we know it, as represented by our desire for something else. Each both clarifies and obscures, both helps and resists the forward momentum that leads to narrative closure. All literary devices—irony, ambiguity, tone, characterization, and so on—may be interpreted based on this metaphoric/metonymic distinction, whose ultimate source resides in a denial-projective double displacement comparable to Freud's model of paranoid consciousness. Syntax is involved, since each word's referential content (metaphoric) offsets the syntactic role it plays (metonymic). Even sound pattern is involved, since pauses, stresses, and resemblances (rhyme, alliteration, etc.) emphasize particular words, thus drawing attention to their symbolic function at the expense of the narrative dynamics by which the attention is drawn forward, lured by the expectations of closure. Usually, but not always, metaphor provides the medium for personal expressiveness, while metonymy absorbs and designifies this expressiveness by means of conventional expectations. Metaphoric representation is projective because it unleashes experiential reserves peripheral to language, while metonymic representation carries out the function of denial by redefining these reserves based on the linear demands of literary form.

The basic distinction between plot and metaphor that I am suggesting replicates the distinction between the projective and denial displacements of paranoia as well as the distinctions emphasized in previous chapters between truth and misrepresentation, positive and negative feedback, and creativity and literary convention—all of which may be categorized by the perhaps more inclusive distinction between expression and constraint, as shown in table 3. Metaphor lets us project unrecognized feelings and inclinations in our experience of a text, thus affording creativity by expressing truths with obvious positive feedback. In contrast, plot denies these projected feelings by drawing upon literary convention that produces negative feedback experienced as pleasure. Both poles are important to fiction. A *before* and an *after* are almost inevitably needed for integrating their antipodal relationship, but they may also be so closely integrated that their sequence is difficult to isolate. In the parallelogram model presented in figure 2, the linear (or metonymic) forward momentum that represents plot as an agent of denial takes place on vector *CB*, while vector *AC* is metaphoric since it represents the full range of feelings projected into a text in order to be denied. *AC* is metaphoric in representing these feelings, while *CB* is metonymic in representing a sequence that ultimately leads to their elimination. *AC* brings feelings to the surface, but only to be reorganized and therefore selectively denied by *CB*.

The orthogonal relationship between these two displacements can be better represented by coordinate axes, as shown in figure 3. Curve *P* in quadrant 2 represents the paranoid sequence *ADB* (denial flowing into the projection of denied feelings), while curve *Q* in quadrant 4 represents the literary sequence *ACB* (vicarious projection rewarded with denial afforded by clo-

TABLE 3. *Distinctions in Literary Form*

Expression	Constraint
Metaphor	Plot
Projection	Denial
Positive feedback	Negative feedback
Truth	Misrepresentation
Creativity	Literary convention

sure). This paradigm also expresses Saussure's vertical axis of simultaneities and horizontal axis of successions, as well as synchrony and diachrony, *langue* and *parole*, signification and syntagma, selection and combination, and illocutionary and perlocutionary effects. Likewise expressed are the distinctions between *animus* and *anima*, Apollonian and Dionysian consciousness, Allen Tate's extension and intension, John Crowe Ransom's structure and texture, and J. Hillis Miller's performative and narrative dimensions of narrative form. Also implied would be the Adlerian distinction between masculine protest and inferiority feelings and Christopher Caudwell's distinction between the natural and social roles that compose one's inclusive identity, with the vertical dimension representing biological need and the horizontal dimension its sublimation based on social and literary convention. For each of the binarisms mentioned here, the horizontal dimension designates an acceptable outcome while the vertical dimension—without which literary experience remains one-dimensional—expresses the anxiety and unconscious needs to be both expressed and denied by imposing such an outcome.

The vertical dimension also designates positive feedback and an open-system accountability to everything we must cope with in life; in contrast, the horizontal dimension traces the denial displacement as closed-system behavior with a plotted syntagmatic transition from *X* to *not X*. Our conscious and unconscious ability to identify with characters as represented by the vertical axis is counterbalanced by the horizontal capacity for producing denial on a sequential basis. One dimension represents leakage, and the other its denial by means of approved closure. The orthogonal integration of these two capacities in fact clarifies a large variety of literary distinctions. The dialectic may pose a conflict as simple as the tension between site and violence, for example, when lush description of a jungle setting expresses *anima* on a

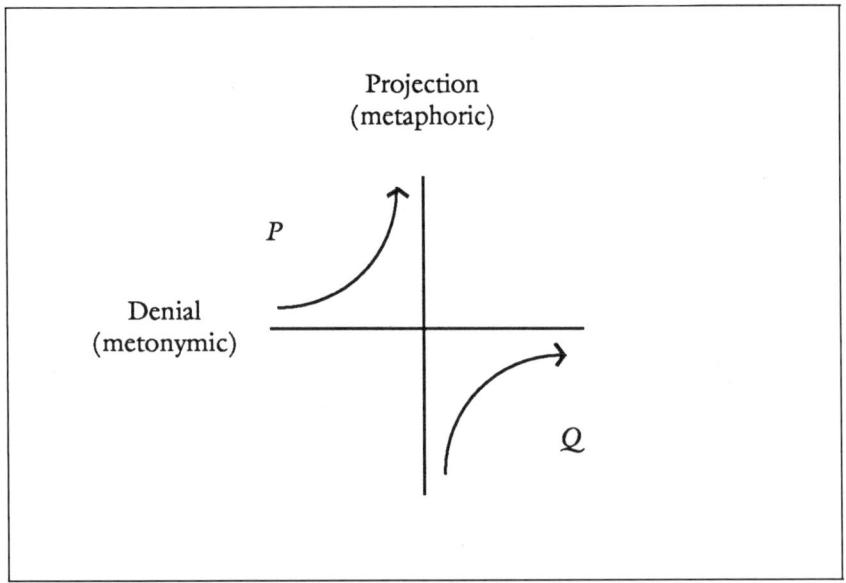

FIGURE 3. *Displacement sequence alternatives*

vertical axis as counterbalanced by *animus* that expresses struggle and victory on the horizontal axis. Caves, mounds, mansions, and bodies of water—even the conventional vision of hell—similarly evoke the threat of polymorphous susceptibility that is denied in paranoid fashion by the conflict among aggressive men who traverse this threatening landscape armed with guns, swords, and other such instruments of phallic aggressiveness. Such a relationship likewise occurs between the sea and a voyager's determination in both *The Odyssey* and *Moby-Dick*, between underground passageways and the quest for secret answers in gothic tales and science fiction.[21] In each instance environmental topology expresses a metaphoric breadth of experience (vertical) that must be harnessed by means of linear achievement (horizontal). With final closure, unacceptable projective implications measured on the vertical axis of simultaneities are denied by a compensatory paranoid victory plotted on the horizontal axis of contiguity.

If the classic Freudian symptoms of homophobic repression aggravate paranoid tendencies, the dialectic tension between metaphor and plot can be particularly dramatic. This happens, for example, when Shakespeare's persistent use of misogynistic innuendos is finally both resolved and denied by means of tragic self-sacrifice. A slightly different version occurs in the popular media, for example, in the so-called buddy movies and TV detective programs in which male bonding between two heroes (metaphoric in its visual immediacy) is both denied and consummated by means of their shared victory at the expense of dangerous criminals. They indirectly fulfill their relationship by acts of justified violence against acceptable scapegoats. This formula first occurred in the *Epic of Gilgamesh* almost five thousand years ago, when Gilgamesh and his sidekick, Enkidu, kill both Humbaba and the Bull of Heaven, and it thrives today as one of the staples of American culture. According to Nietzsche's theory of tragedy, Apollonian success (a masculine accomplishment) transcends Dionysian polymorphousness once the homo-aversive repression of homosexuality can be displaced and denied through justified acts of violence. Drawing upon Allen Tate's theory of tension, I also propose that the intension of plot that documents the struggle for justice effectively counterbalances an extension of unacceptable latent homosexual innuendos. The resulting formal tension is resolved by shared victory in defense of orthodox values.[22] Finally, if the linguistic terms of Roman Jakobson are extended to narrative form, the metonymic inertia of plot counterbalances its metaphoric spectrum of androgynous significations that produce anxiety and the compensatory rage for order.[23] Plot co-opts anxiety through self-signification, the advancement from deficiency to sufficiency, i.e., from felt inadequacy to the apprehension of criminals as a self-defined intrareferential success.

In popular fiction, plot predominates; in high fiction, it is challenged and at times seemingly blocked. Nevertheless, there is always at least a modest sense of an ending. This is true of Thomas Pynchon's novels, for example, in which the rejection of conventional narrative structure is balanced against an ingenious and obsessive use of paranoid thematic content. The denial displacement reemerges as paranoid expectations based on evidence of an insane international conspiracy. Paranoid form is abandoned, but the story expresses a paranoid vision, so it continues to interest readers, if on a slightly different plane. There is no coherent organization of events, but at least an elaborate "plot" is exposed, which more or less brings the novel to its conclusion. Other postmodernist fiction (for example, that of Katz, Sukenick, and Federman) escapes paranoia by eliminating form, sequence, and closure, and without salvaging paranoia in its thematic content. However, as I indicated earlier, this fiction's total freedom from the denial displacement serves as an exception to prove the rule, since it draws only the tiniest audience with the patience to appreciate its merits as aesthetic accomplishment. Most readers are bored with postmodernism's disembodied verbal evocations. Instead, they seek out authors unashamedly willing to invoke metonymy at the expense of metaphor, masculine protest at the expense of inferiority feelings, and paranoid contour at the expense of formless accuracy. In fact, there seems to be a rather high correlation: the more paranoid the vision of experience, the more likely its widespread success. The pathological righteousness of *Jaws, Star Wars*, the Rambo and Schwarzenegger films, and all the spin-offs that now fill our movie theaters during the summer is obviously exaggerated, but a comparable dependence on paranoid form can also be found—if more effectively modulated—in the works of Shakespeare, Dickens, and most of the authors who dominate our literary tradition. We should not forget that *Titus Andronicus* was Shakespeare's most popular play during his lifetime—more popular, even, than *Hamlet*.

six

YOUNG GOODMAN BROWN

Whenever evil, mortal danger, and the courage of lone protagonists seem important, we can surmise that fiction verges on paranoid delusion. As in the case of paranoia itself, free-floating anxiety is diverted and given focus by the fear of hostile forces that must somehow be defeated. In effect, life is simplified and redefined as a primitive conflict to be won by primitive means. Habit, anxiety, indecisiveness, and intropunitive guilt are allayed by extropunitive righteousness that lets negative feedback prevail at the expense of positive feedback, plot at the expense of complexity of characterization, and pleasant illusion at the expense of any genuine effort to come to terms with our personal inadequacies. This pattern of metonymic designification is commonplace in such popular genres as mysteries, westerns, detective stories, gothic thrillers, and the like, but it also occurs in high fiction from ancient epic and tragedy to most of the contemporary novels that presumably transcend escapist conventions. Serious fiction's paranoid dynamics might be attenuated and more effectively obscured, but its appeal derives from a comparable dependence on psychological displacements: not my problem but the story's; not the hero's individual problem but a struggle against outside forces; not empty compromise but total victory over these forces. Whenever this hierarchy of displacements takes precedence, paranoid tension reduction occurs and is experienced as pleasure—the satisfaction of having participated in the outcome of a lively and compelling work of fiction.

Occasionally a particular poem, story, or novel maps out a major portion of this dialectic. Like other works of fiction, it draws on paranoid needs, but it additionally offers itself as a prototype, or working model, that documents most or all of the process and charts the interrelationship among its parts. Its denial-projective machinery is almost entirely visible, so it both deploys and clarifies the dynamics that give literature its paranoid appeal. Blake, Dostoevsky, and Kafka come to mind as authors capable of works that fit this description, but perhaps the most remarkable such work is Nathaniel Hawthorne's "Young Goodman Brown," a short story whose ethical crisis epitomizes the themes and conventions of American literature. Its sometimes painfully obvious Freudian symbolism that dominates the story lays bare a more basic paranoid syndrome that has, in fact, played a dominant role in American fiction since its very beginning. As a relatively brief tale of Young Goodman Brown's nightmarish experience in the forest, it provides the *locus classicus* of the wilderness quest in a tradition that has persisted from Natty Bumppo and Huckleberry Finn to the detectives, cowboys, and antiheroes crowding the media today. In the case of Young Goodman Brown, the choice between heterosexual love and its rejection is sufficiently disguised to be acknowledged, then reformulated as a Manichaean choice between good and evil. Young Goodman Brown briefly tests possibilities symbolized by his journey into the forest, and then rejects them completely and irrevocably for their sinful implications. His story ritualizes frontier challenge, but with the unique outcome that he returns to civilization a reluctant husband who meets but despises his family and community obligations. His brief excursion into the wilderness reveals an identity crisis too dangerous to acknowledge. Once exposed to this crisis, he renounces the possibility of confronting the choice ever again.

The story of Young Goodman Brown tells of his journey into the forest to fulfill his overnight assignation with Satan. Faith, his young bride, pleads with him to tarry with her at their house in the village, but he is determined to fulfill his mysterious mission. Upon reaching the forest he meets Satan, and the two proceed toward a mysterious destination where some kind of a midnight ritual is to be conducted. Soon they overtake his old nurse, Goody

Young Goodman Brown

Cloyse, who had taught Young Goodman Brown his catechism as a child. He discovers to his astonishment that she is traveling to the same ceremony and that she has been a long-standing friend of Satan. When she suddenly climbs on Satan's staff and flies ahead, Young Goodman Brown is shocked by her sinfulness and refuses to cooperate any further with Satan. Left alone, Young Goodman Brown hears cloud-borne voices passing overhead, evidently of other women flying to the same event. One of these voices sounds like Faith's, and a pink ribbon that drops from the sky seems to be the one she was wearing when he left her at their doorstep. Upon this discovery, he loses his composure and frantically rushes to join the evil proceedings, spurred on by the voices of two respectable local clergymen also riding to the same destination.

Eventually Young Goodman Brown stumbles into a clearing illuminated by four burning pines and full of local citizens, many from the most pious and prosperous families he knows. He learns that the crowd has been waiting to baptize Faith and himself as two new converts into what Satan describes as "the communion of their race." Only one figure, probably his mother, motions to him not to participate, but she seems to be lost in the crowd. Satan begins his invocation before a blood-filled basin when Young Goodman Brown suddenly changes his mind and cries out to Faith, who stands beside him, to join in resisting "the wicked one." Instantly, the entire gathering disappears, Faith included, and Young Goodman Brown finds himself alone, swallowed up in darkness. The following day he returns to his village disillusioned with humanity. He fulfills his marriage vows and raises a family of children and grandchildren, but without learning if his extraordinary experience was a dream. He withdraws into himself and finally dies a bitter old man still unreconciled with his family and neighbors.

Young Goodman Brown's suspicious retreat from family and friends almost perfectly exemplifies paranoid decompensation as the degenerative transition from an *acute* phase dominated by the struggle to cope with unmanageable feelings to a *chronic* phase dominated by intractable delusions of persecution. The first phase is represented by Young Goodman Brown's crisis in the forest and the second by his subsequent vigilance against the people he lives with for the rest of his life. The story's narrative provides a completely intact delusional system, an elaborate explanation of events that justifies Young Goodman Brown's hostility toward his presumed enemies. Every detail confirms his suspicion that a conspiracy is taking place at his expense, a conspiracy so pervasive that everybody, even his trusted bride, is probably involved. It is only his complete dedication to virtue that prevents him from capitulating, and because of his refusal he becomes alienated from the entire town, now a pseudocommunity of satanic enemies. Other elements of the story that reinforce a paranoid diagnosis may be listed as follows:

> There is paranoid centrality in the illusion of playing a role of crucial importance. Young Goodman Brown's evil communion is celebrated by all society, and his salvation becomes a temporary battlefield in the cosmic struggle between God and Satan.

> Supernatural interference is too enormous to be withstood except by extraordinary means. Young Goodman Brown finds himself in the clutches of Satan and can escape only by an act of unusual willpower.

> The Manichaean choice between sin and virtue is unduly exaggerated. Young Goodman Brown stakes his life and happiness upon an ethical struggle between evil and purity, and he remains steadfast in his commitment to purity despite the evil temptations to which everyone else has capitulated.

> Young Goodman Brown's judgment of others discloses a pronounced tendency toward premature closure, which is typical of paranoid consciousness. Following his single evening's ordeal, he feels absolutely justified in rejecting his family and neighbors for the rest of his life. Nobody is given a second chance.

> There is a total humorlessness that results from Young Goodman Brown's inability to laugh at himself and to judge himself objectively.

> The possibility of compromise is also excluded. Young Goodman Brown's fate is determined once he has made his choice, and there is no room for accommodation ever again.

> Secret clues are important in exposing the conspiracy against Young Goodman Brown: cryptic allusions, peculiar resemblances, his wife's lost ribbon, etc. Only by sifting this evidence can he expect to save himself from the fate that otherwise awaits him.

> Young Goodman Brown hears the disembodied voices of the clergymen on horseback and the women passing by on a cloud overhead. Hearing

voices is typical of paranoid derangement, even if special circumstances (for example, forest darkness) are adduced to explain the source of these voices.

In the final analysis, it is not clear whether events are real or imaginary. The story of Young Goodman Brown's experience always seems to be at the edge of delusion. He is confident of his ethical judgment, but he cannot be entirely certain that his evidence supports this judgment.

Sexual roles are reduced to simple stereotypes, as is typical of paranoid thinking. Women are divided into paragons of virtue, such as Young Goodman Brown's mother, and threatening temptresses and/or witches, such as Goody Cloyse. Torn between these extremes, Faith becomes a dangerous temptress once she decides to join the devil's party.

Most of the imagery bears surrealistic implications suggestive of delusional extravagance. Young Goodman Brown journeys along a dark and threatening trail to participate in a ghastly ritual dominated by the paraphernalia of witchcraft. Satan presides, and only the voice of Young Goodman Brown's mother can be heard. An enormous crowd has gathered to watch the young couple's initiation, but it suddenly disappears, leaving Young Goodman Brown stranded in total darkness.

Finally, the story is told with disarming candor, emphasizing the truth at one level of interpretation in order to obscure it at another. Young Goodman Brown seems dedicated, as does the narrative itself, to the careful distinction between fact and supposition. However, the story's central motivation seems inexplicable until it is deciphered, whereupon it becomes almost painfully clear.

Perhaps the most intriguing paranoid symptom is the way Young Goodman Brown's story links delusions of persecution to sexual aversion based on unresolved Oedipal difficulties. As Frederick Crews has maintained, the devil plays the role of an unacceptable father surrogate who is trying to initiate his son to the mystery of sex.[1] Together, Satan and Young Goodman Brown are described as looking like father and son, and Satan's close resemblance to Young Goodman Brown's grandfather doubles, and thus reinforces, his paternal role. Similarly, Goody Cloyse, Young Goodman Brown's evil nurse, plays the role of a bad or licentious mother, the willing mistress of his father's designs. The witches' sabbath in the woods symbolizes the consummation of Young Goodman Brown's marriage with Faith, which would allow him to identify with his father according to patriarchal custom and expectations. He and Faith are newlyweds, and their church rites must be completed by sexual union, imposing upon Young Goodman Brown the sinful role his father once enjoyed with his mother. The various individuals attending this ceremony have apparently lost their virginity in comparable fashion.

Hawthorne specifies that the young couple has been married for exactly three months, ample time to have consummated their relationship. This postponement, the length of a season, seems intended to let the story be told by disguising and sublimating its implications. Nevertheless, the status of the two as newlyweds is at stake, and what occurs is the symbolic rejection of sex except for the unpleasant necessity of bearing children. Conjugal intimacy is accepted for the limited purpose of raising a family, not for any satisfaction Young Goodman Brown might find in his physical relationship with his wife. Here, once again, an antiepithalamium discloses itself, for, like Hamlet, Young Goodman Brown is led to reject his designated wife in order to liberate himself from what seems an evil compact between his parents, in his case Satan and Goody Cloyse. Moreover, like the wedding guest in "The Ancient Mariner," he approaches the threshold of matrimony but then withdraws because of the lesson that he has learned from his surrealistic experience. And like Frost's protagonist in "Mending Wall," he erects a barrier to limit human contact—in his case, between himself on one side and Faith, Satan, and the rest of humanity on the other.

The threat of carnal temptation is suggested by the story's initial tableau, in which Young Goodman Brown leaves his house to venture into the forest despite Faith's pleas that he remain with her. "Pray tarry with me," she seductively entreats him as she "thrusts her own pretty head into the street, letting the wind play with the pink ribbons of her cap." As in "The Ancient Mariner," Young Goodman Brown stands poised at their doorway, symbolizing at least the possibility of consummation, and then makes his departure despite Faith's overtures. Young Goodman Brown's preliminary rejection of Faith thus prefigures his more symbolic (and permanent) rejection of marriage later in the story, as does his receding image of Faith still waving from their doorway as he begins his journey. Her benign image recedes even further from his mind by the story's conclusion, though the two continue to live together as a married couple until his death many years later. When Young

Young Goodman Brown

Goodman Brown passes behind the town meetinghouse, thereby blocking his view of Faith, it also seems as if this building, replete with community values, symbolizes the shared assumptions of society that irreparably isolate him both from his wife and from those neighbors who are able to live in normal conjugal union. But here cause and effect are reversed. Contrary to most interpretations of the story, it is not Young Goodman Brown's suspicion of society that dictates his alienation from Faith; rather, it is his rejection of the marriage rite with Faith that dictates his alienation both from her and from society. By gladly accepting his role as Faith's husband, Young Goodman Brown could join this community, but this he refuses to do. His emotional rejection of his wife therefore guarantees his social isolation for the rest of his life.

The sexual implications of Young Goodman Brown's decision are also symbolized by his journey in and out of a primeval forest with almost blatant sexual implications, as explained, for example, by the pubic suggestiveness of trees in Freudian dream symbolism: "He had taken a dreary road, darkened by all the gloomiest trees of the forest, which barely stood aside to let the narrow path creep through, and closed immediately behind." The comparable symbolism of the harmless doorway that Young Goodman Brown refuses to enter at the beginning of the story has been supplanted by a dark and threatening forest path whose penetration supposedly leads to a mysterious ritual consummation. The threat of consummation likewise seems plain in Satan's invocation at the forest ritual, when he stands as a minister in front of the two as if in the act of marrying them:

> By the sympathy of your human hearts for *sin* ye shall scent out all the places—whether in church, *bedchamber*, street, field, or forest—where crime has been committed, and shall exult to behold the whole earth one *stain of guilt*, one mighty *blood spot*. Far more than this. It shall be yours to *penetrate*, in every bosom, the *deep mystery of sin, the fountain of all wicked arts*. (Italics added)

Here, Satan's displaced images of sexual consummation as a fountain of blood from the earth itself suggest, whether Hawthorne quite realized what he was saying, both the classical personification of the earth as the female Ur-goddess Gaea and, in biblical tradition, the "face of the waters" in the second verse of Genesis, which may be traced to the Sumerian Ur-goddess Tiamat, whose "waters" Marduk divides from the rest of her corpse after killing and butchering her, affording the firmament of the universe and later, apparently, the wellspring of feminine temptation.

The specific crimes listed by Satan combine sex, parenthood, and Oedipal confusion in a scrambled but otherwise barely disguised combination susceptible to Freudian analysis:

> [H]ow hoary-bearded elders of the church have whispered wanton words to the young maids of their households; how many a woman, eager for the widow's weeds, has given her husband a drink at bedtime and let him sleep his last sleep in her bosom; how beardless youths have made haste to inherit their father's wealth; and how fair maidens—blush not, sweet ones—have dug little graves in the garden, and bidden me, the sole guest, to an infant's funeral.

Reorganized on a narrative basis, these episodes recounted by Satan predict the fate rejected by Young Goodman Brown. If Young Goodman Brown, a "beardless youth," can identify with his father in his satanic role (i.e., "inherit his father's wealth"), he would have no trouble in consummating his marriage to Faith by penetrating "the fountain of all wicked arts" to produce "one mighty blood spot." But this "stain of guilt" would also provide the drink that lets him "sleep his last sleep in her bosom," the sole guest at the funeral of his own innocence. This Young Goodman Brown wants to avoid, so the ritual is interrupted. In effect, *coitus interruptus* takes place, justified by his cosmic struggle against the devil who only circumstantially resembles his grandfather. Throughout this passage, Satan's imagery exposes the repulsiveness of patriarchal responsibility and the acceptance of an adult role. It almost seems as if Satan, too, shares Young Goodman Brown's revulsion against sex but has learned to accept its necessity.

As Hamlet differentiates his good from his bad father, Young Goodman Brown remains loyal to his good mother, now little more than a half-recognized gesture of restraint, and despises his bad mother, Goody Cloyse ("good" becomes "Goody"), a witch who has lost her broom and eagerly accepts in its place the father figure's writhing serpentine staff. When Satan repeatedly tries to pass on his phallic staff to Young Goodman Brown as if it were his rightful inheritance, his gesture suggests the Oedipal demands implicit in the identification with a father figure who can regard conjugal love as being acceptable, even desirable. But Young Goodman Brown cannot make this adjustment, so the parental figures who encourage his efforts must be rejected in their grotesque heterosexual caricature as Satan and Goody Cloyse.

Classic Freudian theory also helps to explain Young Goodman Brown's close affinity to his mother as the efficient cause of his inability to identify with his father.[2] It is no accident that he rejects Satan's staff or that the single individual who succeeds in dissuading him from accepting communion is probably his good mother, who "with dim features of despair, threw out her hand to warn him back." She alone resists the ceremony that would initiate his maturity, and in doing so she makes her appeal to his regressive and infantile feelings. His conscience, or inner voice, is hers, not his father's, and it is this inner voice that protects him from the ritual demands of Satan. Because of his mother's influence, Young Goodman Brown spurns his young bride, who threatens his dependency, which borders on total identification. In effect, Young Goodman Brown's attachment to his mother has verged on mother-identification, but homosexuality remains unthinkable, leading to anxiety and identity confusion that must be brought under control by accusing others of evil designs against him. His gender crisis is replaced by an obsessive vigilance against presumed enemies associated with the heterosexual temptation to be rejected. What is fascinating about the story of Young Goodman Brown is its economy of means in plotting this transition from his preparanoid innocence to the relatively narrow cathartic gratification that derives from Young Goodman Brown's having exposed his persecutors.

Yet Young Goodman Brown cannot fully identify with his mother. Such a choice would be no less unspeakable, so he finds himself in limbo and must bring his role confusion under control by means of delusional experience that carries out the double displacement of denial and projection typical of paranoid logic: "Not that my mother-identification prevents me from loving Faith; rather, it is she, my presumably loyal bride, who is involved in a universal conspiracy, led by my father, to destroy my soul." Young Goodman Brown's sexual ambivalence can accordingly be disguised by the moral choice between sin and virtue that puts everyone else at fault, not himself. These are trying to deprive him of his virtue, and their designs can be thwarted only by his maintaining a desperate vigilance for the rest of his life. His single night's ordeal in the forest thus dramatizes his crisis, the acute stage of paranoia in which extreme anxiety is triggered by unacceptable conjugal demands. When this crisis is resolved by his emphatic rejection of these demands, his paranoid decompensation has advanced from its acute to its chronic stage. The narrative action pivots on this transition from severe anxiety to a midnight experience—perhaps delusional, perhaps not—that lets Young Goodman Brown recognize his enemies, though in fact he can neither defeat them nor acknowledge the threat they pose as projections of his personal difficulties.

Young Goodman Brown's infantile expectations in marrying Faith are disclosed when he promises, "I'll cling to her skirts and follow her to heaven," exactly as would have been expected in his early childhood relationship with his mother. However, "good" Faith, chosen for her potential benefits as a mother surrogate, reveals "bad" faith when she makes physical demands exceeding those of his mother. These demands become overt when she pleads with him to "tarry" with her because "a lone woman is troubled with such dreams and such thoughts that she's afeard of herself sometimes." By implication, however, Young Goodman Brown has more to fear from her nocturnal fantasies than she herself, and he must find a defense acceptable to his conscience, one that would let him, true to his name—and true to his story's title—find the best means to be both "good" and "man" at the same time. Paranoid delusion is the answer, a wilderness quest that eliminates his problem in two clearly defined stages: first by leaving Faith to journey into a world of shadows where her demands can be disguised as satanic ritual, and second by abruptly terminating this ritual because it is satanic. The first stage culminates with the projective displacement, "They're *all* sinners," while the second stage culminates with the denial displacement, "But *not* me!" Now Young Goodman Brown can withdraw from his wife fully protected from confronting his identity confusion. He and Faith can go on to raise children and grandchildren, but their marriage will never be a union of kindred souls, since she cannot be trusted to satisfy his innermost regressive needs. Young Goodman Brown's internal crisis has been replaced by a fear of evil temptation, an easier and less threatening problem to cope with than sexual role confusion. By means of the paranoid double displacement, his story shifts from his misguided early expectations to a maturity that disposes of his uncertainty through ceaseless vigilance against the evil influence of others. At the brink of heathen ritual, Young Goodman Brown can withdraw from marital consummation for reasons of profound moral significance.

Neither tragedy nor comedy is involved in Young Goodman Brown's ordeal. The threat is too dangerous to be acknowledged, for example, in the context of conventional Menandrine comedy. Hawthorne's Satan, it turns out, is less convincing than Prospero, Theseus, Undershaft, and other such father figures who are eager to present their children in marriage. The mother's desperate warning gesture fortifies Young Goodman Brown's resistance, and then he cuts short the forest ritual to confirm his escape from his wife. Never again will there be any threat of his tarrying with her or sharing with her the communion of their race. No longer tempted, he commits himself to a simpler task, his acceptance of marriage as a perpetual struggle against the threat of satanism. On the other hand, if Hawthorne's symbolism were fully tragic, Young Goodman Brown's story would emphasize his confrontation with a father figure comparable to Laius, Claudius, etc.—in his case through Miltonic warfare against the devil himself. And if a young woman such as Faith were caught up in such a conflict, she would probably be destroyed, like Ophelia, by the almost cosmic release of Oedipal violence, and her elimination would necessarily remain subordinate to Young Goodman Brown's effort to come to grips with the crisis of mother-identification. However, neither comedy nor tragedy takes place. Notable for its brevity, the story of Young Goodman Brown offers little more than a parable or bad dream, a nightmarish enactment of psychosexual ambivalence that justifies the perpetual defense of his inner chastity. The apparition of his good mother gives Young Goodman Brown the courage to deny heterosexual marriage but not to investigate substitutes, so his narrative (as opposed to his life) is quickly brought to its unhappy conclusion. An abortive transition has taken place from a bridegroom's frightened expectancy to the resounding abstinence of a "stern, a sad, a darkly meditative, a distrustful, if not a desperate man." Nothing is left but gloom as Young Goodman Brown tries to live out an undeclared compact with his mother that falls short of homosexual identification.

Typical of paranoid behavior, the story intermittently confesses itself in a variety of partial contexts leading to a resolution whose righteous self-justification may be felt without being understood—the primary obligation of paranoid delusion. No single passage provides a comprehensive explanation of Young Goodman Brown's problem, yet its components may be combined and evaluated in a clinical diagnosis of surprising comprehensiveness. What emerges is akin to *folie à deux*, because the reader can share Young Goodman Brown's paranoid experience without suffering from it and without exactly comprehending it. Moreover, Young Goodman Brown's heterosexual aversion almost entirely crowds from consideration the homoaversive attitudes that may likewise be expected as a by-product of his psychological disposition. There is a rejection of both alternatives, male and female, in his effort to play a mature role. Nevertheless, the abundance of pathological symptoms is almost too obvious to be ignored. If a distraught young gentleman, Y. G. Brown, were to walk into a psychiatrist's office and confide that he had recently talked to the devil disguised as his grandfather, that the devil had lured him into the woods to steal his soul at a witches' sabbath, and that he knows that everybody except his mother participated in the conspiracy, even his bride he can no longer love—the diagnosis, I think, would be plain: a classic case of paranoia, almost too classic to be true except in fiction.

But of course, Young Goodman Brown may be interpreted only as a fictional character, the figment of somebody else's imagination. The entire paranoid syndrome cannot be attributed to his characterization, so he is necessarily less paranoid than might be indicated by his story. At times he seems almost complex enough to be evaluated in psychoanalytic terms, but he remains a literary figure without the polydimensional assortment of coping mechanisms typical of real people, even the most rigid victims of paranoid decompensation. Moreover, though he might suffer from conspiratorial delusions, he cannot escape his status as the figment of his author's imagination, so what he suspects might actually be happening to him. In the story told of his ordeal, the devil probably does approach him disguised as his grandfather, and he probably does find himself at a witches' sabbath. What he sees he sees, and he must deal with this as best he can. He lives in a paranoid world concocted by his author, Hawthorne, and as its reluctant inhabitant he can hardly be blamed for the conclusions he draws. A figment of Hawthorne's imagination, he is ultimately innocent of the circumstances imposed by his creator. Of course, such claims of innocence typify paranoid thinking, but they happen to be true in the case of Young Goodman Brown.

Does this mean that Hawthorne and his readers can instead be diagnosed as being paranoid? Not necessarily. To enjoy a work of fiction with paranoid tendencies, we as readers need not suffer from paranoia. Fiction lets us take advantage of its cathartic benefits without totally imposing its values upon us. As readers we can suspend disbelief without giving full credence to the delusions we provisionally accept while engrossed in reading a story. We can engage the paranoid syndrome on a literary basis, and with a pleasure and flexibility that elude the genuine victim of paranoia. We can try out any projective mechanisms that appeal to us and discard them once they have served

Young Goodman Brown

their purpose. We are able to take advantage of these mechanisms, assured that our lives need not be dominated by them. Limited to fiction, paranoid form may be enjoyed for its strictly aesthetic benefit.

Hawthorne himself may have suffered from mild paranoid tendencies suggestive of the circumstances depicted in his story. He somewhat resembled his character Young Goodman Brown, if his description by Henry James, Sr., was at all accurate: "He has the look all the time, to one who doesn't know him, of a rogue who suddenly finds himself in the company of detectives."[3] Also suggestive of Young Goodman Brown's role was the way Emerson described Hawthorne in his diary entry the day after Hawthorne's burial: "Clarke [the minister who presided at the funeral] . . . said, that Hawthorne had done more justice than any other to the shades of life, shown a sympathy with the crime in our nature. . . . I thought there was a tragic element in . . . the painful solitude of the man—which, I suppose, could not longer be endured, & he died of it."[4] The words "painful solitude," which Emerson applied to Hawthorne, could just as easily have been used to describe Young Goodman Brown in his later years.

Young Goodman Brown's central crisis, symbolized by the forest ritual he rejects, also seems to recapitulate in the context of fiction Hawthorne's relatively slow emancipation from his mother's household once he reached maturity. His father died while Hawthorne was in his infancy, and thereafter, except for the years he spent as a student at Bowdoin College, he lived with his mother until he was thirty-three years old. A year later, in 1834, he wrote "Young Goodman Brown," and four years later, in 1838, he met Sophia Peabody, his future wife. The two were secretly engaged in 1839, apparently to avoid offending his mother, and they finally married in 1842. Apropos of this family background, it seems relevant to cite the clinical findings of J. Nydes, which indicate that there is often a close connection between paranoia and permanent feelings of guilt arising from an unusual attachment to one's mother:

> [T]he absence of a rational authority figure of the same sex has fostered the illusion during childhood that forbidden incestuous impulses may actually be realized. This is accompanied by feelings of guilt and fear of the father, who is perceived unconsciously as a formidable giant who must be defended against.[5]

It seems possible that Hawthorne's close affinity with his mother, especially at the time he wrote "Young Goodman Brown," might indeed illustrate this relationship. It also seems significant in this light that Hawthorne depicts Satan as a father figure who returns from another realm, presumably hell, to insist upon sealing Young Goodman Brown's marriage to his wife. However, as opposed to Young Goodman Brown, Hawthorne deeply loved his wife, and his son, Julian Hawthorne, asserted that there was considerable difference between Hawthorne's domestic role and his narrative persona: "The man and the works were, in Hawthorne's case, as different as a mountain from a cloud."[6] This difference seems particularly striking in the case of "Young Goodman Brown," which was written after Hawthorne had left his mother's house but before he met and married Sophia. The story may consequently be understood as an intermediate exploration of possibilities entirely different from the satisfaction Hawthorne was eventually to find in marriage. He might have experienced mild paranoid tendencies at the time he wrote his story, but even then they were well under control, limited to his use of fiction to explore forbidden alternatives. Like Milton, he was probably able and willing to put himself in Satan's party, just as bothered as his readers by Young Goodman Brown's unhappy decision at the forest clearing.

As a result, neither the author, his readers, nor Young Goodman Brown may be diagnosed as being paranoid, despite their participation in a narrative dominated by witchcraft and devilish conspiracy. All are touched by the paranoid condition, but none exactly fits its profile. Where, then, is the story's paranoid machinery situated? Clearly, it is the story itself as a narrative account of Young Goodman Brown's ordeal that embodies the denial-projective displacement typical of paranoia. As I indicated in chapter 5, fiction plays the same role as the paranoid syndrome in organizing our feelings, but in a temporary and relatively healthy fashion. The basis for a story such as "Young Goodman Brown" might derive from a hypothetical experience its author shares with its readers, but it distills and intensifies this experience with almost diagnostic purity. Its narrative structure provides what amounts to a portable delusional system in which a great variety of personal problems may be brought to focus and discharged by intense conflict against hostile forces supposedly bigger than life.

By exaggerating this conflict and then bringing it to its resolution, "Young Goodman Brown" stirs the negative vision typical of paranoia, but unlike paranoid delusion, its narrative apparatus remains accessible to balanced and healthy vicarious involvement. Events unfold in a nightmarish sequence almost totally devoid of affirmative appeal, yet the story provides the benign and relatively normal benefits of literary experience—unified, intensified, and, as it were, both purposeful and ethically determined. Unacceptable feelings are denied, but without turning to alternative experience, such as might be associated with male bonding and frontier adventure. An enemy is created to give flesh and blood to fearful temptations, but there is no sense of final triumph because of victory over this enemy. As a result, Young Goodman Brown's circumstances possess singular negative appeal. Readers project themselves into the story to share in almost a pure act of denial, since its sexual implications are well enough disguised for their symbolic rejection to be accepted simply as a ritual encounter by which an entire community may be contaminated for presumably inexplicable reasons. There is grim commitment to a closed-system plot that features ritual as the necessary disclosure to justify Young Goodman Brown's misanthropic suspicions. Moreover, the open-system expression of real problems is kept sufficiently cryptic to justify the plot's negative accomplishment based on a personal choice unacceptable to most readers.

The same pattern seems at work in other fiction by Hawthorne. Over and over again, a sensitive young man is thwarted in the ritualization of love for a young woman—by his choice, by hers, or by the force of circumstances. Young Goodman Brown's rejection of the forest ritual parallels the death of Beatrice exactly at the moment when Rappaccini informs her that she and Giovanni can finally share her special poison flower. Essentially the same interruption happens in *The Scarlet Letter* when Pearl forces Hester to replace her scarlet letter and then her hair in her bonnet, thereby postponing and defeating her marriage with Dimmesdale. The same also happens in *The Blithedale Romance*, if somewhat disguised, when Zenobia assures Miles Coverdale that there is nothing he can do for her just before she commits suicide. Reprobate father figures who encourage marriage, such as Satan and Rappaccini, dissolve into Faustian questers, such as Ethan Brand and Hollingsworth, and evil scientists, such as Chillingworth and Westervelt. These stories of evil, undefiled purity, pacts with the devil, and struggle against patriarchal authority afford enough guilt-ridden consistency (described by Frederick Crews as an "underlying sameness") to make further explication almost an exercise in belaboring the obvious.

Parallels may also be found in the mature fiction of Melville, especially in *Moby-Dick*, which he completely revised in manuscript after he came under

Hawthorne's personal and artistic influence. According to friends, Melville was on the brink of publishing *Moby-Dick* at the time he met Hawthorne, but he spent another year revising his manuscript, and in the novel he finally published he substantially expanded the role of Ahab and incorporated cosmic symbolism suggestive of Hawthorne's influence.[7] However, a major difference emerged between their perspectives, since Melville's homoerotic celebration of fraternal love substantially deviated from Hawthorne's vision of paranoid despair.

As Leslie Fiedler has demonstrated, Melville's final version of *Moby-Dick* bears phallic symbolism that is patently androgynous, suggesting that it altogether exceeds Hawthorne's fiction in its resistance to patriarchal identification, and with hostility intense enough to culminate not in perpetual vigilance, but in tragic self-destruction comparable to Hamlet's.[8] By the end of the novel, it becomes obvious that Ahab's pursuit of Moby-Dick expresses his eager commitment to his own destruction by forces beyond his control—exactly the martyrdom repugnant to Young Goodman Brown. More fortunate is Ishmael, the ship's only survivor, who seems to escape Ahab's fate because he can acknowledge his androgynous tendencies. Ishmael's disposition is passive and accepting, exactly the opposite of Ahab's dedication to a mortal conflict—in effect, a homophobic conflict—that he cannot even begin to understand. Ahab and his entire crew—just as much a community as Young Goodman Brown's township—are destroyed by this obsession, but Ishmael's pleasure in handling sperm (the flesh of whale, an intended pun that dominates chapter 94) and his willingness to consummate his blood brotherhood with Queequeg (having been hugged "in that matrimonial sort of style") when they go to bed together at the beginning of the novel earn his use of Queequeg's coffin when the *Pequod* sinks.

The theme or message at the heart of *Moby-Dick* almost seems as if it were intended as a reply to Hawthorne's cautionary tale, suggesting the substitution of Ishmael's androgynous affinities for the paranoid isolation of Young Goodman Brown. Young Goodman Brown's inability to either accept or escape marriage is revised and enlarged in *Moby-Dick* as the choice between Ahab's tragic quest and Ishmael's homoerotic emancipation. Like Young Goodman Brown, Ahab stakes his existence on his struggle against evil forces beyond his control—in his case, actually letting himself be destroyed by this force; in contrast, Ishmael represents as an alternative the friendship that might be possible between Hawthorne and Melville. *Moby-Dick* becomes a cosmic love letter in which Ahab dies, but Ishmael survives—a narrative outcome expanded to epic proportions that demonstrates the modified *carpe diem* theme that true rapport between two men (like Hamlet and Horatio, or Kurtz and Marlow in *Heart of Darkness*) affords salvation from the homo-aversive constraints imposed by heterosexual love. Of course, Ishmael ends up alone, like Young Goodman Brown, but without bitterness, and without enemies and devilish conspiracies to guard against.

That Melville might have consciously or unconsciously intended *Moby-Dick* as a reply to Hawthorne's attitudes (best illustrated by the thematic content of "Young Goodman Brown") might be indicated by Melville's description in his essay "Hawthorne and His Mosses," published in *The Literary World* shortly after he met Hawthorne:

> Already I feel that this Hawthorne has dropped germinous seeds into my soul. He expands and deepens down, the more I contemplate him; and further and further, shoots his strong New England roots in the hot soil in my Southern soul.[9]

Melville's effort to imitate Hawthorne is generally recognized, but it can also be demonstrated, I think, that he sought not just to imitate Hawthorne but also to depict their relationship in the context of the novel he was writing, investing in Ahab the traits he observed in Hawthorne. Melville clearly identified with Ishmael (provocatively, he began his novel by telling the reader, "Call me Ishmael"), and his physical description of Ahab, for example at the end of chapter 16, bears a close resemblance to his description of Hawthorne in both his correspondence and "Hawthorne and His Mosses." In addition, Melville dedicated his book to Hawthorne and ascribed to him, in one of his letters, the same Faustian role he gave Ahab in *Moby-Dick*: "There is a grand truth about Nathaniel Hawthorne. He says No! in thunder; but the devil himself cannot make him say yes." Coincidentally, this defiance against the devil was likewise Young Goodman Brown's achievement in the story of his ordeal. In another of his letters to Hawthorne, Melville consecrated his novel with Ahab's baptism of the harpoon in the name of the devil, "*Ego non baptizo te in nomine patris, sed in nomine diaboli!*" In doing so, Melville truncated his sentence, "This is the book's motto (the secret one), *Ego non baptizo te in nomine*—but make out the rest for yourself." Apparently he was trying to suggest that he considered Hawthorne singularly competent to understand the fullest implications of Ahab's victimization by satanic demands. In "Hawthorne and His Mosses," Melville more directly drew Young Goodman Brown into the comparison by paraphrasing one of the story's sentences in his praise of Hawthorne, "It is yours to penetrate in every bosom the deep mystery of sin."

But of course, Hawthorne could not benefit from Ahab's example. There is no direct evidence why Hawthorne permitted his brief friendship with Melville to lapse, but it can be speculated that the novel *Moby-Dick* might have played a major role. As Melville had asked, Hawthorne fathomed the novel's allegory, but he did not like what he read. Like Young Goodman Brown, he penetrated the deep mystery of sin and then withdrew, in his case by all the more exclusively restricting his companionship to his beloved wife, Sophia, with whom, it turns out, he preferred to share his innermost feelings.

In the broadest sense, Young Goodman Brown epitomizes America's cultural heritage of adolescent heroes who reject mature heterosexual compatibility by taking flight into the wilderness. Both in fiction and in our cultural heritage, we turn out to have been a nation of immature escapists from family obligations. In Fiedler's words, ours has been a tradition of boy explorers who pursue "that strategy of evasion, that flight from society to nature, from the world of women to the haunts of womanless men, which sets our novel apart from that of the rest of the Western world."[10] Perhaps the explanation for this adolescent fixation has been the relatively high level of mobility—both horizontal and vertical—among Americans, since our forebears have migrated among new jobs and new homes at a rate perhaps unprecedented in modern world history. Not only has American civilization expanded as a frontier, but, behind this growing perimeter, there has been sustained restlessness, a cultural "Brownian movement" that has encouraged continuing mobility. The nuclear family has necessarily been vulnerable to this trend, as demonstrated by the large number of American authors who lost their fathers when they were children, including Emerson, Hawthorne, Melville, Poe, Twain, Crane, London, Frost, Roethke, and Berryman. Most of them also had close relationships with their mothers that postponed and somewhat inhibited their social adjustment as adults. Our educational system has likewise been unique in its heavy dependence on female teachers, perhaps explaining the split-identity Van Wyck Brooks found between sharp business practices and transcendental posturing.[11] Those males who have quickly abandoned matriarchal authority—as imposed both by their mothers and by the public schools—have pursued the first of these alternatives, while those who have retained their filial ties (authors, moralists, etc.) have pursued the second, but not without resisting its influence—in the case of Hawthorne, Melville, and their successors by compulsively reenacting the choice imposed upon them within the context of fiction.

As epitomized by Young Goodman Brown's ordeal in the forest clearing, the domestic responsibility associated with matriarchal authority has been avoided by fiction emphasizing a frontier quest in which Oedipal difficulties could be acted out by the struggle of good against bad or virtuous solitude against nefarious conspiracy. Timidity has been heroically reconstructed as a moral battle against forces that disguise the domestic virtues found repugnant—conciliation rejected as intrigue, job responsibility as oppression, and heterosexual compatibility as abject surrender to the opposite sex. Reconstructed by fiction, the conflict has become one of virtuous youth pitted against patriarchy (i.e., the acceptance of a mature identity imposed by conjugal responsibility), pure mobility pitted against corrupt entanglements, and innocent peer affinities pitted against social convention and domestic entanglements. Womanhood has been appreciated primarily in beautiful virgins who are worshiped and defended but left unmarried. Happy marriage would trap the wilderness hero, so instead he has engaged in a presumably ethical struggle on whatever frontier he has found useful in justifying his avoidances. By confronting and defeating identifiable enemies, he has escaped the tranquility he has presumably defended, bypassing the unpleasant recognition that this tranquility has been in fact the enemy he has feared the most. Through paranoid displacement, he has divided his successful escape into two stages: victory against evil, followed by an excusable departure from those he saves from evil—exactly reversing Young Goodman Brown's midnight expedition to determine his future with Faith. The same transgression has been symbolized, but in a sequence that has been revised to permit a satisfying outcome. Young Goodman Brown ventured *into* the woods on a single occasion but immediately returned to become an embittered husband for the rest of his life. In contrast, the frontier hero has frequently emerged *from* the woods, thwarted evil, and then escaped to the woods once again, purified by his victory. The principal benefit of this reversal has been that culpability could be more effectively shifted from heroes to those whom they abandon, or, better yet, to enemies whose defeat has been preliminary to these heroes' abandonment of those they have thought they were protecting—more often than not the women in their lives. Evasiveness has become pardonable—sometimes admirable—entirely within the tradition of American literary history.

Such figures as Rip Van Winkle, Natty Bumppo, and Huckleberry Finn are able to take more prolonged journeys than Young Goodman Brown precisely because their Oedipal crises are better disguised as adventures. Their stories are more optimistic and better ritualized in their effort to liberate themselves from forces beyond their control. Recent counterparts in popular fiction include space travelers beset by extraterrestrial creatures, jaded (but basically innocent) detectives confronted by sinister schemes, and befuddled citizens caught up in international conspiracies, saved from destruction by their naive integrity as Americans. During the twenties such heroes, devoid of recognizable enemies, included "lost generation" innocents such as Gatsby, Jake Barnes, and Babbitt, the latter having strayed into a gratifying extramarital affair before returning to the fold no less chastened than Young Goodman Brown. After World War II, they have included Holden Caulfield, Augie March, Benny Profane, Rabbit Angstrom, Cacciato, and dozens of others, each incapable of a sustained heterosexual relationship because of his pursuit of supposedly more fundamental values.[12]

Young Goodman Brown is unique in this tradition because he ventures into the wilderness just once, and very briefly, before returning to his onerous domestic obligations. As opposed to the other literary frontiersmen, he makes what amounts to a one-night stand—with his wife, no less—and the farthest he penetrates is the clearing where ritual hellfire provides the turning point in his life. He resents his domestic responsibilities even more than do Babbitt and Willy Loman, but he learns to accept his conditional surrender, resentful of his sacrifice to the "petticoat government" ridiculed by Washington Irving in "Rip Van Winkle." He is trapped but innocent, and he knows his only salvation is his successful defense of his innocence. His circumscribed effort exposes the escapist achievement of our less thoughtful frontier heroes, for, singular in his isolation, he reveals the barrier they depend upon, most of them without understanding why. And his ordeal takes precedence historically, set in the earliest colonial times hundreds of years before our frontier closed in on itself and shattered into a variety of bizarre displacements. In the very infancy of our culture, Young Goodman Brown tests its perimeter, judges possibilities, and finds it a "dream of evil omen."

seven

THE AFFIRMATIVE FALLACY

When something is affirmed to deny something else ("What a pleasant day," for example, as one's refusal to talk about anything more), a transition necessarily takes place by which one idea, feeling, or potential word combination is displaced by another that believably serves as its opposite. Between the two a threshold occurs, and like the focal point of a lens, this threshold disperses experience in its original manifestation and then gathers it up again by reversing it. Approaching the focal point, the right-side-up image becomes fuzzy, but on the other side a new image emerges, clear, reduced, and plainly inverted. An upside-down clarity—precise but transposed—has supplanted the original field of vision. To the extent that this analogy may be applied to fiction, narrative form imposes reversal stretched out into a gradual realization, as organized by the unity of action; but elsewhere, for example, in literary criticism, reversal dynamics may be instantaneous, sporadic, or mixed with other conscious operations. In all cases, discomfort initiates scanning activity for alternatives, and after a period of uncertainty—perhaps a moment, perhaps the duration of a novel, perhaps the duration of a career—these alternatives impose themselves in an acceptable manner. Almost as if by magic, unpleasant matters have been eliminated from the agenda, replaced by benign harmlessness.

The Affirmative Fallacy

Unavoidably, to ignore what is happening when denial takes place requires a certain amount of effort. Energy must be committed to the act of oversight, as evidenced by willful ignorance. Just as an image hazes over while moving through its focal point, the act of denial in both fiction and literary criticism cannot be observed while it happens. There must be temporary obfuscation while the choice to deny prevents the awareness that such a choice is being implemented. As E. H. Gombrich has explained in *Art and Illusion*, "though we may be intellectually aware of the fact that any given experience *must* be an illusion, we cannot, strictly speaking, watch ourselves having an illusion" (italics in the original).[1] Charles Sanders Peirce has observed virtually the same dynamics in the shift from doubt to belief:

> However the doubt may originate, it stimulates the mind to an activity which may be slight or energetic, calm or turbulent. Images pass rapidly through consciousness, one incessantly melting into another, until at last, when all is over—it may be in a fraction of a second, in an hour, or after long years—we find ourselves decided as to how we should act under such circumstances as those which occasioned our hesitation. In other words, we have attained belief.[2]

In his novel *1984*, George Orwell somewhat complicates the dynamics of obfuscation in his explanation of "Doublethink" as the individual's conscious internalization of totalitarian political orthodoxy: "And if it is necessary to rearrange one's memories or to tamper with written records, then it is necessary to *forget* that one has done so."[3] The trick, Orwell says, is this:

> [T]o use conscious deception while retaining the firmness of purpose that goes with complete honesty. To tell deliberate lies while genuinely believing in them, to forget any fact that has become inconvenient, and then, when it becomes necessary again, to draw it back from oblivion for just so long as it is needed, to deny the existence of objective reality and all the while to take account of the reality which one denies—all this is indispensably necessary.

Reduced to its simplest dynamics, any reversal in thinking must go unobserved that depends on imposing as a substitute an acceptable positive alternative—one that might bear no obvious connection with the experience denied. The rational act of comparison, "This *but* that," is diminished, if not altogether obliterated by "This [what I want to see] *instead of* that [what I

The Affirmative Fallacy

choose to ignore]." As in the case of metaphor defined by I. A. Richards, a process of signification takes place by which a clear and eidetically coherent experience (the vehicle) expresses another experience that might be relatively shapeless and hard to define (the tenor). The principal difference with Richards's concept of metaphor is that this initial experience is denied and thereby *designified* by a respectable alternative that eliminates it from consciousness. Signification occurs in the sense that this experience is symbolized by a recognizable substitute, but, paradoxically, what results is the obliteration of this signified experience rather than its clarification. According to Peirce, belief designifies doubt; according to Gombrich, illusion designifies the ongoing recognition that illusion is taking place; according to Orwell, politically correct ("PC") thinking designifies one's knowledge of events and relationships that defy orthodox explanation.

Designification can be instantaneous, like metaphor, or it can be stretched out in metonymic fashion with successors gradually crowding from consciousness their predecessors. Probably the most dramatic of metonymic designification is the use of narrative closure to designify local metaphoric suggestiveness, as already explained in earlier chapters. As a story unfolds, the details that reinforce momentum toward its acceptable resolution gather and gain relative strength in the long-term memory, while those that resist this outcome are briefly perceived and then crowded from the short-term memory. In effect, the closure dynamics of the long-term memory have designified both the original state of affairs (the plot's beginning) and the short-term memories that potentially obstruct closure. If and when the vagrant implications of these short-term memories are more true to life than the closure dynamics that deny them, literary misrepresentation occurs.

A comparable use of designification characterizes the paranoid syndrome. As explained by Freud and Swanson, paranoid decompensation depends on a transition from self-doubt to compensatory self-vindication. There is an advancement from denial to the discovery of compensatory alternatives, but with the normal and relatively abstract purpose of imposing a more appropriate thought or feeling. Alternative goals are found in a different area of concern and with apparently different objectives in mind. But if reversal is to occur, it must go unrecognized, i.e., disguised to seem unintended or not to have taken place. This is the only way the denial displacement can function in letting us avoid our problems with a positive outlook—an outlook which in effect denies that denial has been our objective. A double negative actually

The Affirmative Fallacy

takes place, denial plus the denial of denial, as explained by Engels's principle of *Negationsnegierung*. I label the use of this double negative to guarantee the benefit of denial the affirmative fallacy, a compensatory dependence on positive answers that is intense enough to be described as belief. Whatever we believe in this manner, even tentatively—as for example when we "suspend disbelief"—obliges the additional psychic energy needed to impose this double negative, obliging an aggressiveness in excess of the energy we devote to normal ideation. This aggressiveness is typical of belief systems, whether of the popular variety (religion, patriotism, free enterprise, etc.) or of variants more acceptable to the intellectual community (Marxism, psychoanalysis, deconstructionism, etc.). Whenever the attachment to a principle or theory seems excessive, its explanation may be sought, I would propose, in the affirmative fallacy. Four phases make up this fallacy, and these are more or less sequential though their occurrence may be virtually instantaneous: (1) being confronted with the unpleasant truth, (2) its denial, (3) the denial that denial is occurring, and then and only then, (4) the positive affirmation of an alternative truth. An example:

1. The truth   "I am inadequate."
2. Denial   "I am not inadequate."
3. Denial of denial   "I am not denying I am inadequate."
4. Affirmative fallacy   "I am a good worker,"
                         "I am an expert in this field,"
                         etc.

In its simplest manifestation, *Negationsnegierung* comprises the double negative implicit in stage three, "I am *not* denying I am inadequate." In its more complex formulation typical of the affirmative fallacy, the fourth stage is needed to confirm the adequacy of whatever diversionary affirmative truths are formulated as a substitute. Only if all four stages are involved can the preliminary *Negationsnegierung* dynamics be of positive benefit, since the recognition of a double negative exposes it to challenge. If and when we acknowledge our compulsion to avoid unpleasant truths, avoidance fails. To make explicit our intentions necessarily undermines them, for there is tender vulnerability to our quest for alternatives, and we resent submitting it to thorough examination.

This programmatic effort to avoid recognizing the occurrence of denial is intrinsic both to literary form and to the retrospective effort of readers and crit-

The Affirmative Fallacy

ics to explain their satisfaction with particular texts. Critics seem especially vulnerable to the tendency, since they devote their energies to the gathering of evidence supportive of narrative form's closure dynamics. Unable to acknowledge the negative appeal of fiction, they seek out the necessary rationalizations to justify what seem its positive qualities. They try to endow their evasiveness with respectability, and success depends on their skill in ignoring their motives while making the necessary substitutions. "Why is this text so redeeming?" they ask themselves, and the good reasons they find are usually restricted to its positive benefits. Excluded from consideration are the problems denied, despite the likelihood that their denial is usually the most important of these benefits. As votaries of the double negative, critics reject the possibility that denied feelings likewise contribute to literary form. In effect, they grant authors the freedom to bring their feelings under control so they too can share in the task of doing so, but from a more protected vantage. When authors get bogged down on their private battlefields, critics help protect them with supportive volleys from the comparative safety of exegetical battlements. For their status and identities are no less at stake. The more affirmative the value of literary inspiration, the more important their role as official guardians of literary insight that compels, yet defies, explanation—call it genius, inspiration, or whatever one pleases.

As might be expected, literary critics usually focus their energy on interpreting texts that pose the greatest threat to their sense of propriety. They seek out fiction at the brink of confessional extravagance, attracted by the challenge of making its unrespectability respectable, its embarrassment something to be proud of. There is little satisfaction in praising a straightforward conventional novel for its freedom from negative appeal (for example, one by Howells or Trollope), so this exercise in the obvious is bypassed for interpreting other novels and poems whose expressiveness tests the limits of decency. Critics seek out the most vulnerable authors, and the most vulnerable of their works, in order to submit their felt disorientation to conventional literary analysis.[4] But what do these critics try to do? Nothing less than to prove that these texts are just as innocent, just as conventional, just as devoid of threat as the stories and poems that can be safely neglected. The bigger the problem, the more skill needed to domesticate its negative appeal. The text's affirmative meaning is thus exaggerated on whatever grounds seem reasonable, so its tension between leakage and narrative closure may be reduced to principles supportive of the closure dynamics alone. Countervailing suggestiveness is all but eliminated from consideration, and the work's profundity becomes very ordinary indeed, like ocean pebbles that lose their shininess once they have been removed from the surf. A few critics have avoided this tendency, but most have surrendered to it, and with good reason. Evasiveness via literary convention is even safer and more comfortable in criticism than in the fiction it describes.

Once a literary text's political subversiveness has been neutralized by history (for example, with Scott's and Disraeli's novels), and once its technical subversiveness has been absorbed and justified by literary convention (for example, with Landor's and H.D.'s poetry), the single remaining danger consists of its denied unconscious implications. The relatively normal poetry of Bryant and Longfellow can be passed over, for example, in favor of Blake's hallucinations, Wordsworth's escapist flight to nature, and Keats's effort to transcend his fear of death by extolling the permanence of aesthetic form. Trollope can be neglected in favor of Dickens and the Brontë sisters, as can Bennett and Galsworthy in favor of Hardy, James, and Conrad, all of whom brought emotional disturbance into the context of literary form. Probably the most disorienting creativity has been Shakespeare's, yet Shakespearean criticism almost invariably features conventional insights based on the assumption that his excesses were typically Elizabethan—which they were not. Critics have almost completely ignored the bizarre connotations of his metaphors and image clusters as well as the androgynous characterization implied by the metaleptic extravagance of his poetry. The homosexuality in his sonnets is ignored as much as possible, and the irrepressible bawdiness of his comedies is politely dismissed as a sop to Elizabethan audiences. His use of multiple transvestitism is likewise disregarded, as are the double entendres expressive of sex nausea that steal into his tragedies. And of course, the suicidal obsession of such masterpieces as *Hamlet* is harmlessly rendered as thematic profundity befitting Elizabethan theater. As for academic responsibility among the teachers and professors of Shakespeare, this usually consists of their skill in dispensing with these presumably vagrant questions as quickly as possible and then spending their semesters bowdlerizing interpretive possibilities with the necessary assortment of explicative distractions for conveying his mysterious and ineluctable appeal.

Raw data are easy to come by to demonstrate this preference by academicians for normalizing the abnormal. In the *1985 MLA Bibliography*, for example, Shakespeare receives an overwhelming 525 entries, few or none of

The Affirmative Fallacy

which betray much excitement with the issues listed above. Meanwhile, Dickens receives 87 entries, Conrad 83, James 79, Wordsworth 53, Blake 42, and Keats 34. In contrast, Trollope receives 7, Longfellow, Disraeli, and Galsworthy 2 apiece, and Arnold Bennett 1, while Holmes, Whittier, Landor, and Scott receive no entries whatsoever. In the 1985–86 *Books in Print*, 87 entries are listed for Edgar Allan Poe and only 23 for Howells; 87 entries are also listed for D. H. Lawrence and only 11 for H. G. Wells. Perhaps differences in creative talent help to explain some of these discrepancies, but the appeal of literature's felt instability also seems to play a major role. As a rule, the more effectively a text brings disorientation under control, the bigger its audience and the more strenuous the effort of critics to confirm its "normal" genius.

Critics themselves have conceded the avoidances besetting their trade by inventing a number of literary fallacies, but they have failed to recognize how and why these fallacies obscure the full implications of the texts they explicate. Each of their fallacies has been singly invoked to expose critical excesses, but the remedy has been to go to the other extreme—excess biography supplanted by no biography at all, excess formal analysis by no formal analysis at all, etc. Fallacies these are, but their total rejection becomes a "fallacy-fallacy," as proposed by Stanley Fish, when one mode of exclusiveness is rejected in favor of its opposite.[5] Interestingly, both fallacies and fallacy-fallacies take on their own evasiveness as extensions that give a specific aim to the affirmative fallacy. For each, the precise locus of the affirmative fallacy might be difficult to establish, but it can be detected whenever there is a displacement from aversion to diversionary affirmation. Whenever denial is coterminous with a critical fallacy's (or fallacy-fallacy's) acceptable distractions comes the affirmative transposition, the inner voice that interjects, "If we cannot admit *this*, let us concern ourselves with *that*!" As if by magic, *that* becomes the issue.

In some respects the affirmative fallacy can be as restrictive as the other literary fallacies, but its implied double negative paradoxically gives it more inclusiveness as well. That is to say, it is more basic, therefore more universally applicable, as may be observed, for example, in the way it initiates and gives impetus to the rest of these fallacies and fallacy-fallacies. The intentional fallacy, for instance, as explained by Wimsatt, resolves the denial displacement by putting undue emphasis on the author's motivation, while its fallacy-fallacy does this by altogether prohibiting authorial motivation from being taken into account.[6] Similarly, the affective fallacy, as explained by Wimsatt

The Affirmative Fallacy

and Beardsley, shifts our attention to our personal feelings, while its opposite altogether prohibits these from being taken into account.[7] And the fallacy of imitative form, as explained by Yvor Winters, exaggerates the importance of mimetic accuracy, while its fallacy-fallacy altogether rejects the value of mimetic resemblances.[8] Each of these fallacies and fallacy-fallacies helps to consolidate the affirmative fallacy's reversal dynamics by giving aim to its diversionary pursuit of acceptable partial truths, and for each, of course, there is partial justification. Just as the denial displacement sets the stage for other psychological displacements, thereby triggering, for example, the projective fantasies of the paranoid syndrome, the affirmative fallacy sets the stage for these other fallacies to occur. It initiates the dynamics of evasiveness, whereupon each of the others provides an affirmative aim elsewhere as guaranteed by artificial constraints of one sort or another.

The affective fallacy, for example, depends on the exploration of extraneous personal associations irrelevant to the text itself. Fiction's potentially embarrassing implications are denied by the reader's emphasis on mostly irrelevant personal associations that are both gratifying and harmlessly meaningful. Paradoxically, readers are encouraged to explore the full range of experience suggested by fiction except to the extent that it bears upon their specific needs—perhaps too embarrassing to be acknowledged—that would be satisfied by the success story it tells. While reading *Pride and Prejudice*, for example, individuals might admit to being charmed by the precision of Elizabeth Bennet's diction or bothered by Darcy's aristocratic pride as a blemish on his appeal as the countryside's (perhaps England's) most eligible bachelor. These are issues that admittedly enhance the story's interpretation. However, they serve as nothing more than distractions unless tied in with the reader's collaborative eagerness for Elizabeth to succeed in romance. This unrealistic payoff dominates our expectations as we read, but there is discomfort in too closely examining its appeal—so we don't. A wide assortment of personal considerations is emphasized to crowd from consciousness the primitive and even more subjective dynamics of wish fulfillment that disclose our vulnerability. Who can admit out loud, "I really, really want to see the hero win," or "I really, really want to see the two fall in love," or "I really, really want to see the victim vindicated?" Loose associational distractions consequently become important as busywork that rationalizes our raw motivation. On the other hand, the stringent avoidance of our feelings becomes itself a fallacy-fallacy if and when it bans from interpretation the text's affective appeal. To completely ignore what a text does for us shifts formal explication to other kinds of busywork, all of which are equally irrelevant to the felt dynamics of literary form.

The intentional fallacy proposed by Wimsatt and Beardsley similarly complements and gives aim to the affirmative fallacy by emphasizing the author's motivation as the key to interpreting creative work. It stresses the author's life situation rather than the use of literary form as an organizing point for the needs and feelings shared with readers. The emotional demands the author incorporates into the plot are disregarded in favor of biographical information loosely associated with these demands. Yet the avoidance of the intentional fallacy becomes just as evasive if the author's specific aim in telling the story is disregarded. Also stemming from the affirmative fallacy is Yvor Winters's fallacy of imitative form, the excessive use of lifelike accuracy regardless of how boring or irrelevant it becomes to the story being told. This time evasiveness occurs through the pursuit of reportorial authenticity: "Not that I am afraid of confronting my fascination with this story; rather, I want to capture the total experience of the *demimonde* [with Zola's *Nana*] or of a murderer right up to the moment of his execution [with novels by Dreiser, Capote, and Mailer]." Exaggerated mimetic thoroughness thus buries fiction's narrative organization of experience in irrelevant detail. Yet the avoidance of the Fallacy of Imitative Form can be equally fallacious if nonrepresentational virtues are sought for their own sake, for example, by emphasizing avant-garde dislocations that totally thwart conventional literary expectation. When antimimetic aesthetic freedom becomes unbearably tedious, a dose of mimesis is probably needed, if without going to the opposite extreme represented by the fallacy of imitative form.

A. C. Bradley's formalist heresy likewise describes the undue emphasis upon formal considerations—rhyme and rhythm, stanza pattern, imagery, irony, and so on.[9] Here denial is sublimated in the harmless study of contextual intricacy peripheral to the shared denial strategy that gives a text its appeal. Yet the use of form to organize the reader's response to the text cannot be ignored. Also evasive is Bradley's paraphrastic heresy, the dependence on paraphrase and plot outline to convey a poem's fullest meaning.[10] This simplification of the text usually neutralizes fiction's complex challenge by glossing over its dangerous connotations in favor of a harmless conventional meaning. Yet it is the text's narrative organization that affords its overt appeal, and this is almost always paraphrasable. To deny this appeal once again imposes a fallacy-fallacy that originates in the affirmative fallacy. In each of the other fallacies—such as Wimsatt's pictorial fallacy, Poe's didactic heresy, Arnold's historic and personal fallacies, Allen Tate's fallacies of communication and mere denotation, and I. A. Richards's fallacy of vulgar packaging—it is denial that initiates the fallacy process, followed by affirmative commitment to a diversionary aim.[11] Each such fallacy may be rejected in favor of its fallacy-fallacy, but with a comparable negative displacement taking effect. As the initial segment of all such displacements, the affirmative fallacy catalyzes the transition.

Sometimes the affirmative fallacy surfaces as a simple and undiluted realization of the denial displacement. With primitive Aristotelian reversal, for example, it tells the story of an inexperienced soldier who proves he is not a coward (e.g., in *The Red Badge of Courage*), of a father who proves to himself that he can help his son (e.g., in *Death of a Salesman*), etc. Moreover, just as denial becomes obvious when it leads to an awkward mixture of new displacements, the affirmative fallacy becomes obvious when it initiates the pursuit of contradictory virtues—for example, beauty and uncompromising mimetic accuracy, or intellectual freedom and profound devotion to a religious or political orthodoxy (including both communism and anticommunism). The purpose of the affirmative fallacy is likewise evident when one fallacy abruptly shifts to another—for example, when the fallacy of imitative form is patched up with the didactic heresy (e.g., in socialist realism), or when the intentional fallacy is buttressed by the paraphrastic fallacy (e.g., in the simplistic interpretation of a story as the replication of its author's personal experience). When these superficial uses of evasiveness converge and disperse—begin with one, then convert into others—the fundamental importance of the affirmative fallacy once again becomes plain. Too often, in fact, these other fallacies become interchangeable in channeling affirmative purposefulness into harmless exegetical alternatives. Each culminates and gives focus to the dynamics of evasiveness, but their shared impetus begins with denial, and its fulcrum and moment of transition are best defined by the affirmative fallacy.

Most schools of literary criticism necessarily feature assumptions based on avoidances rooted in the affirmative fallacy. They all feature one or more literary virtues, for example, emotional growth, social responsibility, improved sensibility, and heightened aesthetic awareness. However, they exclude from consideration the psychological dynamics by which these literary

The Affirmative Fallacy

virtues (and virtues they are) are rooted in denial, negation, and unrecognized evasiveness. Each approach accordingly glosses over the negative value of literary form by emphasizing its unique range of positive alternatives. In each instance, a positive vision of literary achievement is emphasized, but with implicit negative underpinnings—its implicit aversions and hostilities—that must be grasped to be able to understand it in its fullest complexity. Six critical perspectives illustrate this pattern of oversight—respectively, the vulgar and sophisticated versions of the Marxist, psychoanalytic, and formalist schools of criticism. I include response theory as a sophisticated psychoanalytic approach and deviationism, deconstructionism, and new historicism as sophisticated formalist approaches. I conclude the chapter with a brief assessment of poststructuralist critical theory as a whole in the academic marketplace today.

THE VULGAR MARXIST MODE

Now discredited except among unreconstructed activists, the vulgar Marxist insistence on the propagandistic value of literature was once effectively promulgated by Jean-Paul Sartre in France, by Christopher Caudwell in England, and, at a more simplistic level, by Michael Gold and Granville Hicks in the United States. Most of the critics listed in Lee Baxandall's impressive bibliography *Marxism and Aesthetics* would fit the description of vulgar Marxists, since they emphasize fiction's political message supportive of revolutionary change.[12] Fiction's responsibility is presumably to expose the self-destructive contradictions of capitalism and to suggest an improved future under a proletarian leadership. Unfortunately, this objective has little relevance to the novels and poems we actually read. In fact, our most revered classics usually cling to the status quo, sacrificing revolutionary commitment for the more compelling need of vicarious self-justification, here and now, in the world we know. If history makes its inexorable passage into the future, these classics resist its impetus, providing an oasis of immediate pleasure during the few hours it takes to read and digest them. For some readers certain illusions might heighten our anger against the status quo, as Sartre, the Zhdanovites (or Stalinists), and others have maintained, but for most they encourage political apathy. When readers devour novels and poems, their success in making the unreal come true in the real world diminishes their interest in imposing social change. They can avoid taking action because the texts they enjoy have taken it for them. By losing themselves in fiction, they actually *take inaction*, having been afforded full gratification from the dry-run *praxis* offered by literary form. As I. A. Richards argued, fiction's "incipient action," which excludes or postpones *praxis*, is its primary benefit to readers.[13] This is how fiction lets us cope with fears and anxieties we cannot otherwise deal with—for example, our fear of death, our doubts about our competence, our sense that we lack any final meaning in life, and our respective sexual difficulties (Oedipal, androgynous, adulterous, etc.). In each instance, literary experience features an enactment of personal adjustment that actually discourages political commitment meriting personal sacrifice. Feeling well becomes more important than making concrete changes, and the arena of conflict shifts to internal consciousness as opposed to political activism.

Of course, the pursuit of radical goals may be advocated as one particular mode of personal adjustment, but this seldom happens in fiction, where success is primarily limited to marriage, self-discovery, and simplistic moral vindication. How many novels deemphasize these personal achievements in favor of political victory? Very few. However, fiction's programmatic evasiveness of politics is ignored by Marxists, who insist upon harmony between literary form and revolutionary dedication. In their judgment both fiction and social change are desirable, so they necessarily reinforce each other—good fiction presumably ushering in revolution, the healthy acceptance of revolutionary goals presumably ushering in good fiction. Unfortunately, this is just not the case, and to pretend otherwise illustrates the affirmative fallacy.

The renaissance of the American novel during the late fifties and early sixties effectively illustrates this basic incompatibility between creativity and revolutionary activism. Spurred on by social disillusionment, heightened alienation, and, for some of them, the opportunity for the first time to use sexual explicitness in expressing their sense of malaise, such authors as Barth, Bellow, Brautigan, Burroughs, Heller, Kerouac, Kesey, Mailer, Malamud, Nabokov, Pynchon, Roth, Selby, Updike, and Vonnegut rose to the challenge in a flurry of literary activity that has not been matched since. A similar renaissance occurred in poetry, including the new poets Bly, Creeley, Dickey, Ginsberg, Kinnell, Levine, Plath, Sexton, Snodgrass, Snyder, Stafford, and Wright. Poets who had already been published—for example, Ammons, Ashbery, Berryman, Duncan, Ferlinghetti, Levertov, Lowell, O'Hara, Olson, and

The Affirmative Fallacy

Rich—also seemed to catch fire, whether through the influence of the San Francisco renaissance or through a growing sense of malaise shared with everybody else. In the decade between 1956 (when Ginsberg's "Howl" was published) and 1969 (when Barth's *Giles Goat-Boy* and Pynchon's *The Crying of Lot 49* were published) there was a resurgence of American fiction and poetry that helped to mediate the transition from nonliterary quietism of the early Eisenhower years to the equally nonliterary activism of the protest movement, which, as much as anything, terminated this literary renaissance. Once protesters (many of them novelists) took to the streets, the first-person convention of heroes pitted against the power structure and bourgeois morality quickly gave way to the antiwar journalism of *Ramparts, The Minority of One, The I. F. Stone Weekly, The National Guardian*, and *The New York Review of Books*, such underground newspapers as *The Village Voice* and *The Berkeley Barb*, such bizarre liberationist magazines as *The Realist* and *Avant Garde*, and dozens of other antiestablishment publications now almost totally forgotten. Fiction had provided a temporary mode of adjustment stretched between two antithetical plateaus, the quietism of the Eisenhower decade followed by the countercultural revolutionary dedication of the 1960s. As social behavior, literature had played an intermediate role lacking the ideological consistency of both political extremes. However, by imposing their own structure, authors and poets substituted their own tentative plateaus in works of fiction, each with its beginning, middle, and end. In effect, they avoided making an absolute choice between bourgeois conformity and its total rejection by redefining this choice according to the conventions of the picaresque outsider who is unable to accept or change the world. They survived as oddball nonconformists, as neither defenders nor attackers of any particular faith. Partially examined individualism was thus featured, as opposed to both the middle-class standards of the fifties and the countercultural activism of the late sixties. Fiction's typical male antisocial hero stood alone, without a plan, and with no clear idea of the forces he was up against. All he knew was that his integrity gave him a voice and plenty of excitement as he moved from one encounter to the next.

The rise and fall of this adolescent success formula between the fifties and sixties may be explained, of course, as an intermediate heightening of consciousness that helped to usher in the revolutionary commitment of the sixties. Denial presumably took place, but without any vision of the affirmative substitutes later to be imposed. Fiction both stirred discontent and inhibited its effective discharge, leading to its rejection when activism became fashionable. Indeed, fiction anticipated this activism, but it also resisted it, and its appeal primarily derived from its effectiveness in avoiding engagement. Such an interpretation of fiction's preliminary role in anticipating political turmoil is consistent with Lucien Goldmann's theory that aesthetic inspiration, without understanding how or why, anticipates comprehensive theoretical analysis. Sophocles, for example, supposedly anticipated Plato; Shakespeare, Locke; and Racine, Marx. In similar fashion, fiction's antiauthoritarianism in the years preceding the Vietnam War expressed the alienation that anticipated later trends. However, this was mitigated by a reluctance to be engaged in either the extravagant antisocial behavior or the organized political resistance of the late sixties and early seventies. There was vocal opposition to the conventional values of the fifties, but this rebelliousness was marketable as fiction because it featured defiant withdrawal rather than confrontation. Not surprisingly, when the escalation of the Vietnam crisis finally led to violence in the streets, the formula lost its appeal, shed by its audience like an earlier hair style, as if its obsession with alienation and rootlessness were out of date when pitted against the FBI, CIA, riot police, and liberal-conservative power structure. It is only with sufficient retrospective distancing that transitional novelists may be appreciated for having captured their ambivalence in the context of literary form with such extraordinary success.

Similar patterns of fictive restlessness can be discovered in earlier periods of social transition, including the transcendental inspiration preceding the Civil War, the spiritual purity emphasized by Tolstoy and his contemporaries preceding the Russian Revolution, and the exaggeration of aristocratic virtues by Shakespeare and his contemporaries preceding the seventeenth-century Puritan revolution. All three of these cultural renaissances lost their momentum when literary denial was followed by turmoil and civil conflict that led toward a new kind of orthodoxy, just as the mood of the sixties almost inexorably degenerated into trends leading to the Reagan eighties. The Gilded Age supplanted the early transcendentalism of Emerson, Hawthorne, and their disciples; Leninism (then Stalinism) supplanted the ethical vision of Tolstoy and his contemporaries; and the Puritan Commonwealth followed by Whig politics supplanted the humanism of Shakespeare and his contemporaries. Each of the preliminary renaissances played its transitional role, but only because it both anticipated and resisted subsequent developments. As might be expected, the outcome it heralded ended its persuasiveness except as art.

THE SOPHISTICATED MARXIST MODE

Best articulated by Georg Lukács, Lucien Goldmann, and a variety of critics identified with the Frankfurt school, this more sophisticated vision of history includes in the canon of valid literary expressiveness any work of fiction that exposes social contradictions without necessarily advocating revolutionary change.[14] An accurate documentation of historic crisis is emphasized, and the premature advocacy of revolutionary commitment is discouraged because it diminishes fiction's accuracy as documentation. This is why Lukács preferred Balzac over Zola as a reporter of social disruptions caused by economic dislocation. Nevertheless, the affirmative fallacy once again takes place if accuracy is emphasized at the expense of escapist value in helping to obscure—in effect to *undescribe*—the stressful conditions that dominate our lives. Fiction appeals to us not because it documents social contradictions but because its narrative machinery lets us cope with these contradictions by forgetting ourselves and seeing our problems in a relatively harmless light. Authors emphasize fantasy at the expense of descriptive accuracy in order to make their stories come to life. They prize verisimilitude only because it gives credence to fantasy content, thereby subordinating historic validity to the more compelling dynamics of wish fulfillment. This motivation must be granted its primary role before fiction's symptomatic value can be adequately assessed, and Marxist literary criticism usually falls short of the challenge. Of course, reportorial accuracy in the depiction of gestures, clothing, speech habits, and nonspecific attitudes of characters can be utilized. However, this accuracy is important only to the extent that it reinforces fiction's escapist appeal, and it may be almost entirely neglected without diminishing the cathartic benefit of romance, historical romance, science fiction, horror stories, and jungle adventures.

Obviously illustrating the predominance of escapism at the expense of accuracy, Hollywood used extravagant theatrical glitter during the Great Depression in order to capitalize upon the emotional needs of the American public without more than a couple of times touching upon the social crisis that produced these needs. For explaining the Depression, treatises on economics and sociology would have been more appropriate, but of course the public did not go to movies to educate themselves about the Depression. Their purpose was to feel better about themselves, and this usually meant utilizing Hollywood's relatively limited variety of escapist formulas. They could enjoy themselves, for example, by immersing themselves in Busby Berkeley's choreography of wealth and happiness, or in the success story of somebody who starts out poor but makes it to the top through earnestness and hard work. Other such formulas included the discovery of slumming aristocrats that impoverished eccentrics can be admired too, and the discovery that the real enemy was greed and that all the "real" people could work together to bring about victory. Conflict of the latter category typified socialist realism, but it also cropped up in the most exploitive westerns, Robin Hood thrillers, and pirate adventures, all of which dramatically evoked this pseudorevolutionary appeal as well. Errol Flynn's swashbuckling victories, as directed by Michael Curtiz (who was also responsible for *Angels with Dirty Faces*, *Casablanca*, and *Mission to Moscow*), offered a sense of engagement just as compelling as Hemingway's *For Whom the Bell Tolls* and Steinbeck's *The Grapes of Wrath*—and just as irrelevant to the palliative successes of Roosevelt's New Deal preceding the economic mobilization of World War II.

The vision of John Dos Passos, James T. Farrell, and Jack Conroy was perhaps more accurate than adventure movies in documenting economic and political trends that culminated in an international conflagration which cost tens of millions of lives, but their fiction did not express the mood of the thirties any more accurately than did the lavish productions of Goldwyn, Selznick, and Louis B. Mayer, the Thorne Smith novels, or the countless formulaic *Colliers* and *Saturday Evening Post* love stories. All was myth, and its appeal did not depend upon accurate diagnosis.

When particular myths ceased to interest the public, new myths were found to replace them. The prompt abandonment of the Depression's inventory of success stories, for example, was inevitable once our nation entered World War II. New myths were needed, new wish-fulfillment strategies to deal with new problems. Literature could spin out its fantasies before, during, and after this transition, but in the late forties (as opposed to its role in the late fifties), it did not—could not—document how this basic transition took place. Where are the novels that document how the American power structure, and indeed our entire culture, stumbled upon Cold War ideology as an effective means of sustaining economic prosperity? Not more than a handful of novels may be cited, including Lionel Trilling's *The Middle of the Journey* and Norman Mailer's *Barbary Shore*. An entirely new variety of lies, distortions, and rewritten history swiftly gained currency in the media. Why were these for the most part ignored in fiction? The obvious answer is that fiction primarily addresses itself to personal need and that its myths are useful only to the extent they do so on a personal basis. Otherwise they tend to bore or confuse readers. Social documentation may be connected with this subjective purposefulness, but only if affirmative conventions can be addressed to individual deficiency. Factual information (or misinformation) about the economic circumstances that produce this sense of deficiency is interesting but optional. Does history or economics help to carry the story? If it does, it may be included; if not, it should be thrown out. This principle applies to Balzac, Zola, Shakespeare, and every other author. Reportorial accuracy might seem important, but primarily to give credibility to plot development in fulfilling the pleasure principle. When Marxist aesthetics ignores this negative purposefulness, it too capitulates to the affirmative fallacy.

THE VULGAR PSYCHOANALYTIC MODE

At its reductionist extreme, psychoanalytic criticism descends to symbol mongering, the pursuit of categories typical of the Freudian, Jungian, and Eriksonian interpretations—phallus and womb, animus and anima, and the standard litany of regressive fixations from oral to Oedipal. For all of these psychological typologies, the same fundamental assumption holds true, that every text may be appreciated for its almost inexhaustible expression of repressed feelings. Fiction is supposedly worthwhile to the extent that it serves this function, and our pleasure as readers supposedly results from letting them appeal to us without necessarily understanding how or why. The role of critics is to bring fiction's unconscious appeal to the reader's attention on a systematic basis. A crude theory of mimesis is accordingly promoted based on the conscious re-creation of themes, images, and symbols rooted in our unconscious. Representational accuracy shifts from external to internal truth based on the assumption that cathartic relief comes from exposing unconscious need to the light of critical inquiry. Once again, however, the affirmative fallacy may be detected, since this approach too often neglects our primary purpose when reading—to enjoy ourselves by escaping from ourselves into an imaginary world where improvements are possible. We identify with literary figures whose resemblance to ourselves *justifies* identification, but whose difference from ourselves also *rewards* identification. Symbols and fixations may be useful, but only to the extent that they help us to disclaim our inadequacies—our felt impotence, isolation, and sense of failure. Once again denial occurs, and the entire psychoanalytic battery of displacements contributes to its achievement. Unless this more inclusive purposefulness is given its due, psychoanalytic criticism's eager pursuit of symbols and fixations becomes stale, indeed almost ridiculous.

Phallic symbols, for example, are often interpreted as the expression of macho boastfulness, but their excessive use usually reveals a compensatory denial of sexual inadequacy. The obsession with phallic imagery derives from a sense of deficiency, not excess, so its literary use (for example, in "Young Goodman Brown") discloses evasiveness rather than masculine pride. Unless this negative strategy is recognized, the vulgar Freudian critic's almost random pursuit of symbolic elongations and penetrations becomes no less compensatory. Oral and anal fixations are likewise escapist. Form, for example, is not imposed to defend us from orality, as Norman Holland maintained in *The Dynamics of Literary Response*.[15] On the contrary, form structures and organizes orality to protect us from more basic anxieties. As a regressive defense mechanism, the oral fixation utilizes helplessness to cope with a mature sense of inadequacy. Once organized by literary form, orality takes on the needed linear structure to deny a host of nonoral anxieties. These anxieties, not orality, encourage our dependence on literary experience, while orality as organized by form helps to dispose of them—for a while at least. All the rest of the regressive defenses—anality, phallic assertiveness, and Oedipal role modeling—must also be judged in relation to the fears and anxieties against which they are deployed. To emphasize their appeal free of this intentional value necessarily illustrates the affirmative fallacy.

THE SOPHISTICATED PSYCHOANALYTIC MODE—RESPONSE THEORY

The convergence of affective criticism and speech act theory has opened up a variety of exciting issues whose investigation is to be wholeheartedly encouraged. Nevertheless, the notion of a reader's "identity theme," as proposed by

The Affirmative Fallacy

Norman Holland in *Poems in Persons*, apparently justifies the investigation of the matchup that takes place between the writer's and readers' characteristic styles. Once again the affirmative fallacy is in evidence, this time because criticism emphasizes how readers seek to confirm their sense of identity in the context of literary pattern. Mimesis is brought to a new level of sophistication with a new and more attenuated set of resemblances, this time between readers' personal traits and those in the text with which they may identify. However, as before, these resemblances are featured by response theory at the expense of differences brought into play by fiction to suggest an improvement upon real life. Response theoreticians overlook the distinction between literary resemblances and differences—that resemblances are needed to let readers project themselves into fiction, but that differences make up the active ingredient of fiction, the reason why readers turn to it with any regularity in their lives. At this level, paradoxically, the single most important resemblance or cluster of resemblances in the experience of fiction consists of the mode and style of authors and readers in their pursuit of differences. Only by stressing how our defenses as readers are reinforced by comparable defenses at work in a text can we begin to understand fiction's appeal. In his book *Poems in Persons*, Holland himself seems to recognize this connection:

> Having created his characteristic defensive structures from the work, the reader has warded off anxiety. He can therefore project into it the fantasies that give him pleasure, and he can use his defenses to transform the fantasies into themes that give the work intellectual cohesion and sense.[16]

Here there can be no disagreement, except perhaps in the sequence that sets in motion first defensive structures and then the transformation of these structures into themes. As I explained in chapter 3, pleasure comes when anxiety is reduced through the use of these defenses, thereby reversing Holland's cause and effect relationship. That is to say, anxieties are not automatically eliminated by the act of turning to fiction; instead, it is the process of reading fiction that masks problems in order to reduce anxiety. Holland also limits transformation to one particular phase in literary experience, but in fact literary experience stretches out the process of transformation in mustering the needed defenses to cope with anxiety. From beginning to end, the literary text reinforces the reader's self-respect ("character armor," in Wilhelm Reich's words) by its conscious manipulation of fantasy content. As organized by form and theme, the text reduces anxieties by providing an alternative context of experience suitably resolved by a happy ending. As before, a psychological version of mimetic equivalence is featured, but differences are what matters, not resemblances. Readers might enjoy recognizing themselves in fiction, but their pleasure derives from an escapist strategy based on self-avoidance—imposing "other" as the essence of self. Only enough similarities are needed to make this imposition seem appropriate. The quest is for an improved outcome couched in identifiable resemblances, and fiction facilitates this escapism with as much honesty as can be deployed in the service of illusion.

One of Holland's most intriguing contributions is a feedback model of literary experience based on William T. Powers's theory of homeostatic behavior.[17] Holland proposes a complex feedback loop, or hierarchy of loops, dominated by stimulus, perception, and behavior. There is a lower loop, or combination of loops, governed by physiology, but it is dominated by an upper loop, or combination of loops, governed by cortical activity. Central to Powers's model as adopted by Holland is the assumption of ego psychology that higher levels almost inevitably control lower levels, cortical activity taking precedence over somatic activity. The conscious predominates at the expense of the unconscious and higher brain centers at the expense of the lower. One's identity theme is supposedly fixed by the unique interaction among these vertically organized loops for each particular individual. As a general rule, Holland claims, three levels predominate in a hierarchy with obvious Freudian implications: personal identity (as ego), internalized culture (as superego), and physiology (as id). Literary experience engages all three levels and thereby helps to refine and stabilize the reader's sense of personal identity. The problem with Holland's hypothesis results from his bias in favor of ego psychology. Holland all but eliminates from his analysis the negative dynamics of both homeostasis and the Freudian unconscious. A harmonious interaction among overt feedback loops dominates his model of homeostatic adjustment, leaving little room for negative feedback in producing tension reduction felt as pleasure. According to Holland's model, nothing is denied and nothing excluded to reduce tension levels to a steady-state minimum. His concept of homeostasis is for this reason incomplete and falls short of explaining literary gratification. If exclusiveness is not included in his paradigm, his inclusiveness excludes—it's as simple as that. For a dedicated Freudian, this point seems fundamental.

The Affirmative Fallacy

As I explained in chapter 3, negative feedback provides the message circuit that restores homeostatic balance by its reduction of nervous tension. This reduction is rewarded by felt satisfaction *if* consciousness is included in the loop, as for example, when reading fiction. But consciousness does its job in order to produce satisfaction (the somatic reward for a job well done), thus reversing Holland's priorities. If any hierarchy is involved, the sequence of Holland's model should be reversed to explain how physiology at the lowest order bestows pleasure at the highest for disposing of neural tension levels harmful to the body itself. As Freud insisted, the ego is a small but activated zone of conscious sensitivity compared to our bodies (or somata) dominated by the id. If conscious demands become excessive, literary experience helps by reducing this excessiveness. This is why we read novels—to stop worrying about ourselves by concentrating our attention on gratifying illusions. Our bodies expect and demand relaxation, and the brain responds by engrossing itself in novels whose false assurances can be believed. The interlinking hierarchy that emerges is finally dominated by this compulsion, since fiction fulfills it by denying unacceptable feelings. The literary text as understood by readers might be defined as the highest of the feedback loops, since it takes control of the entire hierarchy of circuits during the reading experience. However, it receives its energy and final orders from below, and the changes it produces harness cognitive recognition to somatic ends.

Once psychoanalysis is eliminated from consideration, response theory falls more in line with the epistemology of Wolfgang Iser, Stanley Fish, and their followers. Here, too, speculation can be promising if denial and the negative imperative are incorporated into their formulations, and if the conative (or motivational) dimension of literary experience is not swallowed up in cognitive puzzle-solving. Both Iser and Fish pay their respects to literary affect, but their emphasis upon conscious meaning tends to diminish affective considerations. Taken to its extreme, this emphasis crowds from consideration both conation and primary process thinking. Iser, for example, divides the literary text into determinate (formal) and indeterminate (affective) meanings, with textual indeterminacies providing gaps whose interpretation must be supplied on an individual basis by readers.[18] Iser defines gaps as negations that "invoke familiar and determinate elements of knowledge only to cancel them out," but with what is canceled remaining in view, thereby revising the reader's attitude toward the text. Because of these negated possibilities, Iser claims, "the reader's attention is . . . fixed, not upon what the norms represent, but upon what their representation excludes, and so the aesthetic object—which is the whole spectrum of human nature—begins to arise out of what is adumbrated by the negated possibilities."[19] Here Iser's paradigm rather closely resembles the model of negative poetics I am proposing, if without specifying the importance of narrative closure in finally completing the act of exclusion. Usually, however, his paradigm implies (or at least accommodates) a narrative homogeneity devoid of closure. To this extent, it resembles a sponge in its spatial network of subjectivity-producing absences honeycombed by a complementary network of textual presences. By filling these absences (or gaps), readers formulate themselves, completing the necessary transaction between the text and their own subjectivity. The spatial constraints of a text supposedly stir self-realization by encouraging the reader's active participation in interpreting literary form. However, Iser's model neglects the repressive dynamics at work in a text and restricts indeterminacies to an arbitrary choice among designated zones, or foci, in any particular text. His model also seems cumbersome because the mixture of indeterminacies he emphasizes at the core of literary experience too easily degenerates into a nonspecific jumble of gaps and nongaps. "Here we must be precise," Iser advises us, pointing to the text's determinate structure of meaning, "but over here, with 'indeterminate' possibilities, we can be appreciative of our individual differences." In other words, we can formulate—or, more appropriately, *reformulate*—ourselves without fear of embarrassment whenever the text provides intermissions that let us ignore its formal constraints. Here again there seems to be an affirmative strategy, a new and more ingenious effort to minimize the subversiveness of literary experience mediated by the text as a whole.

The deficiency is resolved, I think, if Iser's determinacy-indeterminacy dichotomy is merged with the plot-metaphor dichotomy I proposed earlier, with form added to provide synthesis. As the agent of denial, plot establishes a determinate organization of experience with a comparable determinate subversiveness felt by both authors and readers. Some of the dislocations that strike Iser as indeterminate might be accidental—in which case they can be ignored—but others express a metaphoric input that resists the plot's overt dynamics of closure. The writer's projection of personal feelings dislocates structure, and sympathetic readers experience rapport because the structural dislocations let them project their feelings too. When these feelings carry threatening implications (a possibility ignored by Iser), the dialectic very

The Affirmative Fallacy

likely intensifies between closure and metaphoric expressiveness. Suddenly gaps combine in a single inclusive void that resists closure except through renewed commitment to determinate structure. With these simple modifications, Iser's theory comes to life. His static and potentially endless plug-in model of literary form becomes a closed dynamic model with exciting possibilities.

In his lively polemic "Why No One's Afraid of Wolfgang Iser," Stanley Fish turns Iser's theory against itself by describing it as "a piece of literature that satisfies Iser's own criteria for an 'aesthetic object.'" As Fish explains, "this is because it is full of gaps and the reader is invited to fill them in his own way."[20] Fish makes his case effectively, but his argument may be extended to apply to other approaches as well. My denial-projective model, for example, is similarly vulnerable, and so, too, is Fish's concept of interpretive communities, based on his classroom analysis of literary texts. What better example of an interpretive community can be found, Fish suggests, than a full class of eager explicators?[21] However, for most readers, who read books in the privacy of their own homes, the literary experience is, if anything, the behavior of an interpretive *uncommunity*, and in many instances an interpretive *anticommunity*. Granted, all readers belong to a community of one sort or another, but most nonacademic readers resort to fiction in the effort to ignore, if not escape, community. They read to reaffirm themselves, and this subjective quest usually puts them in a temporary *pseudocommunity* established by the text itself. The words they use might be social events, but unless fiction is read aloud, both the generation and the absorption of these words remain private acts. As a result, any evidence pertaining to the private reading habit is usually a better indicator of literary norms than the classroom dialogue emphasized by Fish.[22] For both author and reader alike, it is solitude, paradoxically, that facilitates sharing in fiction's linear momentum toward closure. Even oral poetry probably depended more than recognized on the teller's reconstitution of the poetic material from one telling to the next. Sooner or later in the bardic tradition, public sharing was submitted to individual judgment—in ancient Greece, for example, when one or more Homers organized the Trojan Cycle into two major epics, *The Iliad* and *The Odyssey*.

According to Fish, there is no determinate core of meaning in fiction beyond the structure of assumptions shared by interpretive communities—those groups of individuals whose common beliefs and experiences lead to common expectations about fiction. Inevitably such groups find what they seek, their interpretation providing a structure of constraints that their members can all accept. If evasiveness is at work, it is evasiveness by consensus. If eighteen or eighteen thousand people choose to deny the latent implications of fiction, these latent implications cease to exist for this particular group. Fish disposes of the extreme relativism that might seem to result from this principle with the assurance that readers cannot escape their common values and feelings even if they want to. Since these values and feelings are the product of society, readers will inevitably share them in their judgment of fiction, and in turn fiction will both confirm and refine their understanding in the minds of readers. Fish's qualified relativism is valid, of course, but he deemphasizes the role of fiction as an agent of group consensus that is dominated less by common values than by comparable wish-fulfillment fantasies. Fiction's true determinate core is its mode of structuring the satisfaction that produces an interpretive community among a scattering of individuals, often from radically different backgrounds. Readers might have a wide variety of feelings to be denied by reading books, but these feelings are denied by the same books in roughly the same way. The point of departure among readers is necessarily different because of the individual experiences they bring to their interpretation of a text, but their destination of felt experience produced by narrative form based on the denial displacement expresses, relatively speaking, a convergence of minds. Community primarily derives, as with sports fans, from shared expectations among an audience that seeks gratification in forward momentum toward acceptable closure. Readers belong to this community as long as they can submerge themselves in the story being told, since consensus is imposed by the text in its motion toward closure. The more effectively it focuses the reader's attention on its outcome, the bigger its potential audience, and the more likely this audience will share the same feelings. Readers can withdraw from this outcome only by prematurely closing the book.

As Fish insists, it is possible to include readers in interpretive communities independent of any particular text, and these readers necessarily judge fiction according to the literary conventions of their groups and subgroups. Consequently, their experience of fiction is inevitably influenced by the more inclusive interpretive community (or communities) to which they belong. However, even this expanded model must be predicated on fiction's manipulation of private feelings, since the norms of all interpretive communities are based on the susceptibility of their individual members to the negative dynamics at work in particular texts. In the most inclusive sense, there is shared experience whenever readers suspend disbelief by concentrating on the prospects of a desirable narrative outcome. This means catching the same ride on the same roller coaster provided by the dynamics of narrative closure. Rapport among readers thus derives from comparable avoidance expressive of more or less comparable needs. The sociological relativism of Fish's model seems appropriate, but fiction's narrative dynamics take effect as a shared mechanism to cope with individual deficiencies. Genuine shared problems (for example, poverty caused by the Great Depression) produce individual needs, whereupon fiction's shared mythology offers shared benefits to satisfy these needs. But the crucial segment in this dialectic is the text's impact in helping readers to deny their problems, and on this limited basis the individual response to a text is both preliminary to group consensus and much more selfish and self-indulgent than anybody would be willing to admit in the company of others. At this level, where fiction as spoken art bears unspeakable impact, the effect of the text is as predictable as the negative feedback circuitry of homeostasis.

THE VULGAR FORMALIST MODE

Never to be underestimated is the critic's ability to exaggerate formal pattern in literary experience, usually by pointing out repetitions of a binary, tertiary, or quaternary character. These may be found in sound pattern, in thematic content, in balanced characterization, in contrasting images, and so forth. The more elaborate their integration, the better, but with aesthetic pleasure restricted to the cognitive satisfaction resulting from extrapolating new and more subtle intrareferential equivalences—additional thises to be compared and contrasted with antipodal thats. This kind of formalist reductionism has probably been taken to its extreme in Roman Jakobson's elaborate binary reconstructions of Shakespeare's Sonnet 129 and Baudelaire's "Les Chats."[23] As to be expected, Jakobson's interpretation reinforces the affirmative content of both works by programmatically ignoring their countervailing undercurrent of threatening associations. The most compelling questions about Baudelaire's poetry remain unanswered by Jakobson's otherwise exhaustive exercise in formal analysis. Everywhere in evidence is a subversiveness that can be traced to the rest of Baudelaire's poems in *Les Fleurs du mal*. However, this subversiveness is disregarded in favor of an extravagant variety of local and mostly accidental binarisms. Once again the affirmative fallacy emerges, this time resulting from the pursuit of empty correspondences to the neglect of real issues. Jakobson extrapolates pattern from Baudelaire's poetry as if this intricate complexity of relationships, many of them accidental, dominated his intentions. We permit our attention to be diverted, and *voilà*, meaning is free to do as it pleases, ignored by criticism. The same outcome results from any formalist approach whose intrareferential complexity obscures fiction's extrareferential value as verbal escapism. Formal equivalences seldom declare a text's basic motivation. Rather, they draw attention to themselves to reinforce a text's overt context of signification at the expense of its rejected implications. At the same time, they open the opportunity for accidental insight (the *lapsus linguae*, or slip of the tongue) whose local impact is absorbed and obscured by the distractive use of symmetry to consolidate evasiveness by means of aesthetic accomplishment.

Structuralist poetics affords essentially the same escapism. The regressive sequence of antinomies Claude Lévi-Strauss finds in primitive myth features a dynamic symmetry based on regressive sequence of contraries displaced to new and more abstract (hence less threatening) levels of contradiction. The presence of this sequence in the Oedipus myth and in the more elaborate story of Asdiwal told by the Tsimshian Indians of the Pacific Northwest suggests that its complex narrative organization of mythology served the simple end of escapism via disguise.[24] Threatening contradictions were successively reformulated until the antithetical terms used to describe them had become so remote from experience that resolution was possible. The same escapism might have been intended with the elaborate organization of inclusive symmetries Cedric Whitman found in the narrative construction of Homer's *Iliad*, apparently inspired by the geometric style of Mycenaean pottery.[25] Once again the reader's collaborative eagerness seems obvious, since formal harmony (Nietzsche's Apollonian pole) diverts our attention from threatening alternatives (Nietzsche's antipodal Dionysian pole), just as it did for our ancient forebears who first stumbled on this escapist strategy. By drawing attention to itself, the text's formal symmetry encourages expressiveness otherwise too threatening to tolerate. Our fascination with pattern lets us vent feelings whose full and direct expression would be offensive if overtly confronted. Hence, the relentless violence of Homer's epic is offset and justified by its intricate formal design. To focus on this design without acknowledging its function is to miss the point of this remarkable epic of cultural suicide at the origin of Western civilization, when slaughter could be ritualized as artistic achievement.

THE SOPHISTICATED FORMALIST MODE: DEVIATIONISM, DECONSTRUCTIONISM, AND NEW HISTORICISM

Theories of stylistic deviation invert formalism's emphasis on resemblances by featuring surprise and disorientation instead of realized pattern. Nevertheless, exactly the same purpose of affirmative evasiveness is served. The deviationist approach likewise features cognitive recognition at the expense of literary denial. Deviationists from Victor Shklovsky to Max Eastman, Michael Riffaterre, and Morse Peckham have restricted feeling and motivation to the relatively simplistic dynamics of surprise. In much the same spirit, Stephen Booth has featured interpretive dislocations in the first scene of *Hamlet*, and Stanley Fish has found them in *Paradise Lost*.[26] In all instances, textual dislocations (or SDs, short for stylistic devices) are featured because they draw attention to themselves with enough impact to produce aesthetic value comparable to that of the plastic arts.

As to be expected, deviation theory's emphasis on local effects puts it in the same dilemma as the other "sponge" theories (of density permeated with gaps, enigmas, etc.) that fail to take into account the importance of narrative closure. Deviation becomes a potentially endless literary skill (why not 800 SDs in a poem instead of a mere 350?) with little value except in generating contrivances that draw attention to themselves at the expense of their context.[27] For deviation to be meaningful, it must somehow express the more inclusive denial displacement—any distraction provided by Y to reject the value of X. Deviation becomes important, for example, with irony's contrasting implications, with images that challenge a poem's theme, or with any figurative device whose overdetermination expresses the contradictions at the core of a text. However, with purist theories of literary deviation, we are asked to believe that these distractions enrich literary experience instead of redirecting our attention without necessarily augmenting it. Moreover, we are asked to investigate stylistic devices in isolation, as if they bear no connection to a text's single most important deviation—its narrative momentum from X to Y as *not X*. Herein lies the weakness of orthodox deviation theory, which ignores the dialectic conflict between declared and undeclared intentions, between the asserted and the denied. To obscure this more inclusive deviationist goal by emphasizing a helter-skelter mélange of local disruptions is in itself diversionary, once again a strategy of affirmative evasiveness.

The latest and most complex version of deviationist theory comes under the rubric of deconstructionism, the study of fiction's escape from its central design through a virtually unending maze of tangential distractions. There is supposedly nothing outside a text, since any particular text's intersignification extends to all discourse in the history of civilization. As a result, nothing is inside the text either, and an infinite multiplicity of significations is featured instead of fiction's concentrated effort to repress a limited number of threatening associations. In effect, a text's remotest allusions are pursued to document its victory over the relatively simplistic constraints of literary form. As explained by Paul de Man, the act of reading affords "an endless process in which truth and falsehood are inextricably combined."[28] However, this exegetical limitlessness falls prey to the affirmative fallacy if exercised at the expense of the text's two dominant loci of meaning: (1) the consciously intended poem or prose work as a linear organization of experience, and (2) its denied meaning—the full nonlinear range of feelings and anxieties brought under control by means of this affirmative accomplishment. Unless this focused interaction is granted its paramount role, deconstructionism becomes a flagrant display of pedantic ingenuity that generates textual contradictions without really explaining them.

Jacques Derrida, the founder and chief proponent of the deconstructionist movement as it exists today, correctly perceived the artificial limitations that result from trying to impose an affirmative center on literary experience through a finite set of rules, guidelines, and conventions.[29] According to Derrida, the effort to trace these constraints to an origin reduces fiction to the endless "play" of games according to a limited set of rules that necessarily lies outside its zone of activity, just as the signified experience of words necessarily precedes and differs from the spoken words that signify this experience. The displacement from presence to absence, from closure to the free exploration of alternatives, therefore both simplifies and complicates literary expression. More occurs, but less is involved in what really happens by means of narrative denial. Derrida has represented the intertextual dynamics he considers important with a variety of terms: decentering as the abandonment of

The Affirmative Fallacy

a central organizing principle, freeplay as explorations departing from this center, trace as the suggestion of an anterior presence (or cause) felt by its absence, erasure as the simultaneous presence and absence of signification, differance as the dialectic interaction between these two based on deferment, etc. As explained by Derrida, a literary text is at first sight dominated by enclosure, logocentrism, and the longing for a center, but with closer inspection one or more "ruptures" (catastrophes, or scandals, in the case of social intercourse) disclose additional levels of signification equally vulnerable to decomposition, upon which explication becomes an expanding pursuit of new and more elusive significations in and among texts. Paradoxically, there is nothing outside the text, but all attempts to stay within it fail, since the open accessibility of signification reveals every text to include our total experience as we know it. The job of criticism is to try to capture and define this paradoxical achievement and the often bewildering maze of relationships it depends upon.

Derrida derives his methodology from an imposing variety of sources, but he is especially indebted to Nietzsche's explanation of our intellectual tradition as a congeries of lies and self-serving misconstructions. Like Nietzsche, Derrida advocates uncompromising freeplay as the best means of transcending the false consciousness that governs every category, every dualism, every conceptual strategy we depend on. Derrida claims each dichotomy, for example, becomes an act of violence on the part of the preferred term against its opposite, and like Nietzsche, he rejects this "semantic imperialism" through his archnihilist commitment to transcendent intellectual freedom. However, doubling, and thus the affirmative fallacy, may likewise be found in Derrida's persistent effort to diminish one sphere of interpretation associated with presence, centering, and logocentrism in favor of another associated with decentering, trace, freeplay, and textuality. These latter terms articulate Derrida's need to escape the constraints imposed by a text's centripetal organization, so once again an imperialism exposes itself in the denial (or negation) of one option in favor of its opposite. As a linear act of denial, the text is denied, but so too, by primary process association (commutation devoid of the negative sign), is the experience denied by the text. As with phobias, fiction's denial displacement is thus eliminated from consideration, permitting a sustained effort (tantamount to the repetition compulsion) to supplant fiction's intratextual avoidance strategy with a more comprehensive and better disguised intertextual evasiveness. Derrida's maximally flexible nomenclature for explaining this strategy expresses an even more uncompromising commitment to affirmative demands.[30] It establishes a new kind of evasiveness whose center is so elusive that it can be defined (or eidetically reduced) only by its rejection of any center imposed by literary form. By denying pattern in favor of explicative liberty, Derrida necessarily imposes his own pattern—coherent in its evasiveness—as his preferred emphasis, in effect his preferred use of pattern.

To a certain extent, Derrida's distinction between a centered presence and the "other" as an infinite regression of traces and erasures resembles the negative model I am proposing, since it pits fiction's linear and thematic organization against peripheral truths that tangentially impinge on consciousness. However, Derrida dispenses with literary motivation by emphasizing a text's "failure of intent" without taking into account its very demonstrable success in carrying out the denial displacement. If there are readers who enjoy a text, it succeeds because it engages their imagination, and for them any failure in signification plays a secondary role to the text's metonymic designification—its plotted action ($X = not\ Y$), which affords its homeostatic appeal. Readers are more likely than not to be bored and/or offended by Derrida's infinite regression of extraneous significations that can only disrupt the surface virtues of form and literary convention. Basic truths of human consciousness might emerge in the exploration of intertextual subtleties, but readers can tolerate this range of possibilities only if it brings their attention back again to a central meaning friendlier and more generous to their sense of personal worth. In fact, it can be proposed in the spirit of Nietzsche's nihilist joy that fiction exceeds the deceptive achievement of philosophy and other modes of discourse because of its pragmatic success in commingling truths and their aesthetic rejection in the context of literary form. Typically, there is a compromise formation between the two, and this may be resolved once literary form organizes truths to precede the fictions that deny them. Temporary centrifugal freedom may occur, but centripetal demands must ultimately prevail.

As Nietzsche explained, philosophy's preeminence results from its misguided pursuit of veracity as an *ignis fatuus* always just out of reach. Fiction's more beguiling deceptive appeal comes from its linear realization of "differance," according to which unpleasant truths may be focused and brought to their resolution by aesthetic lies. As Nietzsche also explained, Dionysian extravagance sets the stage for Apollonian reaffirmation through the dynamics of literary form. In terms more appropriate to Derrida's approach, textuality both liberates and compounds significations so they might be all the more effectively harnessed in support of centering and a renewed faith in enclosure. If and when the virtues of centering and enclosure seem forgotten, their temporary neglect can be valued for postponing reaffirmation so it may later be achieved on a more convincing basis. Nietzsche's deceptionist vision therefore reduces Derrida's concept of freeplay to one leg of a dialectic that gives fiction its appeal—not beyond but well within the boundaries of good and evil that Nietzsche finds important to the common reader. Falling short of Nietzsche's transcendent lucidity, fiction promotes simplistic morality—hence dishonesty—by featuring relatively crude solutions to complex problems.

Granted, freeplay gives temporary exposure to polyvalent truths, but this sets the stage for closure sooner or later through an artificial resolution with obvious conventional appeal. In effect, each text deconstructs itself, since its closure dynamics deny and thereby designify its broader compass of associations, both personal and intertextual. Its organization of experience appeals to readers on a zero-sum basis by the way it resolves (i.e., denies) itself, reducing its decentered interrelationship with other texts to the observation of nonfunctional sources and analogues rather than any intrinsic participation in the specific function the text provides with homeostatic impact. There is accordingly no necessary sequence among texts, no skein of intertextual associations so vital that its comprehension plays any role in the appreciation of a particular text. Fiction may be read in any order the reader pleases, and with any inclusions and exclusions the reader wants to impose relevant to discourse as a whole. By ignoring the primacy of denial, hence centering, in literary experience, deconstructionists necessarily play out one more variation of the affirmative fallacy.

Derrida concedes the importance of anxiety in fiction, but he seems unable to recognize how it manifests repressed feelings that oblige a countervailing emphasis on centering, enclosure, and other such compensatory affirmative strategies. Here Derrida's theory may be challenged on strictly "economic" grounds. Balanced against the coherence of the text is an undercurrent of rejected experience that is actually clustered and intensified by the dynamics of exclusion. This locus of disavowed subversiveness (Freud reifies it as the unconscious) is also built in to the text, necessitating the use of centering to curtail the total range of textual and intertextual allusions important to the deconstructionist. If centering necessarily limits the play of experience within the formal organization of a text, it does so in order to maximize the text's effectiveness in withstanding the metaphoric threat of this intertextual subversiveness. As a result, paradoxically, centering occurs at both levels. The tighter a text embraces its acknowledged material, the greater the countervailing importance of the material it denies. These two antipodal zones of activity feed on each other, preventing the expansion of one independent of the other except through designification imposed by narrative closure. Like the standoff between cathexis and countercathexis as defined by Freud, they are locked in combat with roughly equal economic commitment. Centering's brute logic eventually prevails over a finer, more attenuated, and thus more pervasive tracework of decentered allusions, since the total expenditure of psychic activity tied in with this tracework cannot exceed the centripetal repressiveness imposed by literary form. The horizon of significations denied by form is thus more limited than Derrida recognizes, and these significations are necessarily tied in with anxieties far more threatening than the compulsive avoidance of formlessness. To the extent that deconstructionism conceals this dialectic, its remarkable and apparently endless ingenuity seems a new and more strenuous commitment to the affirmative fallacy.

Likewise indebted to the principle of decentering, the emergent critical school described as new historicism (or cultural poetics, the term proposed by Stephen Greenblatt, its generally recognized founder) is more subtle in its use of the affirmative fallacy. Among those who adhere to its doctrine there is a reluctance to theorize, and Greenblatt himself has gone so far as to insist, "It's no doctrine at all."[31] Instead, methodology predominates, and, as prescribed by Jerome McGann, its gathering of data has entailed a relatively conservative investigation of relevant published histories and biographies, documentary evidence about the author's motivation, the work's reception among its original audience, and its potential significance for today's reader.[32] But in its use of these data, new historicism depends upon theoretical assumptions that may be traced to the usual assortment of poststructuralist sources, including Derrida, Bakhtin, Benjamin, Foucault, both Marx and Nietzsche, the metahistorian Hayden White, the ethnographer Clifford Geertz, and, as the *éminence grise* of the principle of indeterminacy, the neopragmatist Richard Rorty. Unlike deconstructionism, new historicism somewhat retains the distinction between text and context, and its pursuit of signification does not programmatically extend to infinity, as Derrida prefers, since its historic milieu must also be taken into account. However, as discourse it entails a cautious and relatively lucid adaptation of Derrida's principle of freeplay as modified by Clifford Geertz's notion of "thick description" for revealing "through the analysis of tiny particulars the behavioral codes, logics, and motive forces controlling a whole society."[33] By means of thick description new historicism gives better focus to thematic materials, but without altogether preventing freeplay in their exploration. It encourages maximum creativity in the exploratory pursuit of analogues and potential sources, but with an adequate convergence of representations to convey a sense of historic context. At times it might verge on gratuitous cleverness, but its historic perspective screens out most of the fugitive associations that might otherwise intrude.

Perhaps the most characteristic debt of new historicism to deconstructionism is its elimination of distinctions among texts that have hitherto been characterized as literary, historical, or outside the scope of either category. Like deconstructionists, new historicists seek to destabilize orthodox boundaries between text and context, but their effort focuses on reducing history to culture and on reducing culture to the interaction among all potentially relevant texts in a system of discourse without a fixed cause and effect hierarchy. This permits them to explore fiction's significance as if it were continuous with other discourse in its more inclusive sociohistorical setting. New historicism's central concerns, according to Greenblatt, "prevent it from permanently sealing off one type of discourse from another or decisively separating works of art from the minds and lives of their creators and their audiences."[34] Greenblatt explains that social action (i.e., history as event) is necessarily imbedded in systems of public signification whose explication requires greater hermeneutic sophistication than would be possible within the constraints imposed by orthodox literary history. The intratextual explicative skills hitherto emphasized by literary criticism must therefore be extended to embrace intertextual significations within their social context, necessitating an entirely new and more inclusive methodology in literary history.

Like deconstructionism, new historicism discourages the interpretation of textual self-referentiality, as featured, for example, by both orthodox formalism and the model of denial and designification that I am proposing in *Negative Poetics*. As McGann declares, "What will not be found in these essays . . . is the assumption . . . that literary works are self-enclosed verbal constructs, or looped intertextual fields of autonomous signifiers and signifieds."[35] The vital paradox that it is the self-referentiality of a text as an act of denial which gives the work an audience and grants it its intrareferential significance seems to elude McGann and other new historicists. The more effectively a text designifies unacceptable experience for its contemporary audience, the more useful it becomes as signification with relevance to other texts published by contemporaries. By limiting fiction to its participation in a broader context of social discourse, McGann precludes its interpretation as structured fantasy in which individual readers might participate. As Edward Pechter maintains, new historicists accordingly tend to ignore "passages whose affective power seems unusually great" (i.e., those portions of a text with emotional appeal).[36] Since the most important of these passages with affective appeal tend to crop up toward the end of narratives as the result of closure, it should be no surprise that new historicists minimize the importance of dramatic (or narrative) outcome, the *sine qua non* of Aristotelian form. Their academic perspective encourages them to investigate fiction as documentation—often enough as a repository of curious information—not as the felt experience that gives fiction its audience. Instead of exploring the formal organization that produces closure, they "valorize" (a favorite verb) coincidences and overlooked paradoxical connections with other texts. Linear sequence is shattered into kaleidoscopic representations, and tropes, ironies, pictures, and symbolisms are "privileged" (another favorite word) at the expense of fiction's intrinsic form. The denial mechanism built into fiction is itself included in the materials to be denied by new historical methodology. Literature becomes textuality, an entirely safe medium for critics, who thereby insulate themselves from both vulgar anxieties and the vulgar coping mechanisms for dealing with them.

New historicism's neglect of form extends to explication itself. Instead of accepting the drudgery and seemingly endless library research needed for particularizing literature's historic context, new historicism resorts to a relatively permissive (dare one say lazy?) essayistic style that maximizes its freedom as discourse relative to its documentation. Tangential associations predominate at the expense of thoroughness. If a particular fact pertinent to the new historicist's thesis eludes research, it may simply be ignored, since the essay it documents bears no pretensions of inclusiveness. As a result, one suspects, new historicists feature an abundance of readily accessible information, but too often at the expense of more pertinent information they choose not to devote the time and energy to excavating from the archives.

The primary justification for new historicism's essayistic emphasis is that it encourages a nonlinear interpretation of texts and inverts the historicity of texts into the textuality of history, converting literary history as both text and event into a shared discourse (or "carnivalistic play") among voices featured by both deconstructionism and Bakhtin's critical methodology. It thereby rejects simplistic cause and effect thinking, but the extremes it resorts to in doing this thinking make it no less vulnerable to evasiveness. For events do occur independent of their documentation, and cause and effect relationships may be at least tentatively proposed to clarify how and why they occur. As a general rule, useful history illuminates motives and likely cause and effect relationships; inferior history ignores or excessively distorts them—or worse yet, restricts itself to thematic posturing entirely dependent upon a variety of unidentified secondary sources as the basis for its assumptions. Indeed, new historicists' essayistic excursions into unfamiliar themes and topics are potentially useful, since these, too, might be helpful in illuminating these relationships, but their use should not be dictated by artificial Draconian standards that deprive the historian of linear resources that crop up even in their own scholarship.[37] Histories and biographies ultimately depend on temporal sequence, despite its limitations, in the organization of their materials. Their dependence on narrative advancement does increase the risk of simplification, if not outright deception, but this risk is worth its benefits in helping to clarify facts and relationships otherwise impervious to definition. Rather than "depriveleging" narrative possibilities, it would seem the better option to compound them, and the more the better. All history, both new and old, benefits from the paradox that a surfeit of perspectives—some more linear than others—is more likely to help in transcending one-dimensional narrative limitations than will their programmatic avoidance.

A second taboo of new historicism that is vulnerable to the affirmative fallacy is its antipathy to reductionism. The aversion encourages an eclectic cannibalism of theoretical systems—Marxist, Freudian, etc.—but without accepting their theoretical core for explaining the progress of history. As a general principle, new historicists avoid tying literary history to the systematic investigation of war, diplomacy, religion, ideology, growth and decay, cultural autonomy, or even climate (as in the case of Ellsworth Huntington's *Civilization and Climate*) or hegemonic overexpansion (as in the case of Paul Kennedy's *The Rise and Fall of the Great Powers*). But of course the primary victim of new historicism's neglect turns out to be the Marxist base-superstructure distinction and related assumptions about class, surplus value, exploitation, economic breakdown patterns, and imperialism and fascism.[38] Instead, new historicism sanitizes Marxism by substituting a sociological perspective that primarily derives from Althusser's and Foucault's emphasis on cultural issues at the expense of economic determinism. Their notion of power, for example, seems particularly useful, since its mixture of Marx and Nietzsche renders both relatively harmless. In the case of Marx, history becomes sociology spiced by Pareto's cyclical elites (potentially fascist) reorganized and sterilized as Gramsci's hegemonic usurpations (fashionably Marxist). A faddish bow to victimology—virtuous power distinguished from its unvirtuous misuse—takes precedence over the interpretation of economic contradictions and the social conflict they produce leading to qualitative change. Once power is isolated in this fashion, the useful base-superstructure distinction between economics and culture may be jettisoned in favor of a relatively superficial interplay between culture and literature that Marxists would limit to the superstructure alone.

In their rejection of Marxist reductionism, new historicists disperse history into what is described by Frank Lentricchia as a "multiplicity of histories," as characterized by "forces of heterogeneity, contradiction, fragmentation, and difference."[39] Theme is emphasized instead of doctrine, diversity instead of ideological monologism, and methodological freedom instead of economic necessity. Nor is economic contradiction granted its impact upon literary contradiction, thereby exiling from fashionable literary history such old-fashioned Marxist literary historians as Christopher Caudwell, George Thomson, Granville Hicks, and Christopher Hill, the latter a biographer of Milton.[40] To his credit, Greenblatt conveys in an extended footnote his ambivalence about Christopher Caudwell's presumably vulgar Marxist explanation in *Illusion and Reality* of Sir Thomas Wyatt's creativity as the outgrowth of his family's social position.[41] As Greenblatt concedes, Caudwell's remarks cannot be rejected out of hand. Though obviously reductionist, they convey genuine insights whose reductionism may be incorporated into a more balanced treatment of Wyatt's poetry. How much of the rest of his criticism deserves the same consideration?

But it is new historicism's devotion to its freedom of textual interreferentiality that dominates its commitment to the affirmative fallacy and links it with other poststructuralist theories of indeterminacy entirely at variance with the dialectic model I am proposing.[42] If literary form bears a determinate psychological effect in its organization of literary response, as I have tried to

The Affirmative Fallacy

demonstrate, this effect and the textual structures that produce it cannot be exclusively judged as the product of indeterminacy (or "intrinsic plurality"). Instead, a dialectic must be sought between fiction's determinate and indeterminate aspects—one that very likely involves deception as an active avoidance of potential significations too threatening to acknowledge. As I indicated earlier, plot may be recognized as being more determinate than metaphor, negative feedback as being more determinate than positive feedback, and, paradoxically, deception as being more determinate than truth itself, since every lie (fiction included) declares itself as a truth, while the truth itself, as both Fish and Rorty must agree, is only provisionally deserving of warranted assertibility.

Usually liars must trade in specifics to make their necessary substitutions ("I sent the check this morning"), but whenever they ask "Who can tell?" and thereby invoke indeterminacy to justify themselves, one must double one's effort to probe their specific intentions. Comparable doubts arise when "Who can tell?" provides the credo of an entire critical generation—one that gained enough momentum during the seventies to reach its culmination, appropriately enough, during the Reagan decade. As rhetorical premise, "Who can tell?" is implicit in the theories of indeterminacy proposed by deconstructionists, new historicists, response theoreticians, neo-Marxists, and the many other schools and sects of the cultural left that have emerged in recent years, all of which collaborate in the neglect of issues amenable to resolution in both literary history and textual explication. A flood of criticism already published has necessarily diminished the opportunity for comparable productivity based on received standards of lucidity and thoroughness, but this impasse has been eliminated—in effect, denied—by the pursuit of indeterminate multiplicity. By undermining the old-fashioned notion of a right theory or explication (or of a right synthesis of theories or explications), the principle of indeterminacy scatters and fragments scholarship, thereby guaranteeing limitless critical productivity and elevating the status of critics to that of a modern priesthood with its customary accoutrements of power and intellectual authority. In ancient times, priests justified their privileged role with magic incantations and access to sacred texts inscrutable to the laity. In the modern university, this relatively simple formula has been supplanted by a more elaborate strategy, if without anybody's quite realizing what has happened. Elusiveness itself, as guaranteed by high turnover, has become the source of intellectual authority, and, appropriately, the elusiveness dominant in critical theory has been confirmed by its pursuit in fiction itself—in both realms as justified by the principle of indeterminacy.

As perhaps might be expected, the critics most closely identified with the concept of indeterminacy in one guise or another have been the most successful in the field of criticism. In their professional affairs their dedication to facts and numbers is often formidable—whether regarding their income, their travel expenses, what is happening to their peers and competitors, the budget and agenda of the conferences in which they participate, or the best use of their calendars to spread themselves among as many audiences as possible. But the lucidity and determinate organizational skills obliged by their professional status are matched by their rigid commitment to the principle of indeterminacy as obliged by their theoretical posture. Why such a paradox? I would suggest because hermeneutic indeterminacy plays a no less determinate role in guaranteeing their status as critics. If exegetical relativism predominates, any critical interpretation or cluster of interpretations may be featured, and, obversely, any critical interpretation or cluster of interpretations may be neglected without any particular sense of loss. The canon of texts worthy of explication may be expanded if qualitative standards no longer apply, and, obversely, new explications of old texts may be ignored, again for the same reason. There is much more room for critics to play, but this is balanced against a more resilient hierarchy in separating the elect from the ordinary among critics. Canonical status may be ignored (in fact, *should* be ignored) in the selection of texts to be explicated, but status itself plays a much bigger role in the transaction among critics, guaranteeing a manageable hierarchy in the field of literary criticism. Those on top stay there, while those below also benefit from the arrangement proportional to the status they enjoy. Once one or more cutting edges have been established, the task of the individual critic is reduced to keeping up with a relatively small percentage of the total output from the profession as a whole, the percentage that is both prestigious and relevant to that critic's own work.

Velocity reinforces indeterminacy in guaranteeing the relative status of the elect. An accelerating intellectual faddishness rooted in elusiveness produces enough theoretical turnover to limit the top to those who can stay on top. No matter how ephemeral, the ideas of prominent indeterminists are almost immediately published, while the productivity of less prestigious critics is more rigorously—and often more arbitrarily—scrutinized by editors, thus impeding its publication and removing it from the cutting edge. Prominent indeterminists are more involved than others, more quoted, more cited in footnotes, brought into more panel discussions, and more often invited to contribute to *Festschriften*. Only the most prominent critics are fully aware of what is happening at any particular cutting edge, as new contributions keep cropping up. Others find out later and thereby participate less, thus confirming their lower status in the profession. Since anybody anywhere can be merely encyclopedic about critical theory or merely thoroughgoing in explications, keeping up predominates instead. High-velocity critical faddishness lets the more prestigious critics and departments retain their status without disproportionately straining their capacity to stay abreast of what is happening that really matters. The same benefit accrues to Ph.D. candidates seeking jobs from the more prominent universities, since the scope of their knowledge is probably comparable to that of students with degrees from less prominent schools. However, their half decade of exposure to the "right" knowledge makes them more desirable as candidates. With not more than a couple shelf-feet of poststructuralist texts (but the "right" couple of feet), they can later make the effort, if so disposed, to acquaint themselves with the rest of literary criticism.

This, of course, has been the tacit arrangement for decades in the field of literary criticism, but the trend has accelerated in recent years. It took the better part of a decade for the T. S. Eliot cult to be cast aside in favor of archetypal theory, then perhaps a half-decade for the transition to Marxist and psychoanalytic perspectives in the mid-sixties, followed in quickening and overlapping clusters by French new criticism, structuralism, response theory, and speech-act theory, then by the deconstructionist, feminist, radical feminist, black, black feminist, and gay perspectives. Now slouching into Bethlehem are neopragmatists, both the anthropological and cultural-materialist new historicists, and the forerunners of what promises to be an ecological school.[43] Each year it seems more difficult to keep abreast of new trends, increasing the stakes for those still able and willing to play the game. The entire movement has become extraordinarily autocratic, even (and with poignant irony) among those who continue to identify themselves as Marxists. Obviously, what is denied by this trend is the cumbersome democratic alternative of conceding too many voices in the academic marketplace without any basis for making the necessary hierarchic distinctions among them. By putting these voices in their place, and by weeding out unfashionable byways in the history of literary criticism (Burke, yes, but why Winters? Frye, yes, but why Wheelwright? Holland, yes, but why Lesser?), rapid turnover separates the in from the out, the high from the low, and those who make it from those who don't. Dominant critical methodologies help to clarify the rationale for maintaining these distinctions based on the principles of freeplay (among those who dispose, anything goes) and indeterminacy (among those for whom anything goes, anything may be said). Appropriately, indeterminists project these distinctions upon literature itself, so the affirmative fallacy permeates both their careers and their interpretation of literature.

eight

ROLAND BARTHES

Roland Barthes affords perhaps the most complex and interesting case of metonymic designification in contemporary criticism. His critical approach introduced an eclectic mixture of concepts drawn from a variety of disciplines, but always with the hidden agenda of excluding from consideration a small assortment of principles he found offensive, including Aristotelian form, narrative continuity, realism (or mimesis), *engagement* (or political commitment), and, most inclusively, *Doxa* as any belief system imposing orthodoxy. From one context to the next (sometimes from one sentence to the next), he shifted among Marxist, psychoanalytic, semiotic, and phenomenological insights, almost always by reducing their full definitions to formalist categories that defied synthesis. Nevertheless, a dialectic finally emerged between the formalist variety dominant in his early career and the confessional and essentially mimetic obsession that terminated his career. Though he despised narrative form, the advancement of his perspective from eclectic formalism to his confessional pursuit of mimesis took on a narrative quality of its own culminating in metnoymic designification, in Barthes's case the worship of the image (specifically his mother's) as a prelude to death.

Barthes's critical approach is particularly useful, since his extraordinary variety of insights both illustrate and explain the dynamics of literary misrepresentation. When engaging in critical evasiveness, thus illustrating the tendency, he drew upon all the resources of contemporary criticism already described in chapter 7, and frequently with extraordinary insight. But when confessing his evasiveness, he declared a number of principles—some fragmentary, some more elaborate—whose systematic combination affords a model of literary experience very similar to the negative model I am proposing here. Not until two of his final books—his autobiography, *Roland Barthes by Roland Barthes*, and *Camera Lucida*—did Barthes fully clarify how and why this elusiveness had dominated his career. In his autobiography he acknowledged the extent to which his aversions could be traced to his homosexual preference, and in *Camera Lucida* he acknowledged that both his androgyny and his formalist restlessness were rooted in his rapport with his mother—a rapport so intense that once she died he no longer wanted to live. With these disclosures, Barthes's critical theory became an autobiographical narrative no less susceptible to explication than a literary text, and with a unity of action that he had sought to reject in his interpretation of fiction throughout most of his career.

What I am proposing here is a brief and necessarily tentative metacritical psychohistory explaining Barthes's career as an act of denial no less compelling than those already discussed in the explications of *Hamlet*, "The Rime of the Ancient Mariner," and "Young Goodman Brown." As in the case of Hamlet, Barthes's inexhaustible elusiveness manifested a vulnerability that anticipated—indeed, predicted—the tragic circumstances of his accidental death, and language culminated in silence when *Doxa* (i.e., homophobic standards introjected as suicidal despair) finally prevailed through Barthes's collaborative eagerness to die, whether or not he intentionally sought out his accidental death.[1] Barthes's rejection of narrative continuity throughout his career therefore assumed a continuity of its own that inverted and stretched to their limit the Aristotelian dynamics of plot. If elusiveness characterized his earlier criticism, his later books confessed personal truths almost too painful to recount, and in his final book, *Camera Lucida*, he repeatedly declared his eagerness to die in order to rejoin his deceased mother beyond the grave. His growth as a critic can accordingly be treated as a magnificent antinovel characterized in its early stages by formalist evasiveness and in the end by a tragic integrity that obtained his final and irreversible freedom from orthodox values. Barthes's epigraph in his own handwriting at the beginning of his autobiography—"It must all be considered as if spoken by a character in a novel"—applies to his autobiography but more, I think, to his entire life—and, indeed, what is "spoken" (Barthes's entire output of criticism) is no less prescient in its elusiveness than Hamlet's antic disposition four centuries earlier.

Barthes's debut in literary criticism began with his relatively modest effort to deny Jean-Paul Sartre's theory of radical *engagement* subsequent to World War II. Like many of his contemporaries, Barthes recoiled from the propagandistic demands implicit in Sartre's theory of existentialism and tried to find a balanced alternative that conceded these demands but subordinated them to an unbiased nonpolitical perspective. The issue of Stalinism divided Sartre from such disillusioned former resistance fighters as Camus and Merleau-Ponty, and Barthes entered the fray more or less aligned with these figures against Sartre. As a young invalid still under the care of his mother, he did not share their background in the struggle against the Nazi occupation of France. Nevertheless, he sympathized with their concerns and joined in their rejection of Sartre's beliefs. Barthes's unique contribution to the debate was his ingenious substitution of literary form for Marxist *engagement*. With a strategy of rhetorical circumvention typical of the affirmative fallacy, he declared his commitment *against* commitment as a misguided distraction that prevents the gratification of ideal form. *Engagement* (writing as *praxis*) was the primary threat, and Barthes responded by hypostatizing *engagement* as a category, history, whose subordination to a more inclusive category, form, designified *praxis* as a literary imperative. In his later books he extended this strategy to reject any social or political orthodoxy that imposes belief at the expense of experiential freedom.

In his remarkable 1949 manifesto *What Is Literature?* Sartre had claimed that the modern "engaged" writer is morally obliged to make a radical commitment to history.[2] According to Sartre, the engaged writer must acknowledge history's unavoidable influence and accept the responsibility of becoming its conscious agent. The objective of the serious writer, in Sartre's opinion, was to serve as a mediator whose *praxis* was the encouragement of social revolution. This role forced writers to "tell it like it is" and to suggest possible avenues toward a satisfactory political solution, no matter how remote in the future. The truth, Sartre implied, was the inevitability of a socialist future, so the ethical obligation of writers was to commit themselves to this truth. Sartre therefore asked writers to accept this responsibility without wasting their talents upon aesthetic objectives inconsequential to the political context of the twentieth century. The counterattack against Sartre's theory of *engagement* was spearheaded by disillusioned leftists who could no longer wholeheartedly support the anticolonial movements in Algeria and Indochina, or, as they had conditionally in the late forties, the Stalinist policies of the Soviet Union. In *The Rebel*, published in 1951, Albert Camus emphasized political commitment as a strictly individual responsibility, and in "On Several Obsolete Notions" and "From Realism to Reality," Alain Robbe-Grillet maintained that commitment is (or was) a fad, and that no further distractions need to be put above the work of the artist. He made the posture of silence an aesthetic imperative and pitted himself against militancy by declaring, "We must challenge this terrorist apparatus brandished under our noses as soon as we speak of anything besides the class struggle or the anti-colonialist war."[3] Like Camus, he unconditionally refused to compromise his artistic freedom of vision to political goals whose ultimate consequence seemed in fact the destruction of this freedom.

But it was Barthes who offered the most ingenious response to Sartre's theory of *engagement* in his first book, *Le Degré Zéro de l'écriture*, published in 1953 and translated in 1967 as *Writing Degree Zero*.[4] Chapters had been published in article form as early as 1947, but the book itself was published after the general reaction against *engagement* had already gained momentum. Also suspicious of Sartre's tendentious demands, Barthes proposed a formal compromise that conceded the importance of *engagement* and then situated it in a more inclusive context whose acceptance almost entirely undermined its importance. His strategy featured extreme rhetorical freedom in a mixture of elliptical pronouncements that ranged from agreeing with Sartre's notion of political commitment at one extreme to maintaining a formal, nonpolitical theory of language and style at the other. From one pole to the other he could move at will, never staying at a position long enough to develop its ramifications with any thoroughness. His political views remained militant enough to provoke attacks by Dieguez and others, but his treatment of politics minimized its impact compared to those of language and style, two sources of literary form independent of history. Barthes also tried to establish a dialectic between Sartre's theory of *engagement* and Saussure's theory of language. Unable to find an adequate synthesis between these alternatives, he nervously shifted between them, his indecisiveness prefiguring the ambivalence he later praised in the tragic hero. By means of this vacillation, he progressively stripped the principle of *engagement* of its moral commitment to the truth and instead featured formal lucidity as the primary objective of literary inspiration.

Barthes's use of affirmation to deny was based on a complex strategy of detours, retreats, and new advancements, but with an overall sequence that may be divided into three stages. First he conceded the political relevance of spoken language (*parole*) and thereby suggested his support of Sartre's demands for the author's participation in history. Next he proposed weighing this propagandistic commitment against literary style and the structure of language (*langue*) as two independent but equally basic influences upon the writer. Finally, he suggested that all three of these influences—history, style, and language—are synthesized by literary form, the most important category of all. By combining these categories in a single overarching paradigm, Barthes hypostatized a regressive sequence from history (concessive) to style (tensive) and finally to language (formalist), the latter as confirmed by literary form, the organizing principle that brings the three together. Apparently the principal benefit of this paradigm was that it let Barthes designify Sartre's version of *praxis* by subordinating *engagement* to "writing degree zero," the perfect equipoise among these three sources that would guarantee form's precedence over the journalistic excesses typical of *engagement*. Barthes could acknowledge with a generous tautology that historic responsibility is an important feature of prose with social implications, which he called *écriture*. Loosely translated, *écriture* meant writing as process—a concept he traced beyond Sartre to Saussure's definition of *parole* as the spoken word. But then Barthes eluded Sartre's social imperatives by emphasizing style and language as additional influences upon *écriture* outside social history, yet loosely connected, or linked, to provide a formal history of literature. Finally, he eliminated partisan commitment from *écriture* in the sense intended by Sartre by arguing that "writing degree zero" is ultimately the most satisfactory mode of *écriture* for contemporary literature, the perfect balance between journalism and literary style, each nullified by its compromise with the other.

According to Barthes, these three sources of literary inspiration—language, style, and journalism (i.e., discourse responsible to history)—provide a basic triad that explains the diachronic history of French literature from classicism to realism, symbolism, and finally existentialism. Barthes explained zero-degree creativity as a sporadic achievement that now and again occurs as literary history makes its incessant circuit among these tripartite extremes. The classicism of Racine and his contemporaries, for example, had featured *langue* as syntactic lucidity, but this was followed by realism in the nineteenth century and then by a stylistic density brought to its extreme in symbolist poetry. By the mid-twentieth century, Barthes claimed, the trend shifted toward the extreme of journalism advocated by Sartre at the expense of both style and language. For a brief, remarkable period, however, he found the pendulum back again at dead center in "writing degree zero," the characterless prose of Camus and Robbe-Grillet, whose syntactic lucidity resembled Racine's purity and timelessness. Without exactly denying Sartre's concept of *engagement*, Barthes characterized it as misguided extremism in contrast to the formal, unmediated balance of zero-degree expressiveness and the Apollonian refuge it offers from social struggle.

Barthes never spelled out his three-stage use of dialectics to deny *praxis*, but it always seems to have been operative in his use of metaphors, ellipses, and paradoxes. A notable example of this strategy may be found in the first chapter of *Writing Degree Zero*, "What Is Writing?" originally published in 1947, in which he almost imperceptibly moved from the first to the second stage within three or four paragraphs, and then brought his argument to rest at the third. He began by militantly declaring *écriture* to be an "act of historical solidarity," a "function" that links form through "human intention" with "great crises of History" (p. 14). In contrast, he found language and style to be "blind forces" and merely "objects" lacking organic validity. At this point he was entirely in accord with Sartre, his theory of *écriture* consistently extending the principle of *engagement*. But when Barthes transposed his terms to a second level of strategy, defining *écriture* as "the morality of form, the choice of that social area within which the writer elects to situate the Nature of his language," he diluted political commitment into making a choice about the nature of language relative to the discussion of pluralistic social problems (p. 14). He divided Sartre's unified theory of history into separate areas within which the writer may choose the most appropriate *écriture*. A variety of causes took precedence over a single cause rooted in class conflict, and the intrinsic virtue of language took precedence over its use as the vehicle for ideas. Barthes next called *écriture* an "ambiguous reality" that "refers the writer back, by a sort of tragic transference, to the sources, that is to say, the instruments of creation," presumably language and style (p. 16). Finally, he claimed in the next paragraph that the freedom of *écriture* is but a moment in time that must be modified by previous usage and that *écriture* is significant "at the level of History" because it provides "a meaningful gesture of the writer." The concept of gesture intended by Barthes necessarily conflicted with Sartre's notion of *praxis*, since it implied expressiveness rather than taking action. In this fashion, Barthes incrementally shifted his approval from *écriture* as a prose of political commitment to the formal "instruments of creation," nonpolitical reifications he had earlier described as the "blind forces" of language and style.

Sometimes Barthes categorically denied the truth-claims of *engagement*, for example when he declared that "any political mode of *écriture* can only uphold a police world" (p. 28). However, he usually hedged his opposition by questioning *écriture*'s sacrifice of formal permanence to the alienation he believed was the necessary product of political commitment: "*Écriture*, free in its beginning, is finally the bond which links the writer to a History which is itself in chains: society stamps upon him the unmistakable signs of art so as to draw him along the more inescapably in its own process of alienation" (p. 40). Here it seems clear that Barthes considered history to consist of perpetual repression without the prospect of resolution and activist writers to be the victims of their own alienation, justifiably forgotten when the programs they advocate are succeeded by others. Also to be noted is Barthes's prelapsarian assumption that artistic freedom was inherited from a Golden Age, a condition "free in its beginning" and mistakenly abandoned over the course of history. This idealization of the past was antithetical to Sartre's conviction that freedom results from struggle toward a utopian future. Barthes proposed that sporadic periods of history regain *écriture*'s nonhistoric lucidity, as has most recently occurred, he claimed, in "writing degree zero." History plays its role, Barthes conceded, but writing degree zero plays its role, too, as both the origin and the recurring pinnacle of history's evolutionary process. With this caveat Barthes could relegate Sartre's revolutionary optimism to a status inferior to the writer's permanent responsibility to the perfection of literary form. By affirming form, he denied the importance of any vision that emphasized political change.

Language (or *langue*) was depicted by Barthes as the force upon *écriture* that is the most impervious to the influence of history. Here again he anticipated the structuralist emphasis upon synchrony that derived from the linguistics of Saussure. According to Barthes, *langue*'s lexicon of rules and definitions exactly counterbalances both *parole* and *écriture*'s ongoing rush of words and locutions in an utterance. *Langue* asserts itself as a corpus of habits and prescriptions internalized by the individual as "a reflex response involving no choice" (p. 9). Sentences might express the truth, but the word combinations composing sentences are entirely the product of habit. If there is any truth to this lexicon of habits, it bears a different origin from the political truths emphasized by Sartre. Obviously borrowed from Saussure, Barthes's concept of *langue* provided fiction with its most basic truth immune to the historic imperative: "This sacral order of written signs establishes literature as an institution and clearly tends to abstract it from history, for no limits can be set without some ideas of permanence" (p. 2). Once again, at the second stage of his strategy, Barthes elevated language to serve as a higher authority that necessarily imposes rules and structures upon the experience of literature. However, the linguistic authoritarianism Barthes promoted here was in conflict with his judgment when he deplored, at the first level of his strategy, "the eternal repressive content of the word 'order'" (p. 26). Considered alone, language could be treated as a benevolent deity, an unmoved mover with an inescapable structural ethic, rather than as a set of rules affording infinite permutations depending on the choice of the author.

Barthes argued that history is also denied by a second category, clearly psychoanalytic in origin—the mystique of personal style: "It is the authority of style, that is, the entirely free tie between language and its fleshly double, which imposes the writer as a 'freshness' above history" (pp. 12–13). Despite the transcendent implications of "above," this innocent authority apparently comes from below, from the thrust of unconscious forces, indeed, from biology itself: "By reason of its biological origin, style resides outside art, that is, outside the pact which binds the writer to society" (p. 12). According to Barthes, the source of style is the deepest region of personality, "where the first coition of words and things takes place," and it expresses drives and feelings that erupt from inside oneself apart from social influence (p. 10). As explained by Barthes, history cannot disclose what is happening inside an author at the moment of writing, since style is "never anything but metaphor, that is, equivalence of the author's literary intention and carnal structure" (p. 12).[5] Barthes found in both style and metaphor an inward awareness more basic than conscious perception, social role, and social context. Historic change in values and attitudes was conceded by the definition of *écriture*, but, like *langue*, the personal matrix of style remained a pure phenomenon independent of social relationships.

But a synthesis was needed, and according to Barthes this could be attained only when literary form succeeds in connecting language and style to history in unmediated equipoise. Through form these three elemental forces—language, style, and history—impinge upon each other to bind the writer to society by shared structural expectations. As the synthesis that combines the three, form necessarily plays a major role in diminishing the relative importance of *engagement* as a literary obligation: "Every mode of *écriture* has thus been an exercise in taming or being repelled by that Form-object inevitably met by the writer on his way, and which he must scrutinize, challenge and accept, since he can never destroy it without destroying himself as a writer" (p. 4). Form is more essential to literature than any of its ingredients and is, in fact, "the first and last arbiter of literary responsibility" (p. 83). For this reason Barthes could praise "writing degree zero" for having liberated form from ideology, not because it permits the abandonment of political commitment but because its perfect equipoise makes this commitment altogether unnecessary.[6] Without retreating from politics, he was marching in a different direction, toward form's zero-degree balance between journalism and the timelessness of style and language.

The concept of a zero degree was actually suggested earlier by Sartre's expression "*l'écriture blanche*," used in his 1947 review of Camus's *L'Étranger*, but Barthes imposed his own definition of a "colorless language," a "style of absence" that transforms itself into a "neutral term or zero element" (pp. 76–77). Zero-degree equipoise becomes exactly the balance between literary style (which Barthes found to be ultimately suicidal in such poets as Mallarmé) and the journalistic clarity recommended by Sartre (which Barthes thought reduces ideology to a question of grammar too much in the "imperative mood"). Through zero-degree symmetry, Barthes claimed, the excesses of journalism and literary density cancel each other out, leaving us with the "absence of all signs," the "style of absence which is almost an ideal absence of style" (p. 77). The zero-degree writer might be aware of modern disorder but anticipates with trepidation the social homogeneity advocated by Sartre (p. 87). The zero-degree writer's disengagement, Barthes claimed, is reflected in an empty style like that of Camus or Robbe-Grillet, which is a "basic speech, equally far from living languages and from literary language proper" (p. 77). The zero-degree writer accepts as an inevitability that the zero-degree balance is only temporary, a fleeting opportunity soon to be succeeded by imbalance toward either journalism or literary style, but also recognizes "that there is no writing which can be lastingly revolutionary, and that any silence of form can escape imposture only by a complete abandonment of communication" (p. 75). Without entirely escaping imposture, the zero-degree writer resorts to literary form, "the way a certain silence has of existing," literature's quintessence free from human struggle (p. 78).

In his subsequent books, Barthes dealt with many topics besides politics, but almost always with the same strategy of disengaging himself through his affirmative pursuit of alternatives, as explained by the affirmative fallacy I discussed in chapter 7. His logic was essentially dialectic, subordinating both logic and induction to the threefold pattern of withdrawal mentioned above: *concessive* in granting a role to whatever tendency or disposition he wanted to deny; *tensive* in establishing a complementary relationship with equally important alternatives; and *formalist* in establishing a structure (or paradigm) among these alternatives that effectively denies (or designifies) the active ingredient presumably acknowledged at the concessive stage of his strategy. The primary benefit of Barthes's formalist strategy, compared, for example, to fiction as organized by narrative form, is that its linear sequence did not depend on obvious metonymic advancement toward closure. Barthes ranged as he pleased among his ideas, leaving it to the reader to comprehend his intentions.

Perhaps the most basic use of this strategy in Barthes's criticism may be found in *Mythologies*, published in 1957 and translated in 1972, in which Barthes proposed that myth is a second-order semiological system that doubles signification, thereby diminishing the influence of raw experience as signified by words and word combinations.[7] He conceded the importance of signification as a representation of whatever is signified, but he subordinated its role to a more inclusive signification based on a "second-order semiological system," the use of the entire sign—comprising both the signified and its full signifier—as an empty signifier to convey myth (pp. 114–16). At the concessive stage of his argument he granted that full (i.e., ordinary) signification is of course essential to literary expression, but he imposed the caveat at the tensive stage of his argument that in signification's literary use as a "global sign" it necessarily becomes empty signification in representing myth. By identifying *meaning* as the final term in ordinary signification and *form* as the final term in the global signification essential for myth, Barthes brought his argument to its formalist culmination. He established a negative polarity between form and what is meant (the first term in ordinary signification) to explain the distinction between literary and nonliterary experience—one necessarily formal and the other necessarily limited to the signification of raw information (pp. 116–18). The interaction is diagramed in figure 4. If the author's signified meaning is full, according to Saussure's theory of signification, it becomes the empty first term of a mythic system essential to literary experience. A word's signification is necessarily compounded by its second referent based on its mythic implications, and this tandem representation gives literary form its precedence over referential accuracy, including, of course, politicized speech. Here, once again, the complementary interaction among alternatives gives precedence to form as a final term that effectively denies the active ingredient of its opposite. In this instance, Barthes's use of form denies raw experience, the first term in ordinary signification, necessarily a more inclusive category of human behavior than the *praxis* implied by *engagement*, whose denial by form was already explained in *Writing Degree Zero*.

To illustrate the tripartite organization of his doubled semiological system, Barthes resorted to the symbolism of the rose:

> Take a bunch of roses: I use it to *signify* my passion. Do we have here, then, only a signifier and a signified, the roses and my passion? Not even that: to put it accurately, there are here only "passionified" roses. But on the plain of analysis, we do have three terms; for these roses weighted with passion perfectly and correctly allow themselves to be decomposed into roses and passion: the former and the latter existed before uniting and forming this third object, which is the sign. (p. 113)

The literary value of Gertrude Stein's rose, for example, depends on linking its primitive (or first-order) signification of the flower usually identified as a rose with its literary symbolism (a second-order signification). The rose as signified at the first level becomes the signification of the mythic rose at the second. As a result, the literary rose becomes both more and less than a real rose. It exceeds the real rose because of its literary status, but it falls short of it because the conventional literary associations linked with this status nullify (or crowd from consideration) most of the direct experience represented by the word *rose*.

What Barthes maintained here was that our plenitude of nonliterary experience is actually designified by the literary use of signification. Raw experience becomes accessible to fiction once it can be incorporated into the formalist meaning-form equation at the core of literary experience. But this equation necessarily asserts itself at the expense of the primary relationship

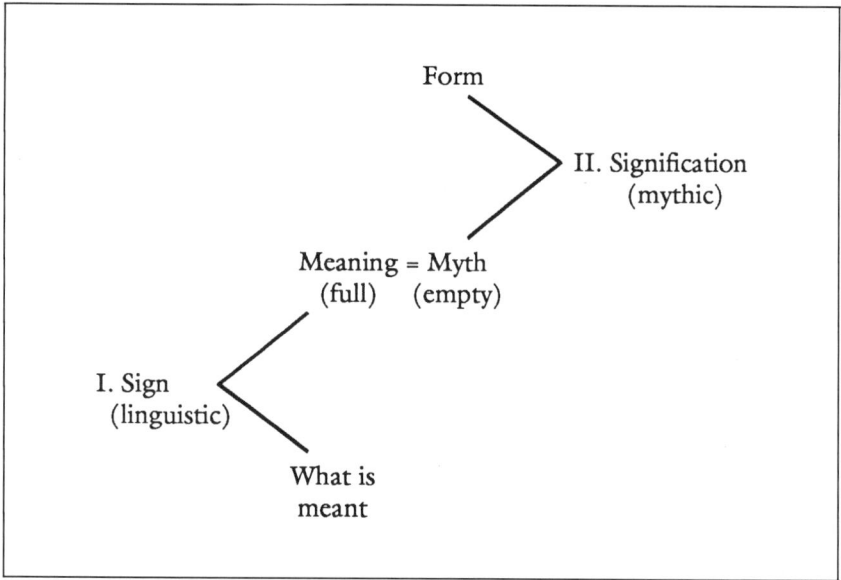

FIGURE 4. *Barthes's model for literary representation*

between signifier and signified—the full experience of the rose evoked by the simple utterance of the word *rose*. Only in poetry, Barthes claimed, is this process of designification resisted, since poets impose a "regressive" semiological system:

> Whereas myth aims at an ultra-signification, at the amplification of a first system, poetry, on the contrary, attempts to regain an infra-signification, a pre-semiological state of language; in short, it tries to transform the sign back into meaning: its ideal, ultimately, would be to reach not the meaning of words, but the meaning of things themselves. This is why it clouds the language, increases as much as it can the abstractness of the concept and the arbitrariness of the sign and stretches to the limit the link between signifier and signified. (p. 133)

Here Barthes's explanation of the presemiological value of poetry apparently converges with my discussion of poetry's metaphoric expressiveness in earlier chapters. It would seem an easy step for Barthes to have explored the tension that might have occurred between the ultra- or hypersignification of poetry and metaphor on the one hand and, on the other, the null-signification of literary form as the organization of myth. However, he neglected this possibility, in part because he wanted to deemphasize the notion of metonymic linear structure (i.e., plot) in the formal organization of myth, and in part perhaps because, as Barthes himself argued in *Writing Degree Zero*, the history of French literature, more than that of English literature, has kept form and metaphor in relative isolation from each other—Racine's mythic ultrasignification, for example, having had almost nothing to do in anticipating Mallarmé's presemiological infrasignification. Barthes therefore conceded poetry a density of signification relatively free of formal constraints, while assigning to all other literature worthy of critical examination an empty signification typical of myth: "The world enters language as a dialectical relation between activities, between human actions; it comes out of myth as a harmonious display of essences. A conjuring trick has taken place; it has turned reality inside out, it has emptied it of history and has filled it with nature" (p. 142). Once again, the full representation of experience based on the relationship between signified and signifier at the first level of signification is purified through its use as a global sign at its second level of signification. A transition has taken place from simple reference to a more inclusive context equating signification with form in the zero-degree equipoise between myth and tangible experience.

Barthes's next major book, *On Racine*, published in 1960 and translated in 1964, was impressive in its range of formalist borrowings.[8] Here Barthes sought once again to elevate form over history, though he turned from the general topic of *écriture* to the more specific investigation of classical French tragedy. He was engaged in the same conflict, but on a different battlefield and with a slightly different strategy. In *Writing Degree Zero*, he had tangentially suggested the tragic element in *écriture* to be the struggle against "allpowerful signs" imposed by history. In *On Racine* he expanded this point by removing tragedy from history because its timelessness supposedly excludes the interior features of process and duration. His new task was to eliminate time and process from tragedy so tragedy itself could be removed from history, establishing what might be described as an aesthetics (or "fallacy") of double timelessness. Once again he emphasized the value of literary form, in this instance by treating it as the vehicle of Racinian transparence "eternally open to signification": "Hence it is ultimately his very transparence that makes Racine a veritable commonplace of our literature, the critical object at zero degree, a site empty but eternally open to signification" (pp. viii-ix). Whereas in *Writing Degree Zero* Barthes would have identified Racine as a classical poet who anticipated literary style's evolution toward the zero-degree lucidity of the twentieth century, he here identified Racine as its most consummate practitioner.

By ignoring the categories of history and style in *On Racine*, Barthes gave the category of language its singular role as the primary source of form in both classicism and modern zero-degree *écriture*. As before, he addressed himself to the question of *engagement*, this time with the somewhat cryptic remark probably influenced by Camus more than by anybody else: "To write is to jeopardize the meaning of the world, to put an indirect question that the writer, by an ultimate abstention, refrains from answering" (p. ix). It might seem that Barthes was echoing Sartre in this remark, but careful scrutiny reveals that he wanted *not* to change the world but to "jeopardize its meaning," a safer and relatively harmless semiotic preoccupation. It posed no obligation to answer questions about current social problems or even to make such an effort. Barthes wanted to ask indirect questions that he himself would not be able to answer—an objective clearly opposite to Sartre's emphasis upon an author's obligation to communicate answers, presumably correct ones, to a less enlightened public. Elsewhere in *On Racine*, Barthes claimed that unanswered questions are the most important contribution of the Racinian tragic hero, as if his seventeenth-century fictive identity perfectly embodied the zero-degree consciousness of today: "Racinian man is *caught* in his disengagement: he is the man of the *que faire?* not of the *faire*; he appeals to, he invokes an action, he does not perform it" (p. 48, italics in original). The Racinian hero thereby prefigured modern disengagement, as did Racine himself, but instead of resorting to zero-degree form, the hero expressed impotent lucidity in the ritual of tragic dénouement. Within the context of tragedy, form manifested itself as the focus of indecision culminating in a silence that afforded "the invasion of the true *praxis*, the collapse of the entire apparatus" (p. 59). Like his twentieth-century counterpart in the zero-degree author, the Racinian hero escaped political struggle through an affirmative commitment to the immanent crisis of language.

The eclectic formalism that pervades *On Racine* gives the impression of a brilliantly disarranged catalog of new dimensions that deny experience by means of form. With a psychocriticism borrowed from Mauron, Barthes investigated primordial family jealousies as the matrix for all tragic action. With the structural anthropology of Lévi-Straùss, he explored unreconciled mythic patterns, for example, the antinomy between the powers of the sun and underground, which he found to be of central importance in *Phèdre*. And with the critical phenomenology of Bachelard and Poulet, he established a spatial dimension for tragedy in its relationship among three sites—the chamber, antechamber, and outside world. Barthes's explanation of the chamber was obviously psychoanalytic, and his explanation of the outside world was just as obviously Marxist, but tragedy, he claimed, is limited to the antechamber, the "site of language," a zero-degree threshold that links these two external realms. The antechamber supposedly reduces tragedy to the empty signification that connects the inner chamber, a psychological "abode of power," with the confused social realities of exterior space. Occupying this intermediate zone, tragedy provides the "media of transmission" from secrecy to effusion, "from immediate fear to fear expressed" (p. 4). Once again we detect Barthes's threefold strategy of disengagement, based on a formalist version of dialectics that recurred throughout his career (table 4). As with his theories of *écriture* and literary signification, Barthes conceded the mimetic element of tragedy that least interested him (exterior space), but he likewise established its antithesis (interior space) and situated tragedy as the formal zone of interaction between the two—in this instance within the antechamber. On this basis, Barthes could draw upon a large variety of reductive approaches to extract tragedy, indeed all literature, from history through its presumably formal timelessness. The truth-value of tragedy was not what it said about real life or what it said about human need but its success in organizing language (and plot) to keep these antithetical demands suspended and unresolved.

Most remarkably, Barthes tried to reduce to formalist guidelines Lucien Goldmann's Marxist interpretation of Racinian dialectics. He acknowledged the value of Goldmann's Hegelian insight that tragic conflict arises from "pure contraries that are never mediated": "The Racinian world is a world of two terms, its status is paradoxical, not dialectical: the third term is missing."[9] But he neglected Goldmann's important qualification that unresolved paradoxes during historic "periods of tragedy" do become resolved by such figures as Plato (for Sophocles), Locke (for Shakespeare), and Marx (for Racine) in later epochs, when the intuitive discoveries of tragedy can be brought into philosophical discourse. This concept of delayed synthesis postpones the mediation advocated by Sartre until destructive contradictions can finally be confronted on an analytic basis, but this, too, Barthes wanted to avoid. He preferred to reject both the direct and the "eventual" theories of mediation

TABLE 4. *Barthes's Strategy of Disengagement*

		Concessive	Tensive	Formalist
1.	*Écriture:*	Engagement	*Contra* style and language	Zero-degree equipoise
2.	Signification:	Concept	*Contra* myth	Form-meaning equation
3.	Tragedy:	Exterior space	*Contra* inner space	Antechamber as the site of language

by instead proposing that human purposefulness is restricted to the vulgar intrusiveness of minor figures such as Oenone, the meddlesome nurse in *Phèdre* (pp. 53–54). Barthes found the pragmatic futility of these characters to be dwarfed by tragic action that fulfills itself in a perfect zero-degree ambivalence of destructive lucidity between contraries that remain unmediated. To this intermediate zone of representation, which is outside history, he restricted his inquiry. In just one sense did he accept the concept of tragic mediation, but his explanation reduced it to futility and absurdity. He claimed tragedy converts *praxis* first to language, providing the illusion of a dialectic, and then to silence, whose dialectic is the "transcendence of failure," the "myth of the failure of myth" (p. 60). On this basis (reminiscent of Hamlet's fate as discussed in chapter 6), Barthes was willing to explain tragic reconciliation, but his concession proscribed both signification and human aspirations in favor of silence.

Barthes largely concentrated his attack upon process and duration to eliminate from tragedy any reference whatsoever to the processes of human behavior culminating in history or narrative closure. In *Writing Degree Zero*, he had boldly proclaimed, "What must be destroyed is duration, that is, the ineffable binding force running through existence."[10] In *Elements of Semiology*, he had similarly tried to eliminate process and density from connotation in language with an ingenious theory of regressive "planes of expression."[11] And in *On Racine*, he made tragic action timeless by explaining duration as a tautological cancellation of terms that only accidentally occupy time: "Racinian duration is never maturative, it is circular, it accumulates and harks back but never transforms anything" (p. 49). He accordingly reduced all tragic process to logical and mathematical formulations outside the dimension of time. For example, he asserted that "Racinian disorder" is essentially a sign or symbol in a "designed," two-dimensional universe, undoubtedly Euclidian. He likewise claimed that tragic conflict is a crisis of space (p. 26), the topographical denial of duration, but also rigidly binary with reversible terms, in this case its algebraic denial (p. 36). He further argued that reversal and discovery are inversions of absolutely no duration (p. 43), that tragic climax does not conclude action but merely "severs" (p. 50), that soliloquy primarily expresses division (p. 36), and that tragic unity consists of ecstatic moments or points in time (p. 37). He claimed that dialogue functions on the level of structure, not of character (p. 36), and that "there are no characters . . . only situations" (p. 13). He also said tragic death is "an empty grammatical category" that "never concerns anyone but the other," since "its constitutive movement is to be inflicted" (pp. 30, 32). Finally, he said that words, though they might arouse hope for mediation, function only as an "illusion of dialectic which brings the audience back to silence, the true praxis without duration" (p. 59). He viewed Racinian tragedy as an "autonomous object" that exists beyond history, process, and human frailties in a limbo of aesthetic perfection, its sublimation the final denial of *praxis* and *engagement* (p. 9). In its perfection it offered the model he wanted of literary commitment as a perfect rejection of human experience.

Barthes's formalist emphasis became increasingly personalized over the years, as became obvious, for example, in *The Pleasure of the Text*, published in 1973 and translated in 1975.[12] But not until his autobiography, *Roland Barthes by Roland Barthes*, published in 1975 and translated in 1977, did Barthes fully draw upon his critical apparatus in explaining the connection between his eclectic formalism and his personal vision of life.[13] A complex syndrome emerged that gave context to many of his theories that had otherwise seemed random and without any clear unity. Central to Barthes's autobiographical strategy was his acknowledgment of his androgynous preference, substituting his own denial strategies as a homosexual for the homophobic and/or homoaversive denial strategies supportive of narrative form.

With typical elusiveness, he finally acknowledged his sexual preference by arguing, for example, that his migraine headaches classified him with the feminine sex (pp. 124–25), that he (like both the Ancient Mariner and Young Goodman Brown) felt peculiarly excluded by weddings (pp. 85–86), and that the phallus should be done away with instead of being treated as a little god (p. 165). More provocatively, he promoted the "sensuous" as a bisexual objective that isolates literary genius from popular opinion. He argued that writing constantly risks vulgarity (p. 126), that it disperses the energy of seduction (p. 143), and that speech and kissing are interrelated outgrowths of bipedalism that cannot be isolated from each other (pp. 140–41). He also advocated a convergence of love and language to triumph over the "dreadful reduction" that language alone imposes on our feelings (p. 114), and he claimed that a writer's block results from the inability to capture the "enchantment" of a seduction (p. 86).

Barthes maintained that art is never paranoid (emphasizing homophobic denial) but is rather fetishistic (emphasizing self-indulgence), and that even the single word expresses fetish as both mana and appetite (p. 68). Here Barthes's rejection of paranoid experience as a component of literature became linked with his programmatic rejection of plot and the rest of the machinery of narrative form. As I indicated earlier, his androgynous bias precluded his acceptance of any synthesis between the "thick" and essentially fetishistic ultrasignification he sought in poetry and its designification by narrative form. Barthes also treated the Oedipus complex as a personal challenge. With obvious relish he quibbled over the relative courage of his earlier remark, in *The Pleasure of the Text*, that fiction should be uninhibited enough to show its "behind" to its political father.[14] "Ass" would be inappropriate, he argued, because it was the child's posterior he had in mind, compounding his obvious disdain for father figures.[15] By spelling out this distinction he claimed to be protesting his innocent intentions, but he also disclosed an infantile defiance reminiscent of both "Young Goodman Brown" and the final image in "Mending Wall."

Barthes identified his primary enemy, the "other" against which he struggled as a critic, to be *Doxa*, or orthodox opinion, thinking's lowest common denominator typical of respectability and patriarchal demands. "The *Doxa*," he argued, "is Public Opinion, the mind of the majority, petit bourgeois Consensus, the Voice of Nature, the Violence of Prejudice" (p. 47). *Doxa* translates from Greek simply as a notion or opinion, but Barthes uses the word to describe any belief system, any righteous cause with popular appeal. In this sense, *Doxa* may be explained as positive belief imposed by the affirmative fallacy, and in turn the affirmative fallacy may be understood as entailing the entire negative displacement that provides the matrix of *Doxa*, guaranteeing its impact among those who believe in it and its offensiveness to others who don't. "I remain behind the door," Barthes claimed. "The *Doxa* speaks, I hear it, but I am not within its space" (p. 123). In effect, Barthes's aversion to leftist politics in his early criticism had expanded to become an inclusive disdain for all *Doxa*—*Doxa* of the left, of the right, and of nonpolitical issues as well. Barthes's affirmative commitment to aesthetic purity as freedom from leftist rhetoric expanded to become a defense of personal freedom from all orthodoxy and social constraint. His campaign against Sartre's existential-Marxist definition of freedom finally led to his own more inclusive definition of freedom—one that was radically iconoclastic, both anti-Marxist and hostile to traditional bourgeois obligations. *Doxa* was the problem, and the role of the intellectual was to help liberate the public from its ubiquitous repressiveness.

But *Doxa* also bore literary implications for Barthes, since he linked it with narrative form, conventional figures and episodes, and, not least, with the "style of a climax" that gives fiction its closure dynamics. Of course, this literary function of *Doxa* offensive to Barthes epitomizes the metonymic function of plot in the model of negative poetics I am proposing, based on a conflict between local metaphoric confession and the narrative sequence of episodes that ends in closure. Barthes enthusiastically praised literature's resistance against conventional narrative closure: "What carries all before it is the flavor of paradox: to be able to suggest that Narrative is not at all projective, to be able to subvert the narrative *Doxa*" (p. 98). But he could not accept the ultimate success of closure as guaranteed by *Doxa*, the demand for a suitable heterosexual resolution by the overwhelming majority of readers. He accordingly declared narrative form to be oppressively tied to both marriage and the Oedipus complex (p. 121), and he argued that the conflicts these impose exaggerate typologies that are best dissolved through "homosexualities . . . whose plural will baffle any constituted, centered discourse" (p. 69). Here again Barthes's explanation of narrative convention falls in line with negative poetics but does not concede the inevitable victory narrative form grants to marriage, the Oedipus complex, and centered discourse at the expense of homosexualities and the celebration of the "plural" as critical objectives. Barthes likewise claimed, predictably, that the dramatic scene, both literary and nonliterary, is generated by a violence that derives from *Doxa*'s heterosexual and patriarchal "insistences" (p. 162). He chose to ignore the fact that this narrative violence is what makes fiction satisfying to most readers and preferred limiting his inquiry to his earlier category of personal style through his pursuit of random *aperçu* and textual curiosities. He thereby ignored the dialectic interaction between narrative *Doxa* and stylistic expressiveness and reduced literary experience deserving of explication to a melange of androgynous significations that resist integration within narrative form's more inclusive structure. If the homophobic imagination absorbs and denies metaphor by means of a cumulative linear structure, Barthes inverted his explicative priorities by disregarding these dynamics in favor of local contexts independent of the dynamics of closure. He conceded that any literary text might be shaped and organized by *Doxa*—for example, Racine's tragedy (heterosexual) or Balzac's "Sarrasine" (transvestite)—but he found more satisfaction in fracturing *Doxa*'s plot-dominated rigidity into myriad fragments, each unique in its escape from "narrative violence."

The escapist strategy of Barthes's antihomophobic commitment was clarified by his probably unconscious use of the regressive antinomies proposed by Lévi-Strauss.[16] Whether by accident or design, Barthes stumbled on his own regressive sequence, first by distinguishing pseudo-Physis (*Doxa*) from anti-Physis, suggestive of his earlier category of style ("all his personal utopias"), then by distinguishing their violence from their neutral coexistence, ambiguously suggestive of both colorlessness and homophilia. Finally, as if by afterthought, Barthes added a final antinomy between virile and nonvirile to complete the regressive sequence for rejecting heterosexual *Doxa* by imposing perfect neutrality. The sequence is diagrammed in figure 5.[17] An unpleasant choice (virile v. nonvirile) was revised as an easier choice (physis v. pseudo-Physis), and then a still easier choice (violence v. neutral), which featured his earlier formalist commitment to zero-degree perfection. But of course, the basic distinction for Barthes spanned this entire field of alternations, between what is virile at one extreme, which he despised, and what is neutral at the other, signifying the style of neutrality (ultimately of silence) he had advocated throughout his career. Barthes accordingly refined his earlier use of the concessive-tensive-formalist interaction by imposing a tandem regression of binarisms expressive of unmitigated aversion. He no longer proposed neutrality as zero-degree compromise but as the single acceptable

Roland Barthes

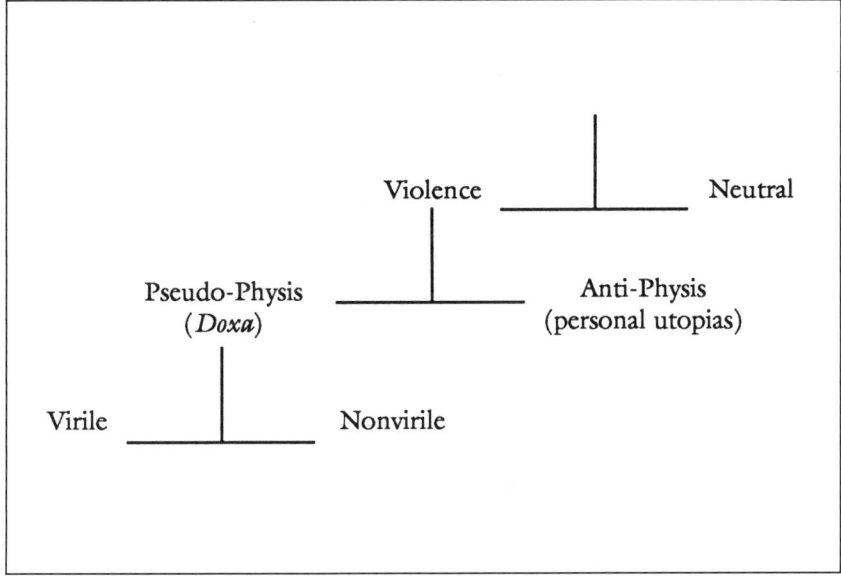

FIGURE 5. *Barthes's sequence of antinomies*

alternative to three enemies, each rendered harmless by its redefinition at a new level of abstraction: virility, *Doxa*, and, the most easily rejected, violence. In effect, Barthes designified all three by organizing them into a hierarchy of binarisms that culminates in neutrality. He expanded equipoise between pure contraries into a regressive advancement among equipoises whose metonymic sequence gives narrative effect to its denial of an unacceptable role—in his case, one that imposed heterosexual rather than homosexual standards.

Barthes claimed he wanted to differentiate "neutral" from zero-degree vacancy because "neutral" afforded "another link of the infinite chain of language" (pp. 132–33). In his earlier criticism he had emphasized neutrality's universal potential as the primary value of zero-degree purification. Now, however, he finally acknowledged that his defense of neutrality was primarily based on his loathing of heterosexual identity as epitomized by pride in masculine sufficiency, deification of the penis, etc. The masculine role was unacceptable to him, and he was at last able to confess his effort to dispose of it through pun, parody, dislocation, and surreptitious quotation. He stressed duplicity as the fantasy to hear not everything but something else—the "other," as discerned by the androgynous critic. There is always a struggle against one's own banality, Barthes claimed, and he described his autobiography as a "Book of the Self" that articulated his resistances to his own ideas by falling away from them to gain new perspective (p. 119). Accuracy was not his purpose but escape—in his case, escape from orthodoxy and the narrative machinery supportive of *Doxa* in the context of fiction. Perversely, because of his escapism, Barthes redefined his criticism as "almost a novel: a novel without proper names" (p. 120). As a novel, his criticism also lacked closure, but this, too, would be provided by the end of his career. Barthes's escapism also justified his role-playing as the assumption of an identity not his own: "The origin of the work is not the first influence, it is the first posture: one copies a role, then, by metonymy, an art; I began producing by reproducing the person I want to be" (p. 99). Barthes complained of being out of place. He was left-handed and of Protestant roots in a right-handed, Catholic nation. Moreover, he was not heterosexual but genderless, not himself but his mother's son, not an author but a role-player. Was he at least a critic? At last he could confess his reductive eclecticism to have been little more than an "echo chamber" of others' theories, each affording escape from a role he refused to play (p. 70).

Perhaps the most remarkable achievement of Barthes's autobiography was his willingness to acknowledge his strategy of evasiveness. Like Hamlet, he admitted dispersing himself to deny his inner vacancy, the "heart of heart" that might explain his almost infinite elusiveness: "To write by fragments: the fragments are then so many stones on the perimeter of a circle: I spread myself around: my whole little universe in crumbs; at the center, what?" (p. 92). It turns out that the fragmentation described by Barthes expressed more fundamental difficulties than his androgynous reaction against *Doxa* and its attendant obligations. Implicit throughout his autobiography was his timidity, his reclusiveness and avoidance of others except those who could share his fragile sensuality. Barthes could boast of at last writing "more openly, more unprotectedly," but he also acknowledged, describing himself in the third person, that he did so "to account for his feeling of insecurity which possesses him today and, still more perhaps, the vague torment of a *recession* toward a minor thing, the old thing he is when 'left to himself'" (p. 102). As in both *Hamlet* and "Mending Wall," the word *thing* bears possible phallic connotations, suggesting a loneliness for homosexual companionship. Barthes had many friendships, but as *Camera Lucida* later made plain, it was primarily his mother who nourished and protected him from his infancy until her death two years before his. Her dominance in his life may be measured by both his reclusiveness and his genderless strategy as critic and iconoclast. Throughout his life, Barthes was intensely dedicated to his role as his mother's boy, and his mother-dependency limited his emotional growth to playing out his own version of her role in his militant commitment against heterosexual adjustment, against *Doxa*, against *engagement*, against all suggestions of orthodox social responsibility.

Here, I think, may be found the essential contradiction at the core of Barthes's identity as a critic that led to his rejection of patriarchal demands. Like both Hamlet and Young Goodman Brown, he justified his loathing of father-identification through his vigilant defense of his mother-cultivated innocence, but unlike Young Goodman Brown, he possessed enough versatility as a gay iconoclast (he described himself as an intellectual "cruiser") to abandon gender distinctions relatively confident of his safety from Oedipal demands (p. 72). Opposed to *Doxa* stood childish vulnerability and infantile anxieties, not the least of which was Barthes's apprehension that he might have grown up: "I no longer feel myself to be sympathetic (to others, to myself). It is at this point of contact between the writing and the work that the hard truth appears to me: I am no longer a child" (p. 137). Obviously, his childhood continued to haunt him. In perhaps the most memorable episode of his autobiography, Barthes told of his mother's saving him from the ruins of a house foundation in which he was trapped, taunted by bullies standing on the walls above him. Likewise, the most memorable photograph included in his autobiography shows him being held in her arms, a ten-year-old child three-quarters her size—he on the brink of tears, she standing proud and sufficient in her motherly protectiveness. It almost seems as if she had just pulled him from the foundation and was parading before the camera his infantile helplessness, which he later overcame by identifying with her, her devoted son *qua* homosexual, *qua* critic, *qua* enemy of orthodox opinion.

In *Camera Lucida*, published in 1980, the year of Barthes's accidental death, Barthes eulogized his mother by linking her memory to his theory of photography as a medium of truth that absolutely transcends literary signification.[18] By emphasizing the absolute mimetic truth of the snapshot, Barthes was at last able to cope with mimesis, a principle he had avoided in his earlier criticism. He could finally accept the value of pure signification in and of itself by featuring the concrete pictorial validity of the ordinary snapshot. Null-signification gave way to ultrasignification, based on his newfound fascination with photography's elimination of the formalist equipoise he had emphasized in his earlier criticism. No longer was avoidance the strategy but a frantic effort to recapture photography's signified experience. Each photograph, Barthes claimed, conveys an indirect but completely accurate transmission of light rays from the subjects photographed to whoever looks at their printed reproduction. The past event recorded by the snapshot is thereby salvaged for the present experience of those who view it. This is true no matter how many photographic surfaces intervene—the lens, film, negative, and print—and no matter how many years have elapsed between the taking and seeing of the picture. Moreover, each photograph conveys certain undeniable truths with obvious existential implications: (1) that the image depicted is from the past, (2) that the subject depicted is already dead or that much closer to death, and (3) that whoever views the photograph is likewise vulnerable to time and eventual death. Here at last were signified truths that the literary dynamics of signification could not distill into formalist evasiveness. A photograph is meaningful, Barthes claimed, if it contains a "punctum"—a detail that stands out, giving tension and unforgettableness to its frozen image. But he added that there is also a more inclusive *punctum* applicable to all photography—the sense of a lost past and the inevitability of death. For Barthes, images of motherhood seemed especially profound in this respect, and the most remarkable photograph Barthes knew of in this respect was the winter garden image of his mother as a five-year-old girl accompanied by her older brother. Already evident in her eyes as a child, Barthes insisted, were the kindness and "sovereign innocence" he would later cherish when trying to rekindle his memories of her. There she stood, fixed in time, his mother as a little girl, though she had already, in fact, lived out her life and died just months before he published his book. The most accurate depiction of her previous existence that remained for him was his small accumulation of snapshots, and their deathly implications provided his best remaining link with his mother.

Barthes could boast of having reversed roles to become his mother's mother in her final years, but this reciprocity culminated in total despair upon her death. Once she died he died too—there was little to live for except her photographs. The Freudian explanation is plain, if bordering on the simplistic. Much earlier in his life, his love for his mother had been displaced to mother-identification, and his intense mother-identification could be sustained only by joining her in death. Like Hamlet, Barthes lucked into self-destruction as both a transcendent gesture of homosexual identification and the ultimate homophobic concession, a final letting go to regain in death a relationship that had prevented his self-realization in life—except as a critic. Throughout his career Barthes had been an enemy of *Doxa*, and he both escaped and acknowledged its obligation by accepting his death. *Doxa* prevailed because he gave up the struggle, but he won, too, because he gladly preferred death to further enduring *Doxa*'s incessant demands. This was Barthes's final and most inclusive act of denial, and, paradoxically, he was brought to this extreme by a theory of mimesis that was antithetical to his earlier critical priorities. By emphasizing photography's ultrasignification, he eliminated (or designified) the mythic doubling of signification crucial to literary form, as explained in *Mythologies*. As a result he relinquished (or designified) his own role as a critic infinitely resourceful in the study of literary form. No longer was there any meaning in denying orthodox values through an affirmative commitment to the avant-garde. Instead, Barthes turned to his tiny collection of amateur snapshots as his only means of reclaiming his inspiration in his relationship with his mother. And his snapshots demanded a renewed commitment to silence, neutrality—and ultimately death.

Death, in fact, became Barthes's new affirmative pursuit, as captured by photography: "I have become Total-Image—which is to say, Death in Person. . . . Ultimately what I am seeking in a photograph taken of me (the 'intention' according to which I look at it) is Death! Death is the *eidos* of that photograph" (pp. 14–15). In a later passage he more specifically tied photography to his grief for his mother and his sense of his own impending destruction entwined with hers:

> With the Photograph we enter into flat Death. One day, leaving one of my classes, someone said to me with disdain: "You talk about Death very flatly."—As if the horror of Death were not precisely its platitude! The horror is this: Nothing to say about the death of one whom I love most, nothing to say about her photograph, which I contemplate without ever being able to get to the heart of it, to transform it. The only "thought"

I can have is that at the end of this first death, my own death is inscribed; between the two, nothing more than waiting; I have no other resource than this irony: to speak of the "nothing to say." (p. 93)

For all practical purposes Barthes's career was finished. Both his literary criticism and mother-dependency ended with this remarkable tribute to his mother based on his theory of photography. She was brought to life, but only by a mimetic worship that featured death. Literary signification had imposed silence and neutrality. Hypersignification demanded death itself—in effect, its transcendence in null-signification, once again illustrating the dynamics of metonymic designification. Perhaps fittingly, Barthes's theory was best illustrated by the winter garden snapshot of his mother that he excluded from both his autobiography and *Camera Lucida*. By her silent but magnanimous smile, his mother, a little girl, perfectly expressed a sense of shared mortality usually reserved to the *Moirai* and Cordelias of literary myth.[19] Barthes's effort to recapture his mother's generous smile was his terminal affirmation, his final contribution to literary criticism. Other projects persisted, of course, but with his theory of snapshot photography he wrote his epitaph. The rest was silence.

Throughout his career Barthes denied masculinity, continuity, closure, belief, righteousness, and political commitment, but most of all *Doxa*, the single overriding principle that summarized the rest. The affirmative values he substituted evolved from early formalist dexterity to an intensely romantic vision of homophile sufficiency—first hinted in *S/Z* and *Pleasures of the Text*, then confessed in his autobiography. When his mother died, his emphasis shifted to an obsessive celebration of death that ended in an avoidable accident when he absentmindedly walked in front of a bread truck. As he had declared much earlier in *On Racine*, the tragic protagonist merely invokes an action but does not perform it—so it does not exactly matter whether Barthes might have intended suicide when he was killed. The circumstances of his fatal accident were perhaps absurd, but its literary appropriateness was no less tragic than the stories of Phèdre, Hamlet, and Oedipus. In a bizarre reversal of narrative form, his effort to retain his mother's memory culminated his pursuit of formalist evasions. The perfectly retrieved image as epitomized by the snapshot (presumably an ultimate act of signification) provided closure to his compulsive rejection of "plotted" closure dynamics over the duration of his career. His earlier formalist strategy based on the sequence of concessive, tensive, and formalist stages was actually reversed, since he had begun his career as a formalist and now ended it in the concessive mode. His theory of the snapshot affirmed life, signification, and indeed his suicidal obligation to both *Doxa* and homophobic closure. As for the intermediate category of tension, this was perhaps best expressed by his many paradigms, all in the tensive mode, whose unavoidable symmetry at least conceded the existence of the energies he wanted to deny—energies to which he would later pay his due. Except for Barthes's inversion of poetry's orthodox sequence—a postponed open-system honesty that succeeded his closed-system defensiveness—his entire corpus of prose from *Writing Degree Zero* to *Camera Lucida* may accordingly be judged as a *supernovel* (not a *subnovel*, as Barthes feared) that established his literary parity with France's major twentieth-century novelists.

Barthes was aware of his achievement. As he stated in the epigraph to his autobiography, "It must all be considered as if spoken by a character in a novel." He was, of course, proposing himself as his own protagonist, with the assumption that his hermeneutic restlessness constituted his story's narrative outline. His insights defied the Aristotelian unities, but once his personal destiny took precedence, these too assumed a linear momentum that necessitated an Aristotelian outcome tantamount to tragedy. Barthes's mother-centered iconoclasm had encouraged his pursuit of criticism, and his final acknowledgment of his indebtedness transfigured his criticism into something akin to fiction. *Doxa* was the enemy and self-discovery his belated victory, as afforded by the regressive mimesis of snapshot photography, actually revising plot as a transition from avoidances to their confrontation, i.e., from designification to its denial. With this postponed and inverted sense of an ending, his career organized itself into a plot (or *muthos*) unparalleled in the history of literary criticism.

nine

THREE AFFIRMISTS AND A BRIEF NEGATIVE MANIFESTO

Emerson once declared, "Our philosophy is affirmative, and readily accepts the testimony of negative facts, as every shadow points to the sun."[1] As he explained almost two decades later, "Once we thought, positive power was all. Now we learn, that negative power, or circumstance, is half. Each defines the other—life and its circumstance—and dialectics explains their interaction."[2] However, Emerson's synchronic dialectic between complementary opposites is apparently resolved when there is diachronic advancement by which one negates or designifies the other, whether in cultural history, as Hegel proposed, in economic history, as Marx proposed, or in fiction's linear unity of action as explained by Aristotle. Here, in my final chapter, it seems appropriate to take into account this negative principle as a historic phenomenon to be observed when literary criticism evolves in response to political trends. Chapter 7 explored denial in a number of critical theories popular in recent years, and chapter 8 focused on the career of a single critic, Roland Barthes. Now, in chapter 9, I want to examine denial in the increasingly dedicated conservatism among three particular works of literary criticism written during the 1970s: Lionel Trilling's *Sincerity and Authenticity*, pub-

Three Affirmists and a Brief Manifesto

lished in 1972, Wayne Booth's *Modern Dogma and the Rhetoric of Assent*, published in 1974, and John Gardner's *On Moral Fiction*, published in 1978. Each is clearly intact and complete unto itself, but the advancement among the three also suggests a more inclusive intertextual unity of action that traces the mounting conservative reaction in the seventies against the liberationist extravagance associated with the protest movement of the sixties. The trend was cumulative, hence linear, so both denial and metonymic designification may be detected even in its initial stages.

All three critics were already prominent in other areas of endeavor, Trilling as the high priest of New York intellectual circles after the thirties, Booth as the most impressive contemporary apologist for what remains of the Chicago neo-Aristotelian perspective, and Gardner as a free-floating author and medieval scholar whose iconoclastic freedom kept him in the news until his unfortunate death in a motorcycle accident in 1982. But the three were also caught up in the maelstrom of controversy that dominated the epoch. As testaments to cultural stability, their respective works of criticism to be discussed in this chapter—especially Trilling's and Booth's—expressed deep personal reservations about the exaggerated, sometimes orgiastic dedication to the cult of authenticity that had typified the protest movement of the sixties. They rejected the virtues usually associated with this cult—courage, integrity, freedom, etc.—by shifting their emphasis to the complementary virtues of intellectual adequacy, social convention, and social responsibility. Their task was obvious: to challenge the value of the sixties by seeking out more acceptable alternatives.

At least the image of antisocial extravagance had characterized the most fashionable authors during the sixties and early seventies: novelists such as Henry Miller, Norman Mailer, and William S. Burroughs; poets such as Sylvia Plath, Allen Ginsberg, and Gary Snyder; philosophers such as Bertrand Russell and Jean-Paul Sartre; social critics such as Wilhelm Reich, Paul Goodman, R. D. Laing, A. S. Neil, Herbert Marcuse, Noam Chomsky, and Frantz Fanon; and literary critics such as Norman O. Brown and Leslie Fiedler. A major cultural revolution had been brought to focus by the Vietnam conflict, and for the better part of a decade an antiestablishmentarianism prevailed that presumably necessitated efforts toward collective recovery. The balanced dissent of Erich Fromm, C. Wright Mills, Arthur Schlesinger, and John Kenneth Galbraith had degenerated into anarchy reinforced by radical journalism's attack upon the power structure, and like Spenser's surrealistic depiction of Error's motherhood, this attack soon replicated itself in scores of new causes, eventually including equal opportunity, environmentalism, nuclear reactors, consumers' rights, gay rights, chicano rights, black capitalism, battered women, battered children, born-again fundamentalism, educational diversity, and, pitted against each other, abortion rights on one hand and the right-to-life movement on the other.

With dialectical predictability, a reaction set in well before the cause mentality subsided (indeed, portions of it still thrive today). Critics and journalists associated with *Dissent* and *Commentary*, such as Irving Howe, Norman Podhoretz, Daniel Bell, Nathan Glazer, and Lionel Abel, led the countermovement through the late sixties, and by the early seventies Trilling and Booth helped to bring its perspective into academic literary criticism. Even radical causes reflected this trend by having become dependent on the success of their respective political infrastructures. Victimization took precedence over breaking the law, and entitlements became the issue instead of escaping the system. Moreover, the radical leadership learned how to restrict their effort to "winnable" issues. Soon the cause mentality evolved into a pursuit of power to implement change, and then into a worship of power in and of itself, presumably as leverage to impose the needed solutions whenever possible.

Eventually there was a vigorous resurgence of productive "selfhood" at levels of mendacity forgotten since the twenties. As Barbara Ehrenreich explains, the reaction against activism finally degenerated into "mere conservatism."[3] Having advanced from creativity to activism in less than a decade, American culture spent the next two decades shifting to careerism followed by entrepreneurial ventures dictated by personal greed. The caricature of populist righteousness epitomized by Abby Hoffman and Jerry Rubin was supplanted by the equally grotesque caricature of free enterprise epitomized by Ivan Boesky, Mike Milken, and Donald Trump. Ironically, the political activism of the sixties produced a sufficient reaction to have led to careerism and intellectual stultification: alienated activists followed by nonalienated activists, and finally nonalienated nonactivists, many of whom parade a style and rhetoric entirely at odds with the ends they pursue. During the sixties a sizable minority "let it all hang out," and procedures and conventions went begging. But within a decade everything was tucked back in again, setting the stage for an entirely different kind of revolution associated with the Reagan presidency. Explained as metonymic designification, political activism

Three Affirmists and a Brief Manifesto

initiated this collective transition from subversive authenticity (metaphoric) to a social climate dominated by status, greed, and hypocrisy (closure as the denial of metaphor). Almost everybody, every movement and intellectual fad, has more or less participated in this slide over the last three decades: liberals no less than conservatives; fiction, poetry, and criticism no less than Washington, Wall Street, and the media.

As I indicated earlier, literary criticism helped to initiate this transition during the seventies by clarifying distinctions and proclaiming the importance of orthodox values (Barthes's *Doxa*) as opposed to the anarchistic excesses of the sixties. A new and improved status quo was sought, and for this purpose books about life were less effective than books about books—books loosely described as literary criticism and intended for a relatively small audience in our major universities. Yet these were the books that told the story. Published in 1972, Trilling's *Sincerity and Authenticity* belabored the choice between uncompromising honesty as demanded by the sixties and the potentially antithetical virtues of prudence and discrimination that had been all but forgotten. Immersed in the sixties, Trilling could not directly claim that authenticity might be dangerous if taken to an extreme independent of these countervailing virtues, but he contextualized his argument to justify such a conclusion. In *Modern Dogma and the Rhetoric of Assent*, published two years later, Booth took a more patently hostile approach, confident of the obvious moral choice between conservative moderation and the radical extravagance that had cropped up on virtually every campus of the nation. Booth supplanted Trilling's struggle to sort out his options with a confident distinction between the Manichaean alternatives of orthodoxy (virtuous) and activism (infantile). Yes, Booth insisted, authenticity could be despised *if* it were coupled with the adolescent mindlessness typical of the protest movement. In *On Moral Fiction*, published in 1978, Gardner nonchalantly blurred Booth's distinctions, disclosing a shared confidence that the battle against uncompromising authenticity had been won. Honesty could once again be cherished as a harmless illusion, and the dialectic in which Trilling immersed himself and which Booth hypostatized as a relatively simplistic dualism was refracted into a variety of relatively mindless prescriptions, many of which seem at least as true in their negative formulations (honesty is *not* the best policy, etc.). If the analogy with the focusing power of a magnifying glass used in chapter 7 may be used once again, Trilling's struggle to define his objections against both sincerity and authenticity may be located almost exactly at the focal point in the trend toward the pursuit of affirmative substitutes—blurred and partaking of both the image and its reversal. In contrast, Gardner's perspective six years later represented authenticity's inversion—lucid, smaller, and unmistakably upside-down, when the pursuit of floater "truths" was a relatively safe means of inhibiting self-recognition. As documented by the advancement among these three critics—all of them entirely reasonable—the intellectual fabric of American culture advanced from one extravagance as epitomized by the sixties to another—essentially its opposite—as epitomized by the eighties. What makes these three critical perspectives fascinating is that, like Barthes's criticism, they both illustrate and help to explain this trend.

Trilling's *Sincerity and Authenticity*, the first of the three affirmist testaments to have been published, was also the most complex because of its ingenious historical treatment of the two concepts linked by its title, sincerity and authenticity.[4] Superficially, Trilling praised the three-hundred-year evolution of sincerity until it was finally reduced to parody by the protest movement of the sixties. In Trilling's opinion, sincerity was always a useful virtue when it was suitably constrained, but once exaggerated out of proportion it became potentially dangerous as a public illusion. According to Trilling, sincerity's status as a virtue first took root at the time of Shakespeare, when the reckless disregard of sincerity, as epitomized by Machiavellian villains, led to its pursuit as an end in and of itself. Trilling sketched the subsequent evolution of sincerity, both in its Continental tradition from *Rameau's Nephew* by Diderot to Hegel, Rousseau, Goethe, Schiller, Robespierre, Nietzsche, and Freud and in its pragmatic English tradition that featured narrative sincerity from Shaftesbury to Austen, Wordsworth, George Eliot, Ruskin, Wilde, and Conrad. Trilling admired English tradition's collective insistence upon a tangible "thereness" in dealing with moral issues, but he was even more fascinated by the relative sophistication of Continental theory, and he attributed its misapplication in the sixties to simplistic trends brought to their culmination in the theories of Laing, Cooper, and Norman O. Brown. Trilling proposed, in any case, that a better balance is needed, and that this can be provided by consulting either the Continental or the English tradition if its implicit constraints are fully understood. Otherwise, he suggested, sincerity can be taken to such an extreme that its pursuit becomes virtually a threat to civilization.

A superficial reading of Trilling's book suggests he was trying to resurrect a balanced theory of sincerity as the basis for social and literary discourse. However, an entirely different picture emerges if his exposition is reexamined in dialectic terms, since his undercurrent of negative assumptions finally overshadowed his numerous affirmative protestations. Not until the last sentence of his book did Trilling provide the key to the entire exposition, but he expressed his final view in a Judeo-Christian allusion so complex that its full implications are easily overlooked:

> The falsities of an alienated social reality are rejected [nowadays] in favor of an upward psychopathic mobility to the point of divinity, each one of us a Christ—but with none of the inconveniences of undertaking to intercede, of being a sacrifice, of reasoning with rabbis, of making sermons, of having disciples, of going to weddings and to funerals, of beginning something and at a certain point remarking that it is finished. (pp. 171–72)

Appropriately, Trilling completed his polemic with the words "it is finished," bringing his argument to a close with a declared sense of an ending based on Christ's final words on the cross according to the Gospel of John. Trilling obviously intended the allusion, but he also used these words to imply his wish to be done with the activistic pretensions of the sixties, since its activists lacked the responsibility to justify any commitment to their particular truths. According to Trilling, their extreme self-indulgence had reduced sincerity to the expression of uncompromising dissatisfaction rather than honest sharing and social responsiveness, as had been its original aim. Once an agent of social cohesion, sincerity instead invited anarchy and economic breakdown, thus coming full circle in its transition from an integrative and vitalizing influence to a destructive force of new and unprecedented levels of mindlessness.

But to what virtue, exactly, did Trilling oppose this decadent worship of sincerity? The answer remains unclear until "it is finished" is fully understood in its more inclusive context, in which he declared the value "of beginning something and at a certain point remarking that it is finished." This linear and essentially Aristotelian virtue of beginning a task in order to end it must be understood in light of Trilling's remark earlier in the chapter that British fiction's narrative excellence depends on its *inauthentic* behavior. Paraphrasing Walter Benjamin, he praised the deceptive benefits of literary illusion: "[T]here is something inauthentic for our time in being held spellbound, momentarily forgetful of oneself, concerned with the fate of a person who is not oneself but who also, by reason of the spell that is being cast, is oneself, his conduct and his destiny bearing upon the reader's own" (p. 135). Trilling also quoted Richard Gilman to the same effect, more specifically putting emphasis on the escapist value of narrative deception:

> [I]t is "precisely that element of fiction which coerces and degrades it into a mere alternative to life, like life, only better of course, a dream (or a serviceable nightmare), a way out, a recompense, a blueprint, a lesson."[5]

Trilling continued:

> A chief part of the *inauthenticity of narration* would seem to be its assumption that life is susceptible of comprehension and thus of management. It is the nature of narration to explain; it cannot help telling how things are and even why they are that way. (p. 135, italics added)

How does narration promote this inauthenticity? For Trilling it does so by imposing a linear sequence of events that promises a significance probably at odds with normal quotidian experience:

> But a beginning implies an end, with something in the middle to connect them. The beginning is not merely the first in a series of events; it is the event that originates those that follow. And the end is not merely the ultimate event, the cessation of happening; it is a significance or at least the promise, dark or bright, of a significance. (p. 135)

For Trilling this inauthentic "significance" or "promise of a significance" typical of literary form could nevertheless be valuable. He asked of this narrative capacity: "Can we, in this day and age, submit to a mode of explanation so primitive, so flagrantly Aristotelian?" His answer to his own question, implicit in his final sentence, was that our destiny does in fact depend on narrative simplifications, turning back the clock to that stage in human development when sincerity could be organized in the insincere context of narrative form. That Trilling saved this answer for his final remark gave narrative impact to his insight as a truth for those willing to accept his assumptions. In effect, his placement of his culminating insight in its terminal position disclosed (or actually boasted of) his realization that he too was engaging in narrative deception by declaring the value of ritualized distortions in strictly positive terms and within his own linear context of narrative form.

Trilling's fascination with insincerity is apparent throughout his survey of the Continental philosophers concerned with the issue. He expressed his admiration of Diderot's *Rameau's Nephew*, for example, because it "lays bare the principle of insecurity upon which society is based and demonstrates the loss of personal integrity and dignity that the impersonations of social existence entail" (p. 31). Trilling likewise called attention to Hegel's definition of culture as the "field of experience . . . by which the disintegrated, alienated, and distraught consciousness expresses a negative relation with the external power of society" (p. 44). To clarify this principle of alienation, Trilling quoted and elucidated Hegel's explanation of truth as one particular mode of deception:

> The truth of the self at a certain stage of its historical development, consists in its being not true to itself, in there being no self to be true to: the truth for self, for spirit, consists precisely in shamelessness. "The content uttered by spirit and uttered about itself," Hegel says, "is . . . the inversion and perversion of all conceptions and realities, a universal deception of itself and others. . . . The shamelessness manifested in stating this deceit is just on that account the greatest truth."[6]

Trilling apparently agreed with Hegel's dialectic explanation that the final truth consists of the shameless acknowledgment of deception's necessity. Moreover, he suggested a need for comparable shamelessness today if we too are to be true to ourselves on a mature basis.

To explain Rousseau's modifications of this dialectic, Trilling summarized the arguments of his *First Discourse* to the effect that literature bears a unique role in perverting and undermining our natural virtues:

> It is literature that is the pre-eminent agent of man's corruption, the essence or paradigm of the inherent falsehood of civilized society. Literature embodies the very principle of society, which is the individual's abnegation of autonomy in order to win the forbearance and esteem of others. (p. 60)

As explained by Trilling, Rousseau attacked literature because it teaches individuals to curtail their natural feelings in order to be accepted by their peers. Trilling obviously agreed with Rousseau's thesis—that fiction bears an inhibitive influence—but disagreed with Rousseau's conclusion that reading fiction should therefore be discouraged. Quite the contrary, Trilling suggested, this inhibitive influence is fiction's most valuable lesson. Trilling was critical of Rousseau's pretensions of honesty in *The Confessions*, but he obviously respected Rousseau's willingness to countenance dishonesty as an important source of social integration. When Trilling finally discussed Rousseau's essay on contemporary drama, one senses his rapport:

> The claim made for the theatre that it advances moral enlightenment is met by Rousseau with impatient incredulity. The purpose of the theatre is to please, and such moral judgment as it makes is accepted to the extent that it is pleasurable, which is to say, so far as it confirms and flatters the settled views of the audience. (p. 63)

By implication, the moral enlightenment attributed to the theater does little more than confirm and flatter one's settled views. This is an opinion Trilling could not bring himself to acknowledge, but he did quote with approval the passage in which Rousseau made this point.

With comparable subversiveness, Trilling resorted to etymology in tracing the word *authenticity* from the Greek word *authenteo*, pointing out that its original definition included both murder and suicide. Trilling also took obvious pleasure in quoting Oscar Wilde's epigrams that the first duty in life is to be as artificial as possible, that all bad poetry springs from genuine feeling, that an individual must first be given a mask to tell you the truth, and that truth in art is that whose contradiction is also true (pp. 131, 118–20). In every instance, Trilling, like Milton, seems to have been in the devil's party, more interested in undermining than in reforming the doctrine of sincerity.

The same perspective emerges in Trilling's discussion of psychoanalysis, which he defined as a narrative science whose awareness of deceptionist contradictions affords its ethical value. Explaining psychoanalysis on a sociological basis, Trilling traced neurosis to the breakdown of the nuclear family and the consequent loss of authority exercised by parents. Drawing upon the work of sociologist David Riesman, he argued that the current abandonment of narrative inauthenticity may directly reflect the decline in traditional family life:

> And perhaps the low status of narration can be thought to have a connection with revisions of the child's relation to the family—traditionally

the family has been a narrative institution: it was the past and it had a tale to tell of how things began, including the child himself; and it had counsel to give. (p. 139)

In other words, the nuclear family is to be praised as an institution because its narrative inauthenticity fosters both ethics and cultural continuity. If uncompromising sincerity leads to the breakdown of the family, the dislocation that results exceeds any of its benefits. Later Trilling favorably quoted Marcuse much to the same effect, contrasting individualization based on adequate parental authority to the nonliterary deficiencies resulting from accelerated peer orientation among preadolescent children:

> But in our contemporary cultural situation, Marcuse says, with the authority of the family, especially of the father, much diminished, the individual's ego "has shrunk to such a degree that the multiform antagonistic processes between id, ego, and superego cannot unfold themselves in their classic form." In the present dispensation "the formation of the mature ego seems to skip the stage of individualization," with the result that "the generic atom becomes directly a social atom."[7]

Trilling's repetition of this argument reinforced his point that diminished patriarchal authority undermines both the Oedipus complex and the early appreciation of narrative form as important stages in gaining full maturity. Instead, there is a disproportionate emphasis upon authenticity, which permits supposedly liberated individuals to justify their antisocial behavior with an exaggerated faith in freedom, self-fulfillment, and hip-relatedness.[8] Trilling was dubious of psychoanalysis as a cure resulting from increased self-awareness. Instead, he suggested, the real benefits of this "narrative science" derive from pitting inhibition against raw impulse, *countercathexis* against *cathexis*, and, most important, conscience (or superego) against the libido and by extension the ego itself.

Trilling contrasted normal expressiveness with the extremes encouraged by an exaggerated commitment to sincerity. Uncompromising sincerity might lead self-confession to the brink of unrestrained psychosis, as advocated by Laing and Cooper, but for the individual with a healthy ego, the basic goal of expressiveness is to be encouraged: "[B]eneath the appearance of every human phenomenon there lies concealed a discrepant actuality and . . . intellectual, practical, and (not least) moral advantage is to be gained by forcibly bringing it to light" (p. 142). Presumably, this "discrepant actuality" may be consulted only if one possesses an ego cultivated by parental identification and the narrative values it implies. And in the final analysis, this capacity is only relative. "We are all neurotic," Trilling declared, establishing as "mature" the necessary dialectic interaction between expressiveness and our narrative commitment to appropriate behavior.

Trilling emphatically disagreed with Jean-Paul Sartre's effort in *Being and Nothing* to reject psychoanalysis because it undermines sincerity rather than encouraging it. As explained by Trilling, Sartre consigned all repressive behavior to the designation of inauthenticity, or bad faith, since, "in order to carry out its function, the censor must engage in purposive acts of perception and discrimination which are of the very nature of consciousness . . . that the censor must have a consciousness of 'being conscious of the drive to be repressed, but precisely in order not to be conscious of it'" (pp. 146–47). Trilling approved of Sartre's explanation of bad faith's censorship dynamics (the double negative of the affirmative fallacy), but disagreed with his conclusion that these dynamics guarantee the failure of psychoanalysis to come to terms with human conduct. Praising psychoanalysis for exactly the qualities offensive to Sartre, he asked, "Must we not say that Freud's theory of the mind and of society has at its core a flagrant inauthenticity which it deplores but accepts as essential in the mental structure?" (p. 154). Here Trilling admitted that he was primarily drawn to Freudian psychoanalysis by its theoretical acceptance of inauthenticity as an organizing principle of consciousness. Because classical Freudian psychoanalysis encourages displacement, sublimation, and a grab bag of other avoidance strategies, it should be immune to the confessional excesses of Laing and Cooper in their simplistic diagnosis of schizophrenia. As in the case of Diderot, Hegel, Rousseau, Freud, Austen, Conrad, and even Marcuse, Trilling granted psychoanalysis a complexity of vision that subordinates raw truth to a civilizing emphasis on misrepresentation.

Why, then, must Trilling be included in the category of affirmists? Trilling's historic treatment of sincerity more or less corroborates the negative principles I have been trying to outline, but like Hegel and Marcuse, Trilling finally believed that fiction's inauthenticity teaches readers to recognize the comparable inauthenticity in the real world, if without entirely rejecting it. According to Trilling, fiction's untruths expose the untruths that dominate our daily behavior, thus encouraging our pursuit of genuine truths. More simply explained, he believed that "the authentic work of art instructs us in our inauthenticity and adjures us to overcome it" (p. 100). With this basically affirmative conclusion I must disagree, if for no other reason than the credulousness of most readers and critics in their appreciation of literary truth. As opposed to Trilling's notion that fiction tells its share of untruths to trigger the recognition of the extent to which untruths dominate our lives, the model I am proposing assigns to fiction a limitless capacity to deceive pleasurably. Readers, for example, do not finish *Pride and Prejudice* delighted because of all the lies and distortions their acceptance of the story has brought to their attention. Instead, they cherish as at least a conditional or suspended truth the results of the story that, as I explained in chapter 2, verge on the preposterous. How many readers scan their memory to recall all the fiction they have read, proclaiming, "What lies, what wonderful lies?" Not even Trilling declares this to be the source of fiction's broad public appeal. But it is only with his final sentence that we fully recognize his attraction to insincerity's virtue as a narrative achievement, and here at last we discover that local insight had been our journey's destination, that the instances of insincerity exposed by Trilling provided, for him at least, the saving grace of the theories he chose to elaborate. Trilling's defense of sincerity consequently both defended and illustrated the positive virtues of insincerity as an affirmative standard. Earlier, Trilling quoted André Gide that one cannot at the same time both be sincere and seem so, or, more to the point, that one cannot be totally sincere in advocating the final necessity of this particular virtue (p. 70).[9] Vice versa, Trilling showed, one cannot be totally sincere in advocating the advantages of insincerity. Too wise to try to bridge the difference, Trilling settled for a narrative statement (insincere) of his crisis (sincere) in the final major work of his literary criticism.

Published two years later in 1974, Wayne Booth's *Modern Dogma and the Rhetoric of Assent* offered a more strident commitment to the affirmative fallacy.[10] Its organization lacked the elegant subversiveness of Trilling's book, but this deficiency was redressed by a unique blend of high ethics and dialectic evasiveness that gave it literary value of its own. Like Trilling, Booth formulated his ideas in reaction to the rhetorical excesses of the Vietnam protest movement in the late sixties and early seventies. In Booth's view, the angry irrationalism of the antiwar protesters was both directly and indirectly the result of scientific method infiltrating the realm of ethics and personal philosophy. He labeled this tendency "scientism," as advocated by "scientismists," and argued that it discourages one's confidence in a world permeated with values. The scientific method's systematic dependence on skepticism and uncompromising behaviorism has so pervasively biased social attitudes, Booth maintained, that a mindless quest for underlying truths, described as "motivism," has come to undermine the very fabric of our society (pp. 24–26). Among other such underlying truths, presumably, would be Freudian metapsychology and the "discrepant actuality" emphasized by Trilling. The abuse of sincerity as defined by Trilling can accordingly be subsumed to another, more fundamental abuse—the relentless pursuit of hidden sources to cast doubt on everything of positive value that can and should be taken for granted in social intercourse. The primary need, Booth proposed, is for a moral renaissance that disposes of this nihilistic extreme by injecting values "back into the domain of knowledge." Many of the social dropouts in the sixties and early seventies might have felt they shared Booth's antagonism to behaviorism, but Booth insisted that their reaction was strictly nihilistic, hence in the spirit of behaviorism. Booth advocated a more responsible commitment to received values as cultivated by appropriate public discourse.

However, there are serious flaws in Booth's argument, many of which may be traced to his use of rhetoric to express his convictions. Throughout his text Booth sacrificed logical consistency to a loosely Socratic methodology based on "the art of discovering warrantable beliefs through shared discourse." Since the ideology of the protest movement had become essentially rhetorical, Booth argued, his refutation of its principles could likewise be restricted to rhetoric, in his case based on orthodox classical standards that link ethics and persuasiveness. As Booth explained in a footnote, his purpose was "only to undermine confidence in the [modernist] dogmas and thus restore practical confidence in a process that might, as one product, buttress a variety of philosophies" (p. 143). But one questions how many philosophies Booth would tolerate, since most theoretical systems oblige a "radical" investigation of roots (*radix* means root), or sources. Some are hidden, and almost all of them may be rejected for their implied motivism.

Moreover, Booth's defense of received opinion takes rhetoric to its extreme as a "supremely self-justifying activity" (p. 138). He claimed to rely on dialectic exchange as the best way to establish the truth, but his approach emphasized audience appeal at the sacrifice of careful verification. Part of his problem may be that his book was based on a series of lectures he presented before a Notre Dame audience. He could have toned down his rhetoric when he revised his lecture notes for publication as a book, but one may speculate that he refrained from doing so because a more balanced presentation would have deprived his ideas of their persuasiveness. Booth's rhetorical exaggerations become evident, for example, in his use of categorical generalizations. At war against the New Left's exaggerations, he himself capitulated to the tendency with sweeping generalizations for which a multitude of exceptions may readily be found. There was obvious categorical excess when he declared with strenuous hyperbole that "modern philosophy . . . has saddled us with standards of truth under which no man can live," or, even more urgently, that "motivism entails fearful consequences with which no one can live for thirty seconds" (pp. xii, 32). His misuse of the non sequitur was likewise sufficiently pronounced that the word *if* at the beginning of any of his sentences probably signals the likelihood that he was drawing a conclusion which exceeded its premises. Randomly chosen examples include the following, each bearing implications that seem clearly fallacious:

> If neither of us has any chance of offering good reasons, I can only trick you, or force you, or blackmail you, or shoot you—and thus change your mind permanently. (pp. 36–37)

> [I]f there are no supra-individual values, there are no values; values can only be found by "individuals" who acknowledge, in responsible discourse, their essential dependence on each other. (p. 127)

> If the whole "scene" of the atomic self, isolated in a cold universe, is undermined, the great liberal, critical fiat, "Make up your own mind," no longer quite makes sense. (p. 141)

Deductions of this sort collapse when exceptions can be found, and each of these bears this deficiency, the first by excluding options based on compromise, the second by excluding undeclared personal values, and the third by ignoring the mixture of altruism and rational skepticism that is dominant in current educated discourse.

Booth's most annoying rhetorical transgression was his unfortunate habit of calling upon his Notre Dame audience to confirm by its silent assent the universal validity of his arguments. In front of a large crowd he challenged dissenters to speak up who might ever have felt, for example, that the first sentence in *Pride and Prejudice* is not ironic or that Bach's B Minor Mass is not a profound and moving experience. From the predictable silence following these questions, he concluded that the universal appreciation of Austen's irony and Bach's cosmic profundity demonstrates the absolute basis of aesthetic standards. This rhetorical tactic might have been effective in holding the attention of Booth's audience, but it is of questionable value in establishing the truth of his argument. Bach's choral music, for example, tends to bore many listeners (it was all but ignored for the better part of two centuries), and Austen's irony no less frequently escapes the attention of unsophisticated readers, as any English professor can confirm who has taught Austen's novels with honest feedback from students at the undergraduate level. Both of Booth's arguments might be challenged in a smaller forum—for example, a graduate seminar—but at the time he gave his lecture series he knew he could depend on the passive indulgence of his large audience, since none in attendance could be expected to blurt out a viewpoint in defense of cultural inferiority. In retrospect careful readers must therefore sift his arguments with more than usual caution to determine their logical, if not rhetorical, validity.

Not surprisingly, Booth rejected stringent verification standards and proposed in their stead the "ancient and natural command to 'assent pending disproof'" (p. 101). He denied the value of empirical methodology by once again resorting to an if-then implication: "If we know only what survives after we have done our best to doubt, we are driven to conclude that most of our action has no cognitive base, since we almost always act on propositions that have not been proved in this sense" (pp. 103–4). However, all knowledge is at least partially verified by repeated observation, and the limitations of day-to-day perceptions do not demonstrate the shortcomings of the scientific method. John Dewey's principle of warranted assertibility, somewhat comparable to that of assent pending disproof, concedes the value of stringent verification standards.[11] When assent pending disproof pertaining to a certain notion (ghosts, Santa Claus, etc.) turns out to be wrong as demonstrated by empirical investigation, its disproof, no longer pending, compels the withdrawal of assent. Assent pending disproof also resembles the concept of *Doxa* loathed by Barthes if this assent compels an acceptance of orthodox beliefs. Booth's cure turns out to have been Barthes's disease, though both were formulated in opposition to leftist political activism—Barthes's rejection of Sartre's concept of *engagement*, and Booth's rejection of the political motivism of the sixties. Perhaps the best explanation of this contradiction is that Barthes rejected radical politics for the equally radical principle of neutrality, while Booth rejected it for a conventional acceptance of the status quo.

Nobody denies that the logic governing our normal behavior probably depends on a happy mixture of habit and accident according to the simplest cognitive function, "it works, so I do it." However, a better and more refined methodology is needed when it comes to buying a house, inventing something, or trying to demonstrate the existence of a god (or gods and goddesses). Even the simplest experience exposes this necessity, as may be illustrated by Booth's example: "If my wife says, 'I have a sudden terrible pain. Call a doctor quick!' I must and will act at once."[12] The natural swiftness of Booth's response suggests an immediate and undeniable connection between his wife's urgent need and his sense of obligation to do something about it. What Booth overlooked was that a different response might be warranted—for example, if his wife were joking, if she were a chronic hypochondriac, if he kept the appropriate medication at home, if a competent doctor were obviously unavailable, or if the cost of medical assistance were too high, as happens to be the case with a majority of the world's population. Sitting at my word processor right now, I perversely ask my wife to repeat Booth's wife's two sentences, word for word, for the sake of argument. She does, but I do not bother to call a doctor, of course because I am confident she is not sick. My point is that language's interpretive contexts are usually more complicated than Booth seems to have been willing to recognize here. As a result, his broad division of knowledge into "assent pending disproof" as opposed to its supposedly value-free alternatives based on scientific induction is necessarily misleading.

Booth did qualify his advocacy of systematic assent with William James's caveat that we cannot permit ourselves to be "flooded with every belief that anyone offers," and that we must begin "only with those beliefs that really recommend themselves to us" (p. 107). Indeed, this qualification seems necessary, but the magnitude of its potential misapplications can be demonstrated by the thousands of collective assumptions "that really recommend themselves" but are proven wrong at a later time. These have included, for example, animist superstitions and the flat-earth hypotheses that still enjoy respectability in some societies. No less erroneous have been widespread assumptions about sex, race, health, personality, physiognomy, religion, history, national destiny, and even simple astronomy and meteorology. According to a recent poll, not more than one-third of the American public realizes the Soviet Union was an ally of the United States during World War II. Randomly ask a group of individuals in the northern hemisphere whether the earth comes closer to the sun in the summer or winter and majority opinion establishes by "systematic assent" that the sun must be closer in the summer, despite the hard astronomical fact that the distance between the earth and sun is the shortest on about January 3. Popular misconceptions about the weather may also be contrasted with the information gleaned from a decent meteorology text, and the same holds true of botany, biology, anthropology, and all the rest of the scientific disciplines. Often, in fact, any particular generation's most widely held "truths" about health, politics, and human nature seem the most fallible to following generations. This vulnerability of popular beliefs has long been noted, and its skeptical recognition provided the basis for both Plato's Allegory of the Cave in philosophy's metaphysical tradition, and, in its empirical tradition, Francis Bacon's systematic catalog of popular misinformation under each of four Idols—of the Tribe (due to human nature), of the Cave (due to individual idiosyncrasy), of the Marketplace (due to language), and of the Theatre (due to traditional doctrine). By advocating uncritical systematic assent, Booth rejected the original guiding principles of both major traditions, metaphysical and empirical, and instead argued for the authoritarian premise with obvious but dangerous populist appeal that shared affirmation must be given prominence to discourage excessive skepticism. "Our society has a sudden terrible pain. Call a doctor quick," cried Booth, so we must rush to systematic assent despite twenty-three centuries of Platonism, despite the last four centuries of scientific discovery.

Of course, one must agree with Booth's contention "that the primary mental act of man is to assent to truth rather than to detect error" (p. xvi). This rush to belief is a compelling human need tantamount to instinct, and it obliges a wholehearted commitment to the psychological machinery I find in the affirmative fallacy. However, it fails to establish on either a logical or an empirical basis the validity of the positive beliefs that appeal to us. In fact, quite the opposite, the "truths" that compel easy assent are more susceptible to error than other truths established by the arduous procedures required for the elimination of error. Booth deplored the "negative pose" that may be associated with resistance to straightforward affirmative commitment, but the exclusion of alternatives is central to accurate judgment, both in science and in daily affairs. Many assumptions or hypotheses must necessarily be rejected in favor of others, and this process of rejection is necessarily based on the negative skills that Booth too readily dispensed with. Whenever two affirmative views come in conflict with each other, one or both must be revised based on a choice that imposes denial. If the simplistic distinction, for example, between freedom and responsibility cannot be resolved, a more sophisticated distinction necessarily arises between compromise and a singular dedication to either of the alternatives, or, more specifically, between two or more alternative balances between the two. When one such balance is affirmed, the other is necessarily denied.

Booth tried to reject the primary value of negation by limiting its function to the choice to be made among positive alternatives. "Assent and affirmation are more fundamental than negation, in both logic and experience," he claimed, and one must concur in the larger sense that this is the goal of all human endeavor (p. 194). But it is also true, as he elsewhere conceded, that "our withdrawals and rejections come always in the light of some affirmation that has been denied or is being threatened" (p. 194). Booth himself explained more abstractly, "Our negatives are learned as we discover violations of our affirmings," to which may be added the important corollary that affirmings in conflict with each other oblige the recognition of negatives (p. 194). This second and more complicated level of perception originates in the earliest stages of infancy (for example, in learning to avoid fire), and its importance cannot be underestimated. To illustrate the extent to which negative thinking has influenced our cultural tradition, Booth himself listed some of the antiheroes who could declare no (or "No, in thunder!"), from Prometheus to Faust and Dr. Rieux in Camus's *The Plague* (p. 195). Moreover, Booth conceded that people are "divided from the rest of animal creation by the capacity to say no . . . by constructing elaborate symbolic structures, some of which will belie what they know to be true" (p. 196). Here Booth, too, seems to have acknowledged dialectical priorities, though he wanted to protect the public from the negative extravagance of both Prometheus and Faust.

However, Booth tried to limit the role of negation by describing it as a process of consciousness that does not otherwise exist in the universe. He treated it as a function without substantive "thereness" and explained its phantom capacity by quoting words attributed to Satan in Kenneth Burke's *The Rhetoric of Religion*, to the effect that the negative constitutes nothing more than the generative principle of both logic and language. Otherwise, Satan declares, "The negative cannot exist. Anything that exists must, by the same token, be positively what it is" (p. 287). Almost exactly the same point was made by Bertrand Russell (it turns out, Booth's intellectual *bête noire*) in his brief cautionary tale "The Metaphysician's Nightmare," in which Satan is depicted as a preposterous phantom whose disappearance confirms negation's identity as an empty term, exposing the truth that the word *not* is superfluous and that its elimination consists of an ethical choice to reject negation's inhibitive implications.[13] Other relevant examples of denial associated with the role of Satan (or of a satanic father figure) include the ghost of Hamlet's father, whose uncertain existence initiates the negative accomplishment of tragedy, and Hawthorne's vision of Satan in "Young Goodman Brown" as a patriarchal apparition whose disappearance symbolizes the rejection of inhibitive Oedipal demands. Still other examples include the Ancient Mariner, who detains the wedding guest only long enough to tell his story; Kurtz, whom Marlow remembers only as a voice; and Frost's fleeting impression of his neighbor's father. All the satans and patriarchal substitutes listed here seem capable of disappearing, and for all of them the no compels designification by ejecting them from tangible experience.

What neither Booth nor any of the literary satans explains is how and why the negative that rejects Y as *not X* bears any positive value for both conceptualization and the principle of life itself. There is no problem in denying negation's existence as a thing, but its more important role seems evident as an exclusionary function that recurs at every level of existence in the physical universe. Of course, negation cannot be reified as an object, but it does constitute an act or process of avoiding, resisting, countermining, pushing away, providing counterthrust, and/or lining up in opposition against the force of circumstance, as mentioned by Emerson. All of these activities manifest a single negative principle crucial to our existence, embodied in process (or *praxis*) as opposed to any particular "stuff" that might be identified independent of process. William Blake explained it with laconic vividness in "The Marriage of Heaven and Hell": "Without contraries is no progression. Attraction and Repulsion, Reason and Energy, Love and Hate, are necessary to Human existence."[14] Both Alexander Oparin and George Wald proposed that the first trace of life probably arose from colloidal resistance to the disintegrative molecular activity of water—biology's most primitive no of all.[15] Mating behavior likewise features its no, as does the fertilized ovum in rejecting all but one of the spermatozoa clustered on its surface. And as explained by Konrad Lorenz, even social cooperation probably derives from inhibited (i.e., denied) aggression.[16]

All behavior, in fact, may be defined as choice-making, with denial necessarily involved in the rejection of unacceptable alternatives. In the case of conscious behavior, thinking means finding substitutes and making comparisons based on perceived differences. The purpose might be affirmative—joining "the Process called existence," as Booth put it—but its means usually consists of a negative strategy based on a complex interplay of avoidances. Booth concedes that learning depends on the use of negatives, but so does other conscious activity, including the experience of literature with its presumably affirmative organization of consciousness. This is also true of ethics and religion, the latter in denying both death after death (as opposed to life after death) and the meaninglessness of a universe too big and too impersonal to imagine. Value itself likewise depends on choice-making in determining which alternatives must be rejected in favor of others. In all instances the goal of consciousness might be affirmative, but its mode of operation for making this goal achievable is negative. This is true even in the most rigorous commitment to affirmative principles—as might be demonstrated by Booth's appeal to systematic assent in order to deny the supposedly negative pose of the Vietnam protest movement.

Booth attributed his rejection of scientism at least partly to his reaction against having flirted with Bertrand Russell's skeptical empiricism during his undergraduate years, and later to his reaction against Russell's controversial identification with the Vietnam protest movement. In Booth's view, Russell opposed the Vietnam War because of his commitment to supposedly immoral and value-free "scientismist" principles, so it had been entirely appropriate that the protest movement inspired by Russell, Sartre, Marcuse, and others gradually had lapsed into bizarre antisocial excesses. These excesses bothered Booth more than the illegal slaughter of perhaps three million people—illegal because the United States had refrained from participating in the 1954 Geneva Accords with the excuse that Vietnam was none of our nation's business, as in fact it was not.[17] The anarchistic effect of Russell's philosophy, Booth argued, may be ultimately traced to Russell's theory of a universe that is deterministic and value-free except for the artificial values imposed by society itself. Booth thus opposed Russell's dependence on facts, logic, and mathematical operations to explain the universe and asked for a different and patently anthropomorphic faith that human values permeate the universe itself.

If human values exist, Booth claimed, they are automatically built in to this universe, *ipso facto* demonstrating a benign and humanistic reality for those who can accept the pervasiveness of this intrinsic relationship. For this reason, evolution has not been strictly purposeless, Booth suggests, but has given humanity the capacity for unique spiritual attainment. This unique blessing, Booth feels, might be explained by Michael Polanyi's "hierarchy of explanatory systems," which, like Bergson's creative evolution, establishes human values as an integral component of the universe regardless of their origin, whether by evolution from below or by divine creation from above.[18] Can such an anthropomorphic notion be seriously defended? Yes, in fact, but only if the exclusionary standards implied by Booth's theory of value can be reformulated to apply to the entire universe. Such a possibility would be confirmed, for example, by the cosmic nihilism of the current so-called Grand Unified Theories (GUTs) that reduce matter to an elaborate scheme of destabilized symmetries whose restoration contributes to new destabilizations, further suggesting the possibility, as explained by Paul Davies, "that the entire universe, including all the apparently concrete matter that assails our senses, is in reality only a frolic of convoluted nothingness, that in the end the world will turn out to be a sculpture of pure emptiness, a self-organized void."[19] In such a scheme the same principles, the same "frolic," pervade all phenomena in a negative universe, an energy field that sustains itself as the denial of its absence. As William James suggests, quoting Chauncey Wright, there seems to be *nothing* behind the bare phenomenal facts, leaving the world "adrift in space, with neither elephant nor tortoise to plant the sole of its foot upon."[20] Absolutely nothing? Nothing but negation itself, the capacity to make something of nothing and, vice versa, nothing of something. If existence itself is God, as both Poe and Allen Ginsberg have proposed, it is a god predicated on "convoluted nothingness," and it offers a very different "matter" from the positivists' universe envisaged by both Kenneth Burke and Bertrand Russell, since both the imaginary satans they refute turn out to be on the right track. Indeed, the yes of consciousness can "no" other yeses without disturbing the affirmative role of the universe itself, but when the total universe's yes is "noed," everything reduces to no, the firmament on which its yeses have done their little dance. Such a dance replicates itself at every level of Booth's and Polanyi's hierarchy of explanatory systems, and its frolic of convoluted nothingness declares an ultimate truth of the universe with room enough for both Russell's physical universe and Booth's built-in system of morals. Thought, like matter, consolidates, then disperses into its void; ethics replicates physics, and physics ethics, both imposing negative structure as a reification (or crystallization) of the dance.

Perhaps in this sense a more inclusive synthesis may be established to give both our morals and physical existence equivalent validity, but only through their negative realization in a vertical hierarchy extending from physics to biology, psychology, ethics, literature, and even the theory of literature. As explained by elementary particle physics, destabilized symmetries underlie force fields that attract and repel each other (i.e., say both yes and no), thereby providing the basis for inorganic and organic molecular structures, for invertebrate life forms, for animal behavior, and for the ethics of human relationships as epitomized by literary deception. In effect, the electrodynamic tension between attraction and repulsion successively replicates itself in colloidal resistances, primitive negative feedback loops, avoidance reflexes, and the dynamics of consciousness, ethics, and even narrative form. In this sense it can indeed be said that there is a fundamental identity between human values and basic physical principles, as argued by Booth. However, the pyramid stands, if at all, on its base, not its apex, and it stands in a physical universe whose negative versatility ultimately predetermines the morals and aesthetic values we emphasize in the conduct of human affairs. The same principles of attraction and repulsion manifest themselves at every level, if with the most attenuated (hence, most complicated) effects restricted to human consciousness and the literature that serves its needs. And if ours is a nihilistic dance at the edge of the void, we possess this literature, as Nietzsche proposed, "lest we perish of the truth." So we dance on, *until* we perish of the truth.

As I indicated earlier, even values depend on an intricate nexus of avoidances rooted in the principle of negation—the choice of X over Y (virtue over vice, culture over anarchy, education over ignorance, etc.). Negative comparisons must be made to establish the desirable attributes of X that are absent from Y. The greater the clamor for value, the bigger the number of possibilities to be rejected. And if values are built in to human motivation, their presence ultimately derives from the denial mechanisms built in to the operation of the brain as an organ that affirms through a complex interplay of exclusions. The evidence it gathers might be positive (both existent and affirmative), but its operation—the way it goes about its business—is basically negative. This may be seen in the all-or-nothing threshold of excitation in particular neurons, in the exclusionary relationship among competitive associative patterns, in the use of negative feedback to produce homeostasis, and finally in the strictly inhibitive role of the neocortex in governing the limbic system's production of emotions. When we become angry, for example, the neocortex inhibits the hypothalamus from inhibiting the amygdalae, whose sudden freedom from constraint produces the behavior commonly associated with anger—presumably a negative response. The same happens when the neocortex inhibits the hypothalamus from inhibiting the septal nuclei so pleasure can be experienced. At least four giant noes have crisscrossed if there is any pleasure in anger, such as in the behavior of the choleric individual as explained by Renaissance psychology.[21] The more complex the emotion, the bigger the switchboard of noes flashing on and off.

Also relevant are the Freudian displacements of repression and denial in the evasiveness typical of neurotic behavior—indeed of all behavior, since unacceptable outlets must first be rejected to shift *cathexis* into acceptable outlets. At every level of neural behavior, therefore, negation exists not as a hypostatized thing but as a dynamic operation at work for producing some kind of improvement. This is what thinking is all about, and it depends upon negative performance rooted in a variety of yes-no operations that occur in the normal activity of the mind. If the universe's everlasting yea (nay's denial) is echoed by our own affirmative values, whether of Russell's or of Booth's philosophy, the harmony among their yeses has been mediated by a complex negative machinery that includes thought, culture, and every dimension of human experience, all of which depend upon the brain's negative operation to produce affirmative results. Affirmation might characterize both the source and the destination of this behavior, but the process itself is in essence negative. Neither values nor literary experience may be adequately defined without giving due recognition to this dialectic principle.

Booth's fierce antipathy to motivism throughout his book was complemented by his unwillingness to submit the issue of human motivation to the balanced and objective scrutiny it deserves. Booth ignored the dialectical speculation of such figures as Hegel, Rousseau, Nietzsche, and Freud, as delineated by Trilling, and almost instinctively rejected contemporary intellectual systems that trace behavior to underlying motives:

"Look for the secret motive" has at least until recently been a slogan of many disciplines, and the unexamined assumption has been that if you can find it—that is, if you can find a class interest or a sexual drive or a kinship interest or a childhood trauma—you have explained away whatever "surface reasons" anyone offers for his beliefs or actions.[22]

Booth's concern seems justified in some instances, but he travestied the three motivational sources he lists (class, sex, and kinship), since few who submit these concepts to systematic analysis claim that they totally explain away the "surface reasons" important to Booth. Careful investigation of the three disciplines Booth suggested—Marxism, psychoanalysis, and structuralism—disposes of his objections. Since Frederick Engels's celebrated letter to J. Black of September 1890, competent Marxists have explained the relationship between economic base and social and cultural superstructure with due allowances paid to the contributions of both. Likewise, since Freud's 1926 paper "Inhibitions, Symptoms, and Anxiety," psychoanalysts and ego psychologists have taken for granted an equilibrium between conscious and unconscious dynamics. And the same goes for cultural anthropologists who have tried to link myth and ritual to underlying kinship systems, as explained by Lévi-Strauss, for example, in chapter 16 of *Structural Anthropology*.

The respective dialectic models established by these three disciplines between surface behavior and its underlying influences did not belittle the importance of any particular surface event through simplistic reference to a single hidden determinant. On the other hand, the economic base featured by Marxist theory never leaves us, nor does the unconscious featured by psychoanalytic theory, nor do syntactic determinations of surface behavior (*parole, syntagma*, etc.) as featured by structuralists. In fact, any suggestion that they can be ignored seems especially susceptible to depth analysis based on exactly the principles found objectionable. As Marxists insist, the vigorous effort to deny culture's interdependent relationship with political economy usually expresses an unexamined commitment to the status quo. As Freudians insist, the vigorous effort to deny any likelihood of unconscious motivation usually expresses the anxious rejection of an entire spectrum of feelings. And as structuralists suggest, the vigorous effort to deny structure as the matrix and design of behavior may itself be judged as a product of such a structure, whether recognized or not. When all three of these sources are collectively denied by an impassioned plea for systematic assent, one suspects a stonewalling typical of authoritarianism, as defined by such figures as Fromm, Adorno, and Wilhelm Reich.[23] Booth neglected to mention the theory of authoritarianism, and, if plied, he would have undoubtedly deplored its exaggeration by the protest movement, but its anti-intellectual misuse does not refute its value as diagnosis of the authoritarian personality.

Much more vulnerable to Booth's critique of motivism would be the theory of negative poetics I am proposing, since it gives motivation a central role in the concept of literary denial. However, the hidden determinant I suggest involves no secret truth beyond the substitutions that take place when one set of feelings is found threatening and replaced by another which is not. Beneath this act of denial particular anxieties are at work—death, humiliation, the sense of entrapment, dissatisfaction with one's role, repressed sexual inclinations, etc. Any of these becomes important whenever its exclusion from consciousness becomes a vested stake for authors and their readers. When homophobia takes precedence, as I try to demonstrate, its repression of androgynous tendencies reinforces the reader's devotion to heterosexual romance and the nuclear family. However destructive its effect among many individuals, it steers the majority of the public toward monogamy and family responsibility, thereby helping to promote the reproduction of the nuclear family (or "traditional family," in the words of Trilling) from one generation to the next. If androgyny becomes too attractive as an alternative life-style, the consequences for society as a whole can be disastrous within a couple of generations. How may one argue otherwise, and with what examples? Here, then, fiction comes to the rescue by reorganizing latent homosexual tendencies to promote homophobic (or at least homoaversive) ends. Homophilia tempts in local contexts, but homophobia absorbs and countermands its temptation by means of literary form. If repressive conflict is minimal, its impact upon literary form will likewise be minimal, as happens, for example, if overt homosexuality is almost entirely approved or almost entirely out of the question. On the other hand, if and when threatening feelings continuously press on consciousness, they oblige a more vigorous dialectic. The more compelling their influence, the more insistent their denial, as typified by our most popular classics.

The organization of Booth's book was argumentative rather than narrative, since it shifted from the protest movement to Bertrand Russell's scientific determinism, then to Booth's own theory of assent followed by a somewhat anticlimactic treatment of art, in which he stressed the importance of the reader's identification with literary characters based on the projective displacement discussed earlier. Nevertheless, a loose cumulative advancement seems apparent as Booth proceeded from his initial attack upon scientism and motivism to his celebration of an affirmative vision in his final chapter on art. From admittedly chilling examples of student anti-intellectualism he turned to their intellectual forebears, then closed with renewed commitment to a positive and life-supportive vision of human purpose. At one point Booth argued that the narrative adequacy of discursive treatises is restricted to "those which, like Pascal's *Pensées*, make narrative heroes out of their authors."[24] This heroism he apparently claimed for himself, and not invalidly, since he offered his book as both a personal testament of a perplexed hero and the story of the hero's struggle to affirm the necessity of systematic assent. Often Booth seems to have been on target, but just as often the truth of the ideas he challenged survived his effort to disprove them, producing a literary vision comparable to Trilling's, if based on a different argumentative strategy and with a different, more obstinate vision of affirmative value.

The third post-Vietnam affirmist testament in critical theory to be discussed is John Gardner's *On Moral Fiction*, published in 1978, when the rejection of the sixties was entirely taken for granted.[25] As a critic, Gardner ignored the antiwar activists and took on the free-floating role of a frontier roustabout ("the only available rules are those of a gunfighter") in combating the pervasiveness of bad art he found in American culture (p. 149). He was not trying to restore orthodoxy but rather took it for granted as the dominant perspective. Instead, he wanted to encourage the recovery of aesthetic and ethical values in contemporary fiction—values that had deteriorated, in fact, through the restoration of orthodoxy over the previous decade.[26] The problem is that his freedom from Trilling's and Booth's sense of imminent crisis diffracted his perspective, randomizing his thoughts to such an extent that his book seems best judged as a breviary of useful but inconsistent insights. Early in his sermonizing, Gardner acknowledged this limitation by declaring, "Criticism, when most interesting and vital, tends toward art, that is, bad science, making up fictions about fictions" (p. 14). Indeed, the tendency toward art pervades the field of literary criticism, but he took it to its extreme by mixing passages of remarkable sensitivity with grand vagaries that are neither artistic nor scientific. This happened, for example, when he extolled the three great virtues of fiction—the Good, the True, and the Beautiful—oblivious of the extent to which these glittering ideals effectively offset each other in life and in most serious works of art (pp. 133, 144). Often, unfortunately, the True is neither good nor beautiful, the Good neither true nor beautiful, and the Beautiful neither true nor good; and, then again, any two of the three may be featured at the sacrifice of the third. Sometimes none prevails, and without diminishing the value of a text, for example, in *Naked Lunch*, by William Burroughs. On one page Gardner attacked literary criticism for trying to universalize "some handy formula" ("What is the simplest formula I can hope to get away with?" he asked, mimicking the strategy), and then he acknowledged on the very next page that "art does the same things age after age" (pp. 129–30). Gardner ignored the possibility that fiction's "same things age after age" might have been explicable by "some handy formula." If literature keeps repeating itself, why exactly must critics be discouraged from seeking out a formula for explaining this recurrence. Obviously, the formulaic obsessiveness of critics might be justified by the comparable formulaic obsessiveness of the literature they try to explain. How could Gardner have simultaneously (within the span of two pages) complained of both except through egregious oversight?

But perhaps Gardner's most serious lapse was the hyperbole with which he concluded his book, "remembering that we live or die by the artist's vision, sane or cracked" (p. 205). He clarified and elaborated his inversion of orthodox Marxist assumptions implicit in this remark near the end of his first chapter in part II: "I am convinced that, once the alarm has been sounded, good art easily beats out bad, and that the present scarcity of first-rate art does not follow from a sickness of society but the other way round" (p. 126). In other words, bad art is not the product of social disintegration but its cause. Here Gardner denied the one-way influence between base and superstructure advocated by "vulgar" Marxists in favor of its opposite, a no less vulgar and top-heavy Hegelian thesis that art single-handedly generates social trends—as if Harriet Beecher Stowe single-handedly caused the Civil War and Fitzgerald and Hemingway invented the roaring twenties. Other more problematic examples would include the notion that modern Zionism was established by Theodor Herzl because of his disappointment as a playwright or that modern Italian fascism was maliciously concocted by poetry, fiction, and journalism as represented by the careers of Marinetti, d'Annunzio, and Mus-

Three Affirmists and a Brief Manifesto

solini. Gardner's argument could likewise be used to maintain that the literary movement terminated by the Vietnam conflict in fact caused both this conflict and the reaction that followed. However, a more complicated dialectic took place in every one of these instances, and the role of fiction was relatively minor compared to those of social and economic trends. In general, it seems obvious that the economic base and its cultural superstructure interpenetrate with shared but disproportionate impact. Artistic trends do beget social and economic consequences—who can deny this? On the other hand, major social trends and catastrophes have had a significantly greater effect upon artistic trends. Chaucer's magnificent poetry bore little influence in causing or postponing the Wars of the Roses, but there can be little doubt that this brutal civil war played a major role in discouraging English literary expression over the subsequent century. Other such examples may be cited almost ad infinitum—the effect of the Thirty Years' War on German culture, of the French Revolution on French culture, of the Civil War on American culture, etc. Depressions, too, have exerted their impact, as have extended periods of relative prosperity.

For the specific historical period important to Gardner's book—our last two decades of social, creative, and economic stagnation—it seems foolish to blame general trends on authors, most of whom are unknown to the public. Popular novelists such as Bellow, Mailer, and Updike may have influenced opinion makers whose response was felt by others in "trickle-down" fashion, but this indirect role seems minuscule compared to the influence of television, spectator sports, and such Hollywood personalities as John Wayne, Clint Eastwood, and Steven Spielberg. Likewise influential has been the inexorable decline in our standard of living since the mid-sixties, resulting from a steady decline in our inflation-adjusted real wages. Other major influences include bureaucratization, technocracy, exploitational trends in the media, the pursuit of unskilled labor abroad by American industry, the creation of urban and rural underclasses, and our economy's chronic dependence on Cold War profits. No less influential have been the government-induced inflationary spiral during President Carter's administration and the false prosperity under President Reagan (the result of a trillion-dollar deficit budget that never quite trickled down). To elevate such authors as Barth, Burroughs, and Stanley Elkin to the status of unmoved movers whose perverse genius somehow authored the malaise of these two decades seems totally disproportionate. Yet this was one of Gardner's principal assumptions—bad science, perhaps, but a charming and wonderful fiction about fiction. Hubris, almost.

The deficiencies that Gardner found in modern fiction may be arbitrarily divided into two categories, the manipulative gimmickry of popular escapism and the esoteric posturing of presumably serious writing. Apropos of popular fiction, Gardner pointed out such defects as commercialism, superficial optimism, simplistic propaganda, failure to imitate people believably, a "comfortable" vision of life, and obvious pandering to a wide market. He contrasted popular fiction's quick and shallow uses of sincerity to the more inclusive honesty expected by sophisticated readers. He also contrasted popular fiction's conformist ideals to genuine individualism tolerant of aesthetic risk. Contrary to Booth's position, Gardner contrasted popular fiction's dependence on universal assumptions (i.e., systematic assent) to the genuine creativity necessary to transcend these assumptions. Gardner argued, "The more appealing or widely shared the doctrine, the more immoral the book" (p. 117). Turning to serious fiction, Gardner deplored pedantry, "creepiness," fake structure, excessive idiosyncrasy, a parochial ethic, an unnatural dependence on texture as opposed to form, the lack of belief, excessive trivia, sleight of hand in the manipulation of characters, overpowering guilt feelings, a death-supportive vision of society, experimentation for its own sake, and "cynical attacks on traditional values such as honesty, love of country, marital fidelity, work, and moral courage" (p. 42). Gardner gave no clear ranking when he listed these defects, and he almost randomly glided from awkward platitudes to remarks of startling perspicacity. Nevertheless, his energy in declaring his aversions—a most negative commitment indeed—helps to rescue his book from its inconsistencies.

But in the final analysis it is Gardner's affirmative vision that one finds most interesting. As in the case of any impassioned articulation of affirmative principles, it is useful to reformulate his "truths" in both their positive and negative significations. By cataloguing his prescriptions for the restoration of fiction as an honest and healthy art, we can systematically expand his arguments for the revival of good fiction, and in terms acceptably dialectic. In fact, a negative manifesto may be proposed for giving dialectic credibility to Gardner's affirmative precepts, with each of his arguments conceded, then enlarged and "resignified" to suggest a more inclusive negative perspective that is at least as relevant to the experience of fiction.

Three Affirmists and a Brief Manifesto

A BRIEF NEGATIVE MANIFESTO FOR AUTHORS BOTH SERIOUS AND POPULAR

1. Literary deception works best if writers can fully believe in the lies they are telling.

"The artist's affirmation, or, more precisely, his search for affirmation, is the work of art," Gardner declared (p. 163). Here, once again, *Doxa* prevails, and indeed the search for affirmation is the most fundamental assumption of the negative poetics I propose. Authors must affirm what seems in their opinion to be true, recognizing that negative possibilities are best realized if kept subordinate to this positive quest. They must focus on their own beliefs—those they think the most important—confident that by making their beliefs come true they are telling their most effective artistic lies. They may acknowledge to themselves at least a few of the lies they are telling, but like Blake, Dostoevsky, and D. H. Lawrence, they must believe in as many of their lies as possible. Also useful is their ignorance of human psychology, since it enhances the lies they believe at the expense of those they can recognize. As a general principle, the aversions and repressed feelings of authors are most effectively fulfilled by being systematically overlooked. Authors can diminish the effect of sincerity crucial to good fiction only if they let themselves be inhibited by doubts and reservations, for above all, they must be confident of themselves in telling their tales. They must believe in the integrity of their work, leaving to others the recognition of how they have manipulated this integrity to suit their needs. And if confronted by such a possibility, they must angrily disavow it. How can readers tell if authors have succeeded in this strategy? Whenever they present stark ethical choices, whenever their characters and situations resonate with unusual appeal, and whenever their negative overtones may be only retrospectively discerned. A premature demand for objective inquiry thwarts this expressiveness. Consequently, it becomes imperative, as argued by Plato in *The Ion*, for authors and their readers to let themselves be inspired unhampered by self-recognition.

2. Writers should make an ethical commitment of their aversion to the truths that disturb them.

"Art is *by its nature* moral. We recognize true art by its careful, thoroughly honest search for and analysis of values," Gardner argued (p. 19). Again, this imperative seems essential, for what is morality but choice-making that features one thought or mode of behavior over another? To profess a morality is to declare the superiority of this conduct to that; to explore morality is to set this against that in active competition; and to write a moral novel is to combine these two obligations, declaring the final advantage of this as compared to the presumed failure of that. Gardner argued against any conflict between good guys and bad guys that is too obvious, but it should also be recognized that moral prescription is no less at stake when the choice is internalized: good guys in possession of more thises than thats, bad guys in possession of too many thats which undermine their conceded thises. A scale of relative complexity may thus be established between Hamlet-style grand uncertainties and Lone Ranger–style popular ethics. Authors may even vary the complexity among their principal characters—perhaps, for example, with one junior-grade Claudius balanced against a Hester Prynne, two Natty Bumppos, and the rest an assortment of Tontos and Blondies. The personal ethics of authors necessarily determine the roles they impose upon their characters, and the subversiveness of their creativity comes from those feelings they can acknowledge by loading the deck for or against characters that illustrate their attitudes. It is this displaced ethical pursuit that gives writing its felt vitality. Ethics (at least indignation) is every author's obsession, and ethics must be provided, mixed with a healthy dose of unexamined motivation.

3. Writers should latch on to as many diversionary truths as possible to hide their most intimate lies from themselves and their readers. The more convincing these diversionary truths, the better.

Gardner argued that "there can be no moral social art . . . without honesty in the individual—the artist—as a premise for just and reasonable discussion" (p. 82). Later he conceded, "We live, necessarily, in a jungle of half-truths and outright lies; if we didn't we'd be forever at one another's throats. . . . Art is our way of keeping track of what we know and have known, secretly, from the beginning" (p. 146). Indeed, Gardner's emphasis upon the importance of honesty and poetic truth may be granted, but with the important caveat that one truth or set of truths almost inevitably appeals to us when it helps to deny another that undermines our sense of personal worth. The literary faults we confess might be important, but even more important are those we cannot confess—of selfishness, meaninglessness, dull-wittedness, and blatant unmitigated ordinariness. A mild dose of literary self-deception thus becomes a useful antidote—like aspirin—to help bring improvements on a temporary basis.

4. Writers must breathe life into the characters that best illustrate and test those problems they themselves want to deny. This is the primary source of growth, complexity, and vital discovery in characterization.

Gardner argued that novelists must experience sincere affection for their characters: "And without compassion—without real and deep love for his 'subject' (the people he writes about and, by extension, all human beings)—no artist can summon the will to make true art" (p. 85). Again, Gardner's prescription seems essential, but with the qualification that this love relationship necessarily exhibits many of the contradictions in the love relationship between real people. For love is more complex than can be comfortably admitted. There must be room for disappointment, ambivalence, and outright aversion. For love to occur, there must also be a sense of real or potential reciprocity, of projective interaction. With authors it is likewise important to cultivate an intimate relationship with their characters. They should be fascinated by their villains and at least a bit worried about their heroes—what kind of people they are as well as what is happening to them. Ignorance about their characters is important too. They should not feel entirely confident and in control of the characters they love. They should give them free rein, at least for a while, to do as they please in their conduct of their affairs. In fact, fiction's negative appeal almost inevitably comes from an author's effective mixture of insight and inspired ignorance in trying to spell out empathy with characters.

5. Writers must remain unashamed of their most intimate, most embarrassing lies, for these are more likely to be appreciated by their readers.

Gardner argued that "the artist ought not to be too civilized" (p. 147), that fiction must be fascist in making the strongest case possible (p. 101), and that the novelist's identity as "poet-priest" ideally expresses the close kinship between primitive artist and primitive priest (p. 155). All of these prescriptions seem useful, but with the qualification that the myth and ritual of primitive religion primarily express taboos to guarantee social cohesion among particular tribes—animist taboos compounded by courtship taboos, warfare taboos, culinary taboos, etc. This primitive machinery persists in modern fiction, transformed by Gardner into something akin to scientific experimentation: "The moral fiction is a laboratory experiment too difficult and dangerous to try in the world but safe and important in the mirror image of reality in the writer's mind" (p. 116). Prohibited alternatives can indeed be tested in fiction—as much as possible, in fact. Whenever authors feel they have something to say but cannot fit it into the story, it is very probably important and they should try to fit it in. Its relevance can be decided later. Moreover, whenever an author is on the brink of saying something too embarrassing to admit—and just saying it seems tantamount to confession—this, for sure, must be added, with its relevance to be decided later. This is the zone of experience oft thought but ne'er so well expressed, and it should be cultivated. The more embarrassed one is by one's ideas—not necessarily because they're sexual but also because they might seem trivial, or selfish, or dumb, or neurotic—the more likely one is on target. The pleasures of fascist viciousness should be tried out by liberals, and the leftist dedication to lost causes (or, worse yet, to soured causes) by conservatives. There is nothing to worry about as long as the dynamics of closure may be counted on to absorb and deny the story's fullest implications.

6. Writers must focus on the story they tell, confident that its presumably realistic outcome will give formal validity to their effort to deceive themselves.

Gardner stressed the importance of form as a dynamic achievement that expresses a new (or renewed) sense of belief: "In literature, structure is the evolving sequence of dramatized events tending toward understanding and assertion; that is, toward some meticulously qualified belief" (p. 65). He praised repetition, the epiphany, and symbolism as essential literary devices, all of which play their role in fiction's struggle against its sworn enemy, chaos. Gardner's qualification that belief be "meticulously qualified" might differentiate serious fiction from the potboiler, but in both instances dramatized events encourage belief within a linear momentum that gives fiction its negative vitality. Chaos (or the lack of form) might threaten at the beginning, but literary structure should culminate in felt belief rooted in the denial imperative.

Three Affirmists and a Brief Manifesto

7. Writers should avoid rehashing obviously stale lies; instead, their self-deception must seem as fresh and precarious as the exploration of new and unrecognized truths.

Gardner argued that "art gropes" (p. 9), that "art deals, at its best, with what has never been observed or observed only peripherally" (p. 13), that there is "endless blind experiment" (p. 14), and that the writer "has nothing to guide him but his feeling as he writes" (p. 170). A particular novelist can take this approach with his materials because he is "a man of maximum sensitivity, a man who sees and feels more things in more precise detail than the people around him, partly because he has excellent emotional and intellectual equipment, including—above all, perhaps—the security which makes for shamelessness and partly because he has special machinery for seeing and feeling: the tradition of art" (p. 167). Indeed, every work of fiction expresses this sensitivity to some degree, and the very greatest works to a considerable degree. However, by itself the willingness to grope, to indulge in shamelessness, and to test the unthinkable is insufficient; fiction must be structured by the inevitable dialectic between threat and denial (X supplanted by Y as *not X*) that justifies a moral outcome based on repressed shamelessness. Otherwise, artistic credibility is vulnerable to awkward ethical dislocations—stories of just deserts perversely thwarted, of conniving trickiness rewarded, etc. What happens too often in real life must be prevented in fiction unless one is truly ashamed of talking about it, and then on a preliminary basis as denied by literary form.

8. Writers should be prepared to test the bounds of sanity in finding a projective context most adequate to the lies that need to be told.

Finally, Gardner stressed the paradox that fiction is both sane and insane: "Art possesses him [the artist], establishing his norms, which are not the world's norms; hence he is saner than the world, and daemonically mad" (p 184). On the one hand, art's "chief quality" is "the good sense and efficient energy with which it goes after what is really there and feels significant" (pp. 176–77); on the other, it "begins in a wound" (p. 181), and the artist must recognize "that the whole thing is a delusion" (p. 194). According to Gardner, "Art imitates insanity and borrows the madman's methods . . . but as long as it is art it is only an imitation" (p. 187). Once again Gardner's thesis—important enough to conclude his book—befits negative poetics, since the psychosis he featured is little more than an unsuccessful coping mechanism for dealing with otherwise unmanageable feelings and impulses. Any pathological syndrome—whether of schizophrenia, paranoia, hysteria, or the sociopathic disorders—comes from the desperate effort to remain intact in the face of these feelings and impulses. In effect, the individual's perceived incapacity expresses failure to control a more fundamental problem, the welter of anxieties and psychological disruptions that otherwise bear a totally disintegrative effect. Like quack medicine, one's insanity provides an insufficient cure. The paranoid delusion, for example, tells stories that help the individual to cope with anxieties that he or she might wish to be dominated, seduced, or violated by others. In lieu of confessional accuracy, a story of victimization is told that pits good guys against bad guys, innocents against conspirators, heroes against brutal villains who seek their destruction. If enough is at stake, anxiety generates the needed delusional thinking to deny felt inadequacy, for only if the fears of paranoid individuals are justified may they consider themselves sane and truly persecuted by their enemies.

Of course, "normal" fiction falls short of bizarre extravagance, but perhaps not as far as many want to think, since its aesthetic "entrancement" (Gardner's epithet) depends on the risks it encourages at the edge of sanity to permit one's withdrawal to a safe but interesting distance. Like the paranoid delusion, fiction works as a coping mechanism to extend and stabilize normal consciousness at the expense of abnormal and unmanageable feelings. Where the id was, let the ego be, Freud declared, and indeed fiction probes and stretches the imagination to its limits so that health and normalcy can finally be paid their due. Experience is reorganized so its most threatening features may be denied by means of a new and more inclusive affirmative commitment. This is the dialectic machinery intrinsic to fiction—its eidetically irreducible ingredient—and fiction's success depends on the writer's courage and ingenuity, matched by a touch of cowardice and obtuseness, in bringing this dialectic to life. Fiction should excite to relax, affirm to deny, and declare those truths that help authors to share with readers their most important lies. And their strategy must go unobserved, most of all by the authors themselves. As Plato explains in *Ion*, writers must be inspired but ignorant of what inspired them, and glad of it. They must keep those thoughts that really matter on the brink of disclosure, imminent but undiscerned.

NOTES

Introduction

1. I do not deny here that deception may also play a major role in other modes of discourse. Its importance in history is suggested by Hayden White's *Metahistory: The Historical Imagination in Nineteenth-Century Europe* (Baltimore: Johns Hopkins University Press, 1973); its importance in autobiography is explored with emphasis on psychiatric interviewing by Donald Spence in *Narrative Truth and Historical Truth* (New York: W. W. Norton & Co., 1982) and with emphasis on published autobiography by Timothy Dow Adams in *Telling Lies in Modern American Autobiography* (Chapel Hill: University of North Carolina Press, 1990).

2. The dichotomy I am suggesting here derives from John Dewey's distinction between truths with "warranted assertibility" and those that derive from "habit" or "apprehension," some of which are more accurate than others. See John Dewey, *Logic: The Theory of Inquiry* (New York: Henry Holt & Co., 1938), pp. 7–14, 143. In both *Philosophy and the Mirror of Nature* (Princeton: Princeton University Press, 1979) and *Consequences of Pragmatism* (Minneapolis: University of Minnesota Press, 1982), the neopragmatist Richard Rorty uses Dewey's concept of warranted assertibility to justify both the skepticism and the antifoundationalism that are featured by Stanley Fish in his recent publications. However, Dewey's definition of warranted assertibility in his *Logic* seems primarily intended to describe truths that may be provisionally confirmed by scientific experimentation. These are necessarily different from the literary truths that I link with misrepresentation.

3. St. Augustine, "On Lying" and "Against Lying," in *Treatises on Various Subjects*, ed. Roy Deferrari (New York: Fathers of the Church, 1952), pp. 47–179, cited by Sissela Bok in *Lying: Moral Choice in Public and Private Life* (New York: Pantheon Books, 1978), pp. 32–35. For the central role of intention in literary deception, see Thomas Roberts, *When Is Something Fiction?* (Carbondale, Ill.: Southern Illinois University Press, 1973), and Clayton Koelb, *The Incredulous Reader: Literature and the Function of Disbelief* (Ithaca, N.Y.: Cornell University Press, 1984).

4. The suspension of disbelief was first proposed by Coleridge; see chapter 6 of *Biographia Literaria*, ed. J. Shawcross, vol. 2 (1907; reprint, London: Oxford University Press, 1958), p. 6.

5. "An Apologie for Poetrie" in *Elizabethan Critical Essays*, ed. Gregory Smith, vol. 1 (1904; reprint, London: Oxford University Press, 1937), p. 184.

6. Ibid., p. 171. Here I associate *praxis* with intention, as opposed to both cognition and affect or emotion. Apropos of the tripartite division among cognition, conation (or intention), and feelings (affect or emotion) as the three principal categories of experience, see James Ward, "Psychology," in *Encyclopaedia Britannica*, 11th ed., s.v.

7. Francis Fergusson, *The Idea of a Theater: A Study of Ten Plays/The Art of Drama in Changing Perspective* (Princeton: Princeton University Press, 1949), p. 36.

8. Northrop Frye, "The Archetypes of Literature," in *Fables of Identity* (New York: Harcourt, Brace & World, 1963), p. 18.

9. Wolfgang Iser, "The Reading Process: A Phenomenological Approach," in *The Implied Reader: Patterns of Communication in Prose Fiction from Bunyan to Beckett* (Baltimore: Johns Hopkins University Press, 1974), pp. 284–85.

10. Wolfgang Iser, "The Play of the Text," in both *Prospecting: From Reader Response to Literary Anthropology* (Baltimore: Johns Hopkins University Press, 1989), pp. 249–61, and *Languages of the Unsayable: The Play of Negativity in Literature and Literary Theory*, ed. Sanford Budick and Wolfgang Iser (New York: Columbia University Press, 1989), pp. 325–39. Once deception is accepted as an "umbrella concept" more inclusive than play (see p. 327 in *Languages of the Unsayable*), the entire apparatus designated by Iser may be used to explain the dynamics of literary deception proposed in this book—"freeplay" and "split signifiers" representing metaphor, "schema" representing plot, etc.

11. I. A. Richards, *Principles of Literary Criticism* (New York: Harcourt, Brace & Co., 1925), p. 266. The relativism implicit in Richards's definition of truth both simplifies and anticipates Dewey's concept of warranted assertibility; cf. n. 2.

12. John Gross, ed., *The Oxford Book of Aphorisms* (Oxford: Oxford University Press, 1983), p. 218. Also replete with quotations that challenge received notions of truth are *The Viking Book of Aphorisms*, ed. W. H. Auden and Louis Kronenberger (New York: Viking Press, 1962), and *The New Book of Unusual Quotations*, ed. Rudolph Flesch (New York: Harper & Row, 1966).

13. White, *Metahistory*, pp. ix, 5–7, 276.

14. E. D. Hirsch, *Validity in Interpretation* (New Haven, Conn.: Yale University Press, 1967), pp. 243–44.

15. It may be argued, of course, that the conventional use of death scenes in Shakespeare's plays was more accurate to the sixteenth century than the twentieth century, now that terminal illnesses are more likely to be prolonged because of professional medical care. Nevertheless, I maintain that the act of dying has not changed to that

extent and that Shakespeare's conventions were inaccurate even for the sixteenth century.

16. Stanley Fish, "Literature in the Reader: Affective Stylistics," *New Literary History* 2, no. 1 (Autumn 1970): 123–62, reprinted in *Reader-Response Criticism: From Formalism to Post-Structuralism*, ed. Jane Tompkins (Baltimore: Johns Hopkins University Press, 1980), pp. 70–100. In the most inclusive sense I argue that lying constitutes the "event" Stanley Fish seeks out in fiction; in other words, the successful act of self-deception is the "something that *happens* to, and with the participation of, the reader" (Tompkins, p. 72).

17. Here I would seem to contradict Heidegger's argument proposed in "The Origins of the Work of Art" (*Philosophies of Art and Beauty: Selected Readings in Aesthetics from Plato to Heidegger*, ed. Albert Hofstadter and Richard Kuhns [New York: Modern Library, 1964], p. 667): "The art-work discloses in its own way the being of what *is*. This disclosure, i.e., this deconcealment, i.e., the truth of what *is*, happens in the work. In the art-work the truth of that which *is* has set itself into work. Art is the setting-itself-into-work of truth" (italics in the original). The best way to bridge my difference with Heidegger, I suspect, is by treating the final literary *what is* as a truth that consists of gladly accepting, if not glorifying, the substitution of *what is not* for *what is* as an inevitable by-product of human consciousness.

18. The similar distinction between fact (*facere*, a thing done) and fiction (*fingere*, a thing shaped or made) is discussed by Adams in *Telling Lies*, p. 10.

19. Wolfgang Iser, "Interaction between Text and Reader," in *The Reader in the Text: Essays on Audience and Interpretation*, ed. Susan Suleiman and Inge Crosman (Princeton: Princeton University Press, 1980), p. 112. That *after* signifies *before* might explain at the most abstract level Jacques Lacan's notion of the displacement of a signifier, in this case with a story's outcome reinterpreting, and thus signifying (or designifying), its origins.

20. See Iser, "The Reading Process," as well as Jacques Derrida, "Structure, Sign, and Play in the Discourse of the Human Sciences," in *The Languages of Criticism and the Sciences of Man: The Structuralist Controversy*, ed. Richard Macksey and Eugenio Donato (Baltimore: Johns Hopkins University Press, 1970), pp. 247–65; Barbara Herrnstein Smith, "Contingencies of Value," *Critical Inquiry* 10 (1983): 1–35; and Gerald Graff, "Determinacy/Indeterminacy," in *Critical Terms for Literary Study*, ed. Frank Lentricchia and Thomas McLaughlin (Chicago: University of Chicago Press, 1990), pp. 163–76. Other concepts now in vogue that emphasize textual indeterminacy include Claude Lévi-Strauss's surplus of signifiers, Jacques Lacan's displacement of the signifier, Jacques Derrida's decentering, Roland Barthes's deferment of the signified, Michel Foucault's writing as absence, Mikhail Bakhtin's loopholes, Hans

Robert Jauss's horizons, Frank Kermode's plurality of signifiers, and Harold Bloom's misprision. All of these may be subsumed in the neopragmatic viewpoint, since they more or less stress William Empson's ambiguity as an intrinsic feature of textual form, reducing literary truth to "null-truth" in the sense that it is neither exactly true nor untrue. The alternative model I am proposing as a postneopragmatic option divides the otherwise apparently indiscriminate category of "null-truths" into relative truths (those with Dewey's "warranted assertibility") and affirmative substitute truths (those with sufficient appeal to be featured in the context of fiction). Any truth may belong to either category, depending on its use, but in general fiction belongs to the latter category and scientific methodology to the former. By means of this distinction, I suggest, the roles of both form and literary truth, which have in recent years been neglected in literary criticism, may be resurrected, the second as a dialectic interplay between relative truths and affirmative countertruths and the first as a linear organization of this dialectic that may be brought to suitable closure.

21. Fish, "Literature in the Reader," p. 83.

22. Frank Kermode, *The Classic* (New York: Viking Press, 1975), chap. 4, esp. p. 139.

23. Stanley Fish, "Interpreting the *Variorum*," *Is There a Text in This Class: The Authority of Interpretive Communities* (Cambridge: Harvard University Press, 1980), pp. 171–73.

24. Stanley Fish, *Doing What Comes Naturally* (Durham, N.C.: Duke University Press, 1989), pp. 11 and 439.

25. In Fish, *Doing What Comes Naturally*, pp. 471–502, reprinted in *Critical Terms for Literary Study*, pp. 203–22.

26. Thomas Kuhn, *The Structure of Scientific Revolutions*, 2d ed. (Chicago: University of Chicago Press, 1970).

27. John Searle, "The Storm over the University," *New York Review of Books* 37, no. 19 (6 December 1990): 40.

28. J. L. Austin, *How to Do Things with Words*, 2d ed. (London: Oxford University Press, 1975).

29. Here I cannot refrain from observing that the programmatic skepticism typical of modern trends in literary criticism has crested during the Reagan decade, when there has been such an abundance of hypocrisy and corruption in every realm of endeavor. A simplistic cause and effect relationship cannot be implied, but if "anything goes" in critical theory, it is easier to accept that "anything goes" in everything else as well.

30. Simon Lesser, *Fiction and the Unconscious* (Boston: Beacon Press, 1957), pp. 201–3.

Notes to Pages 11–23

31. Northrop Frye, *The Educated Imagination* (Bloomington: Indiana University Press, 1964), p. 55.

32. The importance of short-term memory limitations is discussed at length in my article "Psychostylistics: The Possibilities of a Behavioral Science," *Style* 18, no. 1 (Winter 1984): 83–97. The negative model I propose shows how the short-term memory of threatening truths is crowded from consciousness by both the long-term memory of conventional truths and the steady stream of new experiences likewise vulnerable to forgetting.

33. Frank Kermode, *The Sense of an Ending: Studies in the Theory of Fiction* (New York: Oxford University Press, 1967), p. 179.

34. Gerald Graff, *Literature against Itself: Literary Ideas in Modern Society* (Chicago: University of Chicago Press, 1979), p. 12.

35. Coleridge, *Biographia Literaria*, vol. 2, pp. 10–11.

36. Sigmund Freud, *Psycho-analytic Notes on an Autobiographical Account of a Case of Paranoia (Dementia Paranoides)*, in *The Standard Edition of the Complete Psychological Works of Sigmund Freud*, ed. J. Strachey, vol. 12 (London: Hogarth Press, 1958), esp. chap. 3, "On the Mechanism of Paranoia," pp. 59–79.

37. I. A. Richards, *The Philosophy of Rhetoric* (1936; reprint, New York: Galaxy Books, 1965), pp. 89–112.

38. E. H. Gombrich, *Art and Illusion* (Princeton: Princeton University Press, 1960), pp. 5–6

39. Roland Barthes, *Camera Lucida: Reflections on Photography* (Paris: Editions du Seuil, 1980), trans. Richard Howard (New York: Hill & Wang, 1981).

40. Lionel Trilling, *Sincerity and Authenticity* (Cambridge: Harvard University Press, 1971).

41. Wayne Booth, *Modern Dogma and the Rhetoric of Assent* (South Bend, Ind.: University of Notre Dame Press, 1974).

42. John Gardner, *On Moral Fiction* (New York: Basic Books, 1978).

1. A Short History of Deception Theories

1. *Plutarch's Lives*, trans. John Dryden and rev. A. H. Clough, vol. 1 (Boston: Little, Brown & Co., 1910), pp. 198–99.

2. Oscar Wilde, "The Decay of Lying," in *The Artist as Critic: Critical Writings of Oscar Wilde*, ed. Richard Ellmann (New York: Random House, 1969), pp. 290–320.

3. Aristotle's words, "through pity and fear *effecting* the proper purgation [i.e., catharsis] of these emotions" (italics added), do not identify pity and fear as catharsis

but as its agents. First come pity and fear, then catharsis as their purgation through what amounts to ritual sacrifice. This distinction helps to integrate the therapeutic explanation of catharsis offered by Jacob Bernays with Else's model of tragic structure as a transition from *hamartia* to *anagnorisis* (p. 385). See the discussion of Bernays's theory in S. H. Butcher, *Aristotle's Theory of Poetry and Fine Art with a Critical Text and Translation of the Poetics* (New York: Dover, 1951), pp. 345–49. Also see Gerald Else's assumption in *Aristotle's Poetics: The Argument* (Cambridge: Harvard University Press, 1967), p. 229.

4. This paraphrase of the view of Italian critic Girolamo Fracastoro is from J. E. Spingarn's *A History of Literary Criticism in the Renaissance* (New York: Columbia University Press, 1924), p. 34. Fracastoro's effort to synthesize Plato and Aristotle in *Naugerius, sive de Poetica Dialogus* (1555) is discussed by Spingarn, pp. 31–34.

5. Saint Augustine, *The Confessions*, in *The Confessions, The City of God, On Christian Doctrine*, vol. 18 of *The Great Books* (Chicago: Encyclopaedia Britannica, 1952), p. 6. The later history of this movement is thoroughly traced in *The Antitheatrical Prejudice* by Jonas Barish (Berkeley: University of California Press, 1981).

6. Francesco Robortelli, in *Librum Aristotelis de Arte Poetica Explicationes* (Florentiae, 1548), p. 86, cited by Spingarn, p. 30.

7. Sir Philip Sidney, "An Apologie for Poetrie," in *Elizabethan Critical Essays*, ed. Gregory Smith, vol. 1 (1904; reprint, London: Oxford University Press, 1937), pp. 159, 161, and 171.

8. Guez de Balzac, "*Réponse à deux questions, ou du caractère et de l'instruction de la comédie*," in *Oeuvres Diverses* (Paris, 1658), pp. 73–96, cited by Barish, p. 204.

9. Thornton Wilder, "On Drama and the Theatre," in *American Characteristics and Other Essays*, ed. Donald Gallup (New York: Harper & Row Publishers, 1979), pp. 118, 122.

10. Bielfeld was cited by Edgar Allan Poe in "*Ballads and Other Poems.* By Henry Wadsworth Longfellow," *Graham's Magazine* (April 1842), in *Edgar Allan Poe: Essays and Reviews*, ed. G. R. Thompson (New York: Library of America, 1985), p. 687. In the same context Poe equated literary invention with the use of "novel combinations" to achieve a "supernal beauty . . . which, perhaps, *no* possible combination of these forms would fully produce" (pp. 211–12). For this reason he praised the German words *Dichtkunst* (the art of poetry) and *dichten* (to feign) for their shared deceptionist etymological implications.

11. In *Friedrich Schlegel 1794–1802: Seine Prosaischen Jugendschnitten*, ed. Jakob Minor, vol. 2 (Vienna, 1882), p. 170, cited by René Wellek in *A History of Modern Criticism, 1750–1950*, vol. 2 (New Haven: Yale University Press, 1955), pp. 8–9.

12. Sir Joshua Reynolds, "Discourse XIII" (based on the 1797 edition), in *Dis-*

courses on Art, ed. Robert R. Wark (San Marino, Calif.: Huntington Library, 1959), p. 244.

13. G. W. F. Hegel, *Aesthetics: Lectures on Fine Art*, trans. T. M. Knox, vol. 1 (Oxford: Clarendon Press, 1975), p. 9.

14. Hegel, *Aesthetics*, p. 4. Schopenhauer later applied this notion to all inspirational discourse: "[T]he most important, the most lofty, the most sacred truths can make their appearance only in combination with a lie, can even borrow strength from the lie as from something that works more powerfully on mankind; and as revelation must be ushered in by a lie." Arthur Schopenhauer, "Religion: A dialogue, etc.," in *The Essays of Arthur Schopenhauer*, trans. T. Bailey Saunders (New York: Willey Book Co., n.d.), pp. 17–18.

15. C. K. Ogden cites this and the following quotation in *Bentham's Theory of Fictions* (London: Kegan Paul, Treuch, Trubner & Co., 1932), p. xciii.

16. Friedrich Nietzsche, *The Will to Power*, trans. Walter Kaufmann and R. J. Hallingdale (New York: Random House, 1967), p. 435.

17. Friedrich Nietzsche, *Beyond Good and Evil: Prelude to a Philosophy of the Future*, trans. Helen Zimmern (New York: Macmillan Co., 1924), p. 9.

18. Nietzsche, *The Will to Power*, pp. 451–52.

19. Mallarmé's words are included in his letter to Henri Cazalis in April 1866; see *Correspondance: 1862–1871* (Paris: Gallimard, 1959), p. 208. Henry James is quoted from "The Art of Fiction," in *Essays: American and English Writers*, ed. Leon Edel (New York: Library of America, 1984), p. 45.

20. H. L. Mencken, *Prejudices: Sixth Series* (New York: Alfred A. Knopf, 1927), reprinted in *Prejudices: A Selection* (New York: Vintage Books, 1955), p. 245. Also see H. L. Mencken, *The Philosophy of Friedrich Nietzsche* (Boston: Luce & Co., 1913).

21. Mencken, *Prejudices: A Selection*, p. 245.

22. Ibid., pp. 246–47.

23. Edward Abbey, *Abbey's Road* (New York: Dutton, 1979), p. xv.

24. Ursula Le Guin, "Introduction," *The Left Hand of Darkness* (New York: Ace Books, 1987).

25. Leo Tolstoy, *What Is Art?* (London, 1898), in *What Is Art and Essays on Art*, trans. Aylmer Maude (London: Oxford University Press, 1930). Also see I. A. Richards, "Tolstoy's Infection Theory," *Principles of Literary Criticism* (New York: Harcourt, Brace & Co., 1955), pp. 186–89.

26. All are excluded from consideration by Sissela Bok in her book *Lying: Moral Choice in Public and Private Life* (New York: Pantheon Books, 1978). Bok's appeal for greater public integrity is mostly based on classical and scholastic philosophy, and she quotes such modern figures as Nietzsche and George Steiner without acknowledging

Notes to Pages 33–38

their treatment of deception as an unavoidable universal tendency. The other indicated texts include Hans Vaihinger, *The Philosophy of "As If,"* trans. C. K. Ogden (1911; New York: Barnes & Noble, 1966); Gustav LeBon, *The Crowd* (1895; New York: Macmillan Co., 1960); Vilfredo Pareto, *The Mind and Society*, 4 vols. (1916, 1923), trans. Arthur Livingston and Andrew Bongiorno (New York: Harcourt Brace & Co., 1935); and Jean-Paul Sartre, "Bad Faith," *Being and Nothing*, trans. Hazel Barnes (1943; London: Methuen, 1957). The current neglect of LeBon's and Pareto's theories may be partially attributed to their association with the Italian fascist movement, since Mussolini, a student of Pareto, used their theories to manipulate public illusion in support of national economic mobilization. Nevertheless, their value in explaining mass psychology seems, if anything, more relevant today than ever.

27. Richards, *Science and Poetry* (1926), reprinted as *Poetries and Sciences* (New York: W. W. Norton & Co., 1970); *Practical Criticism* (London: Routledge & Kegan Paul, 1929), pp. 280–91.

28. Christopher Ricks, "Lies," *Critical Inquiry* 2, no. 1 (Autumn 1975): 121–42; Lionel Trilling, *Beyond Culture* (New York: Harcourt Brace Jovanovich, 1965), pp. 201–2; Lionel Trilling, *Sincerity and Authenticity* (Cambridge: Harvard University Press, 1971, 1972). I discuss the latter more thoroughly in chapter 9.

29. Sigmund Freud, *The Interpretation of Dreams*, in *The Standard Edition of the Complete Psychological Works of Sigmund Freud*, ed. James Strachey, vol. 5 (London: Hogarth Press, 1958), p. 567, hereafter cited as *Standard Edition*. Freud's pleasure principle suggested in this passage is more thoroughly discussed in chapter 3.

30. William James, *The Principles of Psychology* (New York: H. Holt & Co., 1890), p. 141.

31. Sigmund Freud, "The Relation of the Poet to Day-Dreaming," *Collected Papers*, ed. Ernest Jones and trans. Joan Riviere, vol. 4 (New York: Basic Books, 1959), p. 174.

32. Ibid., p. 183.

33. Ibid.

34. Norman O. Brown, *Life against Death* (Middletown, Conn.: Wesleyan University Press, 1959), p. 56.

35. Herbert Marcuse, *One-Dimensional Man: Studies in the Ideology of Advanced Industrial Society* (Boston: Beacon Press, 1964), pp. 238–39.

36. Herbert Marcuse, *Counter-Revolution and Revolt* (Boston: Beacon Press, 1972), p. 97.

37. *Counter-Revolution and Revolt*, pp. 98–99.

38. Fredric Jameson, *Marxism and Form* (Princeton: Princeton University Press, 1971), pp. 309, 319, and 327. Subsequent topics are discussed on pp. 329–30, 338, 360, and 374. Jameson's analysis of literary deception is substantially in accord with

Notes to Pages 38–46

mine despite his neglect of the dialectic implications of Aristotelian form (p. 328), and despite his relatively artificial distinction between class ideology and idealism as a psychological alternative (p. 368). I also disagree with his conventional use of deviationism based on the notion that art forces the reader into abrupt self-consciousness (p. 375), and I am bothered by some of his rhetorical excesses, for example, when he declares that the novel regenerates itself out of its impossibility (p. 352). However, many of Jameson's arguments suggest a theoretical model substantially in accord with the principles of negative poetics I am proposing here.

39. Ibid., pp. 397–98.

40. Ibid., pp. 401–2, 406.

41. Ibid., p. 408.

42. Roland Barthes, *Critical Essays* (1964; Evanston, Ill.: Northwestern University Press, 1972), p. 126. It may be added that Brecht's overriding emphasis on the necessity of conveying a revolutionary truth finally and definitively excludes his theory of epic theater from the canon of deceptology. He talks of art exposing the lie, not telling or sharing it.

43. Ibid., p. 137.

44. Ibid., p. 160.

45. Ralph Waldo Emerson, "Nominalist and Realist," in *Emerson: Essays and Lectures*, ed. Joel Porte (New York: Library of America, 1983), p. 585.

46. John Barth, *The End of the Road* (1967; New York: Bantam Books, 1969), p. 119.

47. George Steiner, *After Babel* (New York: Oxford University Press, 1975), pp. 217–18.

48. Ibid., p. 220.

49. Ibid., p. 227.

50. Ibid., p. 229.

51. Ibid., p. 233.

52. Anthony Brand, "Lies, Lies, Lies," *Atlantic Monthly* 240 (November 1977): 62.

53. Ibid., p. 63.

54. D. H. Lawrence, "Studies in Classic American Literature," in *The Shock of Recognition*, ed. Edmund Wilson (New York: Modern Library, 1955), p. 908.

55. Norman Mailer, "Appeal to Lillian Hellman and Mary McCarthy," *New York Times Book Review*, 11 May 1980, p. 3.

56. Nina Darnton, "Taking Risks: The Writer as Effective Teacher," *New York Times*, 13 April 1986, sec. 12.

57. Sir Francis Bacon, *Novum Organum*, in *Advancement of Learning, Novum Organum, New Atlantis*, vol. 18 of *The Great Books* (Chicago: Encyclopaedia Britannica, 1952), pp. 109–13.

Notes to Pages 46–54

58. Ralph Waldo Emerson, "Intellect," in *Emerson: Essays and Lectures*, p. 424.

59. Sidney, "An Apologie for Poetrie," p. 184.

60. Samuel Taylor Coleridge, *Biographia Literaria*, ed. J. Shawcross, vol. 2 (1907; reprint, London: Oxford University Press, 1958), p. 6.

61. Richards, *Science and Poetry*, p. 60.

62. René Wellek, *Theory of Literature* (New York: Harcourt, Brace & Co., 1949), p. 14.

63. Northrop Frye, *Anatomy of Criticism: Four Essays* (Princeton: Princeton University Press, 1957), pp. 33–35, 162, 223–39.

64. Gerald Graff treats these and other critics with similar beliefs in "How Not to Talk about Fictions," chapter 6 of his *Literature against Itself: Literary Ideas in Modern Society* (Chicago: University of Chicago Press, 1979). In his paper "Determinacy/Indeterminacy" (in *Critical Terms for Literary Study*, ed. Frank Lentricchia [Chicago: University of Chicago Press, 1990], pp. 163–76), Graff seems to take an entirely different tack, and without mentioning the discrepancy.

65. Graff, *Literature against Itself*, p. 12.

66. Few are more exposed to the truths of fiction than English professors, yet we are hardly paragons of candor and integrity.

67. William James's *Pragmatism* (Cambridge: Harvard University Press, 1975) was first published in 1907; *The Meaning of Truth* (Cambridge: Harvard University Press, 1975) was first published in 1909. The cited passages from *Pragmatism* occur on pp. 3, 4, 38, and 54, and from *The Meaning of Truth* on pp. 103, 108, and 110. James represents a peculiar convergence of Continental and American traditions. He basically agrees with Nietzsche's moral and intellectual relativism; he escapes Nietzsche's nihilistic indignation, however, by accepting expediency as a matter of course in human affairs, but with the confidence that scientific truth will ultimately prevail. As for his American background, James extends Emerson's transcendental revision of Puritan ideology one step further by making a virtue of belief itself, whatever it entails. Deception theory takes this tendency to its limit by emphasizing belief's avoidance dynamics as epitomized by literary experience.

68. Chief Justice John Marshall, *Marbury v. Madison*, 1 Cranch, 137 (1803), quoted in *Documents of American History*, ed. Henry Steele Commager (New York: Appleton-Century-Crofts, 1948), p. 193.

69. The most extreme of these displacements, the worship of virgin purity to deny death, was usefully explored by Freud in "The Theme of the Three Caskets," in *Collected Papers*, vol. 4, pp. 244–56. Among his sources was August Weissman's biological hypothesis that sexual reproduction perpetuates the "immortality principle" of unicellular organisms, making sex and death interdependent in more advanced species. We reproduce so our germ cells might persist—hence romantic love; but we

must die once our capacity for reproduction ends—hence, according to Freud, our obsessive vision of romantic love to deny this inevitability.

70. Sigmund Freud, *Psycho-analytic Notes on an Autobiographical Account of a Case of Paranoia (Dementia Paranoides)*, in *Standard Edition*, vol. 12, pp. 59–79; Robert Waelder, "The Structure of Paranoid Ideas," *International Journal of Psychoanalysis* 32 (1951): 167–77.

71. Stanley Fish, "Literature in the Reader: Affective Stylistics," in *Reader-Response Criticism: From Formalism to Post-Structuralism*, ed. Jane Tompkins (Baltimore: Johns Hopkins University Press, 1980), p. 83.

72. Jean-Paul Sartre, *Nausea* (Norfolk, Conn.: New Directions Paperback, 1959), pp. 57–58. Here Sartre stresses the importance of closure in the linear advancement from beginnings to ends: "Nothing happens while you live. The scenery changes, people come in and go out, that's all. There are no beginnings. Days are tacked on to days without rhyme or reason, an interminable, monotonous addition. . . . Neither is there any end. . . . *But everything changes when you tell about life*; it's a change no one notices: the proof is that people talk about true stories. As if there could possibly be true stories . . . you seem to start at the beginning. . . . And in reality you have started at the end. It was there, invisible and present, it is the one which gives to words the pomp and value of a beginning" (italics added).

73. Sometimes this comfortable alternative meaning seems demonstrably uncomfortable, for example, in novels and movies of horror, sadism, and grim failure. My assumption would be that these excesses nevertheless produce satisfaction by denying even less gratifying experiences, such as fear, anxiety, and intense feelings of inadequacy in interpersonal relationships. The relative health of any society seems to be indicated by the extent to which the popular arts feature bizarre viciousness to cope with the public's repressed sense of helplessness. The more violent a society's use of fiction, one suspects, the bigger and more widespread the problems eventually to be confronted.

2. Austen, Dickens, Conrad, and Stein

1. Adrienne Rich, "When We Dead Awaken," in *Claims for Poetry*, ed. Donald Hall (Ann Arbor: University of Michigan Press, 1982), p. 355.

2. Denise Levertov, "On the Function of the Line," in *Claims for Poetry*, p. 271.

3. Some readers can be gratified that Bellow suggests at least the possibility of Herzog's avoiding any precipitous commitment in his future relationship with Ramona. Herzog seems to have learned enough to avoid a repetition of the problems he has already endured at the hands of his first two wives, both having very heavily

Notes to Pages 65–79

penalized him for his romantic impetuosity. However, Herzog's final diffidence while waiting for Ramona to come for dinner—giving the novel its conclusion—should more obviously set the stage for another botched seduction effort, since his ingrained romantic extravagance precludes any dramatic improvement in self-control. A more honest dénouement—or a more obviously ironic one—would show his virtuous resolve already disintegrating as he toys with fantasies of salvation in the arms of a new woman.

4. Joseph Conrad, "Heart of Darkness," in *Youth and Two Other Stories* (New York: Doubleday, Page & Co., 1923), p. 82.

5. Gertrude Stein, *Four in America* (New Haven: Yale University Press, 1947), quoted by Thornton Wilder in his introduction, p. vi.

6. Ralph Waldo Emerson, "Self-Reliance," in *Emerson: Essays and Lectures*, ed. Joel Porte (New York: Library of America, 1983), p. 270.

7. Friedrich Engels, *Herr Eugen Dühring's Revolution in Science (Anti-Dühring)*, trans. Emile Burns (New York: International Publishers, 1939), p. 155.

8. I have already discussed the quasi-deceptionist stance of these three authors in chapter 1.

9. Contemporary reports out of Zaire are hardly encouraging; as many as two to three million killings are reported to have taken place since its independence in 1960. Nevertheless, this is an improvement compared to the five million or so inhabitants who were killed during the twenty years of King Leopold's personal rule.

10. This mercantile quality in Jane Austen's prose is extensively discussed by Mark Schorer in "Fiction and the 'Analogical Matrix,'" in *Critiques and Essays on Modern Fiction*, ed. John Aldridge (New York: Ronald Press, 1952), pp. 83–98, and by Dorothy Van Ghent in *The English Novel: Form and Function* (1953; New York: Rinehart & Co., 1961), p. 102.

11. There is a curious parallel to Conrad's treatment of sex in the fiction of V. S. Naipaul, who has expressed his indebtedness to Conrad's influence. Like Conrad, Naipaul has organized his stories of the third-world experience so as to identify women as liberals dangerously misguided by the values of the white world. In *Guerrillas* (New York: Alfred A. Knopf, 1975), Jane rejects Roche, her timid white liberal boyfriend, for Jimmy, a sadomasochistic black nationalist revolutionary, only to be killed by Jimmy as his sacrifice to his homosexual relationship with Bryant, a boy staying with him on his run-down plantation. A comparable triangle occurs in *A Bend in the River* (New York: Alfred A. Knopf, 1979), located in Kisangani (once Stanleyville), approximately the site where Marlow first meets Kurtz. Unfaithful to her husband, Raymond, Yvette tries to prove herself by having an affair with Salim, hero of the novel, but she is violently rejected, since he prefers peace of mind living in his bachelor quarters with Metty, his ex-slave. In both of these novels heterosexual love

is punished, and the physical humiliation of a woman initiates the hero's escape, chastened but liberated, from primitive madness to London civilization. For Marlow the situation is reversed, since his jungle adventure affords temporary escape from the liberal women who await him in Europe, but except for these differences, the novels of Naipaul resemble *Heart of Darkness* in their combination of misogynistic assumptions and third-world self-discovery, each brought to light by the other.

12. Ford Madox Ford emphasized his close collaboration with Conrad in his paper "Heart of Darkness," *Portraits from Life* (Boston: Houghton Mifflin, 1937), and in "Working with Conrad," *Yale Review* 75, no. 1 (February 1986): 13–18. Their relationship at the time *Heart of Darkness* was written is also discussed by Olivia Coolidge in *The Three Lives of Joseph Conrad* (Boston: Houghton Mifflin, 1972), pp. 151–55, and by Bernard C. Meyer in *Joseph Conrad: A Psychoanalytic Biography* (Princeton: Princeton University Press, 1967), p. 154. Curiously, most of Conrad's biographers treat both Conrad and Hueffer's collaboration and the composition of *Heart of Darkness*, but they do not attempt to sort out the contributions of Conrad and Hueffer to the writing of this novel.

13. Gertrude Stein, *Lectures in America* (1935; New York: Random House, Vintage, 1975), p. 231.

3. A Homeostatic Model

1. Ralph Waldo Emerson, "Intellect," in *Emerson: Essays and Lectures*, ed. Joel Porte (New York: Library of America, 1983), p. 425.

2. Kenneth Burke, *The Philosophy of Literary Form* (1941; Baton Rouge: Louisiana State University Press, 1967), p. 299.

3. S. H. Butcher gives the classic explanation of catharsis in "The Function of Tragedy," chapter 6 of her book *Aristotle's Theory of Poetry and the Fine Arts* (New York: Dover Publications, 1951), pp. 242–59. Here Butcher proposes a "lustrative" theory of purification comparable to Jacob Bernays's theory of catharsis as pleasurable relief, first proposed in 1857.

4. Karl Menninger, Martin Mayman, and Paul Pruyser, *The Vital Balance: The Life Process in Mental Health and Illness* (New York: Viking Press, 1963), pp. 83–84.

5. Quoted by Sigmund Freud in "Beyond the Pleasure Principle," in *The Standard Edition of the Complete Psychological Works of Sigmund Freud*, ed. James Strachey, vol. 18 (London: Hogarth Press, 1953–1966), pp. 8–9, hereafter cited as *Standard Edition*.

6. Freud, *Standard Edition*, vol. 14, p. 356.

7. Freud, *Standard Edition*, vol. 18, p. 62.

8. Claude Bernard, *Leçons sur les propriétés physiologiques et les alterations pathologiques des liquides de l'organisme* (Paris: J.-B. Baillière et fils, 1859).

9. Walter Cannon, *The Wisdom of the Body* (1939; revised and enlarged, New York: W. W. Norton & Co., 1939).

10. Ives Hendricks, *Facts and Theories of Psychoanalysis* (1934; New York: Alfred A. Knopf, 1958), pp. viii, 96–100; Otto Fenichel, *The Psychoanalytic Theory of Neurosis* (New York: W. W. Norton & Co., 1945), p. 13; G. L. Freeman, *The Energetics of Human Behavior* (Ithaca, N.Y.: Cornell University Press, 1948); Ross Stagner, "Homeostasis as a Unifying Concept in Personality Theory," *Psychological Review* 58 (1951): 5–17. Other useful articles with psychoanalytic applications of the theory of homeostasis include Douglass W. Orr, "Is There a Homeostatic Instinct?" *Psychoanalytic Quarterly* ll (1942): 322–35; John M. Fletcher, "Homeostasis as an Explanatory Principle in Psychology," *Psychological Review* 49 (1942): 80–87; and R. M. Lindner, "Psychopathic Personality and the Concept of Homeostasis," *Journal of Clinical Psychopathology* 6 (1949): 517–21.

11. Critical evaluations of the theory of homeostasis are offered by J. R. Maze, "On Some Corruptions of the Doctrine of Homeostasis," *Psychological Review* 60 (1953): 405–12, and "Psychology: A Review and Critique," *Psychiatry* 18 (1955): 81–91; Robert W. White, "Motivation Reconsidered: The Concept of Competence," *Psychological Review* 66 (1959): 297–333; and Ludwig von Bertalanffy, "General System Theory and Psychiatry," chap. 43 in *American Handbook of Psychiatry*, ed. Silvano Arieti, vol. 3 (New York: Basic Books, 1966), pp. 704–21. Bertalanffy's position is stated at greater length by Charlotte Buhler in "Theoretical Observations about Life's Basic Tendencies," *American Journal of Psychotherapy* 13 (1959): 561–81. Chapters 5 and 6 of Menninger et al., *The Vital Balance*, pp. 76–124, offer a more dispassionate appraisal of the concept as applied to psychology. Stagner, it should be added, anticipated and disposed of many of the arguments against a psychological concept of homeostasis in his 1951 article, which deserves a more sympathetic reading than it has received by his critics.

12. R. C. Davis, "The Domain of Homeostasis," *Psychological Review* 65 (1958): 8–13.

13. Robert Waelder, "The Principle of Multiple Function," *Psychoanalytic Quarterly* 5 (1936): 45–62, cited by Norman Holland in *Poems in Persons* (New York: W. W. Norton & Co., 1973), pp. 45–48.

14. There has recently been considerable effort to determine the specific effect of enkephalins and endorphins (amino acid molecules located exclusively in the brain) upon the experience of both pleasure and pain. Apparently, opiate receptors in the brain's limbic system evoke the sense of pleasure when stimulated by these mole-

Notes to Pages 92–93

cules, suggesting that tension reduction somehow causes the production of these molecules to provide the signal demanded by R. C. Davis (i.e., energy carried in the reverse direction) for indicating that nervous deactivation has been satisfactorily carried out.

15. Bertalanffy acknowledges that homeostasis can occur in an open system, but he claims in his paper "General System Theory and Psychiatry" (in *American Handbook of Psychiatry*, pp. 704–21) that there are particular limits to its application at this level: "In general, the homeostasis scheme is not applicable, (1) to dynamic regulations, that is, regulations not based upon fixed mechanisms but taking place within a system functioning as a whole (for example regulative processes after brain lesions), (2) to spontaneous activities, (3) to processes whose goal is not reduction but is the building up of tensions, and (4) to processes of growth, development, creation, and the like. We may also say that homeostasis is inappropriate as an explanatory principle for those human activities which are non-utilitarian, that is, not serving the primary needs of self preservation and survival and their secondary derivatives, as is the case with many cultural manifestations" (pp. 710–11). Obviously, one may disagree with these exceptions listed by Bertalanffy. The existence of homeostasis does not depend upon the ability of psychologists or neurologists to trace its pathways, any more than falling trees need to be heard for sound waves to have been emitted. Moreover, if consciousness is involved (i.e., included in the loop), the experience of pleasure can be loosely accepted as evidence of its occurrence regardless of whether the source of this pleasure can be exactly identified. In answer to item 2, spontaneity usually affords relaxation; in answer to item 3, suspense stories build tension so it can ultimately be reduced; and in answer to item 4, creativity brings about a gratifying sense of accomplishment. None of the exceptions Bertalanffy mentions seems to preclude the principle of homeostasis.

16. Stagner, "Homeostasis as a Unifying Concept in Personality Theory." Harmony's advantage over disharmony was first demonstrated by Parmenides at the expense of Heraclitus, by the Goddess Nature at the expense of Dame Mutabilitie in Spenser's final cantos of *The Faerie Queene*, and later (and most problematically) by Marx at the expense of Adam Smith and Say's Law in explaining the result of unconstrained growth in social crisis.

17. The misguided ideological aversion to this simple thesis is obvious, for example, in Robert R. Holt's paper, "A Review of Some of Freud's Biological Assumptions and Their Influence on His Theories," in *Psychoanalysis and Current Biological Thought*, ed. Norman S. Greenfield and William C. Lewis (Madison: University of Wisconsin Press, 1965), p. 119, in which Holt advocates as an economics of abundance an open-system approach that "allows one to observe that loving tends to be a

positive feedback system: the more we give, the more we have both for ourselves and for others." Professor Holt's analogy between love and "an economics of abundance" rather effectively dates his argument as a product of the fifties, previous to our collective recognition of both zero-sum limits and retrenchment's occasional necessity in both economics and personal adjustment. If love means perpetual growth, it also means perpetual adjustment to dislocations produced by this growth.

18. Gerald Else, *Aristotle's Poetics: The Argument* (Cambridge: Harvard University Press, 1967), pp. 224–32, 378–85. As I indicated in note 6 of chapter 1, my emphasis of conation (drive or motivation) derives at least in part from James Ward's taxonomy in *Encyclopaedia Britannica* (11th ed., s.v. "Psychology"), in which he proposes a tripartite division of psychology into three complementary dimensions, cognitive, affective, and conative. In my opinion, one of the principal defects of current literary criticism is its virtual abandonment of conation in favor of either affect, as in the case of response theory, or cognition (i.e., the pursuit of perceived associations), as in the case of most poststructuralist approaches.

19. The catalytic function of a literary text was of course first suggested by T. S. Eliot in both "Tradition and the Individual Talent" and "Hamlet," in *Selected Essays of T. S. Eliot* (New York: Harcourt, Brace & World, 1950), pp. 7–8, 124.

20. Else, *Aristotle's Poetics*, pp. 224–32, 378–85.

21. Peter Brooks, "Freud's Masterplot: Questions of Narrative," *Yale French Studies* 55/56 (1977): 291.

22. Samuel Taylor Coleridge, *Biographia Litteraria*, ed. J. Shawcross, vol. 2 (1907; reprint, London: Oxford University Press, 1954), pp. 10–11.

23. I explore this pattern based on statistical samples in my article "Psychostylistics: The Possibilities of a Behavioral Science," *Style* 18, no. 1 (Winter 1984): 83–97.

24. Stanley Fish, "What Makes an Interpretation Acceptable," in *Is There a Text in This Class?* (Cambridge: Harvard University Press, 1980), p. 353.

25. David Hume, "Of Tragedy," in *Essays: Moral, Political, and Literary* (Oxford: Oxford University Press, 1963), pp. 231–55.

26. Morse Peckham, *Man's Rage for Chaos: Biology, Behavior, and the Arts* (Philadelphia: Chilton Books, 1965).

27. In a recent conversation, I was told by Kenneth Burke that the only two texts that really matter now in his opinion are the Bible and the American Constitution. I respectfully treat his opinion as a mature judgment not too dissimilar from what I myself might conclude at his age.

28. Sir Francis Bacon, *Novum Organum*, First Book, 46, in *The New Organon and Related Writings*, ed. Fulton Anderson (Indianapolis: Bobbs Merrill, 1960), p. 51; also in *Advancement of Learning, Novum Organum, New Atlantic*, vol. 30 of *The Great Books* (Chicago: Encyclopaedia Britannica, 1952), p. 110.

Notes to Pages 103–109

29. In chapter 7 I discuss this use of the double negative as the affirmative fallacy.

30. W. K. Wimsatt, *The Prose Style of Samuel Johnson* (Hamden, Conn.: Yale University Press, 1972), p. 38.

31. The hierarchy I am proposing here is not to be confused with the "hierarchy of actualizations" discussed by Francis Fergusson in *The Idea of a Theater* (Princeton: Princeton University Press, 1949), p. 36, which features the relatively superficial categories of plot, characterization, and language, all of which play major roles in the more inclusive hierarchy I am proposing.

32. The deviationist theory of literary style suggested here is usually associated with Victor Shklovsky, Michael Riffaterre, and a host of other critics. Its psychological effect is also explained by Max Eastman in *Enjoyment of Poetry with Anthology* (New York: Charles Scribner's Sons, 1951). To Shklovsky's explanation of attention triggered by distraction, Eastman adds the explanation of how attention then dissolves into inattention.

33. Paul Ekman, *Telling Lies: Clues to Deceit in the Marketplace, Politics, and Marriage* (New York: W. W. Norton & Co., 1985).

34. Ernest Jones, *Hamlet and Oedipus: A Classic Study in the Psychoanalysis of Literature* (New York: W. W. Norton & Co., 1949; Anchor, 1954).

35. These and other regressive displacements important to Eriksonian analysis are cataloged by Norman Holland in *The Dynamics of Literary Response* (New York: Oxford University Press, 1968), chap. 2.

36. Angus Fletcher, *Allegory: The Theory of a Symbolic Mode* (Ithaca, N.Y.: Cornell University Press, 1964), esp. chap. 6.

37. Hans and Shulamith Kreitler, *Psychology of the Arts* (Durham, N.C.: Duke University Press, 1972), chap. 1. The visual arts are emphasized by the homeostatic model proposed by the Kreitlers and by D. E. Berlyne in *Aesthetics and Psychobiology* (New York: Appleton-Century-Crofts, 1971), but nothing is said in either book about the homeostatic dynamics of narrative form.

38. Even in the story of Oedipus, though, artistic simplification dominates, since Oedipus's tragic flaw consists of little more than having murdered his father and married his mother, having refused to believe the oracles that predicted his fate, and having relied on his own judgment to solve his problems. How naive and simplistic these deficiencies seem compared to the favors, payoffs, unkept promises, rhetorical evasions, ethical pretensions, preemptive strategies, expedient coalitions, unprincipled trade-offs, and lucrative sidelines that have gnawed at the consciences of most successful politicians from Pericles (upon whom Sophocles probably modeled Oedipus) to the guardians of our political system today. The flaws of real politicians seem entirely too refractory to be represented by Oedipus's victimization, which resulted from pride and fate alone.

4. Shakespeare, Coleridge, and Frost

1. This distinction between metaphor's image and meaning is essentially the same as I. A. Richard's distinction between metaphor's vehicle and tenor in chapter 5 of *The Philosophy of Rhetoric* (New York: Oxford University Press, 1936). Unfortunately, Richards refrains from dividing the tenor (or intended meaning) into its conscious and unconscious components.

2. The sequence I suggest here reverses the sequence proposed by critics of the deviationist school. Their emphasis upon stylistic devices (or surprises) almost entirely features the interaction between these devices and their local contexts. While I concede the importance of this interaction, I subordinate it to the interaction between these devices as situated in their local contexts and narrative closure as a dominant and more inclusive context. In the final analysis, a text's impact depends, I think, on the preliminary function of these devices (metaphor, etc.) in setting the stage for this more inclusive context. If CX represents context, SD represents stylistic device, and FC represents final closure, the following formula represents the more inclusive sequence that I am proposing:

$$(CX_1 \to SD \to CX_2)(CX_3 \to SD \to CX_4), \text{etc.} \to FC$$

Reduced to its minimum, this formula simplifies to become

$$(CX) \, SDs \to FC$$

A metaphor's acceptability thus depends on how well its primary process connotations are absorbed and nullified in both its particular context and the text as a whole, as dominated by the dynamics of conventional form.

3. Philip Wheelwright, *The Burning Fountain* (Bloomington: Indiana University Press, 1968), pp. 85–86, 99.

4. Ernst Kris, "Aesthetic Ambiguity," *Psychoanalytic Explorations in Art* (New York: International Universities Press, 1952), pp. 243–64; Norman Holland, *The Dynamics of Literary Response* (New York: Oxford University Press, 1968), esp. chaps. 4 and 6.

5. Holland's thorough explication of "Dover Beach" in *The Dynamics of Literary Response* (pp. 115–33) reduces this sexual content to the primal scene fantasy of sexual intercourse between father and mother figures, in effect treating Oedipal fixations as one type of oral spectacle.

6. W. H. Clemen, *The Development of Shakespeare's Imagery* (Cambridge: Harvard University Press, 1951).

7. Here I am obviously drawing upon the theory of Ernest Jones in *Hamlet and Oedipus: A Classic Study in the Psychoanalysis of Literature* (New York: Doubleday & Co., 1949). Beyond Jones, it seems useful to recognize how the Oedipus complex

helps to define the difference between tragedy and comedy, based on the unsuccessful displacement from mother attraction to father identification associated with heterosexual love and its ritual consummation in marriage. *Oedipus Rex*, for example, is pure tragedy restricted to the early Oedipal struggle preceding the presence of a prospective bride to compete with Jocasta, the mother. In *Antigone* and *Ghosts*, Aricia and Regine unsuccessfully compete with their prospective mothers-in-law, while in *Romeo and Juliet*, described as comedy with a tragic conclusion, the mother plays a minor role and the prospective bride wins her husband, but only in death. In *The Tempest*, the impending ritual of marriage dominates the story, and the mother disappears, replaced by the father able to bestow his blessings on marriage. Prospero, the bride's father, makes the necessary arrangements for the marriage while the mother figure is all but forgotten. The tragedy of Hamlet is more disturbing than any of these because he cannot locate himself in this fundamental transition from frustrated love of his mother to identification with a father figure through his pursuit of Ophelia. One father is too perfect to emulate and the other too wicked. Moreover, Hamlet cannot be attracted to his mother any longer because of her relationship with his wicked father, or to Ophelia because of her similarity to his mother. A homosexual alternative might be possible, as suggested by his friendship with Horatio, but to consummate this relationship means identifying with his mother, who both draws and disgusts him. The result is severe ambivalence asserted through metaphor and tentatively resolved by means of tragic dénouement.

8. *Selected Letters of Robert Frost*, ed. Lawrance Thompson (New York: Holt, Rinehart & Winston, 1964), p. x. In his introduction Thompson also declares that Frost's central insight was that one should "confront, recognize, and accept the circular relationship between constructive and destructive forces of personality." He quotes Frost to the effect that creativity provides "a momentary stay against confusion" and that form protects him from the "larger excruciations." A more challenging remark of Frost, and one to which this might be considered a reply, is his cryptic statement, "I have written to keep the over-curious out of the secret places of my mind both in my verse and in my letters." Paradoxically, it is this effort that exposes his strategy to the over-curious.

9. Frost's subtlety in doing so escaped even Thomas when Frost sent him the poem, but Frost's ironic shift in tone (and thus role) was actually intended to be the crux of the poem, more important than its moral that either choice would do. Nevertheless, the shift in tone is explained by its moral, for like the two paths, either role would do (see Frost, *Selected Letters*, pp. xiv-xv).

10. The explication of "Birches" can be almost as elaborate as that of "Mending Wall." Frost's preferences for boyhood when fetching cows, his description of the solitary boy at play who rides trees until he takes the "stiffness" out of them, his

comparison between climbing these trees and filling a cup over the brim—all these images can be explained too easily as extended double entendres.

11. Norman Holland, "The Unconscious of Literature: The Psychoanalytic Approach," *Contemporary Criticism*, in *Stratford-upon-Avon Studies*, vol. 12 (London: Edward Arnold, 1970): pp. 130–53, and *The Brain of Robert Frost: A Cognitive Approach to Literature* (New York: Routledge, 1988), pp. 23–33.

12. Frost's frequent practice of linking fairies and elves in the tales he told his children is cited by Lawrance Thompson in *Robert Frost: The Early Years* (New York: Holt, Rinehart & Winston, 1966), pp. 302–4. Also to be noticed in "Spoils of the Dead" (uncollected but included in *The Early Years*, p. 558) is the connection between homosexual anxiety and death, the latter a fundamental concern in "Stopping by Woods on a Snowy Evening." In fact, "Spoils of the Dead" may be treated as a sequel in the event the poet had decided to stay and die in the snow instead of returning home to his heterosexual obligations.

13. During the frequent and prolonged absences of his father, Frost slept in the same bed with his mother until he was about eleven years old, and then in a cot at the side of her bed throughout his high school years (see Thompson, *Robert Frost: The Early Years*, p. 205). Frost's close attachment to his mother is possibly significant, based on Freud's attribution of homosexuality to the influence of a dominant mother in the absence of the father (see Freud, *Leonardo da Vinci: A Study in Psycho-sexuality*, trans. A. A. Brill [New York: Random House, 1947], esp. pp. 65–83). Current research has traced homosexuality to other causes too, but Oedipal confusion seems to predominate in fiction, especially if homophobic reservations occur.

14. By making this switch, Frost compounded the projective mechanism that makes myth (or story) a paranoid structure, as explained by Otto Rank in his book *The Myth of the Birth of the Hero* (New York: Vintage Books, 1932, 1964), p. 78. Likewise, both Carl Jung, in *Aion*, trans. R. F. C. Hull (Princeton: Princeton University Press, 1968), and Gaston Bachelard, in *The Poetics of Reverie* (New York: Orion Press, 1969), treat art as a means of coming to terms with "anima" by means of fantasy. However, neither takes paranoia into account as perhaps the most effective means of organizing fantasy for this purpose.

5. The Paranoid Dialectic

1. Simon Lesser, *Fiction and the Unconscious* (Boston: Beacon Press, 1962), pp. 148, 201–4, 242. The denial-projective model I am proposing here more closely approximates Lesser's argument that fiction features projective mechanisms (p. 61) than Norman Holland's essentially antithetical position that fiction is introjected by

Notes to Pages 134–142

the reader. See also Holland's *The Dynamics of Literary Response* (New York: Oxford University Press, 1968), pp. 86–87.

2. Sigmund Freud, *Psycho-analytic Notes on an Autobiographical Account of a Case of Paranoia (Dementia Paranoides)*, in *The Standard Edition of the Complete Psychological Works of Sigmund Freud*, ed. J. Strachey, vol. 12 (London: Hogarth Press, 1958), esp. chapter 3, "On the Mechanism of Paranoia," pp. 59–79. Otto Fenichel traces the subsequent development of the concept of paranoia in psychoanalytic theory in *The Psychoanalytic Theory of Neurosis* (New York: W. W. Norton & Co., 1945), pp. 427–36.

3. David Swanson, Philip Bohnert, and Jackson Smith, *The Paranoid* (Boston: Little, Brown & Co., 1970), pp. 275–77. The authors summarize research pertinent to the question of homosexual repression as the source of paranoia on pp. 255–57 and 261–65. Despite high positive correlations established by many of the cited experiments (cf. those of Gardner, Page and Warkentin, Klaf and Davis, Moore and Selzer, etc.), the authors express the cautious judgment that "some association" exists between homosexual repression and paranoid disorder but that a cause and effect relationship has not yet been established. Interestingly, however, their own model incorporates the two displacements proposed by Freud and virtually all the theories of paranoia they cite feature the projective displacement with at least the implications of denial. In itself this displacement mechanism might not offer a cause and effect relationship between paranoia and homosexual repression, but it does help explain the prevalence of latent homosexual jealousies among the paranoid cases discussed throughout *The Paranoid*.

4. Robert Waelder, "The Structure of Paranoid Ideas: A Critical Survey of Various Theories," *International Journal of Psychoanalysis* 32 (1951): 167–77. Waelder supports the theory of double displacement by demonstrating that projection can occur only as an outgrowth of denial. In effect, the denial mechanism initiates the process of displacement, and then projection gives it aim in the substitution of more acceptable feelings.

5. Norbert Cameron, "The Paranoid Pseudo-Community," *American Journal of Sociology* 49 (1943): 32–38; and "The Paranoid Pseudo-Community, Revisited," *American Journal of Sociology* 64 (1959): 52–58.

6. John Keats, letter to George and Thomas Keats, December 21, 1817, in *The Poetical Works and Other Writings of John Keats*, ed. H. Buxton Forman, vol. 6 (New York: Charles Scribner's Sons, 1939), p. 104. For Keats, negative capability embraced the willingness to accept "uncertainties, Mysteries, doubts, without any irritable reaching after fact & reason." By implication, logic and empirical justification may be ignored, and in fact they are best eliminated from the poet's use of materials. As Herbert Marcuse explains in *One-Dimensional Man: Studies in the Ideology of Advanced*

Industrial Society (Boston: Beacon Press, 1964), this freedom may paradoxically occur within an otherwise repressive matrix of experience: "Transcendence beyond the established conditions (of thought and action) presupposes transcendence *within* these conditions. This negative freedom—i.e., freedom from the oppressive and ideological power of given facts—is the *a priori* of the historical dialectic; it is the element of choice and decision in and against historical determination" (p. 223). Literary denial is thus beneficial because it challenges established conditions by exposing readers to a better world of possibilities at odds with the inhibitive constraints otherwise dominant in our lives.

7. Here I combine passages from two papers by Sigmund Freud—"The Unconscious," in *Collected Papers*, ed. Ernest Jones and trans. Joan Riviere, vol. 4 (New York: Basic Books, 1959), p. 119, and "Negation," vol. 5, p. 182. Probably the best explanation of this negative mechanism outside of psychoanalysis may be found in Henri Bergson's *Creative Evolution* (New York: Random House, 1944), pp. 297–324. Bergson concludes, "[W]e seek a thing only because we feel a lack of it. Our action thus proceeds from 'nothing' to 'something,' and its very essence is to embroider 'something' on the canvas of 'nothing'" (p. 323). Apropos of the narrative model I am proposing, closure's affirmative messages embroider "something" on the denial displacement's rejection of deficiencies, and this "something" gains its appeal from having reduced a "something" elsewhere to "nothing."

8. Holland, *Dynamics of Literary Response*, pp. 104 ff.

9. Kenneth Burke, *Counter-Statement* (Los Altos, Calif.: Hermes Publications, 1953), pp. 31, 124. There is no difficulty in subsuming Burke's six categories of literary form in his "Lexicon Rhetoricae" to the negative model I am proposing here. Plot contains traits of both *conventional form* (the form that specifically appeals as form) and *syllogistic progression* (the form dominated by premises that force conclusions), since both form and plot make their appeal only because their premises force the necessary conclusions. Anything conventional is thereby syllogistic; vice versa, anything syllogistic is potentially conventional. This interaction also subsumes both *qualitative progression* (the presence of one quality prepares us for the introduction of another) and *repetitive form* (the restatement of the same thing in different ways) to the dominant *conventional-syllogistic* pattern explained above, since both of these primarily heighten suspense in anticipation of an acceptable resolution. Burke's sixth category, of *minor or incidental forms*, which includes metaphor, paradox, disclosure, etc., may be divided into plotted devices that contribute to the forward momentum of a text and metaphoric resistances that impede this momentum but make it all the more necessary. For example, the overt tenor-vehicle interaction of a metaphor is often congruent with the plot, but its latent implications might be countervailing, hence metaphoric.

Notes to Pages 144–147

10. Gerald Else, *Aristotle's Poetics: The Argument* (Cambridge: Harvard University Press, 1967), pp. 378–85; G. W. F. Hegel, "On Art" (a translation of his *Vorlesungen über die Aesthetik*), in *G. W. F. Hegel: On Art, Religion, Philosophy*, ed. J. G. Gray (New York: Harper & Row Publishers, 1970), pp. 22–127. Plot may also be explained as an "action chain" that brings about an anticipated result and as the transition from initial "discrepant awareness" (the reader's knowledge of the characters' relative ignorance) to its resolution by a process of discovery that restores the characters' level of knowledge to that of the reader. Both of these models are likewise Aristotelian in their linear explanations of literature.

11. Ezra Pound, *Fortnightly Review* (September 1914): 465, 467, quoted by K. K. Ruthven in *A Guide to Ezra Pound's Personae 1926* (Berkeley: University of California Press, 1969), pp. 152–53.

12. John Ciardi, *How Does a Poem Mean?* (Boston: Houghton Mifflin Co., 1959), pp. 994–1007. Many fulcrums can of course be found—even, for example, in the relationship between an attributive adjective and the noun it modifies—but in general I would define plot as consisting of the single basic transition to which all other transitions are subordinated unless there is a fundamental violation of the principle of unity.

13. Robert Penn Warren, "Pure and Impure Poetry," in *Selected Essays* (New York: Random House, 1951), p. 27.

14. Northrop Frye, *The Secular Scripture* (Cambridge: Harvard University Press, 1976), p. 35.

15. J. Hillis Miller, "Narrative," in *Critical Terms for Literary Study*, ed. Frank Lentricchia and Thomas McLaughlin (Chicago: University of Chicago Press, 1990), p. 74.

16. Roland Barthes, *S/Z*, trans. Richard Miller (New York: Hill & Wang, 1974), p. 75.

17. Umberto Eco, *A Theory of Semiotics* (Bloomington: Indiana University Press, 1976), p. 7. Quoted at greater length, Eco's remark supports my thesis that truth and deception are necessarily interdependent in the explication of fiction: "Semiotics is concerned with everything that can be *taken* as a sign. A sign is everything that can be taken as significantly substituting for something else. This something else does not necessarily have to exist or to actually be somewhere at the moment in which a sign stands in for it. Thus *semiotics is in principle a discipline studying everything which can be used in order to lie.* If something cannot be used to tell a lie, conversely it cannot be used to tell the truth: it cannot be used 'to tell' at all' " (italics in the original).

18. Jacques Lacan, "Agency of the Letter in the Unconscious," *Écrits: A Selection*, trans. Alan Sheridan (New York: W. W. Norton & Co., 1977), pp. 146–78, esp. pp. 164, 166–67. This aspect of Lacanian theory is also explained by François Meltzer in his paper "Unconscious," in *Critical Terms for Literary Study*, pp. 159–61.

19. Ralph Waldo Emerson, "Experience," in *Essays and Lectures* (New York: Library of America, 1983), p. 484.

20. Roman Jakobson, "Two Aspects of Language and Two Types of Aphasic Disturbances," in *Fundamentals of Language*, by Roman Jakobson and Morris Halle (The Hague: Mouton & Co., 1956), pp. 55–82.

21. In "The Name of Odysseus," (*Hudson Review* 9 [Spring 1956]: 52–70), George E. Dimock ingeniously supports this model of coordinate interaction. Throughout *The Odyssey* there is persistent tension between *odyssasthai* (to cause pain and be willing to do so) and *Kalypsamenos* (to be covered, suggestive of engulfment by the sea, feminine blandishments, etc.). Only because of *odyssasthai* (horizontal struggle) can Odysseus prevail against *Kalypsamenos*, which is vertical in signifying vulnerability to feminine entrapment as represented by Circe, Calypso, Nausicaa, Scylla and Charybdis, etc. The same distinction is more or less applicable to *Moby-Dick*, as explained by Leslie Fiedler in *Love and Death in the American Novel* (New York: Stein & Day, 1966), pp. 369–88, in which Ishmael's homosexual tendencies offset Ahab's heterosexual mission. In both epics, of Homer and Melville, struggle is metonymically plotted as a horizontal quest with enough momentum to avoid vertical surrender. In one instance the threat is heterosexual, in the other homosexual.

22. Allen Tate's categories are cited from his article "Tension in Poetry," *Essays of Four Decades* (Chicago: Swallow Press, 1968), pp. 56–71. Most of the rest of the New Critical nomenclature as applied to practical criticism—for example, irony, paradox, ambiguity, wonder, tone, etc.—can be reduced, like metaphor, to a doubling of experience offset by plot and theme according to the dialectic approach I am proposing here.

23. Roman Jakobson argues that "the poetic function projects the principle of equivalence from the axis of selection to the axis of combination" in "Linguistics and Poetics," *Style in Language*, ed. Thomas Sebeok (Cambridge: M.I.T. Press, 1960), p. 358. But it should also be obvious that the ultimate (and perhaps impossible) act of denial would be to dispense with the axis of selection by making a text strictly intrareferential in plotting its own denial as a one-dimensional commitment to silence.

6. *Young Goodman Brown*

1. Frederick Crews, *The Sins of the Fathers: Hawthorne's Psychological Themes* (New York: Oxford University Press, 1966), pp. 98–106.

2. Young Goodman Brown's characterization integrates Freud's explanation of homosexuality as identification with one's mother (in his study *Leonardo da Vinci: A Psychosexual Study of an Infantile Reminiscence*) with his explanation of paranoia as

Notes to Pages 167–174

repressed homosexuality (in his study of the Shreber case, *Psycho-analytic Notes on an Autobiographical Account of a Case of Paranoia* [*Dementia Paranoides*]).

3. Henry James, Sr., letter to Ralph Waldo Emerson, 1861, in Ralph Barton Perry, *The Thought and Character of William James*, vol. 1 (Boston: Little, Brown & Co., 1935), p. 88.

4. *Emerson in His Journals*, ed. Joel Porte (Boston: Harvard, Belknap Press, 1982), p. 522.

5. J. Nydes, "The Paranoid-masochistic Character," *Psychoanalytic Review* 50 (1963): 216, cited in David Swanson, Philip Bohnert, and Jackson Smith, *The Paranoid* (Boston: Little, Brown & Co., 1970), p. 261.

6. Julian Hawthorne, "The Salem of Hawthorne," *Century Magazine* 28 (May 1884): 6, quoted by Crews, *Sins of the Fathers*, p. 6.

7. For a sketchy but relevant description of *Moby-Dick* preceding Melville's meeting with Hawthorne in August 1850, consult Evert Duyckinck, "Melville's Moby Dick; or, The Whale," *Literary World* 251 (22 November 1851): 403–4.

8. Leslie Fiedler, *Love and Death in the American Novel* (New York: Stein & Day, 1966), pp. 369–88.

9. Herman Melville, "Hawthorne and His Mosses, by a Virginian Spending a July in Vermont," *Literary World* (17 and 24 August 1850), repr. in *The Shock of Recognition*, ed. Edmund Wilson (New York: Modern Library, 1955), pp. 200–201. Also see Merrell Davis and William Gilman, *The Letters of Herman Melville* (New Haven, Conn.: Yale University Press, 1960), pp. 124, 115, 133, 140, etc.

10. Fiedler, *Love and Death*, p. 76. Fiedler discusses his interpretation of the female perspective as represented in American fiction in his book *What Was Literature: Class Culture and Mass Society* (New York: Simon & Schuster, 1982).

11. The predominance of female primary and secondary school teachers in the United States compared to Europe is discussed by Richard Hofstadter in *Anti-Intellectualism in American Life* (New York: Alfred A. Knopf, 1963), pp. 316–22. Though overlooked, this basic difference between the education of Americans and Europeans seems an important variable in defining our unique cultural heritage.

12. John Updike's *Rabbit Run* (New York: Alfred A. Knopf, 1979) seems especially useful as a modern example of this trend, since the novel's protagonist, Harry Angstrom, runs back and forth between domestic responsibilities imposed by two women. The frontier is reduced to its microcosm—a mountainside patch of woods that Harry must traverse at the end of the novel in escaping Janice, his wife, to return once again to Ruth, his pregnant lover (p. 296). As he dashes through underbrush in broad daylight (in contrast to Young Goodman Brown's nocturnal experience), the sky seems to leap between treetops shaped like a disapproving blue monkey—undoubtedly a female monkey, as implied earlier when Tothero, Harry's mentor and former

coach, describes females as creatures that drop out of the trees at night (p. 53). The heart of the novel—in its thematic explanation, at least—occurs when Harry suddenly reaches the brink of an ancient foundation overgrown by trees. As he momentarily stares into its cavity, he recognizes it was once a house, a domicile with parents and children, and he is bothered by its symbolic value in representing the family obligation he has violated. The angry blue monkey above and the gaping foundation below both convey the same message—a primordial matriarchal insistence upon the importance of family. The message, of course, is at odds with his effort to justify his irresponsibility as a pursuit of Christian perfection more important, he had thought, than family and social responsibility.

7. The Affirmative Fallacy

1. E. H. Gombrich, *Art and Illusion: A Study in the Psychology of Pictorial Representation* (Princeton: Princeton University Press, 1960), pp. 5–6.

2. Charles Sanders Peirce, "How to Make Our Ideas Clear," in *Collected Papers of Charles Sanders Peirce*, ed. Charles Hartshorne and Paul Weiss, vol. 5, *Pragmatism and Pragmaticism* (Cambridge: Harvard University Press, 1934), p. 253.

3. George Orwell, *1984* (New York: Harcourt, Brace & Co., 1949), pp. 215–16.

4. Our best evidence of this tendency in our criticism is probably our strenuous indignation when we are confronted with such an explanation. Nothing less than genuine indifference justifies our claims of objectivity.

5. Stanley Fish, "Literature in the Reader: Affective Stylistics," *Reader-Response Criticism: From Formalism to Post-Structuralism*, ed. Jane Tompkins (Baltimore: Johns Hopkins University Press, 1980), p. 82.

6. W. K. Wimsatt, "The Intentional Fallacy," *The Verbal Icon: Studies in the Meaning of Poetry* (Lexington: University of Kentucky Press, 1954), pp. 3–18.

7. W. K. Wimsatt and Monroe Beardsley, "The Affective Fallacy," *The Verbal Icon*, pp. 21–39.

8. Yvor Winters, *In Defense of Reason* (Denver: University of Denver, Swallow Press, 1947), pp. 41, 87.

9. A. C. Bradley, "Poetry for Poetry's Sake," *Oxford Lectures on Poetry* (New York: St. Martin's Press, 1965), p. 24.

10. Ibid.

11. These fallacies are respectively discussed in the following texts: Wimsatt, *The Verbal Icon*, p. 33; Edgar Allan Poe, "The Poetic Principle," *Edgar Allan Poe: Essays and Reviews*, ed. G. R. Thompson (New York: Library of America, 1984), p. 75; Matthew Arnold, "The Study of Poetry," *Essays in Criticism* (New York: A. L. Burt

Notes to Pages 185–195

Co., n.d.), pp. 279–307; Allen Tate, *Essays of Four Decades* (Chicago: Swallow Press, 1968), pp. 63–64, 58; and I. A. Richards, *So Much Nearer: Essays Toward a World English* (New York: Harcourt, Brace & World, 1968), p. 174. More exotic fallacies and heresies include A. C. Bradley's heresy of the separable substance, "Poetry for Poetry's Sake," *Oxford Lectures*, p. 17, and four fallacies proposed by Northrop Frye: the fallacy of existential projection and the fallacy of a theory of mythological contract, *Anatomy of Melancholy: Four Essays* (Princeton: Princeton University Press, 1957), pp. 63, 108; and the representational fallacy and the fallacy of premature teleology, *Fables of Identity: Studies in Poetic Mythology* (New York: Harcourt, Brace & World, 1963), pp. 10, 14. Not to forget John Ruskin's pathetic fallacy, *Modern Painters*, in *Ruskin's Works*, vol. 2 (Boston: Dana Estes & Co., n.d.), pp. 200–218; repr. in *The Genius of John Ruskin*, ed. John D. Rosenberg (New York: George Braziller, 1963), pp. 61–72. All of these fallacies prescribe avoidances and hence denial, the initial displacement in the affirmative fallacy.

12. Lee Baxandall, *Marxism and Aesthetics: A Selective Annotated Bibliography* (New York: Humanities Press, 1968).

13. I. A. Richards, "Attitudes," *Principles of Literary Criticism* (New York: Harcourt, Brace & Co., 1955), chapter 15.

14. My confessedly simplistic distinction between vulgar and sophisticated Marxist criticism is based on George Steiner's perspective in his excellent, if dated, article "Marxism and the Literary Critic," in *Language and Silence* (New York: Atheneum, 1967).

15. Norman Holland, *The Dynamics of Literary Response* (New York: Oxford University Press, 1968), pp. 34–38. Despite my criticism of many of Holland's arguments in this book, I treat it as one of the major works of psychoanalytic criticism.

16. Norman Holland, *Poems in Persons* (New York: W. W. Norton & Co., 1973), p. 83.

17. Holland explains the feedback loop in four articles: "Criticism as a Transaction," in *What Is Criticism?*, ed. Paul Hernadi (Bloomington: Indiana University Press, 1981), pp. 242–52; "The Brain of Robert Frost," *New Literary History* 15, no. 2 (Winter 1984): 365–85; "Driving in Gainesville," *University of Hartford Studies* 16, nos. 2–3 (Winter 1984): 1–15; and "The Miller's Wife and the Professors: Questions about the Transactive Theory of Reading," *New Literary History* 17 (1986): 423–37. I disagree with Holland's treatment of the feedback loop as a strictly cognitive activity that performs no function beyond its reinforcement of the reader's identity theme. In contrast, the homeostatic feedback loop I am proposing limits behavior to the pursuit of results (or consequence, in Holland's terminology) by which tension is reduced and pleasure experienced.

18. Wolfgang Iser, "Interaction between Text and Reader," in *The Reader in the*

Text: Essays on Audience and Interpretation, ed. Susan Suleiman and Inge Crosman (Princeton: Princeton University Press, 1980), pp. 106–19. Also useful is Iser's essay "The Reading Process: A Phenomenological Approach," *The Implied Reader: Patterns of Communication in Prose Fiction from Bunyan to Beckett* (Baltimore: Johns Hopkins University Press, 1974), pp. 274–94.

19. Wolfgang Iser, "Interaction between Text and Reader," p. 117.

20. Stanley Fish, "Why No One's Afraid of Wolfgang Iser," *Diacritics* 11 (1981): 13.

21. Stanley Fish, "Interpreting the *Variorum*," *Critical Inquiry* 2, no. 3 (Spring 1976): 483.

22. David Bleich's version of response theory also features the use of students as interpretive communities, but within a more definable psychoanalytic frame of reference. Bleich's approach depends on gathering a large sample of response statements from students so that the text's "negotiable" affective appeal can be determined based on resemblances among these responses. Bleich's methodology may be commended for its empirical thoroughness, but one doubts that response statements are validly negotiable (i.e., useful to other readers) unless shared omissions and misreadings are given at least as much importance as what is said. It seems likely, in fact, that certain kinds of oversights might be the most negotiable of all, for example, when embarrassing connotations are overlooked by all respondents. If all protocols from a particular class ignore connotations—for example, the intended sexual connotations of ploughing a field in a seventeenth-century *carpe diem* lyric poem—as Bleich has reported, evasiveness seems likely as the dominant motivation. And if the affirmative substitutes that are dredged up (spring planting, digging for the truth, etc.) vary to a significant degree, the cause and dynamics of avoidance should be considered more important as a negotiable feature than the specific substitutions that are made.

23. Roman Jakobson and Claude Lévi-Strauss, "Charles Baudelaire's 'Les Chats,'" in *Structuralism: A Reader*, ed. Michael Lane (London: Jonathan Cape, 1970), pp. 202–21.

24. Claude Lévi-Strauss, "The Structural Study of Myth," *Structural Anthropology* (New York: Basic Books, 1963), pp. 206–31; "The Story of Asdiwal," in *The Structural Study of Myth and Totemism*, ed. Edmund Leach (London: Tavistock Publishers, 1967), pp. 1–47. By explaining this strategy, Lévi-Strauss escapes its evasiveness. However, any critical model that features regressive antimonies without taking into account their purpose can likewise be explained according to this purpose.

25. Cedric H. Whitman, "Homer and Geometric Art," *Homer and the Heroic Tradition* (1958; reprint, New York: W. W. Norton & Co., 1965), pp. 87–101.

26. The authors listed here are cited for their theories of deviationism: Victor Shklovsky, "Art as Technique," in *Russian Formalist Criticism: Four Essays*, trans. Lee T. Lemon and Marion Reis (Lincoln: University of Nebraska Press, 1965), pp. 3–24;

Max Eastman, *The Enjoyment of Poetry* (New York: Charles Scribner's Sons, 1936); Michael Riffaterre, "Criteria for Style Analysis" and "Stylistic Content," in *Essays on the Language of Literature*, ed. Seymour Chatman and Samuel Levin (Boston: Houghton Mifflin Co., 1967), pp.412–41; Morse Peckham, *Man's Rage for Chaos: Biology, Behavior, and the Arts* (Philadelphia: Chilton Books, 1965); Stephen Booth, "On the Value of *Hamlet*," in *Reinterpretations of Elizabethan Drama*, ed. Norman Rabkin (New York: Columbia University Press, 1969), pp. 137–76; and Stanley Fish, *Surprised by Sin: The Reader in Paradise Lost* (Berkeley: University of California Press, 1971).

27. I explain and chart how stylistic devices designify, or crowd from consciousness, preceding stylistic devices by diverting attention to themselves in my article "Psychostylistics: The Possibilities of a Behavioral Science," *Style* 18, no. 1 (Winter 1984): 83–97.

28. Paul de Man, *Blindness and Insight* (New York: Oxford University Press, 1971), p. ix. De Man's deconstructionism emphasizes the departure from a text's center by exploring an endless web of tangential displacements. Needless to say, these displacements also help to deny the existence of a second center, both extratextual and outside discourse, which is dominated by an individual's inhibitions and repressed memories. Theoretical diffusiveness likewise prevents any kind of focusing and thus erects one more barrier against unpleasant exposure. De Man's deconstructionist speculation may accordingly be treated as an appeal to maximum freedom of discourse (decentering) to disavow an authoritarianism perhaps best represented by his youthful fascism.

29. Jacques Derrida, "Structure, Sign, and Play in the Discourse of the Human Sciences," in *The Languages of Criticism and the Sciences of Man: The Structuralist Controversy*, ed. Richard Macksey and Eugenio Donato (Baltimore: Johns Hopkins University Press, 1970), pp. 247–72; and Jacques Derrida, *Of Grammatology* (Baltimore: Johns Hopkins University Press, 1976).

30. As cryptic and involuted as such figures as Barthes, Lacan, and Lévi-Strauss might seem at times, Derrida exceeds them in his dazzling eclectic elusiveness. He thoroughly deserves his self-proclaimed status as the Mallarmé of philosophy.

31. Stephen Greenblatt, "Toward a Poetics of Culture," in *The New Historicism*, ed. H. Aram Veeser (London: Routledge, 1989), p. 1.

32. Jerome McGann, *The Beauty of Inflections: Literary Imaginations in Historical Method and Theory* (Oxford: Clarendon Press, 1985), p. 62.

33. H. Aram Veeser, "Introduction," *New Historicism*, p. xi. In chapter 1 of *The Interpretation of Cultures* (New York: Basic Books, 1973), Clifford Geertz himself proposes how "thick description," a notion or methodology first characterized (and named) by Gilbert Ryle, applies interpretation to the most specific acts of observation. What the ethnologist seeks with this approach, Geertz maintains, is "a stratified hier-

archy of meaningful structures" (p. 7), "many of them superimposed upon or knotted into one another, which are at once strange, irregular, and inexplicit, and which he must contrive somehow first to grasp and then to render" (p. 10).

34. Stephen Greenblatt, *Renaissance Self-Fashioning: From More to Shakespeare* (Chicago: University of Chicago Press, 1980), p. 5.

35. Jerome McGann, *Historical Studies and Literary Criticism* (Madison: University of Wisconsin Press, 1985), p. 3.

36. Edward Pechter, "The New Historicism and Its Discontents: Politicizing Renaissance Drama," *PMLA* 102, no. 3 (May 1987): 299.

37. As an example of the difficulties in trying of trying to avoid cause and effect relationships, the principal episode Geertz uses from his notebooks to illustrate thick description is an elaborate story of an incident in Morocco (*The Interpretation of Cultures*, pp. 7–9). Approximately seven hundred words in length, his account contains, I would estimate, perhaps as many as fifty examples of stated or implied cause and effect reasoning. The effort to establish an inductive basis for guaranteeing historic objectivity has been mounted by such twentieth-century figures as Carl Hempel, Patrick Gardiner, T. A. Goudge, and W. B. Gallie, only the latter of whom is mentioned, and he only in passing, by Hayden White in his influential book *Metahistory: The Historical Imagination in Nineteenth-Century Europe* (Baltimore: Johns Hopkins University Press, 1973).

38. One searches in vain among new historicists, neo-Marxists, and others now identified with the cultural left for references to such classic explanations of Marxist economic theory as Paul Sweezy's *The Theory of Capitalist Development* (New York: Monthly Review Press, 1942), Paul Baran's *The Political Economy of Growth* (New York: Monthly Review Press, 1957), Paul Baran and Paul Sweezy's *Monopoly Capital: An Essay on the American Economic and Social Order* (New York: Monthly Review Press, 1966), or Ernest Mandel's *Marxist Economic Theory*, 2 vols., (New York: Monthly Review Press, 1968).

39. Frank Lentricchia, *After the New Criticism* (Chicago: University of Chicago Press, 1980), pp. xiii–xiv, cited by Louis Montrose in "Professing the Renaissance: The Poetics and Politics of Culture," *New Historicism*, ed. Veeser, p. 20.

40. Christopher Caudwell, *Illusion and Reality* (New York: International Publishers, 1937), esp. chapters 4–6, and *Romance and Realism: Study in English Bourgeois Literature* (Princeton: Princeton University Press, 1970); Georg Thomson, *Aeschylus and Athens* (New York: Haskell House Publishers, 1967); Granville Hicks, *The Great Tradition: An Interpretation of American Literature since the Civil War* (New York: Biblo & Tannen, 1967); and Christopher Hill, *Milton and the English Revolution* (New York: Viking Press, 1977).

41. Stephen Greenblatt, *Renaissance Self-Fashioning*, p. 282.

Notes to Pages 210–217

42. The dominant role of indeterminacy (or *aporia*) in contemporary criticism was established by a variety of texts and terms, including William Empson's ambiguity, proposed in *Seven Types of Ambiguity: A Study of Its Effects in English Verse* (London: Chatto & Windus, 1963); Mikhail Bakhtin's "loopholes," proposed in *Problems of Dostoevsky's Poetics*, ed. Caryl Emerson (Minneapolis: University of Minnesota Press, 1984), pp. 233–34; Jacques Derrida's "ruptures" and "decentering," proposed in "Structure, Sign, and Play in the Discourse of the Human Sciences," in *The Languages of Criticism and the Sciences of Man: The Structuralist Controversy*, pp. 247–65; Jacques Lacan's "displacement of the signifier," proposed in "Seminar on 'The Purloined Letter,'" *Yale French Studies* 48 (1972): 59–60; Roland Barthes's "deferment of the signified," proposed in "From Work to Text," in *Image—Music—Text* (1977), pp. 158–59; Wolfgang Iser's "gaps," proposed in "The Reading Process: A Phenomenological Approach," in *The Implied Reader* (Baltimore: Johns Hopkins University Press, 1974), pp. 279–80; Frank Kermode's "intrinsic plurality," proposed in *The Classic* (New York: Viking Press, 1975), pp. 117–41; Harold Bloom's "misprision," proposed in *The Anxiety of Influence* (New York: Oxford University Press, 1973), pp. 94–95; Michel Foucault's "writing as absence," proposed in "What Is an Author?" in *Language, Counter-memory, Practice: Selected Essays and Interviews* (Ithaca, N.Y.: Cornell University Press, 1977), pp. 113–38; Hans Robert Jauss's "horizons," proposed in "Literary History as a Challenge to Literary Theory," in *Toward an Aesthetics of Reception* (Minneapolis: University of Minnesota Press, 1982), p. 25; Barbara Johnson's "cognition as an act of violence," proposed in "Melville's Fist: The Execution of Billy Budd," in *The Critical Difference: Essays in the Contemporary Rhetoric of Reading* (Baltimore: Johns Hopkins University Press, 1980), p. 106; and Barbara Herrnstein Smith's "radical contingency," proposed in "Contingencies of Value," *Critical Inquiry* 10 (1983): 1–35. Also consult Gerald Graff's "Determinacy/Indeterminacy," in *Critical Terms for Literary Study*, ed. Frank Lentricchia and Thomas McLaughlin (Chicago: University of Chicago Press, 1990), pp. 163–76.

43. Listed by Stanley Fish in his interview "Learning to Love the PC Canon," *Newsweek* (24 December 1990), p. 51.

8. Roland Barthes

1. Compare what happened with Barthes's description of the tragic protagonist as one who "appeals to, . . . invokes an action, he does not perform it." *On Racine*, trans. Richard Howard (1963; New York: Hill & Wang, 1964), p. 48.

2. Jean-Paul Sartre, *What Is Literature?*, trans. Bernard Frechtman (New York: Philosophical Library, 1949).

3. Albert Camus, *The Rebel*, trans. Anthony Bower (New York: Knopf, 1956); Alain Robbe-Grillet, *For a New Novel: Essays on Fiction*, trans. Richard Howard (New York: Grove Press, 1965), p. 38.

4. Roland Barthes, *Writing Degree Zero*, trans. Annette Lavers and Colin Smith (New York: Hill & Wang, 1968). In several contexts I have simplified the excellent translation by Lavers and Smith for the purposes of greater accuracy.

5. Barthes's equation between metaphor and the unconscious dynamics of style is more or less in accord with my treatment of metaphor in earlier chapters (especially chapter 4), thus supporting the notion of a dialectic tension between plot and metaphor. This possibility seems especially fruitful if combined with his later treatment of narrative form as the primary source of deception, for example, in *Roland Barthes by Roland Barthes*, trans. Richard Miller (New York: Hill & Wang, 1977), p. 98. Unfortunately, the two concepts—metaphor and narrative denial—do not cross paths in Barthes's writings, but their connection seems inevitable.

6. Here Barthes's theory of literary experience as an alternative to *praxis* bears a close resemblance to the model of negative poetics I have proposed in earlier chapters. However, I cannot concur with Barthes's explanation of writing degree zero as a style of perfect lucidity undisturbed by social, psychological, and linguistic impurities.

7. Roland Barthes, "Myth Today," *Mythologies*, trans. Annette Lavers (New York: Hill & Wang, 1972), pp. 109–59, esp. pp. 111–31.

8. Roland Barthes, *On Racine*, trans. Richard Howard (1960; New York: Hill & Wang, 1964).

9. Ibid., pp. 41, 49. Also see Lucien Goldmann, *The Hidden God: A Study of Tragic Vision in the "Pensées" of Pascal and the Tragedies of Racine*, trans. Philip Thody (New York: Humanities Press, 1964), p. 46.

10. Barthes, *Writing Degree Zero*, pp. 38–39.

11. Barthes, *Elements of Semiology*, trans. Annette Lavers and Colin Smith (1964; New York: Hill & Wang, 1968), p. 39.

12. Roland Barthes, *The Pleasure of the Text*, trans. Richard Miller (1973; New York: Hill & Wang, 1975).

13. Roland Barthes, *Roland Barthes by Roland Barthes*.

14. Barthes, *Pleasure of the Text*, p. 53.

15. Barthes, *Roland Barthes by Roland Barthes*, p. 79.

16. The resolution of conflict by regressive schemata is explained by Claude Lévi-Strauss in both "The Story of Asdiwal," in *The Structural Study of Myth and Totemism*, ed. Edmund Leach (London: Tavistock Publishers, 1967), and "The Structural Study of Myth," in *Structural Anthropology* (New York: Basic Books, 1963). The application of his model seems necessarily limited in modern literature, but Barthes's regressive

use of binarisms that culminate in "neutrality" perfectly illustrates its possibilities, if without Barthes's having recognized his indebtedness to Lévi-Strauss.

17. Barthes, *Roland Barthes by Roland Barthes*, pp. 132–33.

18. Roland Barthes, *Camera Lucida*, trans. Richard Howard (1980; New York: Hill & Wang, 1981).

19. Perhaps relevant here is Freud's theory of the ambivalent death symbolism of silent, smiling maidens—on the one hand predicting death by their silence, on the other hand symbolizing its denial by their capacity to bear children. Barthes modified this archetype by featuring his mother as a little girl before his own conception was possible. He thereby assigned her all three roles of the legendary *Moirai*—bearing him, providing him with companionship through life, and finally symbolizing (and neutralizing) his acceptance of death. For King Lear the silent maiden was his daughter Cordelia; for Barthes it was the snapshot of his mother as a child, which completed the circle that eliminated patriarchal authority from his life.

9. Three Affirmists and a Brief Negative Manifesto

1. Ralph Waldo Emerson, "Spiritual Laws," in *Emerson: Essays and Lectures* (New York: Library of America, 1983), p. 318.

2. Emerson, "Fate," *Essays and Lectures*, p. 949.

3. Barbara Ehrenreich, *Fear of Falling: The Inner Life of the Middle Class* (New York: Pantheon Books, 1989), p. 82.

4. Lionel Trilling, *Sincerity and Authenticity* (Cambridge: Harvard University Press, 1972).

5. Ibid., p. 135, cited from Richard Gilman's *The Confusion of Realms* (New York: Random House, 1969), p. 78.

6. Ibid., p. 44; Trilling quoted Hegel from J. B. Baillie's translation of *The Phenomenology of Mind*, rev. and corr. 2d ed. (New York: Humanities Press, 1967).

7. Ibid., p. 165; the passage cited is from Marcuse's *Eros and Civilization* (Boston: Beacon Press, 1955), pp. 96–97.

8. Roland Barthes's aversion to *Doxa* illustrates how this emphasis on authenticity might result from the absence of a father figure.

9. Gide's insight here is exactly antithetical to E. H. Gombrich's insight, which I quoted in chapter 7 to help explain the affirmative fallacy. that one cannot have an illusion and be aware of doing so at the same time. See also E. H. Gombrich, *Art and Illusion: A Study in the Psychology of Pictorial Representation* (Princeton: Princeton University Press, 1960), pp. 5–6.

10. Wayne Booth, *Modern Dogma and the Rhetoric of Assent* (Notre Dame, Ind.: University of Notre Dame Press, 1974).

11. John Dewey, *Logic: The Theory of Inquiry* (New York: Henry Holt & Company, 1938), pp. 7–9, 11, and 143.

12. Booth, *Modern Dogma*, p. 104.

13. Bertrand Russell, *Nightmares of Eminent Persons* (New York: Simon & Schuster, 1955), pp. 29–35.

14. William Blake, "The Marriage of Heaven and Hell," in *The Poems of Blake*, ed. John Sampson (London: Oxford University Press, 1960), p. 248.

15. A. I. Oparin, *The Origins of Life*, trans. Serrgius Morgulis (New York: Macmillan Co., 1938); George Wald, "The Origin of Life," *Scientific American* 191, no. 2 (August 1954): 44–53. Also see Robert Shapiro, *Origins: A Skeptic's Guide to the Creation of Life on Earth* (New York: Summit Books, 1986).

16. Konrad Lorenz, *On Aggression*, trans. Marjorie Wilson (New York: Harcourt, Brace & World, 1963).

17. Lest we forget, the Vietnam War was a blatant intrusion in the affairs of another nation and routinely featured saturation bombings, search-and-destroy missions, and the continuous use of Phoenix torture centers. By refusing to sign the 1954 Geneva Accords (supposedly because Vietnam was none of our business), John Foster Dulles was able to prevent the 1956 plebiscite election these accords stipulated—an election that President Eisenhower acknowledged would have given Ho Chi Minh a landslide victory. Instead, our government installed a puppet government and brought to its defense more firepower than that expended during World War II. For the tens of thousands of Americans involved in the antiwar movement, our government's Vietnam policy posed an ethical choice radically at odds with Booth's conclusions.

18. Booth, *Modern Dogma*, n. 8, p. 51. Booth says he derives his argument from Michael Polanyi, *Personal Knowledge: Towards a Post-Critical Philosophy* (London: Routledge & Kegan Paul, 1958), pp. 381–405.

19. Paul Davies, *Superforce: The Search for a Grand Unified Theory of Nature* (New York: Simon & Schuster, 1984), p. 165.

20. William James, *Pragmatism* (Cambridge: Harvard University Press, 1975), p. 126. James's theory of pragmatism obviously fits deceptionist standards by encouraging beliefs useful to those who hold them regardless of their scientific inaccuracy. Earlier in his text, James makes this extreme relativism abundantly clear: "'The true,' to put it very briefly, is only the expedient in the way of our thinking, just as 'the right' is only the expedient in our way of behaving" (p. 106).

21. The full complexity of the limbic system is only beginning to be understood, and popular treatments of brain physiology necessarily simplify the explanation of current research for the lay reader. Nevertheless, it can be generalized at this point

that our emotions are controlled by a complex interaction among the neocortex, hypothalamus, and limbic system. Apparently the hypothalamus coordinates other portions of the limbic system (most important, the amygdalae) by means of nerve circuitry whose message content is inhibitive instead of stimulative, and the neocortex imposes its own controls with a comparable inhibitive signal system. As an impulse, each message from one center to another is necessarily stimulative, but as a signal its impact is inhibitive. If true, this means that negation (i.e., the *no* message) is multiply operative in even our most transcendent flights of affirmative certitude.

22. Booth, *Modern Dogma*, pp. 24–25.

23. Wilhelm Reich, *The Mass Psychology of Fascism*, trans. Vincent Carfagno (1933; New York: Farrar, Straus & Giroux, 1970); Erich Fromm, *Escape from Freedom* (New York: Holt, Rinehart & Winston, 1941); and T. W. Adorno et al., *The Authoritarian Personality* (New York: Harper & Brothers, 1950).

24. Booth, *Modern Dogma*, p. 186.

25. John Gardner, *On Moral Fiction* (New York: Basic Books, 1978).

26. The aesthetic and intellectual stultification of the late seventies becomes clear if one compares any list of publications from 1975 to 1980 with a list of publications from 1959 to 1964. Things were even worse in the eighties.

INDEX

Abbey, Edward, 31, 45
Abel, Lionel, 244
Adams, Timothy Dow, 277n.1, 279n.18
Adler, Alfred, 151
Adorno, J. W., 266
Adventure stories, 109–10
Affirmation, 138, 264–65; affirmative words deny, 53–54, 103; and Barthes, 219; and denial, 261, 264, 310n.21; in death, 239–40; and negation, 6, 103–104, 271, 310n.21; its quest in art, 271; and plot, 196; as truth that denies more basic truths, 17
Affirmative fallacy, 13, 16–17, 178, 191; basic to the other fallacies, 182–84; as escapism prevents accuracy, 189; and Gide, 253, 309n.9; and Gombrich, 16, 176, 309n.9; and literary criticism, 178–81, 214; and literary form, 178–79; and Peirce, 176. *See also* Designification; Metonymic designification; *Negationsnegierung*
Ali ibn Hazm, 87
Allopathic focusing. *See* Homeostatic literary response
Althusser, Louis, 210
Ambiguity, 55, 148, 149; in "Mending Wall," 126–29; Shakespeare's double entendres, 120–21, 180
Ammons, A. R., 186
Androgyny, 17–19, 118, 266; and Barthes, 231–37; and fantasy,

296n.14; in *Hamlet*, 121–22; in *Moby Dick*, 170; in "Rime of the Ancient Mariner," 118; in "a rose is a rose," 80–83; in Shakespeare's plays, 180. *See also* Male bonding
Antiepithalamium, 19; and Barthes, 232; in *Hamlet*, 119; in *Heart of Darkness*, 84; in "Rime of the Ancient Mariner," 117–19; in "Young Goodman Brown," 160
Anxiety: and disorientation 181; encourages the lie, 57–58; homophobic, 266; and response theory, 193
Aphorisms, 4
Aristotle, 45; on art's imitation of the ideal, 25; and Barthes, 215–16, 241; catharsis, 14, 18, 22–23, 55, 87, 94, 281n.3; character as the agency of action, 139; and Else, Gerald, 93; and Plato, 7, 22–23, 56, 75; plot an imitation of an action, 2, 6–7, 22–23, plot's linear advancement, 6–7, 55, 74–75, 95, 144, 147, 208, 242; reversal and the affirmative fallacy, 184; and Trilling, 247–48; unity of action, 22, 138, 144, 175. *See also* Mimesis; Plot
Arnold, Matthew, 114–15
Ashbery, John, 186
Augustine, St., 2, 24, 45
Austen, Jane, 102, 246, 252. *Pride and Prejudice*, 6, 19, 63–64, 99, 101, 253; its irony, 255–56; its sexual

Austen, Jane (*continued*)
  judgment, 83–84; its subversive truths, 76–77; its transition from truth to untruth, 74–75; its truth, 64; its untruth, 69–70
Austin, J. L., 9–10
Authenticity, 243, 250, 309 n.8. *See also* Truth
Authoritarianism, 266
Avant Garde, 187

Bach, Johann Sebastian, 255–56
Bachelard, Gaston, 229, 296 n.14
Bacon, Sir Francis, 46, 103, 258
Bad Faith. *See* Sartre, Jean Paul
Bakhtin, Mikhail, 206, 209
Balzac, Guez de, 25, 26, 189, 234
Barish, Jonas, 282 n.5
Barth, John, 40, 186, 187, 269
Barthes, Roland, 19, 43–45, 51, 215–41; and Bachelard, 229; and Balzac, 234; and Booth, 256–57; career as a novel, 216, 236, 241; and closure, 230–31, 233, 241; and death, 238–41; and dialectics, 219–20, 224, 227, 229–30; on *Doxa*, 19, 142, 215–16, 232–37, 239, 245, 256, 271, 309 n.8; on duration, 230; on *écriture*, 220–21, 223, 227; on *engagement*, 215, 217–18, 220–21, 225, 228, 229, 231; evasiveness of (concessive, tensive, and formalist), 219, 224, 230, 240–41; and father figures, 232–34, 237; on fetishistic art, 232; on form, 222–23, 224–25, 227, 228, 229; on history, 217, 219–22; and homosexuality, 216–17, 231–37, 239, 240, 241; on Kafka, 39; on language, 40, 221–22, 228, 232; and Lévi-Strauss, 228; and Lévi-Strauss's regression of antinomies, 234–35; and Marxism, 39, 233; and Mauron, 228; on metaphor, 222, 308 n.5; and metonymy, 233; on mimesis, 229, 237–40; and his mother, 236–40; and narrative form, 231, 233–34, 308 n.5; and Oedipus complex, 232–33; on *parole*, 219; on photography, 237–41; and Poulet, 229; on praxis, 217, 219, 220, 231, 308 n.6; and Sartre, 217–23, 233; and Saussure, 219; and selectivity, 39–40; on signification, 224–27, 229, 237–40; on style, 222, 308 n.5; on symbolism of the rose, 225; on tension between story and hermeneutic code, 145–46; on tragedy, 227–31; on truth, 22, 238; and weddings, 232; on writing degree zero, 220, 235, 308 n.6. *Camera Lucida*, 19, 216, 237–41; *Elements of Semiology*, 230–31; *Mythologies*, 224–27, 239; *On Racine*, 227–31, 234, 240; *The Pleasure of the Text*, 231, 240; *Roland Barthes by Roland Barthes*, 216, 231–37; *S/Z*, 240; *Writing Degree Zero*, 218–24, 227, 230, 241
Baudelaire, Charles, 199–200
Baxandall, Lee, 185
Beardsley, Monroe C., 181–83
Beckett, Samuel, 11
Belief: and affirmative fallacy, 178; as assent pending disproof, 256; and Booth, 254–59; and denial, 274; and fiction, 271; and Peirce, 176; as pseudostatement, 33, 47–49; and Schopenhauer, 283 n.14; in serious fiction, 270; as suspension of disbelief, 33,

Index

199; warrantable, 254
Bell, Daniel, 244
Bellow, Saul, 62, 174, 186, 269, 287n.3
Benjamin, Walter, 206, 247
Bennett, Arnold, 180–81
Bentham, Jeremy, 28, 43
Bergson, Henri, 262, 298n.7
Berkeley, Busby, 190
Berkeley Barb, 187
Berlyne, D. E., 293n.37
Bernard, Claude, 89
Bernays, Jacob, 282n.3
Berryman, John, 172, 186
Bertalanffy, Ludwig von, 92, 291n.15
Bielfeld, Baron von, 26, 43
Blake, William, 156, 180–81, 271; on dialectics, 260
Bleich, David, 36, 96, 304n.22
Bly, Robert, 186
Boesky, Ivan, 244
Bohnert, Philip. *See* Swanson, David
Bok, Sissela, 277n.3, 283n.26
Booth, Stephen, 96, 201
Booth, Wayne, 19–20, 243, 244, 245, 253–67; an affirmative vision, 267; on assent pending disproof, 256, 258–59, 266; on Austen, 255–56; on Bach, 255–56; and Barthes, 256–57; and behaviorism, 264; on belief, 254, 257–59; on a hierarchy of explanatory systems, 20, 262; as his own hero, 267; and Marxism, 265–66; and "motivism," 254, 264–66; on negation, 258–59, 264; and psychoanalysis, 265–66; rhetoric of, 254–56; and Russell, 260, 261–62; and "scientism," 254; Socratic methodology of, 254; and structuralism, 265–66; and Trilling, 267; on values

and knowledge, 254; on warrantable belief, 254
Bradley, A. C., 183
Brand, Anthony, 41–42
Brautigan, Richard, 186
Brecht, Bertolt, 39, 40, 285n.42
Brontë, Charlotte and Emily, 180
Brooks, Cleanth, 48
Brooks, Peter, 94
Brown, Norman O., 36, 243, 246
Brücke, Ernst, 87
Bryant, William Cullen, 180
Burke, Kenneth, 213, 292n.27; form and desire, 143; the negative as strictly a logical function, 259–60, 262; six categories of literary form, 298n.9; success confirmed by the reading experience, 86
Burroughs, William S., 186, 243, 268, 269
Butcher, S. H., 282n.3, 289n.3
Butler, Samuel, 77

Camus, Albert, 218, 223, 228, 259
Cannon, Walter, 89–90
Canon, literary, 212
Capote, Truman, 183
Catharsis, 14, 18, 22–23, 55, 87, 94, 189, 191, 281n.3. *See also* Homeostasis
Caudwell, Christopher, 37, 151, 185, 210
Characterization: the agency of action, 139; analogizing with, 11, 133–34; Austen's bias, 69–70, 76–77; Dickens's caricatures, 70–71, 77–78; and evil overload, 12, 69–71, 76–78; and frontier evasiveness, 174; metaphoric, 149; with motivation exaggerated,

Characterization (*continued*)
62; and reversal of genuine experience, 15; simple and complex, 105–106; simplified by ethical righteousness, 62; simplification defied by, 13

Chaucer, Geoffrey, 269

Chomsky, Noam, 243

Ciardi, John, 145, 299n.12

Civil War, 188

Clemen, W. H., 120

Closure, 7, 12–13, 55–56, 73–76, 106, 142, 145, 147–49, 179; audience united by, 99–100, 198; and Barthes, 230–31; and Derrida, 202–205; and freeplay, 203–205; in *Hamlet*, 119; Kermode on, 12–13; and memory, 177; and metonymic designification, 148; and new historicism, 208; as pseudosolution, 7; in "a rose is a rose," 75; Sartre on, 56, 297n.72; versus stylistic devices, 294.n.2

Cognitive theory of literary form. *See* Models of Literary experience

Cold War, 190

Coleridge, Samuel Taylor, 15; "Rime of the Ancient Mariner," 18, 19, 117–19, 160; willing suspension of disbelief, 47, 277n.4

Collier, Jeremy, 24

Colliers, 190

Commentary, 244

Conation. *See* Intention

Concrete poetry, 145

Conrad, Joseph, 72, 73, 80–81, 246, 252. *Heart of Darkness*, 11, 19, 63–64; its composition, 80; Kurtz's negative role, 260; its sexual judgment, 84; its subversive truths, 78–80; its truth, 64–65; its untruth, 71–72, 74, 288n.9

Conroy, Jack, 190

Convention, literary: and the avant garde, 181; and closure, 7, 179–80; a falsehood agreed on, 25; as "some handy formula," 268; syllogistic, 298n.9

Cooper, David, 246, 251, 252

Cooper, James Fenimore, 156, 174

Crane, Stephen, 106, 172, 184

Creeley, Robert, 186

Crews, Frederic, 108

Culler, Jonathan, 48

Curtiz, Michael, 190

Davies, Paul, 262

Davis, R. C., 90–91

Death: and art, 29, 263; and Barthes, 238–41; in *David Copperfield*, 71; and denial, 286n.69, 309n.19; in *Hamlet*, 122–24; literary, 5–6; in "Ode on a Grecian Urn," 114, 180; and religion, 261; in Shakespeare's plays, 5, 278n.15; as a void on which we dance, 262–63, 298n.7

Deception, 4, 21–22; in discourse, 277n.1; and the material implication, 49–50; new lies to meet new historical needs, 191; as paranoid coping mechanism, 134–36; and play, 278n.10; and truth, 249, 299n.17. Theories of: by Augustine, 2; by Bacon, 46; by Barth, 40; by Eco, 146, 199n.17; by Ekman, 107; by Emerson, 46; by Freud, 34–35; by Gombrich, 176; by William James, 24, 52–53; by Mencken, 31; by Nietzsche, 29–30; by Orwell, 176; by

Index

Rich, 59–60; by Richards, 47; by Schopenhauer, 183 n.14; by Steiner, 41–43

Deception, literary, 1–17, 21–58; acceptable if conceded to be false, 47–49; and anxiety, 57–58; and Barthes, 215–16; believable alternatives imposed, 86; as choice among untruths, 8, 58; and contradictory propositions, 53–55; and dishonesty, 21–22; by distortion, 2; by exaggeration, 62, 98; as fresh and precarious, 275; in language, 40–43, 63; and logic's material implication, 49–50; and personal worth, 51; shared between authors and readers, 8; as source and final outcome of fiction, 8; and truth, 8, 45–47, 53; as untelling, 1. *See also* Truth. Theories of: by Abbey, 31; by Augustine, 14; by Barthes, 39–40, 43; by Bentham, 28, 43; by Bielfeld, 26, 43; by Coleridge, 47; by Freud, 34–36, 43; by Gardner, 272; by Hegel, 27–28, 43; by Humboldt, 39; by James, 30; by Jameson, 38–39; by Lawrence, 45; by Le Guin, 31; by Mailer, 45–46; by Marcuse, 37–38, 43; by Mencken, 30–31, 43; by Nietzsche, 28–30, 43; by Paley, 46; by Plato, 22–23, 43; by Poe, 24, 43, 51; by Reynolds, 26–27; by Rich, 59–61; by Richards, 33, 43, 47; by Ricks, 33; by Robortelli, 25; by Rousseau, 26; by Schlegel, 26, 43; by Sidney, 25, 43, 47; by Solon, 21; by Tolstoy, 32–33, 43; by Trilling, 33–34; by Wilde, 21, 43; by Wilder, 25, 43. *See also* Negative poetics

Deceptionism (deceptology), 13; four categories of, 43–45

Deconstructionism, 185, 202–207, 209, 213, and indeterminacy, 211. *See also* Derrida, Jacques

De Man, Paul, 48, 305 n.28

Denial, 13, 54–57, 61, 73, 192, 206; and affirmation, 103–105, 261; and the affirmative fallacy, 175–78, 184; and Barthes, 216, 231, 235, 308 n.5; and belief, 274; and Booth, 266; and critical faddishness, 213–14; as a critical strategy, 211; in criticism between the sixties and eighties, 242–43; and Derrida, 205–206; as the function of consciousness, 264; in genres, 109–10; and Holland, 194; intrareferential, 300 n.23; as literary displacement, 101–105, 107–108, 142; and negative expressiveness, 142; neglected by new historicism, 208; as a paranoid displacement, 134–38, 142; and plot, 6–7, 11, 105–106, 151; and projection, 134–38, 297 n.4; self-referentiality of, 207; and social decline, 287 n.73; and social upheaval, 188; in the universe, 260–64; and Vietnam, 187–88; in "Young Goodman Brown," 169. *See also* Negation; *Negationsnegierung*

Derrida, Jacques, 8, 202–207, 305 n.30

Designification, 177–78, 242; and Barthes, 226; when fiction "undescribes" what bothers readers, 189; Iser on, 7; like metaphor, 16; and plot, 56, 147; from the sixties to the eighties, 242–46. *See also* Metonymic designification

Detective stories, 109

Deviationism, 185, 201–202, 293n.32, 304n.26; its neglect of narrative, 201–202, 294n.2; offset by conflict among stylistic devices in the short-term memory, 305n.27

Devil. *See* Satan

Dewey, John: and Richards, 278n.11; and Rorty, 277n.2; warranted assertibility, 277n.2, 280n.20

Dialectic form, 12, 55–57, 199; in Barthes's criticism, 145, 219–20, 224, 229–30, 234–35; and Blake, 260; and Frye, 145; and Warren, 145. Antitheses: between accidental insight and symmetry, 200; between the acknowledged and denied, 206; between affirmation and denial, 264; between anima and animus, 131–32, 151–52; between Apollonian and Dionysian, 151, 153, 200; between asserted and concealed truth, 72–73; between centering and decentered allusions, 206; between centrifugal and centripetal, 203; between closure and freeplay, 202–205; between combination and selection axes, 151; between contiguity and simultaneity axes, 151–52; between creativity and literary convention, 150; between denial and projection, 137–38, 149–50; between denial and verbal affirmation, 103–104; between expression and constraint, 150; between illocutionary and perlocutionary, 151; between intension and extension, 153; between intertextual and intratextual, 203; between *langue* and *parole*, 151; between leakage and closure, 179; between linear form and peripheral truths, 204; between masculine protest and inferiority feelings, 151; between metaphor and metonymy, 147, 149–50, 153; between metaphor and plot (narrative closure), 112–13, 143, 146, 150, 196–97; between motion and countermotion, 146; between nagging loose ends and final clarity, 145; between narrative and performative, 151; between natural and social, 151; between negative and positive feedback, 107, 150; between negative freedom and historical determinism, 297n.6; between open- and closed-system dynamics, 106; between plot and New Critical explicative criteria, 153, 300n.22; between short- and long-term memory, 96, 281n.32; between signification and syntagma, 151; between simultaneities and successions, 151; between site and violence, 151–52; between the sixties and eighties, 242–246; between story and innuendo, 113; between structure and texture, 151; between synchrony and diachrony, 151; between syntax and referential content, 150; between truth and its aesthetic rejection, 29, 204; between truth and untruth, 3–4, 150, 272; between versions of the truth, 10–12, 61

Dickens, Charles, 71, 154, 180–81. *David Copperfield*, 15, 19, 63–64, 99; its subversive truths, 77–78; its truth, 64–65; its untruth, 70–71

Dickey, James, 186

Dickinson, Emily, 5

Diderot, Denis, 246, 249, 252

Dimock, George, 300n.21

Disraeli, Benjamin, 181

Dissent, 244
Distortion. *See* Deception, literary
Donne, John, 113–14
Dos Passos, John, 190
Dostoevsky, Fyodor, 63, 76, 102, 109, 156, 271
Doxa. *See* Barthes, Roland
Dreiser, Theodore, 183
Dumas, Alexandre, 102
Duncan, Robert, 186

Eastman, Max, 201, 293n.32
Eastwood, Clint, 269
Eco, Umberto, 146, 299n.17
Ecological criticism, 213
Écriture. *See* Barthes, Roland
Ehrenreich, Barbara, 244
Eighties, the, 188, 244, 280n.29, 311n.26
Eisenhower decade. *See* Fifties, the
Ekman, Paul, 107
Eliot, George, 246
Eliot, T. S., 24, 213, 292n.19
Elkin, Stanley, 269
Ellis, John, 48
Else, Gerald, 93, 144, 282n.3
Emerson, Ralph Waldo, 23, 40, 46, 47, 67, 86, 102, 172, 188, 242
Empson, William, 280n.20
Engagement. *See* Barthes, Roland
Engels, Friedrich, 67, 103, 142, 265; letter to J. Black, 265. *See also Negationsnegierung*
Escapism, 12, 186–87, 189–91, 200
Ethics. *See* Morality
Evil: in *David Copperfield*, 77; in *Heart of Darkness*, 78; in Melville's review of Hawthorne, 172; in *Pride and Prejudice*, 76–77; in "a rose is a rose," 82; in "Young Goodman Brown," 156, 158, 172, 174. *See also* Characterization; Paranoia; Freud

Fallacies, literary, 181–85, 302n.11. *See also* Affirmative fallacy
Fanon, Frantz, 243
Fantasy: Freud on, 35–36; Holland on, 142–43. *See also* Freud, "Relation of the Poet to Day-Dreaming"; Holland, on form as defense
Farrell, James T., 190
Faulkner, William, 76
Fechner, Gustav, 87
Federman, Raymond, 48, 153
Female archetypes and personae, 301n.11; and Barthes's mother, 238, 240; and denial of death, 54, 286n.69; in *Hamlet*, 120–21; in *Heart of Darkness*, 78–80; in "Mending Wall," 127–28; as natural terrain, 152; paranoid depiction of, 141; in *Pride and Prejudice*, 69; in "Rime of the Ancient Mariner," 117–18; in "Young Goodman Brown," 161–63, 165
Feminist criticism, 213
Fenichel, Otto, 89, 297n.2
Fergusson, Francis, 2
Ferlinghetti, Lawrence, 186
Fiction: escapist, 12; fallacious, 14; popular and serious, 270; popularity dependent on plot, 153–54; serious as opposed to popular, 12; as substitution of imaginary world, 11; superior to history, 23
Fiedler, Leslie, 243; on adolescent escapism in American fiction, 172; on male bonding in frontier fiction, 19,

Fiedler, Leslie (*continued*)
131; on *Moby Dick*, 170, 300n.21; *What Was Literature*, 301n.10
Fielding, Henry, 6, 99, 104–105
Fifties, the, 186–89
Fish, Stanley: on Austin, 9–10; on criticism, 56; on fallacy-fallacies, 181, 183–84; on indeterminacy, 197–98; on interpretive communities, 8–9, 197–99; on Iser, 197; on Kuhn, 9; on memory loss while reading, 96; neopragmatism of, 8–10; his question, "What does a text do?," 6–7, 279n.16; response theory of, 195; and Rorty, 8, 277n.2. *Doing What Comes Naturally*, 9; "Interpreting the Variorum," 8; "Rhetoric," 9; *Surprised by Sin*, 201
Fitzgerald, F. Scott, 22, 174, 268
Fixations, 192
Flaubert, Gustav, 5
Fletcher, Angus, 109
Ford, Ford Madox, 80, 289n.12
Forgetting, 7
Form: and Barthes, 219, 222–25, 227; and Burke, 298n.9; as a center imposed, 204; as a communicable whole, 60; in criticism, 199–210; denies horizon of significations, 206; and Gardner, 274; and new historicism, 208; as synthesis of plot and metaphor, 143
Form, narrative. *See* Models of literary experience; Plot
Formalism, 109, 185, 199–200, 207; Barthes's eclectic approach, 215
Foucault, Michel, 206, 210
Fracastoro, Girolamo, 24, 56, 282n.4
Frankfurt school, 189

Freeman, G. L., 89
French New Criticism, 213
Freud, Sigmund, 34–36, 246; on cathexis and countercathexis, 206; on the conscious, 34–35; on ego and id, 17, 195; on image of silent young women, 54; inauthenticity the core of his doctrine, 252; motivism of, 264–65; on negation, 142; and negative poetics, 17; on paranoia, 15, 55, 134–35; on pleasure principle, 87–89, 91, 106; on the unconscious, 205. "Inhibitions, Symptoms, and Anxiety," 265; *Interpretation of Dreams*, 34, 112; *Leonardo da Vinci*, 300n.2; "Negation," 298n.7; *Psycho-analytic Notes on an Autobiographical Account* (the Schreber case), 15, 134–35, 297n.2, 300n.2; "Relation of the Poet to Day-Dreaming," 35–36, 43, 45, 51; "Theme of the Three Caskets," 286n.69; "The Unconscious," 298n.7
Fromm, Erich, 243, 266
Frontier, American, 156, 172–74, 301n.12
Frost, Robert, 124, 131–32, 172; his dependence on form, 295n.8; his relationship with his mother, 130, 296n.13; his secrecy, 295n.8; his use of paranoid structure, 296n.14. "After Apple Picking," 125; "Birches," 125, 295n.10; "Mending Wall," 19, 125–32, 160, 232, 236, 260; "Mowing," 128; "The Road Not Taken," 125, 295n.9; "Spoils of the Dead," 128, 296n.12; "Stopping by Woods on a Snowy Evening," 125
Frye, Northrop, 145, 213; archetypes

Index

diminish the value of truth, 48; content as otherness, 145; fiction to avoid being fair-minded, 139; fiction to avoid one's identity, 11; real versus conceivable, 2

Gaea, 161
Galbraith, John Kenneth, 243
Galsworthy, John, 180–81
Gardner, John, 20, 243, 245–46, 267–75
Geertz, Clifford, 206–207; on cause-and-effect, 306n.37; on thick description, 207, 305n.33, 306n.37
Genesis 1:2, 161
Gibran, Kahlil, 102
Gide, André, 253, 309n.9
Gilded Age, 188
Gilgamesh, 18, 76, 153
Gilman, Richard, 248
Ginsberg, Allen, 186, 187, 243, 262
Glazer, Nathan, 244
Goethe, Wolfgang von, 39, 63, 246, 259
Gold, Michael, 185
Goldmann, Lucien, 188, 189, 229
Goldwyn, Samuel, 190
Gombrich, E. H., 16, 176, 309n.9
Goodman, Paul, 243
Gosson, Stephen, 24
Graff, Gerald, 13–14, 48–50, 286n.64; on fiction's propositional content, 49
Gramsci, Antonio, 210
Greenblatt, Stephen, 206, 207, 210

Haiku, 145
Hardy, Thomas, 180
Hawthorne, Nathaniel, 172, 188; and his mother, 167–68; paranoid tendencies of, 167–68; underlying sameness in the stories of, 169. *Blithedale Romance*, 169; *Scarlet Letter*, 169; "Young Goodman Brown," 19, 156–69, 172–74, 232, 236, 237, 260, 300n.2
Hegel, G. W. F., 27–28, 37, 43, 45, 242, 246, 252, 264, 268; from abstraction to absolute knowledge, 144; culture defined, 249; on literary deception, 27–28; pure contraries that are never mediated, 229
Heidegger, Martin, 279n.17
Heller, Joseph, 186
Hellman, Lillian, 45
Helmholtz, Hermann, 87
Hemingway, Ernest, 174, 190, 268
Hendricks, Ives, 89
Heraclitus, 291n.16
Heroes, 12
Herzl, Theodor, 268
Heterosexual love: in *David Copperfield*, 71, 83–84; and death, 286n.69; in "Dover Beach," 114–15; in *Hamlet*, 121–22; in Hawthorne's marriage, 172; in *Heart of Darkness*, 79–80; in *Herzog*, 62; and homophobia, 266; in *Pride and Prejudice*, 69–70, 73, 76–77, 83–84; in *Rabbit Run*, 301n.12; in "a rose is a rose," 81–82; in tragedy, 294n.7; in "A Valediction: Forbidding Mourning," 113–14; in "Young Goodman Brown," 159–61, 164, 172–73; *See also* Antiepithalamium
Hicks, Granville, 185, 210
Hierarchy of actualizations: a closure-denial-homeostatic model, 106, 293n.31; of Francis Fergusson, 2

Hill, Christopher, 210
Hippocrates, 87
Hirsch, E. D., 4–5
Hoffman, Abby, 244
Hofstadter, Richard, 301n.11
Holland, Norman, 214; on anal and oral fixations, 108, 192, 293n.35; on "Dover Beach," 294n.5; his feedback model of literary experience, 194–95, 303n.17; on form as defense, 113, 142–43; on identity theme, 192–95; on introjection, 133, 296n.1; on "Mending Wall," 125. *Dynamics of Literary Response*, 36, 96, 192, 303n.15; *Poems in Persons*, 193
Hollywood, during the Depression, 189–90
Holmes, Oliver Wendell, 181
Holt, Robert, 291n.17
Homeopathic intensification. *See* Homeostatic literary response
Homeostasis, 86–110, 195, 199; as adjustment, 292n.17; in autonomic nervous system, 89–91; Bertalanffy on, 291n.15; and consciousness, 89–91; its debate in professional literature, 290n.11, 291n.15; and growth, 92–93; and harmony, 291n.16; Holland on, 194–95; Holt on, 291n.17; and literary experience, 93–110; through negative feedback, 90–91; as negative versus positive feedback, 91–92; and the pleasure principle, 93; references, 290n.10, 290n.11
Homeostatic literary response: through allopathic focusing, 97–98; and Aristotle, 95; and Coleridge, 95–96; through homeopathic intensification, 98–100; and the Kreitlers, 109; through narrative form, 94; open-system surprises denied by closed-system literary convention, 105; and plot, 94–100; and positive feedback, 106–107; the text an external source of negative feedback, 93–94. *See also* Negative feedback
Homer, 62, 110, 152, 197, 200–201, 300n.21
Homoaversiveness. *See* Homophobia
Homophobia, 17–19, 83–84, 116–17, 134, 141, 234; and Barthes, 216, 231, 234; in "Mending Wall," 129–31; in *Moby Dick*, 170–72; in "Young Goodman Brown," 165–66
Homosexuality, 116–32; and Barthes, 231–34; as Dionysian polymorphousness, 153; in *Hamlet*, 120–22; in "Mending Wall," 125–29; in "Rime of the Ancient Mariner," 118; in "a rose is a rose," 68, 80–83; in Shakespeare's sonnets, 115–16, 180; and the word *thing*, 126; in "Young Goodman Brown," 163
Howe, Irving, 244
Howells, William Dean, 181
Hueffer, Ford Madox. *See* Ford, Ford Madox
Hugo, Victor, 102
Humboldt, Wilhelm von, 39
Hume, David, 98
Huntington, Ellsworth, 209

The I. F. Stone Weekly, 187
Ibsen, Henrik, 295n.7
Identity theme. *See* Holland, Norman
Imagery, 12; and closure, 107; in Shakespeare's plays, 120, 180

Index

Indeterminacy, 8, 10, 211–14; Iser on 196; proponents of, 279n.20, 307n.42; and velocity, 212–13

Intention, literary, 2, 57, 97; exaggerated motivation, 62; fiction the instrument of praxis, 34–35, 278n.6; Freud on, 34–36; William James on, 52–53; and response theory, 195; Steiner on, 41–42

Interpretive communities. *See* Fish, Stanley

Irony, 55, 148–49

Irving, Washington, 174

Iser, Wolfgang, 3, 7, 195–97; on determinate and indeterminate, 196; Fish on, 197; on forgetting, 7; on gaps, 8, 12, 195, 197; and negative poetics, 7, 197; on play, 3, 278n.10

Jakobson, Roman, 149, 199–200, 300n.23

James, Henry, 30, 180–81

James, William, 34, 286n.67; and Emerson, 286n.67; and negative poetics, 286n.67; and Nietzsche, 286n.67; his pragmatism as applied to fiction, 52–53; on the world adrift in space, 262

Jameson, Fredric, 38–39, 284n.38

Johnson, Rose, 68

Johnson, Samuel, 27, 103–104

Jones, Ernest, 108, 294n.7

Jung, C. G., 296n.14

Kafka, Franz, 39–40, 156

Katz, Steve, 153

Keats, John, 114, 180–81; on negative capability, 142, 297n.6

Kennedy, Paul, 209

Kermode, Frank, 8

Kerouac, Jack, 186

Kesey, Ken, 186

Kinnell, Galway, 186

Koelb, Clayton, 277n.3

Kreitler, Hans and Shulamith, 109; 293n.37

Kris, Ernst, 113

Kuhn, Thomas, 9

Lacan, Jacques, 147–48, 279n.19

Laing, R. D., 243, 246, 251, 252

Landor, Walter Savage, 181

Langue (Saussure), 219, 221–23. *See also* Vocabulary

Lawrence, D. H., 45, 46, 68, 76, 77, 102, 181, 271

LeBon, Gustav, 33, 145, 284n.26

Le Guin, Ursula, 31–32, 45

Leninism, 188

Lentricchia, Frank, 210

Lesser, Simon, 108, 214; on "analogizing," 11, 133–34; fiction's projective mechanisms, 296n.1

Lessing, Gotthold, 56, 75

Levertov, Denise, 60–61, 186

Levine, Philip, 186

Lévi-Strauss, Claude, 200, 265, 304n.24, 308n.16

Lewis, Sinclair, 174

Linearity, 208–209. *See also* New historicism

Literary criticism: its evasiveness, 179–214, 302n.4; itself fiction in Barthes, 216, 236, 241; itself fiction in Booth, 267; the negative avoided, 184–85. *See also* Fallacies, literary

Locke, John, 188

London, Jack, 172

Longfellow, Henry Wadsworth, 180–81
Lorenz, Konrad, 261
Lowell, Robert, 186
Lukács, Georg, 189
Lying. *See* Deception, literary

McCarthy, Mary, 45
McDougall, William, 34–35
McGann, Jerome, 206, 207–208
Mailer, Norman, 45, 46, 68, 183, 186, 191, 243, 269
Malamud, Bernard, 186
Male bonding, 153; in *Hamlet*, 121, 171; in *Heart of Darkness*, 79–80, 171; in "Mending Wall," 125–31; in *Moby Dick*, 170; in "Rime of the Ancient Mariner," 118–19. *See also* Androgyny
Mallarmé, Stephane, 30, 32
Marcuse, Herbert, 37–38, 43, 45, 243, 251, 252, 261, 297n.6
Marduk, 161
Marinetti, Filippo, 268
Marshall, John, 1, 53
Marx, Karl, 188, 206, 210, 242, 291n.16
  Marxist critical theory, 36–39, 185–86, 189, 191, 213, 303n.14; and Barthes, 215; inverted by Gardner, 268–69; and new historicism, 209–10; and religion, 36–37; its "vulgar" commitment to revolutionary change, 185–89
Mauron, Charles, 228
Mayer, Louis B., 190
Melville, Herman, 172; and Hawthorne, 169–72; *Moby-Dick*, 110, 152, 169–72; as reply to "Young Goodman Brown," 170–72

Mencken, H. L., 30–31, 32, 43, 46, 52
Menninger, Karl, 89
Metaphor, 55, 111–13; connotations of, 111–13, 116, 234; and metonymy, 147, 149–50; and narrative closure, 12, 107, 112, 113, 143, 146, 150, 298n.9, 308n.5; as positive feedback, 107, 112, 146; as projection, 150; in Shakespeare, 73, 115–16, 120–21, 180; as signification, 146–49; and style, 222; as a stylistic device, 294; tenors of, 146, 148; verbal economy of, 7, 111–12. *See also* Richards, I. A.
Metonymic designification, 7, 16, 56, 147–48, 155; and interaction between long- and short-term memory, 177; and the trend from the sixties to the eighties, 243, 245. *See also* Designification
Metonymy: and Barthes, 233, 235; in *Moby Dick*, 300n.21; in *The Odyssey*, 300n.21; its plateau effect, 148; as plot, 7, 56, 106; as signifier of desire, 147–48
Meyer, Bernard, 108
Milken, Mike, 244
Miller, Arthur, 174, 184
Miller, Henry, 243
Miller, J. Hillis, 145, 151
Mills, C. Wright, 243
Milton, John, 12, 210
Mimesis, 6, 19, 22–23; and Barthes, 215; when exaggerated, 183; failure in popular fiction of, 270; and identity theme, 193–94; as reportorial accuracy, 189, 191; as resemblance to impose differences, 193–94; and virtues, 25–26

Index

Minimalism, 98–99
Minority of One, 187
Misinformation. *See* Deception, literary
Misrepresentation. *See* Deception, literary
Models of literary experience, 13–17; a closure-denial-homeostatic hierarchy, 106; cognitive, 2, 13, 17, 195; cognitive, affective, and conative, 292 n.18; critical deception theories categorized, 43–45; deceptionist, 51–58; expression versus constraint, 150–52; form integrates plot and metaphor, 143; homeostatic, 13, 14–15, 17, 93–110; Iser and negative poetics, 196–97; negative poetics' hyperreductionism, 17; paranoid, 13, 15–16, 17, 133–54. *See also* Designification; Homeostasis; Metonymic designification; Paranoid literary form; Signification
Morality in fiction: Aristotle on, 25; Balzac on, 25; Booth on, 262–64; in *David Copperfield*, 71, 77–78; and deception, 25–26; in "Dover Beach," 114–15; in Frost's poetry, 124; Gardner on, 271–72, 274; in *Heart of Darkness*, 66, 71–72, 78–80; Hegel on, 29; in "Mending Wall," 129–30; its negative function, 261–64, 271–72, 274; and paranoia, 140, 155; in *Pride and Prejudice*, 69–70, 76–77; Sidney on, 25; Steiner on, 41; Tolstoy on, 32–33; Wilder on, 25; in "Young Goodman Brown," 158, 162–63, 173
Motivation. *See* Intention
Mussolini, Benito, 268–69
Muthos. *See* Plot

Nabokov, Vladimir, 186
Naipaul, V. S., 288 n.11
Narration: discouraged by Barthes, 215 16; discouraged by new historicism, 208–209; encouraged by Trilling, 248; as a recurring formula, 5. *See also* Closure; Plot
National Guardian, 187
Negation, 258–64, 274; between literary freedom and historical determinism, 142, 297 n.6; and brain physiology, 310 n.21; and the dance, 262–63; versus affirmation, 6, 271, 310 n.21; versus Polanyi's "hierarchy of explanatory systems," 262–64. *See also* Denial; *Negationsnegierung*
Negationsnegierung 67, 103, 142, 177–78; Gide's explanation, 253
Negative feedback, 15, 90–92, 106, 195, 199; and metaphor, 112; versus positive feedback, 106–107, 112, 119. *See also* Homeostasis
Negative manifesto, 20, 270–75
Negative poetics, 1–17; and the affirmative fallacy, 175–78; and cosmology, 258–64; and deception, 51–58, 61–64; and homeostasis, 93–110, 111–13; as "motivism," 266; and paranoia, 136–54, 155–56. *See also* Dialectic form; Metonymic designification; Models of literary experience; *Negationsnegierung*; Plot; Praxis
Neil, A. S., 243
Neo-Marxism: and indeterminacy, 211; its neglect of classical Marxist economics, 306 n.38. *See also* Marxist critical theory
Neoplatonism, 23–24; and Christianity, 24–25; and Hegel, 28

Index

Neopragmatism, 4, 213, 277 n.2
New Deal, 190
New historicism, 185, 206–11, 213; and indeterminacy, 211; and Marxism, 209–10; and textual intrareferentiality, 208, 210–11
New York Review of Books, 187
Nietzsche, Friedrich, 28–30, 43–45, 46, 51, 58, 206, 210, 246, 264; art versus truth, 29–30, 31, 32; and Derrida, 203–205; Dionysian versus Apollonian, 113, 153, 200, 204–205; and Mencken, 30–31; and Plato, 29–30
Normal fiction, 276
Nydes, J., 167

O'Brien, Tim, 174
Oedipus complex, 108, 129; in American authors, 172; in Barthes, 232–33, 237; in *Hamlet*, 122, 237; and Holland, 294 n.5; and Lévi-Strauss, 200; a minor flaw in Oedipus compared to politics, 293 n.38; and tragedy, 294 n.7; in "Young Goodman Brown," 162–65, 237. *See also* Patriarchal authority; Satan
O'Hara, Frank, 186
Olson, Charles, 186
Oparin, Alexander, 260
Orwell, George, 176

Paley, Grace, 46, 68
Paranoia, 134–36, 155, 182, 275–76; different from its use in fiction, 138–39; homeostatic explanation of, 135–38; and homosexual repression, 134–35, 297 n.3; models of, 136, 137; and role of mother, 167. *See also* Freud, Sigmund
Paranoid literary form, 133–54, 155–56; and anxiety, 155; and Barthes, 232; in Freud's and Swanson's models, 135–36; in literary conventions, 139–42; in popular fiction, 154, 155; and projection, 136–38; in Pynchon's novels, 153; in "Young Goodman Brown," 156–69, 172–73. *See also* Denial; Models of literary experience
Pareto, Vilfredo, 33, 51, 210, 284 n.26
Parmenides, 291 n.16
Pascal, Blaise, 267
Patriarchal authority, its rejection: by Barthes, 232–34, 237, 309 n.8; in *Hamlet*, 122, 127, 237; in Hawthorne's fiction, 169; in "Mending Wall," 127–29; in "Young Goodman Brown," 159–65, 237. *See also* Oedipus complex; Satan
Pechter, Edward, 208
Peckham, Morse, 100–101, 201
Peirce, Charles Saunders, 176
Petrarch, 24
Phenomenological criticism. *See* Barthes, Roland
Photography. *See* Barthes, Roland
Plath, Sylvia, 186, 243
Plato, 22–24, 25, 30, 32, 40, 43, 45, 75; and Aristotle, 56, 75; and Sophocles, 188. Allegory of the cave, 51, 65, 258; *Ion*, 271, 276; *Symposium*, 23
Platonism, 23–24, 26–27; and Hegel, 28; and Marcuse, 37
Pleasure, literary, 1, 86–89, 93, 99, 106, 110, 134; biological explanation

Index

of, 290 n.14; Kenneth Burke's theory of, 143. *See also* Freud, Sigmund, on pleasure principle, "Relation of the Poet to Day-Dreaming"
Pleasure principle. *See* Freud, Sigmund
Plot: as action chain, 299 n.10; and affirmative fallacy, 175; before and after, 7; and Burke, 268 n.9; and closure, 7, 145; and denial, 8, 15, 55–57, 61, 73–74, 105–106; focuses response, 98, 107; and homeostasis, 94–100; as imitation of single action, 22; linear, 15, 57, 75, 104, 143, 145; as metonymy, 7, 147; as *muthos*, the *mimesis* of *praxis*, 6–7; and New Critical explicative criteria, 300 n.22; and new historicism, 208; and popular fiction, 153; and projective displacement, 137–38; resistances of, 145–46; as reversal, 10, 56, 175; in "a rose is a rose," 75, 148; as transition from abstraction to absolute knowledge, 144; as transition from discrepant awareness to shared discovery, 299 n.10; as transition from problems to their solution, 143–44; and truth, 55; versus story, 149. *See also* Aristotle; Closure; Lessing, Gotthold; Metaphor, and narrative closure; Metonymic designification; Metonymy
Plotinus, 23–24, 39, 45
Podhoretz, Norman, 244
Poe, Edgar Allan, 26, 43, 51–52, 102, 172, 181, 262; on *Dichtkunst* (the art of poetry) as *Dichten* (to feign), 282 n.10
Polanyi, Michael, 262
Porter, Katherine Anne, 5

Postmodernism, 153, 183. *See also* Minimalism
Poststructuralism, 185
Poulet, George, 229
Pound, Ezra, 144–45, 148
Pragmatism: and absolute truth, 4; James's theory as applied to fiction, 52–53
Praxis: and consciousness, 34–35; and the denial displacement, 105; and fictive change, 133–34; and *gnosis*, 2; and Hamlet, 121, 123; imitated by fiction, 6–7; and intention, 278 n.6; postponed by fiction, 186; projected to plot, 137–38; when the lie *happens* instead of being told, 56–57; and writing, 217. *See also* Plot
Projection, literary, 15, 97–98, 133–34, 182, 196, 273; of guilt, 139; and metaphor, 150; and narrative form, 138; and paranoid displacement, 134–38; when identification is rewarded, 192
Prometheus, 259
Propositions, in fiction, 14
Prynne, William, 24
Psychoanalytic criticism, 185, 191–95, 213; used by Barthes, 215. *See also* Freud, Sigmund
Puns, 12; as resistance to closure, 107
Puritan commonwealth, 188
Pynchon, Thomas, 153, 174, 186, 187

Racine, Jean, 188, 219–20, 227–31, 234
Ramparts 187
Ransom, John Crowe, 151
Reader's response: a choice among un-

Reader's response (*continued*)
truths, 8; in interpretive communities, 8–9; and new historicism, 208; as a use of the author's lies, 14, 73
Reagan eighties. *See* Eighties, the
Realist, 187
Reductionism: negative poetics as a hyperreductionist model 17; new historicism's rejection of, 209
Reich, Wilhelm, 193, 243, 266
Repetition. *See* Formalism
Repetition compulsion, 109; through intertextual evasiveness, 203
Representation, 7. *See also* Signification
Repression, 4, 36
Response. *See* Reader's response
Response theory, 185, 191–99, 213; and indeterminacy, 211. *See also* Fish, Stanley; Holland, Norman; Iser, Wolfgang
Reynolds, Sir Joshua, 25–26
Rich, Adrienne, 187; poetry as the pursuit of meaningful differences, 59–60
Richards, I. A., 4, 16, 43, 96; and Dewey, 278n.11; on fiction's incipient action, 186; on metaphor, 177, 294n.1; on pseudostatement, 33, 47–49; on sincerity, 33, 113. *Practical Criticism*, 33; *Science and Poetry*, 33
Richardson, Samuel, 106
Ricks, Christopher, 33
Riesman, David, 250–51
Riffaterre, Michael, 201
Robbe-Grillet, Alain, 40, 218, 223
Roberts, Thomas, 222n.3
Robespierre, Maximilien, 246
Robortelli, Francesco, 25, 26
Roethke, Theodore, 172
Rorty, Richard, 8, 206, 277.n2

Roth, Philip, 186
Rousseau, Jean-Jacques, 26–27, 246, 249–50, 252, 264
Ruben, Jerry, 244
Ruskin, John, 246
Russell, Bertrand, 102, 243, 260–63, 264, 266; his rejection of *not*, 260
Russian Revolution, 188

Salinger, J. D., 174
Salvianus, 24
San Francisco renaissance, 187
Sartre, Jean Paul, 33, 37, 185, 217, 243, 261; and Barthes, 217–23, 228, 233; on closure, 297n.72; and Trilling, 252
Satan: in *Moby Dick*, 171; in *Paradise Lost*, 12; quoted by Burke, 259–60; quoted by Russell, 260; in "Young Goodman Brown," 157, 159–65, 169
Saturday Evening Post, 190
Saussure, Ferdinand de, 151, 218, 219
Schiller, Friedrich von, 246
Schlegel, Friedrich, 26, 43, 55
Schlesinger, Arthur, 243
Schopenhauer, Arthur, 283n.14
Schwartzenegger, Arnold, 154
Scott, Sir Walter, 181
Selby, Hubert, 186
Selznick, David O., 190
Semiotics, used by Barthes, 215
Seventies, the, 242–45, 311n.26
Sexton, Anne, 186
Shaftesbury, Earl of, 246
Shakespeare, William, 102, 154, 180; and death, 5, 278n.15; and Locke, 188; metaleptic complexity, 120; and the Puritan revolution, 188; sex nau-

Index

sea of, 120, 152, 180; and Whig politics, 188. *Antony and Cleopatra*, 15; *As You Like It*, 18; *King Lear*, 5, 309 n.19, *Othello*, 5; *Romeo and Juliet*, 67, 295 n.7; Sonnet 73, 115–16; Sonnet 129, 199; *The Tempest*, 295 n.7; *Titus Andronicus*, 154. *Hamlet*: 5, 10, 15, 19, 96, 98, 105, 119–24, 146, 148, 154, 216–17, 236; as antiepithalamium, 119, 121–22; its celebration of death, 122–24; its denouement, 121–22; its formalist appeal, 109; its ghost, 260; its homophobic obligation, 119, 295 n.7; its metaleptic complexity, 120; and the Oedipus complex, 108, 122, 165, 237, 295 n.7; its plot-metaphor dialectic, 119; sex nausea of, 120–21

Shaw, George Bernard, 145
Shelley, Percy Bysshe, 102
Shklovsky, Victor, 201, 293 n.32
Sidney, Sir Philip, 2, 13, 24, 25, 26, 43, 47
Signification: and Barthes, 224–27, 232, 238–40; deception of, 146, 299 n.17; and denial, 7; displacement of the signifier, 279 n.19; and metaphor, 146; regression of significations, 204
Sin. *See* Evil
Sincerity, 271. *See also* Trilling, Lionel; Truth
Sixties, the, 186–88, 243–45; and Booth, 253–55; followed by economic decline, 269; protest movement of, 243, 261; and Trilling, 247; Vietnam unjustified, 310 n.17
Smith, Barbara Herrnstein, 8
Smith, Jackson. *See* Swanson, David

Smith, Thorne, 190
Snodgrass, W. D., 186
Snyder, Gary, 186, 243
Solon, 21, 30, 45, 50
Sophocles, 102, 109, 188, 295 n.7
Speech act theory, 213
Spence, Donald, 277 n.1
Spenser, Edmund, 291 n.16
Spielberg, Steven, 269
Stafford, William, 186
Stagner, Ross, 89
Stalinism, 185, 188
Stein, Gertrude, 81–83. "A rose is a rose," 19, 63–64, 144; its grammatical ambiguity, 83; its plot, 75, 148; its sexual implications, 83–85; its signification, 225; its subversive truths, 80–83; its transition from truth to untruth, 75; its truth, 67–68; its untruth, 68; in *The World is Round*, 82
Steinbeck, John, 190
Steiner, George, 40–42, 43–45, 51; language as instrument of deception, 40–41; on Marxism, 303 n.14
Story, when in conflict with plot, 149
Stowe, Harriet Beecher, 268
Structuralism, 200, 213
Style: explained by Barthes, 219, 222–23; resists closure, 13
Sukenick, Ronald, 153
Swanson, David, Philip Bohnert, and Jackson Smith, 135, 297 n.3
Symbols, 192

Tate, Allen, 151
Textuality, 208. *See also* New historicism
Theme: defense against metaphor in "Mending Wall," 129–30; featured by new historicism, 210

Index

Thespis, 21
Thomson, Georg, 37, 210
Thoreau, Henry David, 22
Tiamat, 161
Tolstoy, Leo, 5, 7, 43, 102, 188; *What is Art*, 32–33
Tone, 149
Tragedy, 22–23, 144, 153; in Barthes's life, 216; in *Hamlet*, 121, 123; in "Young Goodman Brown," 164–65
Transcendentalism, 188
Trilling, Lionel, 19–20, 33–34, 191, 264; his dialectic view of the truth, 247, 253; on fiction's authenticity, 253; on the inauthentic, 247–49; on inauthenticity as the core of Freudian doctrine, 252; on linear sequence as an agent of the inauthentic, 248; on the nuclear family, 250–52, 266; on psychoanalysis, 250; on Rousseau, 249; on Sartre, 252; on the sixties, 247; on the truth as deception, 249, 253; on truth's Continental and English traditions, 246. *Beyond Culture*, 33; *Middle of the Journey*, 191; *Sincerity and Authenticity*, 19–20, 33–34, 242–53
Trollope, Anthony, 180–81
Trump, Donald, 244
Truth, 1, 3, 67, 271; affirmed versus rejected, 55; assent of, 258–59; avoidance of as an ethical commitment, 271; basic versus superficial, 4, 270; close approximations, 4; confessional, 7; constative and performative, 9–10; conventional literary, 7, 14; as deception, 249; as denial, 11, 53; to disguise the lie, 6; and English professors, 286n.66; fashionable and unfashionable, 61–62; and fiction, 50; hard versus benign, 4, 57; as harmless illusion, 245; and Heidegger, 279n.17; in the lie, 283n.14; limited versus inclusive, 6; and literary form, 61; and metaphor, 7; and negation, 259–60; negative, 258–64; paranoid, 141; and photography, 238; relative, 8–9; and repose, 86; repressed personal, 5; scientific versus both literary and religious, 14; subversive, 76; in tragedy, 229; as undistorted reference, 4; as valid if it may be construed as a lie, 299n.17. *See also* Authenticity
Twain, Mark, 156, 172, 174

Updike, John, 174, 186, 269, 301n.12

Verisimilitude, 51, 189; through pseudostatement, 47; through willing suspension of disbelief, 47
Vietnam. *See* Sixties, the
Village Voice, 187
Villains, 12. *See also* Evil; Characterization, and evil overload
Violence, depiction of, 148
Vocabulary, 40–43, 56, 63; and love, 212; and "a rose is a rose," 75, 83; as a sign, any word lies, 146. *See also* Langue
Vonnegut, Kurt, 186

Waelder, Robert, 55, 91, 138, 297n.4
Wald, George, 260
Ward, James, 34–35, 278n.6, 292n.18
Warren, Robert Penn, 145

Index

Wayne, John, 269
Webb, Beatrice and Sidney, 145
Wellek, René, 48
Wells, H. G., 145, 181
Wheelwright, Philip, 113, 214
Whig politics, 188
White, Hayden, 206, 277n.1, 306n.37
Whitehead, Alfred North, 8
Whitman, Cedric, 200
Whitman, Walt, 24
Whittier, John Greenleaf, 181
Wilde, Oscar, 29, 32, 43–45, 50, 246, 250; that life imitates art, 21
Wilder, Thornton, 25–26, 43
Wilderness. *See* Frontier, American

Wimsatt, W. K., 103–104, 181–83
Winters, Yvor, 48, 183, 213
Wish fulfillment, 97, 182, 198. *See also* Freud, Sigmund, on pleasure principle
Words. *See* Vocabulary
Wordsworth, William, 24, 180–81, 246
World War II, 190
Wright, Chauncey, 262
Writing degree zero. *See* Barthes, Roland
Wyatt, Sir Thomas, 210

Zhdanov, Andrei, 185
Zola, Émile, 183, 189

OHIO UNIVERSITY